India In 1500 AD
The Narratives of Joseph The Indian

India In 1500 AD
The Narratives of Joseph The Indian

ANTONY VALLAVANTHARA

GORGIAS PRESS
2001

First Gorgias Press Edition, November 2001

Copyright © 2001 by Gorgias Press LLC.

All rights reserved under International and Pan-American Copyright Conventions. Published in the United States of America by Gorgias Press LLC, New Jersey. Originally published in India by the Research Institute for Studies in History (RISHI), Mannanam, in 1984.

ISBN 0-9713097-0-1

GORGIAS PRESS
46 Orris Ave., Piscataway, NJ 08854 USA
www.gorgiaspress.com

Printed in the United States of America
10 9 8 7 6 5 4 3 2 1

PREFACE

Love for documents and a sense of criticism are authentic signs of true search for history. Though the Indians in general and the people of Kerala in particular do not have the habit of preserving documents of the past, today many people and centres are interested in collecting and preserving historical documents. Unlike in the recent past more and more people are making critical study of history with the help of authentic documents. Care for the past and the practice of documented criticism was lacking in studies on Kerala history in general and history of Christianity in Kerala in particular. Writing of history of Kerala, especially of the Christian communities, has to take a new turn of becoming more documented. Many people have realised the need for such a change in writing history. Many have moved in those lines. It is in pursuance of this target that I decided to make an in-depth study of the Narratives of Joseph the Indian, a magnificent description of India in 1500 AD, as it came from the lips of an Indian and recorded by a European.

This study is the result of three years of research. I have conceived this study as a first step toward the realisation of a cherished plan for publishing what I used to call the *Documenta Malabarica*, a series of publications of historical documents of Malabar or Kerala origin. My researches into the sources of the Liturgical Year of the Thomas Christians, made me conscious of the value of Malabar documents, both in print and in manuscript, for the study of the history. It was in 1979 that I first began to think in this line and I worked on the Narratives of Joseph the Indian to publish this document as the first in the series *Documenta Malabarica*. Now after five years I have great pleasure to publish this as the first in the first series called

"Kerala Documents Series" published under the auspices of the *Research Institute for Studies in History (Rishi)*, Mannanam, an Institute for the study of socio-cultural and religious history of India, especially of Kerala.

This work was presented at the Catholic University of Louvain-la-Neuve, Belgium, for obtaining the degree of Licenciate in Historical Sciences. Many people have helped me in this work. First of all I express my gratitude to Professor Roger Aubert, of the Catholic University of Louvain-la-Neuve, Belgium, who guided me in this work. I remember with gratitude Professor Bahna de Andrade of the University of Portugal, who was good enough to put at my disposal all the knowledge and documentation he had on the topic, even the manuscript of his own translation of the documents. I remember with thanks Fr. Jose Bacelar Oliveira, Rector of the Catholic University of Portugal and the Jesuit fathers of the Provincial House, Rua da Lapa, Lisbon. It was at the Jesuit house at Rua da Lapa that I wrote the first draft of this work. I thank very cordially all my friends and colleagues, especially the members of my community, who have helped me to realise this work.

Nazareth Carmel House,   **Fr. Antony Vallavanthara CMI**
Muhamma P. O.,
Alleppey – 688 525
15-8-1984

To
My Beloved Mother

TABLE OF CONTENTS

	Page
Preface	vii
Table of contents	xi
Foreword	xv
Introduction	xix

PART I

Sources of the Narratives of Joseph the Indian

1.0.0.	**Search into the Sources**	3
1.1.0.	**Preliminary survey of the three sources**	3
1.1.1.	Paesi Nouamente Retrouati and its translations	5
1.1.2.	Itinerarium Portugallensium and Novus Orbis	6
1.1.3.	Sonderlinge Reysen van Joseph	7
1.1.4.	The question of Fasciculus Temporum	7
1.1.5.	The Problem of the Portuguese text	10
1.1.6.	The limits of our study of the sources	10
1.2.0.	**Paesi Nouamente Retrouati and the Italian text of the Narratives of Joseph the Indian**	11
1.2.1.	The first edition of Paesi, 1507	12
1.2.2.	The contents of Paesi	13
1.2.3.	The division of the work	13
1.2.4.	Remarks on the division of the work	15
1.2.5.	The editions and translations of Paesi	16
1.2.6.	The Editor / Compiler of Paesi	17
1.3.0.	**Itinerarium Portugallensium and the Latin text of the Narratives of Joseph the Indian**	24
1.3.1.	Description of Itinerarium Portugallensium	26
1.3.2.	The contents of Itinerarium	27
1.3.3.	The division of the work	27
1.3.4.	Interdependence of Itinerarium and Paesi	29
1.3.5.	Itinerarium and Paesi, a comparative study	32
1.3.6.	Common source of Paesi and Itinerarium	37
1.4.0.	**Novus Orbis and the Narratives of Joseph the Indian**	42
1.4.1.	Novus Orbis	42
1.4.2.	The description of Novus Orbis	44

1.4.3.	The contents of Novus Orbis	45
1.4.4.	The division of Novus Orbis	46
1.4.5.	German and Dutch translations of Novus Orbis	48
1.4.6.	The Three re-editions of Novus Orbis	49
1.5.0.	**Sonderlinge Reysen van Joseph**	50
1.5.1.	The origins of the text of Sonderlinge Reysen	52
1.6.0.	**Interrelation of the sources and the texts**	52

PART II

Joseph the Indian and His Narratives

2.0.0.	**Joseph and his Narratives**	57
2.1.0.	**The Person of Joseph**	57
2.1.1.	The Narratives of Joseph the Indian	60
2.1.2.	The origins of the Narratives of Joseph the Indian	61
2.1.3.	Importance of the Narratives of Joseph	63
2.1.4.	Joseph the Indian and his Narratives down the centuries	64
2.2.0.	**The Travels of Joseph the Indian**	71
2.2.1.	Joseph the Indian meets Pedro Alvares Cabral	71
2.2.2.	Joseph travels to Lisbon with Cabral and visits Rome and Venice	74
2.2.3.	Joseph the Indian meets the Pope	76
2.2.4.	Did Joseph go to Jerusalem and Babylon?	78
2.2.5.	When did Joseph return to India?	81
2.3.0.	**Joseph and His Narratives**	81
2.3.1.	Did Joseph write the Narratives?	82
2.3.2.	Date and Place of the Narratives	83
2.3.3.	What language did Joseph speak?	84
2.3.4.	The writer of the Narratives	87
2.4.0.	**The contents of the Narratives of Joseph the Indian**	94
2.4.1.	The voyage of Cabral and travels of Joseph the Indian	94
2.4.2.	The person of Joseph	94
2.4.3.	The description of the city of Cranganore, a description of Kerala in 1500 AD	95
2.4.4.	The city of Cranganore	96
2.4.5.	The structure of the society, social classes of the Hindus, their temples and their worship	96

2.4.6.	The customs and manners of the king and the people of Cranganore	96
2.4.7.	The St Thomas Christians of Cranganore	97
2.4.8.	Climate at Cranganore, ships, navigation	99
2.4.9.	The monetary system and the flora and fauna	99
2.4.10.	The city of Calicut	100
2.4.11.	The west coast of India and the islands and cities in the Arabian sea, Gujarat, Ormus and Cambay	100
2.4.12.	The King Narsindo and the Body of St Thomas in the Church of Mylapore	101

PART III

The Texts of the Narratives of Joseph the Indian

3.0.0.	**The Three Texts**	105
3.1.0.	**History of the three texts**	107
3.1.1.	The Italian text of Paesi	107
3.1.2.	The Latin text of Itinerarium	108
3.1.3.	The Dutch text of Sonderlinge Reysen van Joseph	109
3.2.0.	**Comparative Study of the three texts**	110
3.2.1.	The division of the chapters	111
3.2.2.	The titles of the chapters	112
3.2.3.	Interpolations and additions	116
3.2.4.	Internal differences	119
3.2.5.	Similarities of the three texts	120
3.2.6.	The value of the three texts	121
3.3.0.	**The Italian and Latin texts: a comparative analysis**	121
3.3.1.	Internal differences	122
3.3.2.	Chapter 1	123
3.3.3.	Chapter 2	124
3.3.4.	Chapters 3 and 4	125
3.3.5.	Chapters 5 and 6	125
3.3.6.	Chapters 7 – 10	127
3.3.7.	Chapter 11	127
3.3.8.	Chapters 12, 13, 14	128
3.3.9.	Differences in the titles of the chapters in the tables of contents	129

PART IV

India in 1500 AD
as described by Joseph the Indian

4.0.0.	The Narratives of Joseph the Indian	139
4.1.0.	Presenting the three texts	139
4.1.1.	The Italian and Latin texts	141
4.1.2.	The Dutch text	142
4.2.0.	The Narratives of Joseph the Indian Italian and Latin texts and translations	145
4.3.0.	The Narratives of Joseph the Indian The Dutch text and translation	219
4.4.0.	Notes and Comments	261
	Appendix I Paesi Nouamente Retrouati	295
	Navigators and their Expeditions.	310
	Appendix II Itinerarium Portugallensium	312
	Appendix III Novus Orbis	316
	Bibliography	328
	Index	338

FOREWORD

There are a few vague references of early visitors to Europe from India; but Joseph the Indian's is the best documented visit. Travelling aboard one of the ships of Pedro Alvares Cabral which set sail from Cochin, Joseph, a leading priest of the St. Thomas Christians, reached Lisbon in June or July, 1501. There he was received by King Manuel. After six months's stay in Portugal, he, with a companion from Lisbon, proceeded to Rome and got an audience with Pope Alexander VI. After Rome he visited Venice quite probably on his way to Jerusalem and Persia. Reports of the interviews Joseph gave in Lisbon, Rome and Venice are extant. But what he told the Venetians was extensively reported. It is this report, under the name 'The Narratives of Joseph the Indian', which Fr. Antony Vallavanthara studies in the present book.

Fr. Antony has succeeded in tracing almost all the available texts and versions of the Narratives, some of which were not known earlier. This has helped him to make a serious attempt to reconstruct the original Narratives. A comparative study of the three earlier texts of the Narratives and their sources, editions and translations leads the author to propose a new hypothesis on the first sources. The understanding among the scholars so far has been that the text in *Paesi Nouamente Retrouati* (1507) was the original written text and the Latin text in *Itinerarium Portugallensium* (1508) and *Novus Orbis* (1532) were corrupt and unreliable translations. The new hypothesis put forward by the author is: *Paesi Nouamente Retrovuati* is not the immediate source of *Itinerarium Portugallensium* and the latter is not the immediate translation of *Paesi*, but they originate from a remote common source, and hence the texts of the Narratives of Joseph the Indian in *Paesi* and *Itinerarium* represent two earlier versions of a remote original text in Portuguese or in some Italian dialect. The hypothesis is a challenging one. However it has to face a volley of questions and considerations like the following.

If an original Portuguese text existed it is very difficlut to understand how Joao de Barros who wrote his *Da Asia* in the middle of the 16th century did not know of it. If the text in *Paesi* was an attempt at a real Italian translation, then there arises a serious problem that needs solution: why did the translator still retain the 'Portuguesisms'? On the contrary, the very presence of 'Portuguesisms' seems to corroborate the position so far held by scholars: *Paesi* represents the minutes taken down by an Italian interviewer of Joseph. It is possible that as the interviewer was putting down notes rather rapidly he did not care to render into good Italian some of the expressions in Portuguese either Joseph himself or his interpreter used. It is likely that Joseph, during his journey and his stay in Portugal, learned enough Portuguese to communicate himself in that language, though possibly not without some difficulty. But we cannot rule out the possiblity that he spoke in Arabic and his companion, probably a Portuguese, translated what he said into Portuguese or Italian. It is also possible that his interpreter/ companion had travelled with him to Lisbon from India. One fact which perhaps needs to be further explored, is the close resemblance of the text of *Paesi* with corresponding passages in Damiao de Goes's *Cronica*. It is also likely that the compiler of the text in *Itinerarium* had at his disposal some sources other than *Paesi* from which he added a few details to the text of *Paesi*.

The present study of Vallavanthara and the new hypothesis he puts forward have opened up a plethora of questions which the scholars are called upon to investigate and answer.

The author has provided very critical materials and many insights for this effort. The Narratives is of special interest for the study of early history of Christianity in India. All the sources available for the period are practically of western origin. The Narratives of Joseph, despite the fact that it was written down by a European and that too not without some distortions, is the only early source which can be called Indian in origin. In it we seem to hear the very words of a 16th century well-informed, educated leader of the ancient Christians of India, about those Christians, their traditions, customs and practices; so too about the wider socio-cultural context in which the Christians lived at the turn of the 16th century.

The very fact that the Narratives ran into 25 different editions and versions in seven European languages is a proof of the importance early scholars attributed to it. The publication of this book must serve as a great incentive for scholarly studies on the history of Christianity in India in general and of the ancient Indian Christians in particular. It is hoped that this book will stimulate similar publications of the immense source materials that are available in many European languages but difficult of access to many in India. Wishing the book wide acceptance among historians I take this opportunity to congratulate Fr. Antony, a former student of mine, for this very worthy but very demanding undertaking.

A. M. Mundadan CMI.

INTRODUCTION

India in 1500 AD is a study on the Narratives of Joseph the Indian. The Narratives of Joseph the Indian originated in the context of the great discoveries of the new world at the end of the 15th and the beginning of the 16th centuries. They are narrations about India in 1500 AD, especially the then newly discovered Indian coasts with the centres of trade and the ports of pepper. They also describe the socio-economic and cultural life of the various groups of people, especially of the Hindus and Christians on the west coast of India with their customs and manners, faith and religions, rites and rituals. They are a very rare and valuable historical document for students of history, geography, sociology, theology and world religions.

The fact that they are narrations of an Indian, a native of Cranganore, in Kerala, a priest and a great personage among the St Thomas Christians of Malabar, who went to Europe in 1501 in the wake of the great discoveries, makes the document a treasure-house of immense value. This great person who described the then India was known in history as Joseph the Indian. With his brother Mathias, also a priest, he went to Europe in Cabral's ship, just three years after Vasco da Gama discovered the new sea routes to India. Mathias died on the way or in Portugal. Joseph visited Lisbon, Rome and Venice. In Portugal he was very solemnly received by the King of Portugal and was the royal guest for almost six months, after his arrival in

Lisbon in June 1501. In Rome he had an audience with the Pope and in Venice he was received by the illustrious Signoria of Venice. With Pope Alexander VI he discussed the questions of the relations of the Malabar Church to the Pope of Rome and the Chaldean Patriarch. With the Signoria of Venice he discussed socio-economic conditions of Kerala.

What Joseph the Indian narrated were recorded by a European, whose name remains unknown in history. Published as they were in the first decade of the 16th century, the Narratives of Joseph the Indian are a rare source for first hand information about the Coast of Malabar as it was when the Portuguese landed there for the first time in history. They were published in Italian, Latin, German, Dutch, and French and had been re-edited more than twenty times within twenty years after their first publication in Italian in 1507 and Latin in 1508.

Students of Indian history will find the Narratives of Joseph the Indian a valuable source of historical information about the kings and kingdoms of the Indian-subcontinent. The Narratives of Joseph are also an important source for the history of the voyages of Cabral as Joseph travelled with Cabral. So far as the historical value is concerned they rank with the descriptions of historians like De Barros, Goes, Dionysio, Osorius, Gasper Correa and other Portuguese historians.

The Narratives of Joseph the Indian contain historical and geographical descriptions of Cranganore, Calicut, Cochin, Gujarat, Cambay, the kingdom of Narsinga with its two cities of Bisnagar and Mylapore, Oriza and the gulf of Oriza, the Cape of Mogolistan and the island of Ormus, the Cape of Diongul Maya and Ely, the Cape of Comerin and the islands of Ceylon and Sumatra, with their geographical positions, climate, flora and fauna, trade and commerce, spices and the ports.

One of the most important and valuable thing that makes the document a very rare document is that they are a source of information about the life and traditions of the Pre-Portuguese Christianity in India. They reveal to us the ecclesiastical system, sacramental and liturgical life of the

St. Thomas Christians of Malabar with their faith and traditions, feasts and fasts, the customs and manners. We also learn from the Narratives about the relation of these Christians to the Pope and the Patriarch of Babylon.

Why this study ?

Almost all the historians of Christianity in India use the Narratives of Joseph as an important source for the traditions of the St Thomas Christians. Specialists like Assemanus, Nilles, Schurhammer and Mundadan often cite Joseph as a valuable source side by side with Goes, De Barros, Dionysio and other Portuguese historians.

Though historians use this document as a valuable and valid source for the study of the history and traditions of the St Thomas Christians, so far no systematic study has been made on the Narratives of Joseph themselves, tracing their origins and history with a view to find out the sources and to make a critical analysis of the Narratives and their texts. As they are such an important document, I think that a critical study of these Narratives is indispensable for further researches in St Thomas Christian traditions. Hence I thought it would be a great contribution to the cause of history to make a detailed study of the Narratives of Joseph the Indian in view of a critical edition of the text.

Though Church historians often use the Narratives as an important source, they are not much known to the specialists of Kerala history and Indian history. One of the reasons is that the Narratives were not easily accessible as all the important editions were in the European languages of the sixteenth century.

There was another reason for this study. I found that all the sources of the Narratives of Joseph the Indian were very rare books and that we do not possess any detailed study or accurate references to the sources. Almost all authors who used the Narratives of Joseph the Indian did not have access to a good many of the texts that I was able to identify and trace out during my research. I, therefore, decided to present the texts and sources which were not known up to the present to the great authorities on the St Thomas Christians studies, and the specialists of Indian History.

Difficulties and Limitations of our studies

I had to face three main difficulties in my research. First of all there exists no real tool of scientific research which could be used to identify all the sources of the Narratives of Joseph the Indian. Secondly, the studies so far made on Joseph were often very meagre and depended on one or the other source. None of the authors had access to all the sources we know today. Even those, who knew about some of them, did not give proper references. Some others who referred to the Narratives did so in the context of the study of the discovery of America or for the purpose of cataloguing. They did not know the importance of the Narratives.

The most important difficulty that I have come across in the study was the problem of the accessibility of the sources. Though we know of some 25 different translations and editions of the Narratives I could not trace out all the different editions. However I was fortunate enough to get the first editions of all the three sources we discuss in this study. I was also lucky to trace out the documents not known to the historians of the Malabar Church.

Organisations of the study.

The study is divided into four parts. Part I is a search into the sources of the Narratives of Joseph the Indian. Part II is a study of the person of Joseph and his Narratives. Part III examines the three known texts, coming from the three sources from which all the known 25 editions and versions originated. In Part IV we present the three texts, (Italian, Latin and Dutch) and their translations with notes and comments.

Part I is a search into the sources. It begins with a preliminary survey of the sources, in which are enumerated the different editions and versions of the texts, their sources, and the problems related to them. Then a detailed analysis is made of the sources, showing the interrelation of the texts and the sources. Special attention is given to the question of the interrelation between the Latin text and the Italian text and their sources, proposing the hypothesis of interrelation of the sources.

Part II is mainly meant to present the person of Joseph the Indian and his Narratives. There we trace the origins of the Narratives, their writer, date and place and the contents. I have shown there the imporatance of this document.

Part III is a comparative study of the three texts from which all the other known texts in the various languages have originated. A special comparative study of the Italian and Latin texts is also made.

Part IV is the presentation of the three texts of the Narratives of Joseph the Indian and through them India in 1500 AD as described by Joseph the Indian is presented. The Italian and Latin texts and their translations are presented in parallel columns, which will be followed by the Dutch text and translation and finally the notes and comments on the texts.

Three appendices at the end will provide further information and documentation on the three sources of the Narratives.

PART I

Sources of the Narratives of
Joseph the Indian

Search into the Sources

The Narratives of Joseph the Indian have come down to us in different languages. We have them today in Italian, Latin, French, German, Dutch, Portuguese and English. The various versions of the Narratives can be traced back to three main sources, one in Italian, another in Latin and the third in Dutch. All the known sources are found in print. We have not yet come across any text of the Narratives of Joseph the Indian in manuscript. Perhaps, there is a fourth source mentioned by some authors.[1] We have not, however, succeeded in tracing any copy of it.

1.1.0. Preliminary survey of the three sources

Of the three known sources, the earliest is Italian. It was first printed and published from Vicentia, in Italy, in 1507 with the title *Paesi Nouamente Retrouati*.[2] It is a collection of voyages of the great discoveries of the "new world" at the end of the 15th and the beginning of the 16th centuries. The second was published in Latin from Milan, in Italy in 1508, seven months after the publication of *Paesi*, under the title *Itinerarium*

---

1. Discussed elsewhere. Cf. 1.1.4.
2. Hereafter *Paesi*. For further details Cf. 1.1.1., 1.2.0.ff, Appendix I.

*Portugallensium.*³ It contains a description of the same voyages as contained in *Paesi*. *Itinerarium* closely resembles *Paesi* in form and organisation of the work. *Novus Orbis Regionum ac Insularum*,⁴ generally known as *Novus Orbis*, first published from Basel in Switzerland in 1532, reproduced all that was contained in *Itinerarium*. Through *Novus Orbis*, the text of the Narratives of Joseph the Indian contained in *Itinerarium* has come down to us in various editions and versions. The third source is in the Dutch language. It is a booklet entitled *Sonderlinge Reysen van Joseph den geboornen Indiaan*.⁵ This booklet was published in 1706 by Peter Vander Aa, a Dutch publisher, in his serialised collection of voyages. According to the title-page of this work, it was then "translated from Portuguese for the first time".

A fourth possible source, perhaps prior to all the above mentioned, was referred to by Gouvea,⁶ Germann,⁷ Nagam Aiya,⁸ and Schurhammer.⁹ This is a collection of chronicles known under the name *Fasciculus Temporum*¹⁰ an appendix of which, according to their reports, contains the Narratives of Joseph the Indian. As already mentioned above, we could not find a text of the Narratives appended to *Fasciculus Temporum* in the two copies we consulted at the Vatican Library in Rome and the Bibliotheque Royale of Brussels. We shall discuss the question of *Fasciculus Temporum* later.¹¹

---

3. Hereafter *Itinerarium*. For further details Cf. 1.1.2., 1.3.0.ff, Appendix II.
4. Hereafter *Novus Orbis*. For further details Cf. 1.1.2., 1.4.0.ff.
                                                                                              Appendix III.
5. Hereafter *Sonderlinge Reysen*. For further details Cf. 1.1.3., 1.5.0.
6. A. De Gouvea, *Jornada do Arcebispo de Goa Dom Frey Aleixo de Menezes Primas da India Oriental religioso da Ordem de S. Agostinho*, Coimbra, 1606, fol. 5.
7. W. Germann, *Die Kirche der Thomaschristen*, Gutersloh, 1877, p. 316.
8. Nagam Aiya, *The Travancore State Manual* Trivandrum, 1906, Vol. II, P. 149.
9. G. Schurhammer, "Three letters of Mar Jacob Bishop of Malabar", in *Orientalia, Bibliotheca Instituti Historici SJ*, Vol. XXI, Rome, 1963 p. 337, note 22.
10. W. Rolevinck, *Fasciculus Temporum, omnes antiquorum chronicas succincte complectens*, Paris, 1512.
11. Cf. 1.1.4.

1.1.1. Paesi Nouamente Retrouati and its translations

As already mentioned above, the earliest known source of the Narratives of Joseph the Indian is *Paesi Nouamente Retrouati*. The full title of the work is *Paesi Nouamente Retrouati et Nouo Mondo da Alberico Vesputio Florentino Intitulato*. It was first published on 3rd November 1507 from Vicentia and was re-edited in 1508, 1512, 1517, 1519, and 1521.[12] A fascimile reprint of the 1508 edition was published from London in 1916.[13]

Paesi was first translated into German by Jobsten Ruchamer and was published from Nuremberg in 1508.[14] In the same year appeared in Lübeck the Dutch translation of *Paesi* based on the German translation of Jobsten.[15] The French translation of *Paesi* was done by Mathurin du Redouer directly from Italian. It was first published in 1515 and was followed by five successive editions, all appearing in Paris (1515-16, 1516, 1521, 1528 and 1529).[16] We do not know of any complete English translation of *Paesi*. However, we have an English translation of the text of the Narratives of Joseph the Indian contained in *Paesi* together with the translation of the parts of *Paesi* related to the voyages of Cabral. It was translated by William Brooks Greenlee and was published by the Hakluyt Society, London, in 1937.[17] A Portuguese translation of the work of Greenlee was published by a Portuguese, Antonio Alvaro Doria, in 1966.[18]

All together we have today 17 editions of the Narratives of Joseph the Indian originating from *Paesi* alone: seven in Italian, six in French, one each in German, Dutch, English and Portuguese.[19]

---

12. For further details about the different editions and translations of *Paesi* Cf. 1.2.5. and Appendix I.
13. Cf. Appendix. I.
14. Cf. Appendix I.
15. Cf. Appendix I.
16. Cf. Appendix I.
17. W. B. Greenlee, *The Voyages of Pedro Alvares Cabral to Brazil and India from Contemporary Documents*, Hakluyt Society, London, 1937. The Narratives of Joseph the Indian appear on pp. 97-113, under the head "the account of Priest Joseph."
18. A. A. Doria, *A Viagem de Pedro Alvares Cabral a Brasil e a India, pelos documentos et relecaos coevas*. Porto, 1966. The Narratives of Joseph the Indian appear on pp. 197-214.
19. Cf. Appendix I.

6   INDIA IN 1500 AD

1.1.2. Itinerarium Portugallensium and Novus Orbis

The second source of the Narratives of Joseph the Indian, as already mentioned above, is *Itinerarium Portugallensium*. The complete title of this work was: *Itinerarium Portugallensium e Lusitania in Indiam inde in occidentem ac demum ad aquilonem*.[20] It was translated by an Italian monk named Archangelo Madrignano (Archangelus Madrignanus), and was published from Milan on 1st June 1508. *Itinerarium* which appeared about seven months after *Paesi*, was regarded by many authors as the translation of *Paesi*. This view, we feel, is not correct. We shall prove it later.[21]

The famous work *Novus Orbis*,[22] first published from Basel in 1532 also contains the Latin text of the Narratives of Joseph the Indian. The first 142 chapters in this well-known collection of voyages is nothing more than a re-edition of *Itinerarium*. Hence, the text of the Narratives of Joseph the Indian in the *Novus Orbis* is simply a reproduction of the text of *Itinerarium*.

Novus Orbis was also published from Paris in 1532 without any addition to the Basel edition of the same year. It was again published in 1537 and 1555, each time adding new materials to the previous editions. It was rendered into German by Michael Herr in 1534, the translation being based on the Basel edition of 1532.[23] The Dutch translation of Cornelius Ablijn was modelled on the German translation of 1534 and was published from Antwerp in 1563.[24]

Thus we have today 7 editions of the Narratives of Joseph the Indian originating from *Itinerarium*, five in Latin, one in German and one in Dutch. All these are reprints or translations of the text contained in *Itinerarium Portugallensium*.

---

20. For further details about the *Itinerarium* Cf. 1.3.0. ff. and Appendix II.
21. Discussed elsewhere Cf. 1.3.4., 1.3.5, 1.3.6.
22. For further details Cf. 1.4.0. ff. and Appendix III.
23. Cf. Appendix III.
24. Cf. Appendix III.

1.1.3. Sonderlinge Reysen van Joseph

The third source that we know of for the Narratives of Joseph the Indian is the booklet *Sonderlinge Reysen van Joseph den geboornen Indiaan*, which appeared in Leyden in 1706 in a serialised collection of voyages in 29 volumes published by Peter Vander Aa, a Dutch, under the title *Naaukeurige Versameling der Gedenk-waardigste Zee en Land Reysen Na Oost en West Indien*.[25] The booklet in question appeared in the third volume of the collection which contains the voyages undertaken between 1500 and 1504. However, the booklet is complete in itself, having a title-page, table of contents and even an index of its own. According to the piece of information given on the title-page it was translated from Portuguese. The Narratives of Joseph the Indian contained in *Sonderlinge Reysen van Joseph* show certain differences from the texts of *Paesi* and of *Itinerarium*.

1.1.4. The question of Fasciculus Temporum

As already stated above[26], we know of *Fasciculus Temporum* as a source of the Narratives of Joseph the Indian from Gouvea, Germann, Nagam Aiya and Schurhammer. Germann and Nagam Aiya seem to depend on Gouvea. Schurhammer cites both Nagam Aiya and Germann in his articles, but does not make any reference to Gouvea. This makes us think that he got this information only from the other two.

Gouvea, in his *Jornada*, speaks of Joseph the Indian and of the Narratives of Joseph the Indian contained in *Fasciculus Temporum*, in the following words:

> "...... of which they had information through the fleet of Pedro Alvares Cabral (which returned) the previous year in which there were two of the same Christians of Cranganor to go to the Kingdom (Portugal) and from there to Rome and then to return through Armenia[27] and Babylonia to meet

---

25. P. Vander Aa, Leyden, 1701-1707.
26. Cf. 1.1.0.
27. This is not Armenia but Aramea.

8   INDIA IN 1500 AD

> their Patriarch. One of these by name Mathias died in Portugal and the other, Joseph, went to Rome and from there to Venice where, according to the information which he gave about this Christianity, an account was written in Latin language, which has been incorporated in the book entitled Fasciculus Temporum."[28]

About the same question Germann says the following:

> "...... Joseph, however, a man of about 40 years of age, had a very benevolent reception at the court and was sent to Rome with a companion and from there he went to Venice. What he narrated appeared in a booklet in Latin language entitled, *"The travels of Joseph the Indian"*, appended to the work *Fasciculus Temporum*. The various collections of descriptions of voyages especially *Paesi Nouamenti Retrouati*, Vicenza, 1507 and the more elaborate *Novus Orbis* from Basel have borrowed from it."[29]

Reading this statement of Germann one gets the impression that he knew nothing about *Fasciculus Temporum* personally. However, he gives the title of the Narratives of Joseph as *"The Travels of Joseph the Indian"*. As to the source of this title one has to ask where Germann got it from. Since he does not mention *Itinerarium*, the two probable sources might be *Jornada* of Gouvea and *Novus Orbis*. However, Gouvea does not give any title to the Narratives. Therefore, if Germann did not have any source other than Gouvea, it seems likely that he simply presumed that the title of the Narratives in *Fasciculus Temporum* should be the same as that of *Novus Orbis*. For, we come across

---

28. Gouvea, *op. cit.* fol. 5. (The translation is mine.) The original Portuguese text reads as follows. "...... do que elles ja tinhao noticia pella armeda do annos atras de Pedralueres Cabral com que tinhao ido dous dos mesmos Christaos de Cranganor para passarem ao Reyno & dahi a Roma & voltarem pella Armenia & Babylonia a verse com seu Patriarcha hu dos quaes per nome Mathias morreo em Portugal & o outro Ioseph que passou a Roma & dahi a Veneza, aonde pella informacao, que deu desta Christianade se compos hu matado (sic) della em lingoa latina, que an da juncto ao liuro intitulado Fasciculus Temporum."
29. W. Germann, *op. cit.* pp. 315-316. (Translation is mine.)

the title *"Navigatio Josephi Indi"* on the top of the pages of *Novus Orbis*, containing the Narratives of Joseph the Indian.

Nagam Aiya definitely depends on Gouvea, for, he clearly mentions Gouvea's name. But we cannot say on whom he depends for the other details he has given, since his account is different from that of Germann. We give below the citation from his *Travancore State Manual*:

> "...... From the information obtained by persons who spoke to Joseph a book was published, which gives a description of the Malabar Christians, which may be taken for what it is worth. The book was in Latin and was appended to the *Fasciculus Temporum*, according to Gouvea, but it was soon translated into other languages. An Italian version appeared at Vicenza in 1507 called *Paesi Nouamente Retrouati*. It is also cited as *Navigatio Novi Orbis* and as *Travels of Joseph the Indian*." [30]

Schurhammer mentions *Fasciculus Temporum* as a source of the Narratives of Joseph the Indian in his article, *Three Letters*, but he does not mention it in the other article where he discusses the testimony of Joseph the Indian.[31] We have tried our best to secure a copy of the Narratives in *Fasciculus Temporum*, but the two copies we could consult did not have the appendix mentioned.[32] At the present state of our research we can say nothing more about the text of the Narratives of Joseph the Indian in *Fasciculus Temporum*. We will be very happy if we succeed in finding a copy of this appendix from some library in the world. Until then we have to be content with what we already have at present.

---

30. Nagam Aiya *op. cit.* Vol. II, p. 149.
31. G. Schurhammer, *art. cit.* p. 337-338; "Malabar Church before the coming of the Portuguese, Joseph the Indian's Testimony," *Orientalia*, *Bibliotheca Instituti Historici SJ* Vol. XXI, Rome, 1963, pp. 351-63.
32. Bibliotheca Apostolica Vaticana, (Inc. II, 472, Barberini, Q, II, 21.) and Bibliotheque Royale de Bruxelles.

1.1.5. The Problem of the Portuguese text

There remains another problem, the question of the existence of the Portuguese text of the Narratives of Joseph the Indian. We have reasons to think that such a text in Portuguese existed prior to all the known texts. Perhaps the very original text was in the Portuguese language. For, in the first place, there is an indication on the title-page of *Sonderlinge Reysen van Joseph* to the existence of a Portuguese text. We read on the title-page the statement that it was "now translated for the first time from Portuguese."[33] Secondly, it is probable that the source common to *Paesi* and *Itinerarium*, of which we shall speak later,[34] which might have been in some Italian dialect, depended on some Portuguese original, at least for the Narratives of Joseph the Indian. (For, Book II and Book III of these works clearly say that they were translated from Portuguese. The dedicatory letter of Montaboldus Fracanus in *Itinerarium* says that he proposes to narrate refering to the materials in Portuguese and then in the Etruscan language. Hence, the Narratives of Joseph the Indian which are very closely connected with the voyage of Cabral contained in Book II and Book III, also might have been in Portuguese.) Thirdly, in all probability, as we shall show later[35], the language that Joseph the Indian spoke when he was in Europe was Portuguese rather than Italian or Latin and hence, he narrated what is contained in the Narratives in the Portuguese language. Further, from the internal evidences in all the texts and the Portuguese influence in the language of the Italian text of the Narratives, we have to conclude that the writer of the Narratives, who recorded what he heard from Joseph, was a Portuguese.[36] The original might have been written in Portuguese. But, no such text has so far been identified.

1.1.6. The Limits of our study of the sources

We have decided to limit our present study to the texts of the Narratives at our disposal coming from the three sources

---

33. The Dutch text is: "Nu aldereerst uyt 't Portugueesch vertaald".
34. Cf. 1.3.6. The common source of *Paesi* and *Itinerarium*.
35. Cf. 2.3.3. What language did Joseph speak?
36. Cf. 2.3.4. The writer of the Narratives.

mentioned above. These three texts differ among themselves in certain details, one text possessing details which the others do not have or giving the same thing in a different way. However, they have many things in common. We feel that these three texts come from three different independent immediate sources. However, they seem to have originated from a remote common source. Therefore, it is of great importance to our study to trace their origin and provenance to evaluate each of the texts and to sort out the Narratives as they came from Joseph salvaging them from all editorial modifications, additions and omissions. Hence, a detailed study of the known sources and their important editions and translations is of great use to our study. In the following pages we try to make such a study of the sources we could identify, namely *Paesi, Itinerarium, Sonderlinge Reysen van Joseph* and *Novus Orbis* which originated from *Itinerarium*. Our study of the sources will be limited to these four documents.

1.2.0. Paesi Nouamente Retrouati and the Italian text of the Narratives of Joseph the Indian

Paesi has been described by Harrisse[37], Fumegalli[38]. Humboldt[39], Brunet[40], Rothschild[41], Thatcher[42], Vignaud[43], Greenlee[44], Tiraboschi[45], Camus[46], and mentioned by a few others, especially

---

37. Harrisse, H., *Bibliotheca Americana Vetustissima*, New York, 1866 (BAV) No. 48, pp. 96-99; No. 55, p. 108; no. 70, p. 130; no. 90, p. 159; no. 94, p. 153; no. 109, p. 184-187; Appendix pp. 469-70; *Additions*, Paris 1890 p. 26; Appendix pp. 469-70.
38. Quoted by H. Vignaud, *Americ Vespuce*, Paris, 1917, p. 19.
39. Homboldt, *Examen Critique*, Vol. IV, p. 80, quoted by Harrisse, *op. cit.* p. 96, Vignaud, op. cit. 19.
40. Brunet, *Manuel de Libraire et de l'amateur de Livres* 1921, Vol. V, p. 1156.
41. Rothschild; *Catalogue*, Vol. II, p. 427 quoted by Vignaud, *op. cit.*, p. 19.
42. Thacher, *Columbus*, Vol. II, p; 526, referred to by Vignaud, *op. cit.* p. 19.
43. *op. cit.* p. 20.
44. W. B. Greenlee, *op. cit.*, p. p. 95-113.
45. Tiraboschi, *Storia della Letter*. Vol. VII, pp. 213, 216, quoted by Harrisse *op. cit.* p. 99.
46. A. G. Camus, *Memoir sur la collection des grands et petits voyages et sur la collection des voyages de Melchisedech Thevenot*, Paris, 1902, p. 342.

cataloguers.[47] Harrisse, Brunet, Thatcher, Rothschild and Vignaud give descriptions of the different parts of *Paesi*. However, certain details given by Harrisse (no. 48) are incorrect,[48] and the opinion about the compiler of this collection needs revision.[49] W.B. Greenlee to some extent speaks of the manuscripts and other sources.[50] Harrisse and Vignaud give details about the different editions of *Paesi*.[51]

Vignaud gives also information about the various translations although incomplete.[52] However, none of the descriptions of these authors is complete and quite a few of their affirmations need revision. Hence, we feel that some detailed analysis of the structure, organisation and the contents of *Paesi* is necessary for our study. We need this especially to assess the value of the text of the Narratives of Joseph the Indian contained in *Paesi*, to solve the problem of the redactor of *Paesi*, to find the relation between *Paesi* and *Itinerarium* and also to trace the origins of the Narratives themselves. Here below, we attempt such an analysis basing it on the first edition of *Paesi*.

1.2.1. The First Edition of Paesi, 1507

Paesi of 1507[53] was quarto in size and consisted of 125 folios.[54] On the cover is given a rectangle in which there is

---

47. Cf. Harrisse and Vignaud. Harrisse gives them under the title direct references, p. 99; Vignaud, *op. cit.*, p. 20.
48. There is a mistake in the dates and the place names given on (BAV) pp. 97-98. Joseph the Indian is qualified as a converted aborigine, but he belongs to the ancient St. Thomas Christian community, which makes a big difference. There is no chapter CXLIII, which Harrisse gives, in any of the copies or editions and translations we have seen. Nor is it mentioned by any others.
49. Cf. below 1.2 6.
50. Greenlee op cit, pp. 95-97.
51. Harrisse, *op. cit.*, pp. 96-99, 130, 159, 163, 184-185, *Additions*, p. 463; Vignaud, *op, cit.* p. 26.
52. Vignaud, *op. cit.* pp. 23-28.
53. We have seen the copy of the National Library of Paris (Res. P. 7, *Catalogue General des livres imprimes de la Bibliotheque Nationale*, Paris, 1929, Vol. 54, Col. 300, under Fracanzano da Montalboddo) and the photocopy of the copy in the British Museum. We have also compared with other editions and translations.
54. Cf. Appendix I.

a globe. A scroll encircles the globe and is contained in the rectangle. On the scroll is written the title of the work: *Paesi Nouamente Retrouati et Nouo Mondo da Alberico Vesputio Florentino Intitulato.* The title-page is followed by 5 folios containing the table of contents, and the dedicatory letter of Montalboddo Fracan. The rest of the folios (7r–125r) contain the descriptions of the voyages. On the verso of the last folio the colophon is given.[55]

1.2.2. The contents of the Paesi

Paesi contains the voyages of Aloysius Ca da Mosto (to Cape Verde and Senegal 1454-1455), of Peter de Cintra (to Senegal, 1462, written by a Ca da Mosto), of Vasco da Gama to the Indian Coast (Calicut on Kerala Coast (1497-1499), of Pedro Alvares Cabral (to Brazil and Calicut 1500-1501), the first voyage of Columbus (1492-1493), the voyage of Alonso Negro (1499), the voyages of the Pinzon brothers, a duplicate of Vespucci's voyage, and the four letters containing matters related to the voyage of Cabral. The last item in the volume is Narratives of Joseph the Indian contained in nine and a half folios or 19 pages of the work.

1.2.3. The Division of the Work

Paesi is divided into six books comprising 141 chapters actually numbered as 142, owing to a mistake in numbering chapter X as XI and so on. (This mistake was repeated in all the later Italian editions, but was corrected in the French translation). Here below we give the division of the work according to the books and chapters.[56]

Book I	Chapters I–XLVII	46 Chapters
Book II	Chapters XLVIII–LXX	23 Chapters
Book III	Chapters LXXI–LXXXIII	13 Chapters
Book IV	Chapters LXXXIV–CXIII	30 Chapters
Book V	Chapters CXIV–CXXIV	11 Chapters
Book VI	Chapters CXXV–CXLII	18 Chapters

---

55. Cf. Appendix I.
56. For details about the division of the work Cf. Appendix I.

14 INDIA IN 1500 AD

Book I (Chapters 1–47)

The beginning of the first Navigation through the ocean to the land of the black, of the Bassa Ethiopia by the command of the most Illustrious Lord Infante of Huric brother of Don Dourth King of Portugal. [57]

Chapters 1–47   The voyage of Aloysius Ca da Mosto to cape Verde and Senegal undertaken between August 1454 and June 1455.[58]

Book II (Chapters 48–70)

The Second Book of the Navigation from Lisbon to Callichut (translated) from Portuguese into Italian.

Chapters 48–50   The voyage of Pietro de Zinzia (Peter de Cintra) in 1462 written by Ca da Mosto as it came from the lips of Cintra's secretary.

Chapters 51–62   The first voyage of Vasco da Gama to India from 9th July 1497 to 19th July 1499.

Chapters 63–70   The first part of the travels of Cabral.

Book III (Chapters 71–83)

Of the Navigation from Lisbon to Calichut (translated) from the Portuguese language into Italian.

Chapters 71–83   The second part of Cabral's travels to India.

Book IV (Chapters 84–113)

Beginning of the Navigation of the King of the Castiglia to the islands and countries newly found: book four.

Chapters 84–107   The first voyage of Columbus (1492)
Chapters 108–111   The voyage of Alonoso the black.
Chapters 112–113   The voyage of Pinzon brothers.

---

57. For the Italian equivalents of the titles of the various books Cf. Appendix I.
58. For the details about the navigators and their voyages mentioned in the different books Cf. Appendix I.

Book V (Chapters 114-124)

The New World: (translated) from Spanish into the Roman language: book five.

Chapters 114-124 The third voyage of Vespucci.

Book VI (Chapters 125-142)

The sixth book containing the things about Calichut which are related to the Navigation of Pedro Aliares described in the second and third books which are proved to be trustworthy by certain letters (given) according to the year collected in this last book.

Chapters 125-128 Four Letters: 1. Letter of a Cretan. 2. A letter of a Spanish merchant about the treaty between the king of Portugual and the king of Calichut, 3. The letter of Peter Pasqualigo to his brother in Lisbon. 4. Copy of the letter Francis de la Saita Cremone to Pasqualigo.

Chapters 129-142 The Narratives of Joseph the Indian.[59]

1.2.4. Remarks on the division of the work.

This division of the work into six books seems to be arbitrary. Often the titles of the books do not correspond to their contents. We find the indication "finis" (end) where it does not have any relevance in the make up of the whole work. For example, Book II contains as indicated above: 1. the voyage of Peter Cintra (chapters 48-50) 2. the voyage of Vasco da Gama (chapters 51-62), 3. the first part of Cabral's travels (chapters 63-70). It has the title: *"The Second Book of the Navigation from Lisbon to Callichut (translated) from Portuguese into Italian."* The travels of Cintra contained in this book have nothing to do with the title *"the Navigation from Lisbon to Calichut."* This was written by Ca da Mosto and had a better place in Book I. A "finis" appears at the end of chapter 50 at the middle of Book II where it is irrelevant. This "finis" is at the end of the travel of Cintra, and this "finis" would have been more meaningful if the chapters 48-50 were

---

59. They are given on $9\frac{1}{2}$ folios 19 pages on fascicles marked B_{ii}, C_{ii-iii}, D_{i-iii}r.

included in Book I. The third item in Book II contained in chapter 63-70 is incomplete. The part of the travels of Cabral, which is the continuation of what is contained in chapters 63-70 is separated and is included in Book III. Book III also has almost the same title as Book II, namely *"Of the navigation from Lisbon to Callichut (translated) from Portuguese into Italian."* As W. B. Greenlee points out, the chapters 63-83 now divided into two books in *Paesi*, originally formed one whole and was known as the *"Anonymous Narrative"*.[60] The work would have been better organised if the chapters 63-70 had been separated from Book II and included in Book III. Then the title of Book II with the travels of Vasco da Gama alone would have been more relevant. And the title of Book III with chapters 63-83 containing only the travels of Cabral with the same title as Book II would have been more meaningful. Then the "finis" at the end of Book III also becomes relevant. The title of Book VI gives no hint that it contains the Narratives of Joseph the Indian, even though they form the bulk of the materials contained there in. The chapters 129-142 have no indication at the beginning that they contain such a valuable document of history.

1.2 5. The editions and translations of Paesi[61]

We have stated earlier that *Paesi* was re-edited in 1508, 1512, 1517, 1519 and 1521. The 1508, 1512 and 1519 editions were published from Milan. They keep the same title as the first while the other two, 1517 and 1521, editions were published from Venice with titles different from that of *Paesi* of 1507. The 1916 edition is nothing more than a fascimile reprint of the 1508 edition from Milan. The German translation of Ruchamer published from Nuremberg had the title: *Newe unbekanthe landle Und ein newe weldte in kurtz verganger zeythe erfunden.*[62] The Dutch translation, based on the German translation and published from Lübeck in 1508, had the title: *Nye unbekande lande unde eine nye Werldt in korter forgangner tyd gefunden.* The French translation

---

60. W. B., Greenlee, *op. cit.* pp. 53-97.
61. For details Cf. Appendix I.
62. Cf. Appendix I.
63. Cf. Appendix I.

of Mathurin du Redouer saw six editions. The first edition is not dated but is supposed to be published in 1515. The later editions appeared in 1515-16, 1516, 1521, 1528 and 1529. The titles of some editions varied from that of the first edition which was entitled: *Sensuyt Le Nouueau Monde & Nauigations faictes par Emeric de Vespuce Florentin* [64] The English and Portuguese translations of *Paesi* are partial whose titles are different from that of *Paesi* as indicated earlier.

1.2.6. The Editor / Compiler of Paesi

Now we come to a very important question in our study, namely the question of the editor / compiler of *Paesi*. This question is raised not out of mere scientific curiosity. Nor are we prompted to discuss it anew, because there was some controversy over this among the specialists of American studies in the past years. We take up this question again because a correct knowledge about the editor / compiler of *Paesi* is of prime importance to us. In the first place, an accurate knowledge about the editor / compiler and the sources he used, is a basic requisite to assess the value of the text of the Narratives of Joseph the Indian in *Paesi*. It will also help us to determine the criteria to be used to compare this text with the texts from other sources. Besides, a precise knowledge about the editor and the sources he used will, perchance, give us some clue to the original source from which all the known texts originated.

Our probe into the identity of the editor / compiler of *Paesi* did not yield the results we wanted. We were not able to identify the editor / compiler of *Paesi*. However, we are happy to note that our research has yielded some very valuable results which we have least expected. It has enabled us to show that the opinion, held by many authors that Montalboddo Fracan. (whose name they find in the dedicatory letter of *Paesi*), was the editor of *Paesi*, is not tenable. It has also helped us to affirm that the views of the authors who regard *Itinerarium* as the translation of *Paesi*, are not correct and that *Itinerarium* does not directly depend on *Paesi*.[65] All these together made

---

64. Cf. Appendix I
65. 1.3.6., also 1.3.4. and 1.3.5.

us posit the hypothesis of a common source of *Paesi* and *Itinerarium*. This, in turn, made us affirm that Montalboddo Fracan. of *Paesi* and Montaboldus Fracanus of *Itinerarium* are one and the same person and that it was he who edited or collected and published the materials in the source common both to *Paesi* and *Itinerarium*.

As already indicated above, there was some controversy among some writers over the question of the editor / compiler of *Paesi*. Two groups of writers were involved in the discussions. The first group comprised editors of catalogues of books and the second consisted of specialists of American studies who were interested in the Columbus and Vespucci questions. Both the groups discussed the question in as much as it was relevant to their studies. Many could not make a serious analysis as the documents were very rare and not easily available. They often had to depend on secondary sources. Hence, their analysis was often partial or incomplete. In general, these writers assumed that the materials contained in *Paesi* existed prior to 1507 in print or in manuscript. But they were put together into one volume and translated into Italian(?) by an Italian whose task, according to them, was one of collecting, translating and editing the materials.

The majority of the writers who made an effort to trace out the editor / compiler of *Paesi*, seem to have depended solely on the indications in the dedicatory letter of *Paesi*. None of them adduces any external evidence to substantiate his view. Only Humboldt who named Zorzi as the editor attempted to look for the editor elsewhere. Those who depended on the dedicatory letter of *Paesi* named Montalboddo Fracan. as the editor. The address of the dedicatory letter would induce any one to take such a position. For it reads as follows: "Montalboddo Fracan. al suo amicissimo ioānimaria Anzotello S". Different authors have expressed their views. In their discussions different writers have given the very name of the editor differently like Fracan.,[66]

---

66. Paesi, 1507.

SEARCH INTO THE SOURCES 19

Fracanus,[67] Fracanzano,[68] Fracanzio,[69] Fracanzo,[70] and the two names together as Montalboddo Fracan,[71] Fracan de Montalboddo,[72] Montaboldus Fracanus,[73] Fracanzio da Montalboddo,[74] Fracanzo da Montalboddo,[75] Montalboddo Fracanzano,[76] Fracanzano de Montalboddo,[77] Fracanzio de Montalboddo,[78] Fracanzo Montalboddo,[79] and even Fracanzio de Monte Albodo.[80] But common to all these we have the invariable Montalboddo together with at least Fracan. Basing oneself the dedicatory letter it is quite possible that one names Montalboddo as the editor or compiler of this collection.[81]

But, Humboldt, counting on the authority of a remark made by Baldelli, believed that Alexander Zorzi, a famous cosmographer and cartographer of Venice was the editor and compiler of this collection. He wrote:

> "The true compiler (raccogiitore) of this curious and important collection of Vicence is, as it was believed for a long time, neither Montalboddo Fraconzio of Venice nor Fracanzio da Montalboddo, that is to say, a native of Monte-Alboddo, in the March d'Ancôna, professor of fine arts of Vicence,

---

67. Camus, *op. cit.*, p. 343; *Itinerarium* fol. I.
68. *Catalogue Generale des livres imprimes de la Bibliotheque Nationale*, Paris 1929; Vol. 54, 299; Humboldt *op. cit.*, Vol. iv. p. 80, Harrisse *op. cit.*, p. 96, Camus, *op. cit.*, p. 5; Compare with Francanzano in Brunet, *op. cit.*, Vol. V, 1159, quoted by Harrisse, p. 185.
69. Humboldt, *ibid.*; Camus, *ibid.*; Vignaud, *op. cit.*, p. 20.
70. Camus, *ibid.*
71. *Paesi.* 1507.
72. Harrisse, *op. cit*, p. 184.
73. *Itinerarium*, fol. 1 Camus *op. cit.*, 343.
74. Humboldt *ibid.*, Harrisse, *op. cit*., 96.
75. Camus, *op. cit.*, p. 5.
76. Brunet, *ibid.*, Humboldt, *ibid.*, Harrisse *op. cit.*, p. 185.
77. Camus, *op. cit.*, p. 342.
78. Vignaud, *op. cit.*, p. 19.
79. Harrisse seems personally to have accepted this, form. Cf. *op. cit.*, p. 187.
80. Brunet, *ibid.*, Humboldt, *ibid.*
81. But the presence of the same letter in the *Itinerarium* will pose certain difficulties with regards to this position and we have a different line thought and hypothesis. Cf. 1.3.6

but (according to the ingenious opinion of Baldelli) Alessandro Zorzi, the famous cosmographer and designer of maps of Venice." [82]

What Humboldt refers to here is the remark of Baldelli, contained in a foot-note to the *Il Millione*, where Baldelli mentions his discovery of the Magliabechi Library collection[83] of voyages and related things, both in print and manuscript form. The foot-note reads as follows:

"Esiste nella Biblioteca Magliabechiana (Class. XIII. var. Palch. 8. Cod. n.21 e 84)[84] la celebre Raccolta Vicentina delle navigazione dei Portughesi, della quale sarà in acconcio in altro luogo il raginare, divisa espressamente in due volumi, uno contenente gli scouprimenti orintali, l'altro gli occidentali. E il primo volume intitolato Nicolò Conti: e ciò perchè il viaggio del medesimo della dettatura originale del Poggio è in fronte del volume. Il secundo è intitolato Alberico, perchè contiene le navigazioni di Americo Vespucci... Ho con diligenza studiata questa raccolta, ed ho scoperto chi ne fosse il raccoglitore. Nel volume secundo... e questi essendo in Venezia diede una carta dei detti scuoprimenti, e la relatione di Bartolommeo ad Alessandro Zorzi, suo amico *e compilatore della raccolta predetta.*" [85]

Taking this statement of Badelli, Humboldt made his affirmation, that Zorzi was the compilor of *Paesi*, which challenged the beliefs held till that time. A resume the view held by many writers up to that time could be found in the statement of Brunet who wrote:

---

82. Humboldt, *Examen critique*, Vol. IV. p. 80 quoted by Harrisse, *op. cit.* p. 96. (Translation is mine.)
83. For a detailed analysis of the documents Cf. Roberto Almagia, *Interno a quattro codici fiorentini e ad uno ferrarese dell'erudito vicenziano Alessandro Zorzi.* Firenze, 1936.
84. Today the signature of this codex is Magl. xiii, 83 & 84.
85. Baldelli-Boni, B., *Il Millione di Marco Polo*, Vol. I, Firenze 1827, p.xxxii quoted by Harrisse. p. 186.

"Ce nom de *Montalboddo Fracân. ou Franc. (anzano)* se lit certainement dans toutes les éditions de ce recueil. Nous voyons même que c'est celui sous lequel est placée l'édition de 1507, dans la *Biblioth. pinell.*, qui passe pour être l'ouvrage de l'abbé Morelli. Cependant ce savant bibliothécaire, dans ses notes sur la lettre de Colomb, dit que le recueil de voyages (*Mondo Novo*) imprimé à Vicence, en 1507 a été donné par les soins d'un certain *Fracanzio*, natif de *Monte Alboldo*, dans la marche d'Ancône, et reprend à ce sujet ceux qui, d'après la mauvaise leçon de l'épître citée, ont attribué ce livre á un prétendu *Montalboddo Francanzano*. C'est aussi ce que répète Zurla, *di Marco Polo* vol. II., p. 108".[86]

The notes on the letter of Colomb, by Abbé Morelli, which Brunet mentions here reads as follows:

"...per opera di un Fracanzio, che ivi professava Lettere, ed era nativo da Monte Alboddo, terra nella Marca Anconitana; non di un Montalboddo Fracanzano Vicentino, siccome scrittori anche di grande merito indotti furono a nominare quel raccoglitore della guasta lezione, che il libro nella lettera dedicatoria, con altre molte d'importanza, presenta: le quali bene spesso vennero adottate da Fra Arcangelo da Madrignano."[87]

This last quotation is very important to understand the belief that existed before Humboldt brought in Zorzi. But, Humboldt's position does not seem to stand the test. Harrisse, discussing the 1521 edition of *Paesi*, was very confident in opposing the view of Humboldt, and even "to substitute the name of Fracanzano Montalboddo, in the place of that of Alessandro Zorzi." He wrote:

"But we always defer cheerfully to the opinion of those in whose experience and erudition we have

---

86. Brunet, *op. cit.*, Vol. V, col. 1159, quoted by Harrisse, *op. cit.*, p. 185.
87. Lettera Rarissima, pp. 45-46, quoted by Harrisse, *op. cit.*, p. 185.

been taught to place confidence, and did not hesitate to substitute the name of Fracanzano Montalboddo in the place of that of Alessandro Zorzi as the author of this most valuable collection of voyages."[88]

But, Henry Vignaud, who follows Harrisse's latest view, affirms:

"The dedicatory letter (of *Paesi*) indicates that the compiler of the collection was Fracanzio of Montalboddo professor of fine arts of Vicence. But, Humboldt, taking the authority of a Baldelli, believed that the true author of this work was Alexander Zorzi, the cosmographer and cartographer of Vicence. (*Examen critique*, Vol. IV, p. 80). *There seems to be an error.* Harrisse, who has seen the original pieces on the spot, assures us that a careful examination shows that Zorzi was only the collectioner of the documents utilised and that Montalboddo was really the author." [89]

But, Robert Almagia, who made a detailed study of the Magliabechi Library collection, [90] (of which Baldelli mentions in the foot-note in his *Il Millione*, which tempted Humboldt to come up with his theory), and who knows all the views of the time about the compiler of the *Paesi*, from Abbé Morelli up to Harrisse, in his work on the Magliabechi collection (*Intorno a*

---

88. Harrisse *op. cit.*, p. 187.
89. Vignaud, *op. cit.*, p. 19. (Translation is mine)
90. The codex 84 of this collection is important for our study of *Paesi* and also of the Narratives of Joseph the Indian. For, the whole codex has five books. The content of books I-III of *Paesi* was planned here to become book III, book VI of *Paesi*, book IV of the collection. And books, I, II, V, contain things not contained in *Paesi*, On the picture (carta) on folio 130v. is written in pen. "Libro Quarto delle Cose Calicut conforme alla Navigatione de Pedro Aliares etc.", which is of importance to our study of Joseph the Indian. Cf. Roberto Almagia *op. cit*, p. 30. We have ourselves seen the photocopy of the collection. The printed pages of the *Paesi* are found in them.

SEARCH INTO THE SOURCES 23

quattro codici fiorentini e ad uno ferrarese dell'erudito, Vicenziano Alessandro Zorzi) denies any relation between Zorzi and *Pacsi*. He very clearly says:

> "Non può affermarsi che lo Zorzi abbia avuto parte diretta nella pubblicazione dei *Paesi nuovamente discoperti* (sic) avvenuta nel 1507 a Vicenza, e attribuita a Fracanzio da Montalboddo......".[91]

This statement of Robert Almagia shatters the view proposed by Humboldt that Zorzi is the editor of *Paesi*. This brings us to the earlier view that Montalboddo Fracan. is the editor of *Paesi*. However, none of the advocates of this view adduces any external evidence. All their arguments are based on the dedicatory letter found in *Paesi*. The salutation of the dedicatory letter reads as follows: "*Montalboddo Fracan al suo amicissimo Ioanimaria Anzetello Vicentio Salutem*". Anyone who finds such an address in the dedicatory letter would immediately be tempted to believe and affirm that Montalboddo Fracan. is the editor of the work. However, such an affirmation becomes untenable from the fact that we find the same words also in the dedicatory letter of *Itinerarium*, whose editor is Archangelus Madrignanus, an Italian monk. In *Itinerarium* we find two dedicatory letters. The first is the dedicatory letter of Madrignanus addressed to Magnifico Iafredo Caroli. The second dedicatory letter occurs after the second title. It begins as follows: "*Io Mariae Vicentino Montabolbus Fracanus Salutem*" Here the difference from the Italian is that the word Anzetello" is missing and that there is a slight difference in the spelling of Montalboddo, which is written as Montaboldus. We shall prove later that the common opinion among the specialists that *Itinerarium* is the translation of *Paesi* is untenable and that there is no interdependence between *Itinerarium* and *Paesi* except that they have a common source.[92] Then the question arises. How are we to explain the presence of the same salutation in the dedicatory letter both in *Paesi* and in *Itinerarium*? Our hypothesis is that both *Paesi* and *Itinerarium* have a common source and that Montalboddo Fracan of *Paesi* and Montaboldus

---

91. Roberto. Almagia, *op. cit*. p. 34. no. 4.
92. Cf. 1.3.3.

Fracanus of *Itinerarium* are one and the same person. The slight differences in the forms of the names can be accounted for by the fact that the first is the Italian form and the second is the Latin equilavalent with the case ending of the nominative case. The differences in the spelling of the name Montalboddo and Montaboldus might have originated from the error of the scribe or of printing. We have cited above the variety of forms in which modern authors have transcribed the name which at most could have had only two forms, namely that of *Paesi* and that of *Itinerarium*. Hence, we conclude that Montalboddo Fracan of *Paesi* is not the editor of *Paesi* but that he is the editor/compiler of the source common both to *Paesi* and *Itinerarium*. We cannot say for sure who translated and edited *Paesi*.

1.3.0. Itinerarium Portugallensium and the Latin text of the Narratives of Joseph the Indian

Itinerarium has been described by Harrisse,[93] Fumegalli[94] Humboldt,[95] Brunet,[96] Tiraboschi,[97] Camus,[98] Vignaud,[99] and Van Paret.[100] Camus gives a detailed description of a copy on Velin kept in the National Library of Paris.[101] As far as we are aware, only Camus and Harrisse give some description of the contents and organization of the work. Humboldt speaks of the other two editions which are not mentioned by Harrisse, Fumegalli, Brunet and Camus.[102] Biddle, in his *Memoir of Sebastian Cabot*

---

93. Harrisse, H., *op. cit.*, no. 58, pp. 113–115.
94. Fumegalli, no. 32 quoted by Vignaud, *op. cit.*, p. 23.
95. Humboldt, *op. cit.*, Vol. IV. p. 85 quoted by Harrisse, *op. cit.* p. 115.
96. Brunet, *op. cit.*, Vol. VIII, p. 474 quoted by Harrisse, *ibid*.
97. Tiraboschi, *op. cit.*, Vol. VIII, p. 123, quoted by Harrisse, *ibid*.
98. Camus, *op. cit.*, p. 5, pp. 342–344.
99. Vignaud, *op. cit.*, pp. 23–24.
100. Van Paret, *Catalogue d's livres imprimes sur Velin de la Bibliotheque du Roi*, Paris, (8 Vols. 1822-28), Vol. V. p. 150. no. 172.
101. Camus, *ibid*. Van Paret, *ibid*.
102. Vignaud, *op. cit.* p. 24 says so. We have seen a copy of the work in the collection of Durate de Souza in Lisbon, which does not have a table of contents. But the copy of National Library of Paris has a table of contents. The index of which Harrisse speaks seems to be the table of contents. Do these differences prove what Humboldt said?

enumerates what Vignaud calls the "erreurs commises par la traducteur de cette collection", (mistakes committed by the traslator of this collection).[103] However, as in the case of *Paesi*, none of the descriptions of the authors cited above are complete Almost all them invariably assumed that *Itinerarium* is the translation of *Paesi*.

We find similarity between *Paesi* and *Itinerarium* as all the writers have seen. But, we find also differnces between the two which none of them could decipher or indicate. This is very clear in the case of the text of the Narratives of Joseph the Indian which occur in chapters 129-142 in Book VI as in *Paesi*, but shows striking difference from the text of *Paesi*. Henry Vignaud who was the most critical of work of Archangelo Madrignauns, does not seem to have noticed these differences. For, he affirmed,

> "Itinerarium Portugallensium comprises the pieces given in Paesi Retrouati......Whatever it be, Itinerarium is nothing other than a translation of *Paesi Retrouati*, a defective and inexact translation and without addition of any other piece."[104]

However, we feel that a negligence in translation in its most contemptible form cannot create all those differences which we find in the two works concerned.

A comparison of *Paesi* and *Itinerarium* is essential for us not only for determining the value of the text of the Narratives of Joseph the Indian in *Itinerarium* and the interrelation between the two, but also for understanding the value of our arguments in postulating a source common both to *Paesi* and to *Itinerarium* and in concluding that Montalboddo Fracan. is not the editor of *Paesi*, but of the source common both to *Paesi* and to *Itinerarium*. Hence, in the following pages we give a detailed analysis of *Itinerarium Portugallensium*.

---

103. Vignaud. *op. cit.*, p. 24, footnote.
104. Vignaud. *op. cit.*, p. 23.

1.3.1. Description of Itinerarium Portugallensium[105]

The work consists of 98 folios. The first 10 folios contain the cover page, the letter of dedication of Madrignanus, and the table of contents. The next 88 folios contain the descriptions of the various voyages which form the subject matter of the work.

On the cover page, at the top, is given the title of the work: *Itinerariū*[106] *Portugallensī*[107] *e Lusitania in Indiā*[108] *& in de in occidentem & demum ad aquilonem*. Below the title there is a map covering the whole page on which is marked, Portugal with Lisbon, Africa with its capes like Cape Debuga, Cape Biancho, Cape Verde, Monte Negro, Cape of Good Hope, Melindo, the Persian Gulf and Arabia with Mecha, the Indian Coast with the three ports, Calicut, Cannanore and Cochin (Calichut, Canan, Cucci) to which references is made in the work. On the verso of the cover page is a dedicatory epigram in a few lines of verse. On the following folios marked Aii–A8 is given the dedicatory letter of Madrignanus who translated the work. The dedicatory letter begins: 'Magnifico Iafredo Caroli ...... Archangelo Madrignanus ...... SDP". It ends on the recto of folio A8. On the next two folios is given the table of contents.

The subject matter of the work, namely the description of the voyages, is contained on the next 88 folios marked I–LXXVIII. The last folio is marked 78 instead of 88 by mistake. On the recto of folio I at the top we have a second title which reads: *Itinerarium Portugallensium ex Vlisbona ī*[109] *Indiam nec non in occidentem ac Septemtrionē*[110] *ex Vernaculo sermone in latinum traductum. Interprete Madrignano Mediolense Monacho Carevalensi.* Below this title is given the dedicatory letter of Montaboldus Fracanus which begins with the address "*Io Maria Vicentino ...... Montaboldus Fracanus Salutem*".

---

105. Our description of *Itinerarium* is based on the copy on paper kept in the National Library of Paris. Res. G. 547.
106. Itinerarium.
107. Portugallensium.
108. Indiam.
109. in
110. Septemtrionem.

SEARCH INTO THE SOURCES   27

1.3.2. The contents of Itinerarium.[111]

The matters described in *Itinerarium* are the same as those of *Paesi*, except for the differences which will be pointed out later. Just like *Paesi*,[112] *Itinerarium* contains descriptions of the expeditions of Ca da Mosto, Peter Cintra, Vasco da Gama, Pedro Alvares Cabral, Columbus, Alonso Negro, Pinzon brothers and Vespucci. The last book contains four letters related to matters connected with the travels of Cabral, and the Narratives of Joseph the Indian.

1.3.3. The division of the work.[113]

Itinerarium is divided into six books containing 141 chapters actually numbered 142 because of a mistake in counting chapter X as XI as in *Paesi*. Here below is given the division of the work into books and chapters.

Book I	Chapters I-XLVII	46 Chapters
Book II	Chapters XLVIII-LXX	23 Chapters
Book III	Chapters LXXI-LXXXIII	13 Chapters
Book IV	Chapters LXXXIV-CXIII	30 Chapters
Book V	Chapters CXIV-CXXIV	11 Chapters
Book VI	Chapters CXXV-CXLII	18 Chapters

Each book is divided into different chapters. All the books except Book I have their proper titles. In some books more than one navigation are treated. As in the *Paesi* the titles do not always correspond with the matters treated within. Below is given the subject matter of each book with the title and the division into chapters.

Book I (Chapters 1-47)[114]
(No title given)

Chapters 1-47   The voyage of Aloysius Ca da Most to Cape Verde and Senegal undertaken between August 1454 and June 1455.

---
111. For details Cf. Appendix II.
112. Cf. 1.2.2. the contents of *Paesi* and Appendix I.
113. Cf. Appendix II.
114. Book I has no title in *Itinerarium*, while in *Paesi* it has a title. *Novus Orbis* gives a title different from that of *Paesi*. Cf. 1.2.3. and 1.4.3.

28 INDIA IN 1500 AD

Book II (Chapters 48-70)

The Second Book of the Navigation from Lisbon to Calechut.[115]

Chapters 48-50   The voyage of Peter de Cintra written by Ca da Mosto as it came from the lips of Cintra's secretary.

Chapters 51-62   The first voyage of Vasco da Gama to India from 9th July 1497 to 19th July 1499.

Chapters 63-70   The first part of Cabral's travels to Calicut.

Book III (Chapters 71-83)

The Third Book of the navigation made from Lisbon to Calechut.

Chapters 71-83   Second part of Cabral's travels to Calicut.

Book IV (Chapters 84-113)

Beginning of the Navigation of the King of Spain through which he discovered many regions of the earth unknown upto now and ordered to inhabit the lands discovered.

Chapters 84-107   The first voyage of Columbus (1492)
Chapters 108-111   The voyage of Alonso Negro (sic)
Chapters 112-113   The voyage of Pinzon Brothers.

Book V (Chapters 114-124)

About the New World: translated from Spanish into Italian.

Chapters 114-124   The Third Voyage of Vespucci known as Mundus Novus.

Book VI (Chapters 125-142)

The sixth book containing the astonishing things about Calichut which are not different from what Peter Aliares wrote in the second and third books which are again collected from the letters of certain noble men as given in the following.

Chapters 125-128   Four letters of the noble men.
Chapters 129-142   The Narratives of Joseph the Indian.[116]

---

115. For the Latin equivalents Cf. Appendix II.
116. Folios. LXXXII - LXX (X) VIII.

1.3.4. Interdependence of Itinerarium and Paesi

The close similarity between *Itinerarium* and *Paesi*, in their subject matter, organisation and division into different books and chapters, made many authors think that *Itinerarium* was the translation of *Paesi*. Under that supposition some writers very severly criticised Archangelus Madrignanus (Archangelo Madrignano) who published *Itinerarium* for the differences they found in these two works. These writers described these differences as mistakes that resulted from negligence and carelessness in translation. The criticism of Humboldt, in his *Examen Critique*, resulted from such a view. Humboldt is not very sympathetic in his comments:

> "The redaction of the Latin translation of Madrignano, however, was done with extreme negligence. The division of the six books is indicated only for the second and third books at chapters 48 and 71, and not for the fourth and fifth books. The chapter 114 deals with Americ Vespuce and the work is without table of contents and the name of the navigator whose voyage is given remains unknown".[117]

This statement of Humboldt about the division of the work into different books is not correct. All the books except the first have titles. We could find a table of contents at least in the copy we have consulted in National Library of Paris.

Tiraboschi, the Italian critique, on his part, affirmed that Madrignanus had purposely changed the title in *Itinerarium*. He criticised him for using the expression *ex vernaculo sermone in Latinum traductum*. He felt that Madrignanus used this expression to make others believe that he had translated it from Portuguese. Camus to some extent defended Madrignanus against the attack of Tiraboschi. Still he too believed that *Itinerarium* was the translation of *Paesi*. Camus writes:

> "In the next year this collection (Paesi) was translated by Archangelo Madrignani of Milan of the order of the Citeaux and was printed in Milan. He changed

---

117. Humboldt. *op. cit.* Vol. IV p. 85 quoted by Harrisse, BAV p. 115

the title and announced his translation as made on the original Portuguese."[118]

And later in a foot-note Camus made his defence of Madrignanus in the following words:

"Tiraboschi seems to me to impute mal-intent on Madrignani for having changed the title of the collection and for having intended to make others believe that he translated it from the Portuguese original. The words "ex vernaculo sermone" employed by an Italian, can signify that he has translated it from Italian. Madrignanus did not want to dissimulate what he had given. For, he translated and printed the very dedicatory letter of Fracan."[119]

Camus seems to be correct in thinking that Madrignanus translated the materials contained in *Itinerarium* from some Italian dialect. But, his statement that Madrignanus translated the very dedicatory letter of Montalboddo contained in *Paesi*, is not correct. For, the letter of dedication in *Itinerarium* is different from that of *Paesi*, though the name of Io Maria is same in both. The letter of dedication of *Itinerarium* seems to imply that the things contained in the work are described referring to the Portuguese language and then to the Etruscan. It can be that Montalboddo prepared what is contained in his collection from Portuguese and Etruscan languages and published in some Italian dialect.

Henry Vignaud it his study of Amerigo Vespucci, gives a resumé of the views that existed upto then and attributes the defects and inexactitude to the work of Madrignanus. He writes:

"Itinerarium Portugallensium comprised the pieces given in Paesi Retrouati, but since this work has in its title the words "ex vernaculo" one could criticize Madrignani, the editor of this collection for pretending that it was from Portuguese that he translated his text. But, Camus has remarked that,

---

118. Camus, *op. cit.*, p. 5 (translation is mine)
119. Camus, *op. cit*, p. 343 (translation is mine)

this expression used by an Italian could mean that it might have been translated from Italian. Whatever it be, Itinerarium is nothing more than a translation of Paesi Retrouati, a defective and inexact translation and without addition of any other piece "[120]

These writers and others who followed similar views were generally led to such conclusions by the similarity between these two works. All these writers seem to have started their analysis with the assumption that *Itinerarium* was the translation of *Paesi*. As indicated above in our study of the editor of *Paesi*, two groups of writers made comparative study of these two works. The first were some specialists of American studies and the second, authors of catalogues of books. The former studied the two works in relation to the discovery of America and the Colombus vs Vespucci questions. These authors studied maily Book IV and V of the two works and advanced their arguments mainly depending on their finding of the comparison of these two books. The cataloguers, on the one hand, made general study of the two works as much as it served their purpose. None of these writers seems to have made a thorough comparative analysis of these works going into the organisation of the books and chapters and of the matters contained them. None of them seems to have ever compared the titles of the chapters of Book VI, let alone going into the differences in the details of the contents of each chapter. The Narratives of Joseph the Indian, the subject matter of our study, contained in the chapters 129–142, reveal striking differences in the titles of the chapters and the details of the descriptions. These writers failed in scrutinizing these areas properly. In many cases these two works in question were not easily available and many of the writers had to depend on secondary sources which were not always accurate. Their information was inexact, their affirmations hasty and hence their conclusions were not accurate and sometimes very defective and faulty.

---

120. H. Vignaud, *op. cit.*, p. 23 (translation is mine). Vignaud gives also a foot-note: "Pour un grande nombre d'erreurs commises par le traducteur de cette collection, voir Biddle sur Sebastian Cabot, London, 1831, pp. 251 ff. We have not been able to consult Biddle.

The question of the relation between *Itinerarium* and *Paesi* is of great importance to our study. It is important for us in determining the value text of the Narratives of Joseph the Indian and also in finding the source of the Latin text which is different from the Italian text in *Paesi*. Perhaps, this will give us some clue to find out the source of all the three texts, without which our study would remain imperfect. Besides a word in defence of Madrignanus, against the common current of opinions with regard to the relation of *Paesi* and *Itinerarium*, is also a scientific must. Hence, in the following section, we make a comparative study of the two works.

1.3.5. Itinerarium and Paesi, a comparative study

As far as the organization, division and subject matter in general, of *Paesi* and *Itinerarium* are concerned, as indicated above, there is great similarity between the two works. Both the works have six books and 141 chapters, wrongly counted as 142 in both. The division of the two works into different books and of the books into different chapters, is similar in both. The subject matter of the different books and chapters of the one agrees with that of the corresponding section of the other. However, striking differences can be marked between the two works in the details and mode of presentation.

Our description of the cover page of *Paesi* and *Itinerarium* clearly shows that there is great difference in the cover designs[121]. The cover design of *Itinerarium* is different from that of *Paesi* of 1507. However, the German and Dutch translations follow the design of the 1507 edition of *Paesi*. The cover design of *Itinerarium* reveals, it seems to us, the originality of Madrignanus and his scientific knowledge. While the picture on the cover of *Paesi* is a globe and a scroll on which the title of the work is printed, in *Itinerarium* we have the map of the world indicating the seas and lands about which descriptions are given, especially, the Kerala Coast with the then known three ports on the west coast, Calicut, Cochin and Cannanore.

---

121. For the description of the cover of *Paesi* Cf. 1.2.2. and Appendix I, and of *Itinerarium*. Cf. 1.3.1. and Appendix II.

If one considers the titles of the two works, one immediately notices that the titles are different. *Paesi* has only one title, *Itinerarium* has two. *Paesi* is entitled "*Paesi Nouamente Retrouati et Nouo Mondo da Alberico Vesputio Florentino Intitulato*". None of the words 'Nouo Mondo', or 'Alberico Vesputio' can be found in the title of *Itinerarium*. Its first title runs: "*Itinerarium Portugallensium e Lusitania in Indiam & inde in occidentem & demum in aquilonem*", and the second reads: *Itinerariam Portugallensium ex Vlisbona in Indiam nec non in occidentem ac Septemtrionem ex Vernaculo sermone in Latinum traductum*".

The tables of contents of the two works agree in general though there are differences too. Similarly, differences and similarities are seen in the letters of dedication. In *Paesi* there is only one letter of dedication, while *Itinerarium* has two, the first on the folios Aii – Aviii and the second on the folio I^r. The first is of Madrignanus to Magnifico Iafredo Caroli and the second of Montaboldus Fracanus to Io Maria Vicentino. This second letter does not agree in content with the dedicatory letter of *Paesi*. However, the writer of the letter and the person addressed to are same, though their names are spelled differently. In *Paesi* it is written 'Montalboddo'; in *Itinerarium* it is 'Montaboldus'.

Coming to the organization and division of the two works, we see that both the works are divided into six books in the same way. Both agree in the total number of chapters. Also in the number of chapters in each of the six books, the two works agree. Book I has 47 chapters in both. However, when *Paesi* has a long title for Book I, *Itinerarium* has neither the title nor even the indication for Book I. Book II and Book III agree in the titles as well as in the subjects treated. The three subjects treated in Book II as well as the number of chapters in each section agree. However, Book IV and Book V do not agree as regards the titles. They were the two books that were studied by the specialists of American studies. The titles of Book VI vary, but the subject matter in general is the same, though there are striking differences in details.

Coming to the organization, we find similarities as well as differences in the numbering of the chapters and their titles. The two works agree in the tables of contents in their division into chapters. There are 142 chapters each in the tables of contents both in *Paesi* and *Itinerarium*; but there are only 141 chapters in both the works. This happened because chapter X was numbered as XI in the text of both the works. This mistake of counting chapter X as XI is seen in both. Chapters XXVI and XXXII are numbered as XXVII and XXXIII respectively in Book I of *Paesi*. These mistakes are not found in *Itinerarium*. Chapter XXXIX of *Paesi* has a title, while that of *Itinerarium* has none. In Book VI we find differences as well as similarities in the organization into chapters.

Again there is similarity and difference between the two works with regard to the four letters given in Book VI, in their sequence and numbering of the chapters. In both *Paesi* and *Itinerarium* they are given in the first four chapters of Book VI. In the tables of contents of both the works they are given in the same order, namely 125, 126, 127 and 128. However, they are given in a different sequence in the body of the text both in *Paesi* and *Itinerarium*. The letter given in chapter 128 in the tables of contents of both the works is given immediately after chapter 125 in the text, with different chapter numbers. *Paesi* counts it as chapter 128, while *Itinerarium* counts it as 126. The other two letters, namely the second and third letters in the tables of contents with chapter numbers 126 and 127, are given as the third and fourth letters in the Book VI keeping the same chapter numbers. Thus, we have two different sequence of chapter numbers. In *Paesi* four letters are in the sequence 125, 128, 126, 127 followed by 129, while in *Itinerarium* we find the sequence 125, 126, 126, 127, followed by chapter 129 having no chapter 128.

We have come across another very interesting difference be-between the two works. It is a diagram found in chapter 39 of *Itinerarium*. This diagram is not found in *Paesi*. The diagram in question appears on folio xxiii^v of *Itinerarium* and it shows the position of stars which are discussed in the chapter. Though there is no diagram in *Paesi*, there is some space left blank which appears to have been meant for some diagram. In the 1508 edition of *Paesi* we do find a diagram in the corresponding chapter. So we feel that the blank space found in *Paesi* was meant for some diagram. (Compare the folios of *Paesi* 1507 and *Paesi* 1508 on pp. 35 & 36).

SEARCH INTO THE SOURCES 35

There is also difference between the diagrams of *Itinerarium* and *Paesi* of 1508. In *Itinerarium* the stars are represented in a

[Note space without picture]

Paesi 1507

The unnumbered folio of *Paesi* with the blank space in chapter 39. *Itinerarium* has a diagram in this chapter (see p.37). *Paesi* 1508 also inserted a diagram in this blank space (see p. 36), which is different from that of *Itinerarium*.

rectangle, while in *Paesi* we find a trapezium. The stars are also marked differently in both the works in question (see the pictures on pp. 36, 37). Though there is difference between *Paesi* and *Itinerarium* with regard to the diagram in chapter 39, they agree very well in the case of the diagrams in chapters 119 and 121, except for the technic of representation (see pp. 36, 37 and 38).

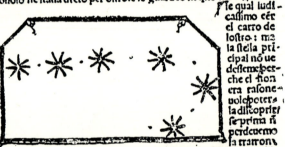

Paesi 1508

The folio containing the diagram given in chapter 39, which is different from that of *Itinerarium* (see p. 37). *Paesi* 1507 has blank space here (see p. 35).

SEARCH INTO THE SOURCES   37

There are also similarity and differences in the division and titles of the last 14 chapters of the two works which contain the Narratives of Joseph the Indian. It is the differences between

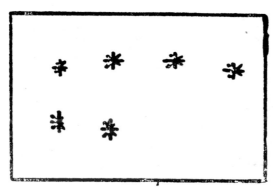

The digaram in *Itinerarium* (1598)
It appears on folio xxiii in chapter 39 of *Itinerarium*. It shows the position of the stars described in the chapter. (The reproduction is ours; reproduced from the copy kept in the National Library of Paris.)

The diagram in *Novus Orbis* 1532
Novus Orbis reproduced what was in *Itinerarium*. (The reproduction is ours.)

the texts of the Narratives of Joseph the Indian in these two works that prompted us to compare the two works in detail. For the details of the differences of the texts Cf. Part III.

1.3.6. Common Source of Paesi and Itinerarium

The comparative analysis of *Paesi* and *Itinerarium* leads us to some interesting conclusions or hypotheses regarding the interdependence of *Itinerarium* and *Paesi*. We feel that direct dependence of *Itinerarium* on *Paesi* is not something that we can confidently defend. The view that *Itinerarium* is the translation of *Paesi* is a supposition which is untenable. The presence

Paesi 1507

The diagram given in chapter 119. Compare the technic of representation with that of the diagrams in *Paesi* 1508 (see p. 36) and *Itinerarium* (see p. 37).

of the differences indicated above, especially these of the texts of the Narratives of Joseph the Indian, cannot be explained away as mistakes of negligence and carelessness in the act of translation. For, such negligence and carelessness in their most contemptible form cannot create a text of the Narratives of Joseph the Indian which is different from that of *Paesi* but similar to that of *Sonderlinge Reysen* which claims to be translated from original Portuguese.[122] Our research has made us posit a few hypotheses on the interdependenc of *Paesi* and *Itinerarium*. We propose the hypothesis of different immediate sources and a remote common source. In the following paragraphs we attempt to explain ourselves.

We begin our comparison with the analysis of the differences in the cover page and the titles of the two works.[123] In itself they do not prove or disprove dependence or non-dependence of the one on the other. It may be that the author of *Itinerarium* changed the design of the cover for some reason or other as did the editor of the second edition of *Paesi*. We can also think that Madrignanus purposefully changed the title, and declared "*ex vernaculo sermone traductum*" to make others believe that he had translated it from Portuguese, as Tiraboshi and others held. Then we would have to answer the question why should he keep in the work, the dedicatory letter of Montalboddo which is different in form and details of the contents, from that of *Paesi*. He could have omitted that and stated in the title directly and clearly "ex lingua Portuguesa traductum". Why should he use the expression "ex vernaculo sermone", if he had not translated it from some Italian dialect? Our opinion is that Madrignanus translated the material contained in some source in the Italian dialect, most probably from the Etruscan dialect as the dedicatory letter gives a clue. That explains better his expression "ex vernaculo sermone traductum". Hence, we argue for a source other than *Paesi*.

Now we come to the question of the dedicatory letters. Camus has said that *Itinerarium* gives the very letter of Montalboddo as in *Paesi*. The first dedicatory letter of Madrignaus

---

122. For details of the differences between the two texts Cf. Part III.
123. Cf. 1.2.1; 1.3.1 and 1.3.5.

to Magnifico Iafredo is the dedicatory letter of *Itinerarium*. The letter of Montaboldus is what was already in the source he used. That is why, this letter occurs after the table of contents and the second title of the work. The fact that the name of the writer of the dedicatory letter is given differently in the two works can be understood better in that way. The name might have been spelled differently in the source which Madrignanus used. This brings us to another hypothesis: the immediate sources of *Paesi* and *Itinerarium* were different. However, they originated from a common source whose editor was Montalboddo Fracan (Fracanus Montaboldus). The similarity in the division of the works and the subject matter of the books, in general, reveal that they have a common source. However, the differences in the descriptions and titles of the books point to different immediate sources. The fact that chapter 10 is omitted in both the works in the text but is given in the tables of contents of both shows that they originate from a common source.

We have indicated above that the mistakes in counting chapter 26 as 27 and 32 as 33 found in *Paesi* are not repeated in *Itinerarium*. It can be argued that Madrignanus corrected these mistakes. Then one should answer why did he not correct the mistake in counting chapter 10 as 11. This was more serious than those two mistakes, because the table of contents gives chapter 10 which is omitted in the text. Or why did he not correct the mistake of giving the 4th letter in the table of contents as the second letter in the text in Book VI just as it is in *Paesi*? Why did he retain the same position and give a different numbering as 125, 126, 126, 127 when *Paesi* keeps the numbering as 125,128,126,127 ? Why did he repeat the mistake of *Paesi* here ? If he corrected one thing he should have been careful and consistent in correcting the mistake of counting the chapters as the French translator has done. We know that Madrignanus was a man of scientific calibre. He had translated many other voyages. So, we feel that Madrignanus did not correct the mistakes of *Paesi* in any case. He translated the source he had. We think that the unity in mistakes points to a common remote source and the differences in mistakes point to different immediate sources. The similarity in the tables of contents and the differences in the texts again point to a remote common source and different immediate sources. Hence, the mistakes in the numbering of chapters point to different immediate sources and a remote common source. Therefore, we feel that the differences in the titles of the different books and chapters, with common corresponding subject matter, and the similarity and differences in the counting of the chapters can better be explained by postulating different immediate sources and a remote common source to *Paesi* and *Itinerarium*.

The differences of the diagrams in their representation and the absence of the picture with the space given for it in the chapter 39 in *Paesi*, and the presence of a picture in chapter 39 of *Itinerarium*, different from that of *Paesi*, point to the existence of a common source from which the immediate sources originated. For, in chapter 39 of the source of *Paesi* there was a picture, which the editor of *Paesi* forgot to give in the space provided. Or it was not in the source of *Paesi* itself. In any case, the presence of the picture in *Itinerarium* shows that either its editor knew the source of *Paesi* or he used a source different from that of *Paesi*.

The differences in the text of the Narratives of Joseph the Indian also point to different immediate sources both to *Paesi* and *Itinerarium*. This will explain the differences in the mode of description of the chapter 129 in the two works. It will explain also the differences in the titles of the chapters and the differences in the spellings of the names of places of the two texts (for details cf. Part III).

Hence, our hypothesis is that the immediate sources of *Paesi* and *Itinerarium* were different and that there existed a source common to both the sources of *Paesi* and of *Itinerarium*. Montalboddo Fracan of *Paesi* and Montaboldus Fracanus of the *Itinerarium* are one and the same person and that he is the editor of the source common to both. The dedicatory letter found both in *Paesi* and *Itinerarium* was the dedicatory letter of this common source. This should have been in some Italian dialect. This will explain the expression "*ex vernaculo sermone*" of the title of *Itinerarium*. The Immediate sources of both *Itinerarium* and *Paesi* were different and they originated from this common source. Hence, we affirm that, unless otherwise proved, it remains proved that *Paesi* in not the immediate source of *Itinerarium* and the latter is not the direct translation of *Paesi*.

1.4.0. Novus Orbis and the Narratives of Joesph the Indian

The ecclesiastical writers of the 18th and 19th centuries knew about Joseph the Indian and his Narratives through another source, *Novus Orbis*.[124] Assemanus, in his works,[125] mentions only the 1555 edition of *Novus Orbis* as the source of the Narratives. So also Nilles, the author of the *Calendarium Utriusque Ecclesiae*,[126] knows about Joseph the Indian and cites in his work the 1555 edition of *Novus Orbis*. Germann, the author of *Die Kirche der Thomaschristen*, very clearly states that the only one source accessible to him of all the known sources was *Novus Orbis* of Grynaeus. Even the Portuguese chronicler-historian De Barros knew of no other source than *Novus Orbis*. In the 16th century, speaking of Joseph the Indian and his Narratives, he wrote:

> "The Italians, who in this area are more curious than we are, have made a summary which is incorporated in a volume entitled *Novus Orbis*, which includes some of our navigations, written not as they merit and as they happened."[127]

This shows that he did not have any knowledge of the 17 editions of *Paesi* and the Latin text in *Itinerarium*. He was aware only of *Novus Orbis* which appeared some 25 years after *Paesi* and *Itinerarium*. The text of the Narratives of Joseph the Indian in *Novus Orbis* depends on *Itinerarium*.

1.4.1. Novus Orbis

Novus Orbis is a collection of accounts of voyages undertaken at the end of the 15th and first half of the 16th century. It was first published in 1532 and had three different editions and German as well as Dutch translations. This collec-

---

124. Cf. 1.1.0., 1.1.2.
125. J. J. Assemanus, *Codex Liturgicus Ecclesiae Universae*, Romae, pp. 229–243.
126. Nilles, *Calendarium Manuale Utriusque ecclesiae Orientalis et Occidentalis*, Romae, 1897, p. 651, "Das Syro–Chaldaische Kirchenjahr der Thomas-christen". *Zeitschrift fuer Katholische Theologie*, Vol.20 (1896) pp. 726-739.
127. De Barros, *Da Asia*, Lisbon, 1774. Dec. I. Bk. V. Chapter viii.

tion is bigger than *Paesi* and *Itnerarium*, and it was further augmented in the subsequent editions. The first part of this work, which consists of six books and 142 chapters, is nothing more than a reprint of *Itinerarium Portugallensium*. Hence, the Narratives of Joseph the Indian contained in the *Novus Orbis*, are simply the reproduction of the text of the Narratives in *Itinerarium*.

Though generally known as *Novus Orbis*, the complete title of the work is *Novus Orbis Regionum Ac Insularum Veteribus Incognitarum una cum tabula cosmografica & aliqot aliis consimilis argumenti libellis quorum omnium catalogus sequenti patebit pagina*. This is also known by the name of Grynaeus, and even of J. Huttich, for it was Simon Grynaeus, who edited, the things collected by J. Huttich. A note written in ink on the copy of the 1537 edition of *Novus Orbis*, kept in the Bibliotheque Rayale de Bruxelles,[128] reveals the history of this collection. This note, which in fact is an adapted citation of Camus, reads as follows:

> Meusel nomme cette collection, 'Collectio Huttico-Grynaeo-Hervagiana,' parcequ'elle a été formée par les soins de Jean Hutticus de Mayence, Chanoine de Strassburg, qui la fit imprimer a Bâle par Hervagius, lequel la confia aux soins de Simeon Grynaeus. On en fit differentes editions a Bâle 1532, 1537, 1555. (Bibl. Hist. t. III, P. 221),[129] (voyez Camus, Memoire sur la collection des grandes et petits voyages. Paris, 1802, p. 6.)

Of course, Meusel and Camus mention there also the Paris edition of 1532,[130] which is not mentioned in the note quoted above. Camus says there that "Editio Parisina est omnium rarissima." *Novus Orbis* was translated into German by Michael Herr, and

---

128 Bibliotheque Royale de Bruxelles, Section of Reserved Books, Call Number, V. H. 14120. This note is on the page after the cover page that forms the part of the binding of November 25, 1825.
129. G. Meusel, *Bibliotheca Historica*, Lipsiae. 1787, Vol. III, pars I, pp. 221-223. On the margin Meusel calls it Collectio-Huttico - Grynaeo-Hervagiana, p. 221.
130. Meusel *ibid*.

was pubished from Strassburg in 1534. The Dutch edition was the last of the editions or translations of *Novus Orbis*, that we know of. The translation was made by Cornelius Ablijn, and it was published from Antwerp ('Thantwerp') in 1563. The Basel 1532 and Paris 1532 editions are same; but Basel 1537 and 1555 editions have certain additions which are not found in the first. The German follows the first edition. The Dutch is different in the organization of the books and chapters. We have examined all the editions of *Novus Orbis*.

1.4.2. The description of Novus Orbis

Meusel,[131] Camus,[132] Brunet,[133] Harrisse,[134] Vignaud,[135] Panzer,[136] Humboldt,[137] and Maittaire,[138] describe *Novus Orbis*. Meusel and Camus give the details of the contents of the work. (We are familiar with all the different editions and translations. Our description of *Novus Orbis* is based on our comparative study of these texts).

Novus Orbis was first published "in the month of March 1532" "apud Io Hervagium" from Basel in Switzerland. This first edition comprised 634 pages (ii+xlvi+584+ii) in folio including the cover page. The first 48 pages numbered in folios comprise the cover page, the table of contents (on the back of the cover page), the preface of Grynaeus, the three sets of indices of materials included in the volume, and the description of the map included together with the tips for its use by Sebastian Muster, the famous German cartograph. (The map said to be included is not found in the two copies we could consult of the 1532 edition, but is found in the 1555 edition.) The following 584 pages numbered from 1 to 584 contain the descriptions of the various travels included in the work.

---

131. Meusel, *ibid.*
132. Camus, *op. cit.* p. 6
133. Brunet, *op. cit.* Vol. IV. col. 132
134. Harrisse, *op. cit.* pp. 296-299
135. Vignaud, *ibid.*
136. Panzer, quoted by Harrisse *op. cit.* p. 297.
137. Humboldt, *op. cit.* p. 222 note quoted by Harrisse. *ibid.*
138. Maittaire, quoted by Harrisse, *ibid.*

SEARCH INTO THE SOURCES 45

Novus Orbis, in none of its editions, is a properly organised work. It is a conglomeration of materials related to the various navigations put together without proper editing or reorganisation. It can be called a mosaic work of the materials already published, presented in the way they were available. For example, the first 153 pages are nothing but a reproduction of the materials found in *Itinerarium Portugallensium*, with the same division of books and chapters and even with the mistakes therein. What follows this section is the navigation of Amerigo Vespucci which is given with its own division without relation to the first chapter numbers and division of books. Each item that follows in the volume is kept as it was published without any editorial change. Therefore, we cannot find any indication of the division of the different materials. However, the indices of materials give us a clue to find some kind of dividing line among the materials. The three indices given represent three groups of materials of three different sources of provenance. If we divide the work accordingly, we can give demarcation into three different sections, besides the introductory folios, as follows:

Introductory Section[139] first 48 pages in folios, in four fascicles marked Alpha, Beta, Gamma and Delta.
    Section 1. pp. 1 – 153. Contains the materials in *Itinerarium*.
    Section 2. pp. 154–297
    Section 3. pp. 297–584:

1. 4. 3. The Contents of Novus Orbis

What interests us most in *Novus Orbis* is the first item in the work, namely, the materials contained in *Itinerarium*. This is followed by an account of the four Navigations of Amerigo Vespucci (1451–1512), the letter of King Emmanuel to Pope Leo X, the 7 books of the travels of Ludivic Varthema, the Roman Patrician, a description of the Holy Land by the monk Brocardo, the three books of Marco Polo, the description of Tartar by Haithon, the Sarmatia Asiana et Europea by Mathias Michou, the letter Paul Jovus to Archbishop Constantine, Peter Martyr's description of the islands and people he discovered, and the antiquities of Erasmus Stella.

---

139. The first 48 pages make up 4 fascicles with folio numbers.

46   INDIA IN 1500 AD

Containing as it does all that is in *Itinerarium*, *Novus Orbis* is a source for the Narratives of Joseph the Indian. It keeps the same order in the first 141 chapters numbered 142 as in *Itinerarium*. The chapters CXXIX – CXLII, contained in pages 142 to 153 of the 1532 Basel edition, are the Narratives of Joseph the Indian.[140] The contents are same as that of the Latin text of *Itinerarium*.

1.4.4. **The division of the Novus Orbis**

As already indicated above *Novus Orbis* is not a properly organised work having its own division into different books and chapters. So we have divided *Novus Orbis* of 1532 into four sections. We cannot give all the details about all the different sections. Our attention will be focused mainly on the 153 pages of the first section. Only very short indications will be given for the other sections.

Introductory Section (first 48 pages)

The title-page	pp. i[141]
The table of contents	pp. ii
The Preface of Grynaeus	pp. iii–v
The first set of index	pp. vi–xiii
The second set of index	pp. xiii–xxiv
The thrid set of index	pp. xxiv–xxxvi
The description of the map and the tips for its use	pp. xxxvii–xlviii

Section 1 (pp. 1–153)

(Reproduction of the materials in the *Itinerarium Portugallensium*. It contains six books and 141 chapters counted 142).

Book I (pp. 1–50)

Navigation of Aloysius Ca da Mosto to the unknown lands.

Chapters 1–47	Travels of Ca da Mosto	pp. 1–50

---

140. The Narratives appear on pp. 125–134 in the Paris edition of 1932, pp. 142–153 in the Basel edition of 1537 and pp. 202–210 in the Basel edition 1555.
141. We have adopted this mode of numbering the first section for convenience. Cf. note no. 139.

Book II (pp. 51-70)

The second book of the Navigation from Lisbon to Calechut translated from Portuguese into Italian.

Chapters 48-50	The voyage of Peter Cintra written by Ca da Mosto.	pp. 51-55
Chapters 51-62	The navigation of Vasco da Gama to Calicut.	pp. 55-64
Chapters 63-70	The travels of Cabral (one part)	pp. 64-70

Book III (pp. 71-89)

The third book of the Navigation made from Lisbon to Calechut.

| Chapters 71-83 | The travels of Cabral (continuation) | pp. 71-89 |

Book IV (pp. 90-121)

Here begins the Navigation of the King of Spain through which many regions upto now unknown were discovered. He ordered to inhabit and frequent the newly discovered regions.

Chapters 84-107	The Navigation of Christopher Columbus	pp. 90-117
Chapters 108-111	About the different peoples and places found by Alonso Negro.	pp. 117-118
Chapters 112-113	About the Navigation of Pinzon companion of the admirant and the things he discovered.	pp. 119-121

Book V (pp. 122-130)

Epitome of the navigation of Alberic Vespuci, De Nouo Orbe translated from Spanish to Italian.

| Chapters 114-124 | Navigation of Vespucci | pp. 122-130 |

Book VI (pp. 130-153)

Memorable things about Calechut, which are similar to those Peter Aliares wrote in his second and third treatises which are collected from the letters of certain nobility.

Chapters 125-128	the four letters	pp. 130-142
Chapters 129-142	The Narratives of Joseph the Indian (*Navigatio Josephi Indi*).	pp. 143-153

Section 2 (pp. 154-297)

The Navigation of Amerigo Vespucci	pp. 154-184
The Letter of King Emmaunel to Pope Leo X	pp. 184-187
The Navigation of Ludivic Varthema (7 books)	pp. 187-297

Section 3 (pp. 297-584)

Brocard Monachus: description of the Holy Land.	pp. 297-329
The Three books of Marco Polo.	pp. 330-417
The Book on the Tartar by Haithon	pp. 419-481
Mathias Michou: Two books of Sarmatia Asiana & Europea.	pp. 482-531
Libellus of Paul Jovus to Archiepiscope Constantine	pp. 532-548
Peter Martyr: About the islands he discovered and about the customs of the people there.	pp. 549-569
The two books of Antiquities by Erasmus Stella	pp. 570-584

1.4.5. German and Dutch translations of Novus Orbis

The german translation of *Novus Orbis* was made by Michael Herr in 1534 based on the Basel edition of 1532. The title of the German translation was: *Die New welt der Landschaften unnd Insulen, so bis hie her allen altweltbeschreybern vnbekant. Jungst aber von den Portugalesern vnnd Hispaniern im Niedergenglischen Meer herfunden.* It was published on 21 September 1534 from Strassburg. The Narratives of Joseph the Indian occur on folios 45v–49r consisting of chapters cxxix-cxlii.

The Dutch translation was the last reproduction of *Novus Orbis*. It was published from Antwerp in 1563. It contains the latest of all translations and editions of the text of the Narratives of Joseph the Indian in the 16th century. It was translated by Cornelius Ablijn. The title of the work was *Die Niewe Weerrelt der Landtschapen ende Eylanden die tot hier toe allen ouden Weereltbeschrijbern onbekent geweest sijn. Waer nu onlac vanden Portugalosiern en Hispaniern.*

From the title it appears that this was the translation of the German of Michael Herr. However, as far as the organization and division of the work are concerned, it agrees neither with the German nor with the Latin *Novus Orbis*. It consists of vi +818 pages. It is divided into 21 sections. The Narratives of Joseph the Indian come as the item 9 on pp. 226-235 with the title *Die Reyse Josephi des Indianers*. In the table of contents, however, this is given as Den *Boecxken der Schipvaerden Josephi des Indianers van der Stadt Caranganora*, (the book of the Navigations of Joseph the Indian from the city of Caranganora). This shows that the editor thought of the Narratives of Joseph the Indian as an independent material. This needs more research before we could say a final word about it.

What is interesting in this Dutch edition is the fact that the first three books of *Paesi* and *Itinerarium* comes as nos. 14,15, and 16. Book IV is given as 11th, 12th and 13th. Book V becomes no. 17 and the four letters of Book VI come as the nos. 7 and 8. The contents in general agree with the contents of *Novus Orbis* of 1532 and the German translation of Michael Herr.

This, in brief, is the description of *Novus Orbis* of 1532 and its versions. Though the title of the work says that a map of the world is given in the volume, the two copies we could consult did not have the map mentioned. Nor could we find it in the Basel edition of 1537, which we have examined. However, the 1555 edition has a map of the world. The Paris edition too has a map. But, this is different from the one found in the 1555 edition we could examine at Köln.

1. 4. 6. The Three re-editions of Novus Orbis.

The Paris edition of 1532 was nothing more than a reprint of the Basel edition of 1532. The title was the same as the first edition. But, the vignette represents a gally bearing the lillies of France with the motto: Vogue la Gale. It was printed "Parisiis apud Galeotum a Prato in aula maiore regii Palatii ad primam columnam." The colophon reads: Impressum Parisiis apud Antonium Augellerum impensis Ioannis Parui & Galeoti A Prato Anno MDXXXII, viii Kalen. Novembris. The format and the pagination of this edition are different from that of the Basel edition of 1532. However, it is nothing more than a re-impression of the Basel edition. There are altogether ii+xxiv+xix+514 pages, including the title-page whose reverse is the table of contents. The Narratives of Joseph the Indian appear in chapters 129-142 on pages 125-134.

The Basel edition of 1537 was published in March. It was also a re-impression of the Basel edition. But there was an addition. The Navigation of Carol Caesar. However, in the table of contents it is not given. The title-page clearly says: "to this last edition is added the Navigation of Carol Caesar". In the division of the work and the pagination it follows the Basel edition of 1532. Altogether there are 48+600 pages. The Narratives of Joseph occur in chapters 129-142, on pp. 142-153.

The 1555 edition also appeared in Basel. This edition had still other additions. The pagination was different from that of the other editions. In the table of content the additions are marked clearly. On the title-page it is marked as Anno MDLV. This is the largest of all the editions of *Novus Orbis*. The Narratives of Joseph the Indian appear in chapters 129-142 on pp. 202-210.

1.5.0. Sonderlinge Reysen van Joseph

We have stated earlier that the third source of the Narratives of Joseph the Indian is the Dutch booklet called *Sonderlinge Reysen van Joseph*. This booklet consists of 23+4 pages including title-page, table of contents, the text and the index in 4 pages at the end, which are not numbered.

On the title-page on top is given the title which reads: "*Sonderlinge Reysen van Joseph den geboornen Indiaan; Bevattende een Aanmerklijke Beschrijvingh der Landen, Steeden, en Inwooners van Caranganor, Calicuth, Cambaja, Narsinga, enz.* Door de Portugeezen uyt sijnen Mond opgetekend, Anno 1501. Nu aldereerst uyt

SEARCH INTO THE SOURCES 51

't Portugeesch vertaald.[142] As we have stated earlier, it was published from Leyden in 1706, by Peter Vander Aa, whom the book qualifies as "Boekverkoper" (bookseller).

This booklet appeared in the second volume of a collection of voyages published by Vander Aa, under the title: *Naaukeurige Versameling der Gedenk-waardigste Zee en Land-Reysen Na Oost en West-Indien*. This volume contains voyages undertaken between 1500 and 1504 and the title-page of the volume gives the date 1707. This means that the booklet appeared first and then it was incorporated into the volume. We have indicated earlier that this formed part of a very big collection consisting of 29 volumes. It contains the expeditions of the Spanish, the Portuguese, the Dutch, the English and other nations of Europe between 1246, and 1696 searching for new lands, islands, peoples, new hoards of gold, pearls and gems, and new trade routes to the greats ports of spices. The whole collection consists of 28 parts in 29 bands. The Narratives of Joseph the Indian is given here as the travel of an Indian with the index "IN" standing for India. It is clearly stated in the table of contents which says: "the letter, which stands before each voyage shows from which nation the Navigator is sent or is himself born.

The work consists of the table of contents, a Foreword, (Vorbericht), 11 chapters (Hoofdstucken) and the index. Of the 23+4 pages, the text of the Narratives of Joseph the Indian is given on pp. 3-23 where the text ends with "EYNDE" (end). After page six a picture is inserted showing the sacrifice of the Hindus in the temples which is being described on pages 6-7 in chapter 3. Each chapter has a chapter heading which is longer than those of *Paesi* and *Itinerarium*. On the margin of each page side-headings are given. The division into chapters do not correspond to that of *Paesi* and *Itinerarium*. The index on the last

---

142. Remarkable travels of Joseph, the born Indian, containing remarkable description of the countries, cities, and inhabitants of Caranganor, Calicuth, Cambaja, Narsinga etc. Noted down from his lips by the Portuguese in 1501. Now for the first time translated from Portuguese.

four pages is named Register, which gives the alphabetical index to the matters contained in the text.

1.5.1. The Origins of the text of Sonderlinge Reysen

The text of the Narratives of Joseph the Indian contained in *Sonderlinge Reysen van Joseph* is different from those of *Paesi* and *Itinerarium*. But it is closer to the text of *Itinerarium* than that of *Paesi*. From internal evidences it seems that the editor of *Sonderlinge Reysen* knew the Latin text of Madrignanus. For, he makes references to that text in IV Hoofdstuk.

The editor of *Sonderlinge Reysen* claims that it was the ntranslated from Portuguese for the first time. Here the question arises. Was it from the original Portuguese text, of which we have spoken earlier,[143] that it was translated? Or was it from the Portuguese translation of the Latin text said to be appended to *Fasciculus Temporum*?[144] Or was it from a Portuguese translation of the text in *Itinerarium* or *Novus Orbis*? The comment of the editor or translator in IV Hoofdstuk, make us think that he knew the Latin text of Narratives of Joseph the Indian. If that is the case, how to account for the differences? It is also possible that the source of *Sonderlinge Reysen* was the common source of *Paesi* and *Itinerarium* of which we have spoken earlier.[145] But, since we have not been able to identify the Latin text of *Fasciculus Temporum*, the probable Portuguese origianal text and the common source of *Paesi* and *Itinerarium* we are not in a position to say a final word about it.

1.6.0. Interrelation of the sources and texts

In the foregoing pages we have made a search into the sources of the Narratives of Joseph the Indian. We have seen that 25 different editions and versions of the text of the Narratives exist in seven different languages. There are 7 texts in Italian, 5 in Latin, 6 in French, 2 in German, 3 in Dutch, one in English and one in Portuguese. We also said that all these texts originated from three main sources. We have analysed and

---

143. Cf. 1.1.5
144. Cf. 1.1.4
145. Cf. 1.3.6

SEARCH INTO THE SOURCES 53

studied all the sources in detail, namely *Paesi, Itinerarium,* and *Sonderlinge Reysen van Joseph,* and also *Novus Orbis* which depends on *Itinerarium*. We also discussed the questions regarding the existence of a Latin text appended to *Fasciculus Temporum*,[146] mentioned by some of the authors and of the original Portuguese text.[147] However we could not identify these two texts.

In all, there are 17 editions of the Narratives of Joseph the Indian originating from *Paesi* alone. 7 in Italian (1507, 1508, 1512, 1517, 1519, 1521 1916), 6 in French (1515, 1515-16, 1516, 1521, 1528, 1529), one each in German (1508), Dutch (1508), English (1937) and Portuguese (1966). There are seven editions of the text originating from *Itinerarium,* 5 in Latin (1508, 1532 1532, 1537, 1555), one in German (1534) and one in Dutch (1563). In our discussion of the sources we have showed that there is no direct dependence of *Itinerarium* on *Paesi,* and that *Itinerarium* is not the direct translation of *Paesi*.[148] We also proposed the hypothesis of a remote common source and different immediate sources for *Paesi* and *Itinerarium*.[149]

Hence our hypothesis on the interrelation of the texts and the sources is that there existed the original in Portuguese or in some Italian dialect. From this originated the source common to *Paesi* and *Itinerarium*. The Latin text of *Fasciculus Temporum,* and the text of *Sonderlinge Reysen* might have depended on the original source or on this common source. From this common source originated the immediate sources of *Paesi* and *Itinerarium* which were different from this common source. Montalboddo Fracan of *Paesi* and Montaboldus Fracanus of *Itinerarium* are one and the same person and he is the editor/compiler of this common source, from which the sources of *Paesi* and *Itinerarium* originated. *Paesi* and its editions and translations directly depend on the immediate source of *Paesi,* while *Itinerarium* and its reproductions depend on the immediate source of *Itinerarium*.

---

146. Cf. 1.1.4.
147. Cf. 1.1.5.
148. Cf. 1.3.6.
149. Cf. 1.3.6.

The Narratives of Joseph the Indian
Schema showing the interrelation of the sources

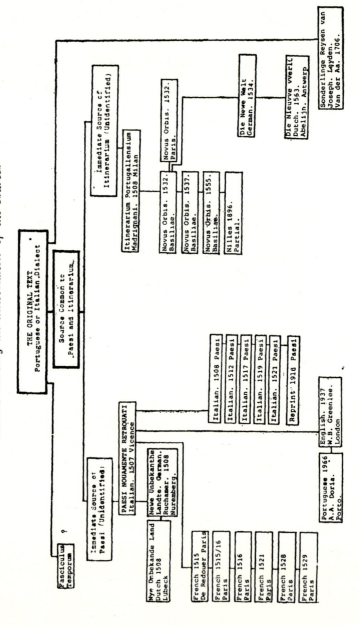

PART II

Joseph the Indian and his Narratives

Joseph and His Narratives

In Part I we have examined and analysed in detail the sources of the Narratives of Joseph the Indian. There we have said that the texts of the Narratives of Joseph the Indian have come down to us in 25 different editions and versions in different languages. We have also stated that all these texts in the various languages originated from three main sources, *Paesi*, *Itinerarium* and *Sonderlinge Reysen van Joseph*. In this Part II we propose to make a study of the person of Joseph the Indian, and of his Narratives, and their origin, importance, writer, date, place and contents.

2.1.0. The Person of Joseph the Indian

Joseph was an Indian by nationality, a native of Cranganore, in Kerala, *dark coloured and medium size*. He was born in 1461 and *at the time when he was in Lisbon* (1501) *he was about forty years old. He was an ingenious man, of high truthfulness who detested nothing so much as telling lies, a sober and reasonable man, of exemplary life, of high integrity and remarkable friendliness.* Those who were acquainted with him acknowledge that *he was a man of whom we will never feel sorry to have made our acquaintance, unwavering and unimpaired in faith.* This is the description of Joseph the Indian that we get if we put together what we have in the three texts of the Narratives of Joseph the Indian as an eye-witness report.

According to the Narratives, Joseph was ordained priest in Mesopotamia, by the Catholicos of Babylon.

> "The said Joseph narrated, that with a Bishop he set out from the city of Caranganora, and on board a ship went to the island of Ormus which is 1500 miles away from Caranganora. From there he went over land for three months, together with the said Bishop and came to great Armenia, to greet their most reverend great Pontiff by whom the said Bishop was initiated in to the sacred order and the said Joseph was ordained priest."[1]

In the historical introduction of the letter of the four bishops from India to the Patriarch Mar Elias written in 1504 we read:

> "In the year of Alexander 1801 (1490 AD) there came three trustworthy Christian men from the remote regions of India to Mar Simeon, the Catholic Patriarch of the Orient, to ask for Fathers (abahata) and take them with them. One of them died on the way according to the will of the Creator. The two others came safely to the Mar Catholicos who was then living in the town Gazarta Bet Zabdai and they were received by him with the greatest joy. One of them was called George and the other Joseph. Both of them were ordained priests in the holy church of St George in Gazarta by the Mar Catholicos. For they were fairly educated."[2]

Authorities, on the subject like Schurhammer,[3] Germann,[4] and Mundadan[5] think that Joseph mentioned in this letter is

---

1. Latin Text, ch. 5, in Part IV.
2. G. Schurhammer "Three Letters of Mar Jacob, Bishop of Malabar", in *Orientalia, Bibliotheca Instituti Historici SJ*, Roma, vol. XXI, 1963, p. 334.
3. G. Schurhammer, *ibid.*
4. W. Germann, *Die Kirche der Thomaschristen*, Gutersloh, 1877, pp. 315-317.
5. A. M. Mundadan, *Thomas Christians*, Bangalore, 1967, pp. 53-59; *The Traditions of Thomas Christians*, Bangalore, 1970, (hereafter *Traditions*) pp. 123 ff.

Joseph the Indian. If that is true, then Joseph was ordained in 1490 when he was 29 or 30 years old.

According to Germann, Joseph made a second journey to Babylon in 1492 with Bishop Thomas one of the Bishops who were consecrated and sent to India by the Catholicos in 1490, at the request of the delegation of Joseph and his companions. Germann thinks that this second journey was to fetch the offerings of the Christians of India to the Catholicos.[6] However, we cannot affirm anything for certain about this journey.

Mathias Mundadan and to some extent, Schurhammer think that Joseph the Indian was the same person as the chief priest of Cranganore whom Penteado mentioned in 1518. Penteado, was a Portuguese priest who often was at variance with the Bishop, priests and people of the community of the St. Thomas Christians. He was in Cranganore. He worte in 1518:

> "As soon as the priest, who returned from Portugal returned from (his pilgrimage to Sao Thomé) he was scandalised with me and asked me what I wanted. I said you should conform to Rome."[7]

Schurhammer, speaking of Joseph the Indian in his article *Three Letters of Mar Jacob*, which we have cited earlier, poses the question: "Is he not the parish priest of Cranganore, who returned from Portugal, mentioned by Penteado."[8] This question of Schurhammer has an affirmative intonation.

Mundadan in his *Thomas Christians* says that Joseph the Indian was the priest mentioned by Penteado. He writes: "The chief priest of Cranganore mentioned here seems to be Joseph the Indian who had been to Portugal."[9]

---

6. W. Germann, *op. cit.*, p. 317.
7. G. Schurhammer, *art cit.* p. 345.
8. G. Schurhammer, *ibid.*, p. 337.
9. A. M. Mundadan, *Thomas Christians*, p. 92., footnote 51.

In his work *The Traditions of Thomas Christians* Mundadan is more affirmative. He writes:

> "Joseph the Indian, whose mission to Babylon in 1490 and his trip with Cabral to Portugal and Venice, etc. was, no doubt, an important man in the community and he was a priest and the rector of the main church of Cranganore."[10]

All these reveal that Joseph the Indian was a very important personality of the community of the St. Thomas Christians of Malabar. What is most interesting with him is his love for his community, which he shows in a very daring manner through his adventurous endeavours for its good and bright future.

2.1.1. The Narratives of Joseph the Indian

The Narratives of Joseph the Indian are an historical document of rare value which contains descriptions of India in 1500 AD. Narrated by an Indian and recorded by a European, in the wake of the discoveries of the new world, they contain fascinating descriptions of the Malabar Coast and the countries, islands, and cities en route to and around the ports of Malabar. They describe various peoples with their customs and manners, faith and religion, rites and rituals, dress and food, as well as the flora and fauna of the places described.

The countries, islands and cities described therein belong to two groups: those lying west of Cranganore, the native place of Joseph the Indian and those lying east of it, east and west being understood in accordance with the geographical concepts of Ptolemy that was prevalent in the 14th and 15th century descriptions of the new world. Among those lying west of Cranganore, are Calicut, the most important city of the Malabar Coast, where Vasco da Gama first landed, the city of Guzerat, the great city of Cambay, the most excellent of Indian cities called the Cairo of India, with its vegetarians, conjurers and celibates, the island of Ormus, with its horses, glass vessels, and hoards of pearls, the cities of Cape Mongolistan like

---

10. A. M. Mundadan. *Traditions* p. 123.

Sebobek, Semath, Chismy. Among the second group, are included the city of Cochin in the Kingdom of Cochin, the Cape of Comerin, the Kingdom of Narsinga, with its two cities of Bisnagar and Mylapore, Oriza and the Gulf of Oriza. Mention is also made in this group, of the island of Sylam or Ceylon, Sumatra called Taprobane and of China which is called "the island with many islands" whose merchants trade with India. The description of the first group is more detailed than that of the second.

The most extensive and most interesting of all the descriptions found in the Narratives of Joseph the Indian, is that of the city of Cranganore, with Hindus and Christians, their temples and churches, the division of the society according to castes, the customs and manners of the king and the people, their dress and food, trade, commerce, and monetary system, ships and navigation. They give us very interesting information about the plants and animals of the Malabar Coast, pepper, ginger, rice and the medicinal herbs. The most interesting of all the descriptions of herbs and plants is that of the palm trees which produce the "Indian Nuts", and the process of making toddy, vinegar, sugar and oil from them.

The most valuable thing which historians and theologians will find in the Narratives of Joseph the Indian, is the accounts of the life of the St. Thomas Christians who trace their origin to St. Thomas the Apostle. We find in them details about the traditions, ecclesiastical system, sacramental and liturgical life of these christians with their fasts, feasts, and celebrations. They reveal also their social customs and religious practices, and their theology of the Papacy as well as understanding of their relation with the Church of Rome.

2.1.2. Origins of the Narratives of Joseph the Indian

The Narratives of Joseph the Indian originated in the context of the great explorations and discoveries at the end of the 15th century, especially the discovery of the trade routes to the Indian subcontinent. Accounts of the new lands and islands, and the various peoples in those regions with their customs and manners, faiths and religions, and trade and commerce were of sensational interest to all in Europe. The discovery of new trade routes to the heavens of pepper and spices of the Malabar Coast were shifting the very course of European trade and commerce to India and the East. The Christians of Prester John and of the other parts of the Orient were the subject of interest to many. Hence, all sorts of descriptions of the newly found lands were being read and studied by people of different walks of life, everyone looking at them from his standpoint and practical purpose.

It is in this context that Joseph the Indian came to Europe in 1501 AD with Pedro Alvares Cabral in his ships returning from India after his historic discovery of Brazil and voyage to India. Joseph boarded a ship at Cochin on 10th January 1501 and landed in Lisbon in June 1501. He was received by the King of Portugal with great honour and travelled to Venice and Rome. He was the first Indian to visit Europe in the wake of the new discoveries and the first Indian Christian, known in history, to have an audience with the Pope of Rome. The person of Joseph was at one time a source of wonder and of first hand information about the newly found Indian Coast, with its people, Hindus, Christians and even Jews. Above all, Joseph the Indian was a direct source of information about the St. Thomas Christians. The fact that he was a member of the community of these Christians, and more especially that he was a priest, gave an added attraction to his person and to what he narrated.

In the year 1500 the fleet of the ships under Pedro Alvares Cabral arrived at Calicut. After the quarrel with the Zamorin of Calicut he came to Cochin and was engaged in loading the ships at Cochin and at the Port of Cranganore. Then Joseph the Indian together with his brother Mathias (as De Barros, Gouvea, Goes, Geddes and Soledade name him) came to Cabral and expressed his wish to tour the western countries in order to go to Rome and Jerusalem. His proposal was accepted by Cabral. On 10th January, 1501 he set out from Cochin with Cabral together with his brother Mathias. On the way Mathias died and Joseph arrived at Lisbon in June 1501. He was received by the king of Portugal and remained in Portugal until January 1502. Then with a companion given by the king he went to Rome and from there to Venice where he arrived in

June 1502, and stayed many days there. When he was in Rome he had an audience with Pope Alexander VI who discussed with him questions related to the Indian Church and its relation to the Catholicos of the Orient.

When Joseph was in Europe he was interviewed by a European whose name remains unknown in history, who published all that he heard from Joseph the Indian. The writer of the Narratives was a man of erudition, with a scientific mind and a vast range of interests. The matters discussed in the Narratives of Joseph reveal the variety of questions that the writer put to Joseph. He asked Joseph about all possible areas of human interest leaving to us thereby valuable and rare information about the Indian continent in 1500 AD.

2.1.3. Importance of the Narratives of Joseph

The Narratives of Joseph the Indian are a very valuable source for the students of history, geography, sociology, trade and commerce, astronomy and navigation, theology and world religions. For the historians of Malabar and of India in the 16th century, they give information about the kings and kingdoms of the Indian sub-continent, especially on and around the coast of Malabar. We learn from them much about the life of the peoples in the various cities and countries, especially their socio-economic life, customs and manners. They are an invaluable source for the history of the voyage of Cabral to Calicut and Cochin, his quarrels with the king of Calicut, and friendship with the king of Cochin.

For students of ecclesiastical history and theology, the Narratives of Joseph the Indian are a mine of information about the life and traditions of St Thomas Christians of Malabar at the beginning of the 16th century. From them we come to know about their ecclesiastical system, liturgical life, sacraments, monastic system and spirituality. We learn from them about the feast of St. Thomas and the tomb of St. Thomas in the Church in Mylapore.

For the students of geography, the Narratives of Joseph provide geographical descriptions of the cities of Cranganore, Calicut, Cambay, Gujarat, Bisnagar, Oriza, Mylapore, of the islands of Ormus, Ceylon, Sumatra, and of the Cape of Mongolistan and Cape Comerin. They give us information about the flora and fauna of these places.

A sociologist will find in them the different social classes in the city of Cranganore which in fact represents Kerala society at the end of the 15th century. There he will also find the social customs and manners of the kings and people of Cranganore, Calicut, Cambay, Guzerat, etc.

The students of economic history and commerce will find in them information about the commercial centres and ports on and around the Coast of Malabar. They give us details about the trade in pepper, ginger and other spices when the Portuguese first landed in India. We are told there about the merchants who used to come to these ports from all parts of the world.

The students of world religions will find in the Narratives descriptions of the religious life of the Hindus and Christians in Cranganore and the religious life of the people of the other cities described in them. They reveal also the western attitude to the non-Christian religions. Above all, the Narratives of Joseph the Indian serve as a source of great value for the study of Christianity in India before the coming of the Portuguese.

2.1.4. Joseph the Indian and his Narratives down the centuries.

There have been references to Joseph, or his travels or his Narratives, in almost every century since his time. The first contemporary document that mentions Joseph's travel to Portugal and Rome is the *Anonymous Narrative*[11] written by an unknown pilot of the fleet of Cabral. After him De Barros and Goes in the 16th century refer to Joseph and his travels. Gouvea, Geddes and Faria y Sousa in the 17th century, and Glen, Assemanus, La Croze, Soledade and Astley in the 18th century speak of Joseph and his travels. In the 19th century we have

---

11. W. B. Greenlee, *The Voyage of Pedro Alvares Cabral to Brazil and India*, London, 1937, p. 86; *Navegacao de Pedro Alvares Cabral*, Lisbon, 1812 p. 135.

three authors Nilles, Hough and Germann who discussed the Narratives of Joseph the Indian. In our own times writers like Nagam Aiya, Schurhammer, Podipara, Greenlee, Mundadan and Banha de Andrade discuss the question of Joseph, or his travels or his Narratives.

Of these, the *Anonymous Narrative* and Faria y Sousa do not mention the name of Joseph or his brother. De Barros is the first to mention the name of Joseph's brother and companion of journey as Mathias. Soledade, Goes, Gouvea, Germann and Hough mention the name of both Joseph and his brother and companion, Mathias. 20th century references and studies are more elaborate than those of the preceding centuries.

The *Anonymous Narrative,* which is the earliest contemporary document other than the Narratives of Joseph the Indian, has the following account to give:

> "And thus we were twelve or fifteen days loading the ships at a distance from Cuchin at a place called Carangallo (Cranganore). In this place there are Christians, Jews, Moors and infidels.... and from these two other christians came with us. They said that they wished to go to Rome and Jerusalem. The captain had great pleasure with these men."[12]

The two other writers who mention Joseph and his travels in the 16th century are Goes and De Barros.[13] Both give the name of Joseph's companion as Mathias. De Barros mentions *Novus Orbis* as the source of the Narratives.

In the 17th century we have Gouvea making mention of Joseph and his brother and companion Mathias, in his *Jornada.* He mentions *Fasciculus Temporum* as containing the Narratives of Joseph the Indian. We have already cited him in connection with the question of *Fasciculus Temporum.*[14]

---

12. W. B. Greenlee, *ibid.* Cf. also Latin Text, ch. 1, Italian Text, ch. 1, Dutch Text, ch. 1, in part IV and the corresponding note in Part IV.
13. Infra p. 75. Cf. A. M. Mundadan, *Thomas Christians* p. 58. De Barros, *Da Asia,* Dec. I. Bk v. ch. viii.
14. Cf. 1.1.4.

Faria y Sousa whom we have mentioned elsewhere is the witness of the second half of the 17th century. *Portuguese Asia* of Faria y Sousa is very brief in its statement. It reads:

"At Cranganore were found some Christians of St. Thomas, under the Armenian Bishops. Two were brought to Portugal, one died on the way and the other returned."[15]

Michael Geddes in *The History of the Church of Malabar* speaks of Joseph and his Narratives. He mentions only *Fasciculus Temporum* as the source of the Narratives of Joseph the Indian. He writes:

"The first news of this ancient, but remote Church, was brought to *Europe* by *Pedralvares Cabral*, who putting into *Cranganor* in the year 1501 and meeting there with several of those Christians, he perswaded two of them, who were Brothers, to come along with him to *Portugal* where the eldest whose Name was Matthias, died at *Lisbon*; and the other whose name was *Joseph*, went first to *Rome*, and from thence to *Venice*. where, upon his information, a Tract was publish'd in Latin of the State of the Church of Malabar, and is printed at the end of *Fasciculus Temporum*."[16]

In the 18th century Assemanus, La Croze, Soledade and Astley made references to Joseph the Indian in their works. Assemanus in the preface of his famous work *Commentary on the Chaldean and Nestorian Patriarchates*[17] and in the *Codex Liturgicus*[18] takes Joseph the Indian as a good authority. He knows about the Narratives only from *Novus Orbis* of 1555. La Croze also

---

15. Faria y Sousa, *The Portuguese Asia or History of the Discovery and Conquest of India by the Portuguese*, translated by *Cap. John Stevens*, London, 1695, p. 59.
16. Michael Geddes *The History of the Church of Malabar*, London, 1694, p. 2.
17. Mentioned by Nagam Aiya, *Travancore State Manual*, Trivandrum. vol. II, 1906, p. 150, probably he means *Bibliotheca Orientalis Clementino Vaticano*, 4 volumes, Rome, 1718-28.
18. J. S. Assemanus, *Codex Liturgicus Ecclesiae Universae*, Rome, pp. 229, 243.

speaks of Joseph the Indian and found the Narratives in several collections of travels.[19]

In his history of the Franciscan Order[20], Soledade mentions Joseph and Mathias and their journey to Portugal. In the index of the work we have a reference to Joseph and Mathias as Caçanars who were sent by the Bishop to effect reunion with Rome. However, this view of Soledade has no value in the face of the historical facts we know.

We have another author in the same century who speaks of Joseph and his Narratives. It is Thomas Astley who published his *Collection of Voyages and Travels* from London in 1745. It is clear from what he writes that he knew only *Novus Orbis*. He attaches very little value to the Narratives of Joseph the Indian. He writes:

> "Thus Joseph lived to get to Portugal and is the Josephus Indus under whose name there is a voyage given by Grynaeus, containing twelve pages: but properly it is no more than an account of Kranganor and its inhabitants, (particularly the Christians and their religious rites), but very short and unsatisfactory. Nor is this any wonder, since Grynaeus, or whoever took the relation from Joseph's mouth, tells us he could scarce understand him."[21]

This quotation from Astley itself shows how biased he was. It reveals his ignorance of the origin of the Narratives, their sources, the person of Joseph and the writer of the Narratives. The following pages will reveal how false his view is.

In the 19th century we have three authors who wrote about Joseph the Indian and his Narratives. They are Nilles,

---

19. La Croze, quoted by J. Hough, *The History of Christianity in India from the commencement of Christian Era*, (5 vols, London, 1839–60), vol. I, p. 153.
20. F. da Soledade, *Historia Seraphica da Ordem dos Frades Menores de S. Francisco na Provincia de Portugal, Continuator da obra de Frei Manuel Esperanca que appresenta este mesmo titulo, III vol.* Lisbon, 1705, p. 523 ff.
21. Quoted by Nagam Aiya, *op. cit.*, vol. II, p. 150.

Germann and James Hough. Nilles [22] takes the Narratives of Joseph the Indian as the source of the liturgical traditions of the St. Thomas Christians. However, he was only acquainted with the Latin text contained in the 1555 edition of *Novus Orbis*. We have cited Germann in detail in relation to the question of *Fasciculus Temporum*.[23] For he mentions *Fasciculus Temporum* and *Novus Orbis* as the sources of the Narratives. According to him "Mathias was the elder brother of Joseph." James Hough, speaking about the voyage of Cabral, mention Joseph the Indian and his companion Mathias. According to him, it was their intention to meet the Patriarch in Mosul. He mentions the Narratives of Joseph the Indian under the title: *Voyages of Joseph the Indian*, and the source of his information seems to be La Croze.[24]

Coming now to our own times, Nagam Aiya, Schurhammer, Podipara, Greenlee, Mundadan, Banha de Andrade have made studies on the Narratives of Joseph the Indian. Nagam Aiya, as already mentioned above considers the Narratives of Joseph the Indian in his *Travancore State Manual*.[25] There he reveals some of the sources of the Narratives, and gives the names of some authors who wrote about it. He gives a short description of the life of the St Thomas Christians as it appeared in the Narratives of Joseph the Indian.

W. B. Greenlee,[26] as stated earlier, makes a brief study of the person of Joseph, his travels and the sources of the Narratives. He gives the Narratives of Joseph the Indian the title *The Account of Priest Joseph*. He gives in his work the translation of the text of the Narratives found in *Paesi*, with notes and references. However, he has made some mistakes in the translation of the texts. He does not seem to have known the Latin or Dutch text, or made any comparative study. However, his study gives us some information about the other sources of the Narratives. He is of the view[27] that the

---

22. Nilles, *Calendarium Manuale Utriusque Ecclesiae*, Roma 1897, pp. 651 ff.
23. Cf. 1.1.4.
24. J. Hough, *op. cit*, p. 153.
25. Nagam Aiya, *op. cit.*, vol. II, pp. 149–50.
26. W. B., Greenlee, *op cit.*, p. 95–113.
27. W. B. Greenlee, *op. cit.*, p. 97.

first chapter of the Italian text was written by Fracanzano himself. He considers him as the compiler or editor of *Paesi*. This view, we have shown earlier, is not correct.

Podipara in his work on the Syro-Malabar Hierarchy uses the Narratives as a source.[28] Vellian,[29] following Nilles, mentions the Narratives as a possible source for the study of the liturgical traditions of the St Thomas Christians.

In his work *Mundos Novos do Mundo*,[30] Banha de Andrade makes a study of the Narratives of Joseph the Indian. He uses as his source the Portuguese translation of the *Account of Priest Joseph* by Greenlee, found in the Portuguese translation of the work by Antonio Alvares Doria, which we have mentioned in Part I in our study of the sources of the Narratives.[31] Banha de Andrade is also familiar with the two studies of Schurhammer which we will discuss below. He has given a good paraphrase of the Narratives. His seems to be the longest study on the Narratives. However, he does not know any source other than the Greenlee, Doria and *Paesi*.

Schurhammer speaks of Joseph the Indian in two of his articles. We have already referred to the first[32] in connection with the question of *Fasciculus Temporum*, and the person of Joseph. In it he mentions *Fasciculus Temporum*, *Paesi* and *Novus Orbis* as sources of the Narratives. He does not mention *Itinerarium* or any translation of the *Paesi* or *Itinerarium*. However, he makes references to the *Navigacão da Cabral*, of De Barros, Nagam Aiya, and Germann.

In his second article, "Malabar, Church before the coming of the Portugese, Joseph the Indian's Testimony",[33] he uses the Narratives of Joseph the Indian as a source for his study of the relation between the Malabar Church and the Church of

---

28. P. J. Podipara, *The Hierarchy of the Syro-Malabar Church*, Alleppey, 1976 p. 32.
29. J. Vellian, *Kurbana Oru Padhanam*, Kottayam, 1968.
30. Banha de Andrade, *Mundos Novos do Mundo*, Lisbon, 1972. pp. 369-377.
31. A. A. Doria, *A Viagem de Pedro Alvares Cabral*, Lisbon, 1966. pp. 194-214.
32. G. Schurhammer, *art. cit.*, p. 339-349.
33. G. Schurhammer, in *Orientalia, sup. cit*, p. 351-363.

Rome. In this article he mentions only *Paesi* and *Novus Orbis* as the sources. He gives the Italian text and the English translation of the relevant texts. Here Schurhammer takes Joseph as an important witness of the tradition of the Malabar Church.

Lastly we have the two works of Mathias Mundadan[34] which we have cited above which refer to Joseph the Indian. Mundadan uses Joseph as a source. He knows *Paesi* and *Novus Orbis* of 1532 as the sources of the Narratives. He knows *Paesi* through the 1916 fascimile edition of the 1508 edition.

About the text of the Narratives of Joseph the Indian, Mundadan makes the following remark:

> "Simon GRYNAEUS's *Novus Orbis* (Basileae 1532) gives an unreliable Latin translation with many striking changes, additions and ommissions, of the same account in chapters 249-292. Cf. Schurhammer 26".[35]

Mundadan seems to have got the information from Schurhammer or some other source. Here the numbers of the chapters given correspond neither to those of *Paesi* nor to those of any edition of *Novus Orbis*. Mundadan being unaware of *Itinerarium* and *Sonderlinge Reysen van Joseph*, it is no wonder he thinks that the text of the Narratives of Joseph the Indian in *Novus Orbis* is the translation of that in *Paesi*. He was only repeating what many others before him mistakenly affirmed. We have shown elsewhere that this position is wrong.

Mundadan gives a broader history of Joseph, connecting the pieces of information from the Narratives with those from other sources. Here he seems to follow the line of thought of Germann and Schurhammer on whom he greatly depends. Basing himself on what is given in the chapter 5 of the Narratives Mundadan affirms that Joseph the Indian is the same person as the Joseph who was in the delegation mentioned in the letter of the bishops from India in 1504. He writes:

---

34. *sup. cit.*, p. 58, note 5.
35. A. M. Mundadan, *Thomas Christians*, p. 59, note 114.

"This Joseph was the same Joseph who was in the Indian delegation of 1490 which went to fetch bishops for the Indian Church and who was ordained priest there".[36]

As we have said elsewhere, Mundadan also identified Joseph the Indian with the chief priest of Cranganore of whom Penteado made mention in 1518. We have already cited the relevant passages from Mundadan in connection with the person of Joseph.[37]

In his *Traditions* Mundadan uses the Narratives as a source for his description of the liturgical, sacramental and other traditions of the St. Thomas Christians.

2.2.0. The Travels of Joseph the Indian

We have stated above that the Narratives of Joseph the Indian originated in the context of the great discoveries. The witnesses that we have cited above testify that Joseph went to Portugal in the ship of Pedro Alvares Cabral together with his brother Mathias who died on the way or in Portugal. The Narratives of Joseph tell us that after reaching Lisbon Joseph went to Rome and Venice, and in Rome he had an audience with Pope Alexander VI.

We find that there are certain differences in the testimonies of these witnesses. Some of them are defective and partial. Hence we propose to discuss here Joseph's travel to Lisbon, Rome and Venice, and his audience with the Pope. We shall also discuss the questions of his travel to Jerusalem and Babylon and also of his return to India.

2.2.1. Joseph the Indian meets Pedro Alvares Cabral

In 1499, Vasco da Gama returned from his first voyage to India. His great success in finding the sea route round the Cape of Good Hope and in establishing trade relations with the Malabar Coast, which up to that time was under the control of the Arabs, made King Emmanuel of Portugal to undertake new adventures in his maritime enterprises.

---

36. A. M. Mundadan, *Thomas Christians*, p. 58; *Traditions*, p. 123.
37. Cf. 2.1 0.

In the year 1500 the Serene King "relying on the words of those who had travelled in those regions in the foregone days", decreed to send a new fleet of ships under Pedro Alvares Cabral. Adequate preparations having been made, the King officially gave the royal standard to Cabral on 8th March 1500, after a solemn liturgical celebration at the Church of Belem, which then was outside the city of Lisbon. On 9th March, Cabral set out with his 13 ships. Among his captains was Bartholomew Dias, who first discovered the Cape of Good Hope.

On the way Cabral had the good fortune of accidentally discovering Brazil and Madagascar. The coast of Brazil was sighted on 24th April. He then sent one of his ships back to Lisbon to report his unexpected discovery. On 2nd May, with his twelve ships, he continued his journey to India, setting sail to cross the Cape of Good Hope. "On the way," the Narratives of Joseph the Indian tell us, "he had to undergo the strain of terrible anxiety and danger", "sailing through very great storms and peril." On 24th or 25th of May[38] he lost four of his ships. "And he went twenty days through this storm without setting sail to the wind", we are told by the *Anonymous Narrative*.[39]

On 16th June he sighted Arabia. He reached the island of Mozambique on 20th June, and Melinde on 2nd August. "At last, by the grace of God, they arrived the city of Calechut on 13th September of the same year with seven of his ships. Four ships of the fleet perished and were sunk by hard tempest and the other one sailed to Zaphala." On 18th Cabral had an interview with Samorin, the ruler of Calicut.

The Narratives of Joseph the Indian tell us that, "for almost three months they tarried at the port of Calechut. By this time there arose some dispute between our people and the inhabitants of the place."[40] Doddwell commenting on this, remarks that "Cabral was eminently unsuited for the diplomatic side of his mission and showed no disposition to consider the

---

38. The *Anonymous Narrative* gives the date 24th, W. B. Greenlee *op. cit.* p. 61; Castanheda and De Barros agree with it, but Goes gives 25th.
39. W. B. Greenlee, *op. cit.*, p. 61.
40. Latin Text, ch. 1, in Part IV.

JOSEPH AND HIS NARRATIVES   73

sentiments and prejudices of those with whom he was sent to trade."[41] Mundadan says: "But soon owing to the envious instigation of the Mohammedan merchants, troubles began."[42] Whatever be the reasons, these disputes "reached a climax with the seizure on 16th December of a ship belonging to the Arabs."[43] But "the Mohammedans retaliated by attacking the Portuguese factory and killing the factor and 53 others. The king did not comply with Cabral's demands for compensation. Therefore, he bombarded the town for two days and killing many in a nearby village named Fundarane, Cabral sailed to Cochin where he arrived on December 24."[44]

The "king of Cuchin received Cabral and his ships very kindly," say the Narratives of Joseph the Indian. The Portuguese loaded their ships at the ports of Cuchin and Cranganore "some twenty miles form Cuchin." There they remained twelve or fifteen days. "In this port of Cranganore, the Portuguese were approached by many Christians of St Thomas."[45] It is here that Joseph and his companion approached Cabral. The *Anonymous Narrative* tells us: "And thus we were twelve or fifteen days loading the ship in a distance from Cochin at a place called Crangallo In this place there are Christians... and from there two other Christians came with us. They said they wished to go to Rome and Jerusalem. The captain had great pleasure with these two men."[46] Therefore they came aboard our ship and travelled with us", say the Narratives of Joseph the Indian.[47] Hardly had they finished loading the ships when news was brought to Cabral that a large fleet was proceeding from Calicut to attack the Portuguese. Soon Cabral set sail for the deep sea on 10th January 1501 "together with the said brothers", leaving about thirty Portuguese in Cochin, among whom was the famous Duarte Barbosa. On the 15th they arrived at Cannanore, where they loaded the ships further and set sail for

---

41. H. H. Dodwell, *The Cambridge History of India*, Cambridge 1929, vol. V, p. 5.
42. A. M. Mundadan, *Thomas Christians*, p. 54.
43. H. H. Dodwell, *ibid*.
44. A. M. Mundadan, *ibid*.
45. A. M. Mundadan, *ibid*. p. 58.
46. W. B. Greenlee, *op. cit.*, p. 86; Cf. *Paesi*, Book III, ch. lxxviii.
47. Latin Text, ch. 1, in Part IV.

Portugal. After two and a half months' voyage they came to the Cape of Good Hope on Palm Sunday, the 4th of April. And at the end of the month of June 1501, Cabral's ships reached Lisbon.

2.2.2. Joseph travels to Lisbon with Cabral and visits Rome and Venice.

We have said above that it was when Cabral's ships were in Cochin and Cranganore that Joseph and his companion approached Cabral. We have several witnesses to this. The Narratives of Joseph the Indian describe it in the following words:

> "As we tarried there doing our trade, as already mentioned in the chapter lxxviii of Book three, two brothers, Indians as well as Christians, came from the town called Caranganora, about twenty miles from Cuchin. They said that they greatly desired to visit the western countries, especially that they vowed to go to visit Rome and the holy city of Jerusalem. Therefore they came aboard our ships and travelled with us."[48]

Here the reference is to the discussion of this fact in the *Anonymous Narratives* as found in chapter lxxviii of Book III of *Itinerarium* and *Paesi*. We have cited above[49] the English translation of the relevant passage of *Paesi* given by W. B. Greenlee. Here we cite the English translation of the Latin text found in *Itinerarium* and *Novus Orbis*.

> "Therefore we remained there about 15 days loading the ships not far from the city of Cuchin where there is a port which is called Carnagallo, where we find Christians... two Christians who said they wanted to go to Jerusalem and from there to Rome (approached the Captain), which pleased the captain."[50]

---

48. *ibid..*
49. Cf. 2.2.1., p. 73, note. 46.
50. *Novus Orbis, Basileae,* 1532. p. 85, (translation is mine).

None of these texts mentions the name of Joseph's companion. But De Barros, Goes, Gouvea, Geddes and Soledade give the name of Joseph's companion as Mathias. Describing how Joseph approached Cabral, Goes tells us that two Indian Christians named Joseph and Mathias, both of them brothers and natives of Cranganore, came to Cabral asking him to take them to Portugal from where they could go to Rome and Jerusalem. Cabral was very pleased at their idea and sent them to be accommodated in the ship.[51]

De Barros gives some more details in the *Da Primeira Decada*, which we reproduce here, as paraphrased by Mundadan:

> "He says that the Portuguese after having established friendly relations with the king of Cochin, were loading their ships in twenty days' time in the river of Cranganore five leagues from Cochin. In this port of Cranganore the Portuguese were approached by many Christians of St Thomas. Of these Christians two brothers named Mathias and Joseph, who had been educated by the Armenian Bishops who resided there, wanted to go with Cabral to Portugal and Rome, and from there to Jerusalem and Armenia to see their Patriarch."[52]

Faria y Sousa referring to Cabral's voyage says:

> "At Cranganore were found some Christians of St Thomas, under Armenian Bishops. Two were brought to Portugal, one died and the other returned."[53]

The Narratives of Joseph the Indian tell us that Joseph the Indian met Cabral at Cochin coming from Cranganore: (he) "came from the town called Caranganora about twenty miles from Cuchin."[54] But Goes, Barros and the author of the *Anonymous Narrative* mention Cranganore as the place where Joseph approached Cabral.

---

51. Goes, I, 135, cited by A. M. Mundadan, *Thomas Christians*, p. 58.
52. A. M Mundadan, *ibid*. p. 58; Barros, *op. cit.*, Bk. V, ch. viii.
53. Faria y Sousa, *op. cit.* p. 59.
54. Latin Text, ch. 1. in Part IV.

Joseph the Indian set sail from Cochin in the ship of Cabral on 10th January 1501.⁵⁵ On the 15th of the month the ships landed at Cannanore to load the ship further. The Narratives of Joseph the Indian do not tell us much about what happened on the way. From the *Anonymous Narrative* we know that on 31st January they were in the gulf of Melinde and on 12th February they had trouble with the storms and then they came to Mozambique where they "took water and wood".⁵⁶

According to the Narratives of Joseph the Indian, Joseph's brother Mathias died on the way. All the three texts agree on this.⁵⁷ The Italian text tells us: "Of these two brothers, one died on the way, the other named Joseph lived." The Latin text is slightly different. It reads, "Of these Indian brothers, whom I remember still, one is alive and the other one died, as we proceeded to Portugal" (dum in Lusitaniam proficisceremur). The Dutch text says simply, "and on the way one of these two Indian brothers died and the other still lives."

But according to Barros, Mathias, Joseph's brother and companion, died after reaching Portugal: "Porem o Mathias depois de ser neste reino faleceo & Josepe foy ter a Roma & a Veneza."⁵⁸ Gouvea also says that Mathias died in Portugal: "hum dos quaes, per nome Mathias morreo em Portugal."⁵⁹ We cannot therefore, say for certain, when Mathias died.

As for the arrival of Joseph the Indian and the ships of Cabral, the three texts of the Narratives of Joseph the Indian have three slightly different accounts to give. The Italian text tells us that Joseph reached Lisbon "at the end of June 1501", while the Latin text says, "aliquando mense Junii." The Dutch text puts it simply "in the month of June."⁶⁰ But all the three

---

55. According to the *Anonymous Narrative* the date is 10th January, but *Cambridge History* gives 9th. Cf. W. B. Greenlee, *op. cit.*, p. 87; H. H. Doddwell, *op. cit.*, p. 5.
56. W. B. Greenlee, *op. cit.*, pp. 89-91.
57. Italian Text, ch. 1, Latin Text, ch. 1, Dutch Text, ch. 1, in Part IV
58. De Barros, *op. cit.*, Dec. I, Bk. 5, ch. viii, 446.
59. A. De Gouvea, *Jornada do Arcebispo de Goa Dom Frey Aleixo Menezes Primas da India Oriental religioso da Ordem de S. Agostinho*, Coimbra, 1606, fol. 5.
60. Italian Text, ch. 1, Latin Text ch. 1, Dutch Text ch. 1, in Part IV

texts have something in common, that is, Joseph came to Lisbon in June. But the *Anonymous Narrative* as found in *Paesi* and *Novus Orbis* gives the date "end of July",[61] and "fere ultima Julii",[62] respectively. Mathias Mundadan, who seems to depend on the *Navagacāo*, gives the date as 31st July.[63] But we see that two letters known to us, the first dated 27th June 1501[64] and the other (of Giovanni Affaitadi) dated 26th June 1501[65], both written from Lisbon, mention the return of the ships of Cabral. This means that Cabral's ships must have arrived earlier than 26th June 1501.

The Latin text of the Narratives of Joseph the Indian tells us that, when Joseph reached Lisbon, he was received by the King of Portugal: "And when we landed there the said Joseph was received by the king."[66] The title of the chapter indicates that he was received with honour by the king: "exceptus a Rege honorifice."[67] According to the Italian text Joseph remained in Lisbon until the month of January 1502. It says: "When they reached the aforesaid place (Lisbon), the aforesaid Joseph remained until the month of January."[68]

About his journey to Rome and Venice we have this report from the Italian text of the Narratives of Joseph.

"And when he departed from the said place there was given to him by the majesty of the Most Serene King, one companion who should accompany him to Rome, Venice and Jerusalem. And thus having been at Rome, then he came to Venice in the year 1502, in the month of June and remained there many days."[69]

---

61. W. B. Greenlee, *op. cit.*, p. 91.
62. *Nouvs Orbis*, Basileae, 1532, p. 88.
63. A. M. Mundadan, *Thomas Christians*, p. 58.
64. W. B. Greenlee, *op. cit.*, 119-123; *Novus Orbis*, Basileae, 1532, pp, 130-133
65. W. B. Greenlee, *op. cit.*, pp. 124-129.
66. Latin Text, ch. 1, in Part IV.
67. Latin Text, ch. 1, in Part IV, *Novus Orbis*, Basileae, 1532, p. 142.
68. Italian Text, ch. 1, in Part IV.
69. *ibid.*

The Italian text has nothing to say of his return to Lisbon or journey to Jerusalem. The travel story ends there. But the Latin and the Dutch texts tell us that Joseph returned to Lisbon. The Latin text reads: "....and then together with a campanion he travelled to Rome and Venice and again returned to Lisbon",[70] while the Dutch text puts the same thing in slightly different words: "... from where Joseph the Indian, with the consent of the king went to Rome and from there to Venice and then back to Lisbon."[71]

2.2.3. Joseph the Indian meets the Pope

We are told in the Narratives of Joseph the Indian that Joseph had an audience with Pope Alexander VI. We do not have any source other than the Narratives for this. From the details given in them we know that Joseph met the Pope who gathered from him information about the Indian Church and asked him about the authority of the Oriental Catholicos to consecrate and appoint Bishops, Archbishops, Patriarchs and thus to rule the eastern regions. In the discussion we find the theologian in Joseph the Indian looming out with his understanding and interpretation of the rights of the Catholicos whom he presents as "vicem gerens Petri" just like the Pope of Rome.

It is in the chapter 5 of the Narratives[72] that we have the reports about the audience with the Pope. Chapter 5 is a discussion of the then existing ecclesial and ecclesiastical system of the St Thomas Christians. There we are informed about the Bishops, Archbishops and the Patriarchs of India and China. It speaks of the Catholicos of Mosul and his rights to consecrate, appoint and send Bishops and other ecclesiastical dignitaries to the different parts of the eastern regions under his authority. It is in this context that the Pope discussed the question of the authority of the Catholicos Patriarch of Mosul and Joseph gave his theological interpretation on the question. Joseph is reported to have answered the Pope in the following words:

"Once St. Peter the apostle was Prefect in Antioch
and when the holy Roman church was troubled

---

70. Latin Text, ch. 1, in Part IV.
71. Dutch Text, ch. 1, in Part IV.
72. Latin Text, ch. 1, Italian Text, ch. 1 and Dutch Text, ch. 1, in Part IV.

under Simon the Magus who left the monuments of his fame, St. Peter was sent to Rome to confound Simon and to confort those suffering from the trouble. Here St. Peter before leaving Antioch for Rome deputed his vicar in Antioch and it is he who governs the oriental parts and is called Catholica and is the vicar of Peter. This Catholica is elected by twelve cardinals in Armenia. They say that they do this with the authority of the Roman Pontiff."[73]

In the Latin text of the Narratives we find an attack on this view, which is an interpolation in the text. We do not have such an interpolation in the Italian text. It is an attack on the view expressed by Joseph the Indian with an affirmation of the classical Roman theology of Papacy. However, it is important to note that Joseph the Indian had his own understanding of the ecclesiology of his Church and of its relation to the Church of Rome.

2.2.4. Did Joseph go to Jerusalem and Babylon?

It is evident that Joseph visited Rome. All the three texts tell us about his audience with Pope Alexander VI. To the visit to Venice also all three texts bear witness. The Italian text very clearly affirms that he came there in the month of June 1502 and remained there many days. But, of his journey to Jerusalem or to Babylon we have no indication whatsoever in the Narratives.

All the known texts of the Narratives of Joseph the Indian and the *Anonymous Narrative* speak of Joseph's and his companion's desire to go to Jerusalem.[74] The Italian text, when it speaks of the companion given by the King of Portugal, speaks of him as "he who should accompany him to Rome, Venice and Jerusalem."[75] This means Jerusalem was included in the programme of Joseph when he was in Lisbon. However there is no mention in any of the texts of their intention to

---

73. Latin Text, ch. 5, in Part IV.
74. Italian Text ch. 1, Latin Text, ch. 1, Dutch Text, ch. 1, in Part IV; W. B. Greenlee op. cit. p 86, Navigacao, sup. cit. ch. xix, p. 134.
75. Italian Text, ch. 1, in Part IV.

proceed to visit the Patriarch of Babylon. Goes speaks only of Jerusalem. [76] However it is De Barros[77] who tells us of their intention to go to see their Patriarch in Babylon. But, none of the texts tells us anything about the actual journey to Jerusalem, or about the trip to Babylon.

Germann thinks that Joseph visited the Patriarch, of Babylon. He presents Joseph as being instrumental to the return of Bishop Mar Thomas to India in the year 1503. [78] According to Germann, this visit of Joseph was the third visit to Babylon. The first was in 1490 when Joseph went to Babylon with two others in the delegation sent from Kerala to Patriarch Simeon asking for bishops, mentioned elsewhere. [79] It was then that Joseph was ordained priest and Bishop Thomas was consecrated together with Bishop John. Germann says that because of the quarrel between the Portuguese and the king of Calicut which the Narratives of Joseph the Indian mention, [80] it was not possible for Bishop John to travel. But in 1492 Bishop Thomas accompanied by Joseph the Indian, came to Babylon "um dem Patriarch die Gaben der Indischen Glaubigen darunter auch einen Sclaven zu uberbringen", to put it in Germann's own words. [81] He feels that this is the journey to which Joseph the Indian refers in the Narratives. [82] And Germann tells us that according to Assemani Joseph returned to India in 1493. Germann writes: "Nach Assemani kehrte Joseph schon in 1493 wieder zurück wahrend wir den Bischop Thomas erst 1503 wieder auf dem Wege finden. Wenn nun Gouvea angiebt Josephs Reiseplan sei uber Portugal, Rom und Venedig (wir konnen aus andern Quellen Jerusalem hinzufugen), nach Armenien gegangen, um dort den Patriarch wieder zu sehen, so liegt es nahe dies Rückkehr des Bischofs in 1503 als durch Joseph veranlasst zu denken."[83] But, Germann himself says, "wir Konnen jedoch seine Reiseroute nicht weiter als Venedig verfolgen, den wenn

---

76. Goes, *ibid*.
77. De Barros, *ibid*.
78. Germann, *op. cit.*, pp. 316-317.
79. Cf. 2.1.0. foot-note no. 2.
80. Latin Text, ch. 1, Italian Text, ch. 1, in Part IV.
81. Germann, *ibid*.
82. Latin Text, ch. 5, Italian Text, ch. 1, in Part IV.
83. Germann, *ibid*.

Hough [84] von seine Rückkehr über Portugal nach Indien zu berichten weiss, so scheint er dafür keinerlei Gewährschaft zu haben." [85] We have the Latin and Dutch texts which say that Joseph returned to Lisbon. But we have not been able to study in detail the position of Assemani and other documents, to evaluate the hypothesis of Germann. It is not unlikely that Joseph went to Babylon, taking into account the enterprising character of Joseph and his position in the community.

2.2.5. When did Joseph return to India?

The three texts of the Narratives of Joseph the Indian have nothing to tell us about the return of Joseph to India. None of the 16th century authors like Goes and De Barros say a word about his return. Only Faria y Sousa tells us that Joseph retunred to India.[86] Germann, in what we have cited above, quotes Hough. But, Hough himself does not give any reference to his source of information. We have only his statement. He writes: "We have no further particulars of this Joseph, than that he returned from Venice to Portugal and thence sailed back to his native land."[87] But as far as we were able search for the documents we have not come across any contemporary document to affirm this.

Mathias Mundadan and to some extent Schurhammer, whom we have quoted elsewhere think that Joseph returned to India and was the chief priest at the main church of Cranganore. These authors, especially Mathias Mundadan, adduce the testimony of Penteado to prove this position.[88] If their views are correct, then Joseph returned to India at a date earlier than 1518.

2.3.0. Joseph and his Narratives

In the foregoing pages we have presented Joseph the Indian and his Narratives. There we have stated that the

---

84. J. Hough *op. cit.* p. 153.
85. Germann, *ibid.*
86. Faria y Sousa, *op. cit.*, p. 59.
87. J. Hough, *op. cit.*, p. 153.
88. Cf. 2.1.3., 2.2.2.

82 INDIA IN 1500 AD

Narratives of Joseph the Indian originated in the context of his voyage with Cabral from Cranganore to Lisbon and of his travels from there to Rome and Venice. Here comes the question: What is the relation between Joseph and the Narratives? Did Joseph write the Narratives? If he did not write them, who wrote them? What language did Joseph speak? In what language were the Narratives written? When and where were they written? What are their contents? We have already given some indication to the answers of these questions. In the following pages we discuss these questions systematically.

2.3.1. Did Joseph write the Narratives?

As far as we know Joseph does not seem to have written the Narratives in his own hand. The Narratives themselves and the testimonies of the witnesses we have cited, indicate that Joseph the Indian did not write the Narratives. All the three texts tell us that the writer recorded what he learned from Joseph. The Italian text puts it as follows:

> "Having been at Rome he then came to Venice in June, 1502 and remained there for many days. During that time information has been gathered from the said Joseph about the things written below."[89]

The Latin text puts it in a different way:

> "At last sometime in the month of June 1501 we came to Lisbon. When we landed there the said Joseph was received by the king. Together with a companion he travelled to Rome and Venice and then returned to Lisbon. By this time we have learned many things worthy of knowing from the some Joseph which we propese to narrate in the following pages."[90]

The Dutch text after describing the travel says:

> "...Joseph....went to Rome and from there to Venice and back to Lisbon. From the same we have

---

89. Cf. Italian Text, ch. 1, in Part IV
90. Cf. Latin Text, ch. 1, in Part IV

received very interesting things which we will present to the reader."[91]

We have many other instances in the text which indicate that the writer put down what he received from Joseph the Indian. For we read in chapter 3, "There are many other sacrifices of which Joseph did not narrate much".[92] The Dutch text says: "More other offerings they have. But not mentioned by Joseph the Indian".[93] "We did not hear much about it from the said Joseph"[94], "because they do not pertain to the narrative of priest Joseph".[95] All these citations from the Narratives of Joseph the Indian imply that Joseph only narrated the things contained in the Narratives which the writer recorded in his own language.

In the title-page of *Sonderlinge Reyesen* there is a statement that it was "noted down by the Portuguese from the mouth of Joseph".[96] It implies that Joseph only narrated and it was written down by a European.

2.3.2. Date and Place of the Narratives

Now we come to the question, when and where Joseph narrated the things, and when were they written. The Italian text has this remark,

> "Having been at Rome he then came to Venice, in June, 1502 and remained there for many days. During that time information has been gathered from the said Joseph about the things written below."[97]

This would mean that Joseph narrated the things in June 1502 or later in Venice. However, the Latin text does not have these dates and the place specified. It says:

> "When we landed there (Lisbon), the said Joseph was received by the king. Together with

---

91. Cf. Dutch Text, ch. 1, in Part IV.
92. Cf. Latin Text, ch. 3, in Part IV.
93. Cf. Dutch Text, ch. 3, in Part IV.
94. Cf. Latin Text, ch. 14, in Part IV.
95. Cf Italian Text, ch. 14, in Part IV.
96. Door de Portugeezen uyt sijnen Mond opgetekend, Anno 1501.
97. Italian Text, ch. 1, in Part IV.

a companion he travelled to Rome and Venice and then returned to Lisbon. By this time we have learned many things worthy of knowing, from the same Joseph, which we propose to narrate in the following pages."[98]

This means that Joseph narrated what is contained in the Narratives during the voyage or after his return to Lisbon We are not in a position to say how these differences arose between the texts.

One thing is clear from the text. Since it describes the audience with Pope Alexander VI, we can say that the Narratives were written after the audience. For, all the texts mention the visit to Rome and Venice. Since the Italian text puts the visit to Venice after the visit to Rome, it may not be wrong to think that the Narratives written at a date later than the visit to Venice, that is, later than June 1502.

2.3.3. What Language did Joseph speak ?

Here we come up against another important question. What language did Joseph use ? Did he make himself understood ? The Italian text gives the impression that Joseph did not understand the language of his interviewer. For, it says:

> "There are many other kinds of sacrifices which Joseph, because he did not have the language and because he had not had many dealings with Gentiles, has not been able to explain entirely."[99]

We have at least one author, Thomas Astley, who thinks that Joseph did not understand the language. He would also explain the Latin text in those lines. He writes:

> "Nor is this any wonder, since Grynaeus or whosoever took the relation from Joseph's mouth tells us he could scarce understand him."[100]

---

98. Latin Text, ch. 1, in Part IV.
99. Italian Text, ch. 3, in Part IV.
100. T. Astley, quoted by Nagam Aiya, *Travancore State Manual*, vol. II p. 151.

This view of Astley is untenable. For the Latin text puts it in another way, which could make a big difference in the meaning It reads:

> "There are many other sacrifices of which Joseph did not narrate much, because on the one hand, we could hardly understand him and more than that, Joseph himself did not have much acquaintance with the gentiles as he was not of the sect."[101]

Here the problem is not necessarily the lack of knowledge of the language on the part of Joseph, but the lack of background knowledge of the religious practices and the temple system on the part of his hearers, or the lack of proper terminology on the part of Joseph. And the Italian expression "non hauer la lingua, ne hauer gran practicha cum gentilii non ne ha sa puto explicare el tutto" and the Latin "... quorum non meminit Ioseph, tum quia uix eum intelligere quiuimus..." in the context do not necessarily indicate Joseph's lack of knowledge of the language.

It would be ridiculous on the part of the writer of the Narratives of Joseph the Indian to say that he could not understand Joseph because of Joseph's lack of knowledge of the language. For in the Narratives he himself makes affirmations as follows:

> "By this time we have learned many things worthy of knowing, from the same Joseph which we propose to narrate."[102]

> "Beyond this is China ... of which we do not mean to speak, for, we did not hear much about it from the said Joseph the Indian."[103]

> "But since they least pertain to what the said Joseph narrated, we abstain from making additions to it lest you should think that we narrate anything other than the truth."[104]

---

101. Latin Text, ch. 3, in Part IV.
102. Latin Text, ch. 1, in Part IV.
103. Latin Text, ch. 14, in Part IV.
104. Latin Text, ch. 14, in Part IV.

Note that when the Italian text uses the expression "ne hauer la lingua",[105] the parallel Latin expression is "quorum non meminit Joseph."[106] There is a world of difference between the two. If the writer of the Narratives meant by the Italian expression "ne hauer la lingua", that Joseph did not know any language which the writer knew so as to make himself understood or that the writer did not understand anything that Joseph narrated because of the language, he is undermining even the very possibility of his writing of the Narratives. How could he write down what Joseph narrated without having a common language. How could the writer make the affirmation "by this time we have learned many things", "we did not hear much from the said Joseph the Indian", and "since they do not pertain to what the said Joseph narrated, we abstain from making any addition", if he did not understand the language of Joseph the Indian. Such a statement on his part would be rediculous and make the whole Narratives of Joseph the Indian a shear nonsense.

Scientific research in the traditions of the St Thomas Christians and in the Kerala history last fifty years have shown that much of the rare and valuable information contained in the Narratives are trustworthy. We find in them accounts of certain traditions of the St Thomas Christians which no other documents prior to it contained, which can be given only by a son of the soil. The writer could get at that time such information from no other source. Hence we have to suppose that what is contained in the Narratives came from the mouth of an Indian, a Thomas Christian of Malabar origin. Hence, we have to affirm that Joseph the Indian had enough knowledge of some language, which the writer could understand, to make himself understood and thereby make the very Narratives possible.

Now comes the question. If Joseph knew the language, what was the language he spoke. The first language that Joseph might possibly have used seems to be Portuguese. As a priest from Malabar we could suppose that Joseph knew Malayalam and

---

105. Italian Text, ch. 3, in Part IV.
106. Latin Text, ch. 3. in Part IV.

Syriac. But, it does not seem that the writer could understand any of them. The three language that the writer possibly knew were Portuguese, Italian and Latin. However, there is greater possibility that Joseph learned Portuguese more easily than Italian, or Latin. For according to the Narratives, Joseph started his journey with the Portuguese on 10th January 1501. We are told by the Italian text that Joseph remained in Lisbon until January 1502, after arriving there sometime in June 1501.[107] That means he had one complete year with the Portuguese, six months in the ship and six months in Lisbon, before he started his journey to Rome and Venice. Being an ingenious man, it was not impossible that he picked up the Portuguese language, sufficiently well to make himself understood. It would be safer to suppose that he learned the Portuguese language more easily than the Italian or Latin language, taking into account the possibilities offered to him. Considering also the Portuguese influences[108] found in the Italian text we have to suppose that the Narratives themselves were first written in Portuguese or at least by a Portuguese. Taking all these facts together, it may not be wrong to assume that Joseph spoke Portuguese and made himself understood, and that he made the narrations in the Portuguese language.

2.3.4. The writer of the Narratives

We do not know for certain who the writer of the Narratives of Joseph the Indian was. Nor can we say with certainty in what language they were first written. From the remarks of De Barros in his *Da Asia* it appears that they were written in Italian. For, he writes:

> "The Italians, who in this are more curious than we are, made a summary which is incorporated in a volume entitled *Novus Orbis* which includes some of our Navigations written not as they merit and as they happened."[109]

However, this statement of De Barros does not seem to be correct. For, in the first place, we find a certain "Portuguesism"

---

107. Italian Text, ch. 1, in Part IV.
108. Cf. 2.3.4. infra, pp. 88–91.
109. De Barros, *ibid*.

or Portuguese influence in all the known texts of the Narratives of Joseph the Indian which leads us to the affirmation that they were at least written by a Portuguese, if not in the Portuguese language. Secondly, we have shown above[110] that in all probability, Joseph made the narrations in Portuguese. Thirdly, there is an indication on the title page of *Sonderlinge Reysen van Joseph.* that it was translated from Portuguese for the first time, which means that there existed a Portuguese text. Hence, if Joseph made the narration in Portuguese and if they were first written in the Portuguese language, then the writer of the Narratives was a Portuguese. Also, there is some possibility that the Narratives of Joseph were first written in some Italian dialect or in the Latin language. Even then it may not be wrong to affirm that the writer of the Narratives of Joseph the Indian was a Portuguese provided Joseph made the narration in Portuguese. But, De Barros did not know any source other than the *Novus Orbis.* And *Novus Orbis* has simply reproduced the text in *Itinerarium.* And we do not know for certain what the source of the text of the Narratives contained in *Itinerarium* was. Hence, De Barros' information was partial. On the other hand, the affirmation that the Narratives were written by a Portuguese will better explain the Portuguesism found in the texts which we discuss here below.

The Portuguesism or Portuguese influence that impels us to conclude that the writer of the Narratives was a Portuguese is revealed in three levels: (1) in the use of the personal and possessive pronouns, (2) in the use of certain Portuguese expressions found in the Italian text, (3) in the use of the Portuguese past participle in the place of the Italian past participles, in the Italian text.

It is in the first chapter of the Narratives that we come across the instances of the use of the pronouns mentioned above. Here personal and possesive pronouns are used in the first person in many instances where the pronouns stand for the Portuguese. All the three sources reveal this phenomenon. However, it is the Latin text that is the most profuse in this use. The first chapter of the Latin text has at least ten expressions

---

110. Cf. 2.3.3.

such as "our king", "our ships", "our fleet", "with us", "we noticed", "we set out", "we landed". "we have learned" etc. where except for the last case the pronouns stand for the Portuguese, and in the last instance for the very writer of the Narratives. If the writer is to use pronouns in first person like "we", "us", "our" to denote the Portuguese he should be a Portuguese. In the Dutch text too we have such expression occuring from the middle of the "Foreword" (Voorbericht) onwards. There we find expressions like "When we were engaged in trade", "entered our ships", "sailed off with us", "against us", "to destroy our ships", "as we became aware", "we gave ourselves", "given to us", "we sailed for Lisbon", "we came to Lisbon" "we received" etc. In all these cases the pronouns stand for the Portuguese. In the Italian text however, such expression occurs only once. However, that single instance is very significant. For, the editor of the Italian text unlike the others has taken care to give the description in Chapter 1 in the third person. However, inspite of his scrupulous editorial care to put his narration in the third person we find in the very title of the Chapter the expression "our caravels". It reads: "How Joseph the Indian came to Portugal on board *our caravels* and the king caused him to be accompanied to Rome and Venice". Here the expression "our caravels" denote the Portuguese caravels and the pronoun stands for the Portuguese. If the writer is to use the pronoun "our" for the Portuguese he was also a Portuguese. In the title the expression "the king" is without specification, unlike what the editor does in other cases such as "the king of Portugal", "other Portuguese", "leaving an equal number of their own Portuguese",[111] etc. where every thing is in the third person. Again, in the Italian text indirect expressions are used where other two texts use first person. For example, we read in Latin, "in so far as we could learn from our dealings with him,"[112] where Italian puts the same as "in so far as could be understood *by them.*"[113] We can adduce similar other examples from the texts. Hence the presence of the expression "our caravels" in the Italian text points to the fact that such an expression existed in the original text which the editor of the source

---

111. Italian Text, ch. 1, in Part IV.
112. Latin Text, ch. 1, in Part IV.
113. Italian Text, ch. 1, in Part IV.

common to all the known texts might have used. Though the editor of the Italian text took care to change the original expressions in the first person, into third person this one instance escaped his attention. Hence, we affirm that the original text of the Narratives of Joseph the Indian used pronouns both personal and possesive in the first person to denote the Portuguese. Hence, we feel that the writer was one among the Portuguese for whom those pronouns stand. Hence, we conclude that the writer of the Narratives was a Portuguese.

This view is further corroborated by the fact that there are certain glaring examples of Portuguese influence in the Italian text of the Narratives of Joseph the Indian. The expressions like "molestade da cadauno", "molto despresiadi", "tagliadi", "tirado", "camino", "veludade", "enclofada" found in the Italian text[114] reveal Portuguese influence. The noun forms like desideracao "brusao", "hercditao", "uzao", in the Italian text[115] also point to some sort of Portuguese influence. They show that the first text was in Portuguese or, at least, that the writer of the first text was a Portuguese.

The most interesting cases of the Portuguese influence are found in the use of the past participles. There are many instances where the past participles are found in the Portuguese form instead of the Italian form. For example, we have participles like sopranominado for sopranominato, parlado for parlato, antenominado for antenominato, despresiadi for despresiati, molestada for molestata, molestadi for molestati, deputadi for deputati, deputado for deputato, consechrado for consecrato, prenominada for prenominata, chiamada for chiamata.[116] Few of such Portuguese forms were corrected in the 1508 edition of *Paesi*, just few months after the 1507 etition. We have five examples where the Portuguese form was corrected into the Italian form like sopranominado into sopranominato,[117] antenominado into antenominato,[118] parlado into parlato,[119] consechrado into

---

114. Italian Text, chapters, 3, 2, 10, 3, 1, 4, 12. in Part IV.
115. Italian Text, ch. 3, 4, 4, in Part IV.
116. Italian Text, chapters, 1, 2, 5, 4, 11, 5, 12, 11, in Part IV.
117. Italian Text, ch. 1, in Part IV.
118. Italian Text, ch. 2, in Part IV.
119. Italian Text, ch. 2, in Part IV.

consecrato,[120] and chiamada into chiamata.[121] It shows that the very editor of the second edition recognised these Portuguese variations or Portuguese influences. What is more interesting is the fact that we have both the forms prenominado[122] and prenominato[123] occuring in the very first edition itself. This is not only the case of past participles. We have two forms pescador[124] and peschatori,[125] (the first Portuguese, and the second Italian), occuring in Chapter 3 of the Narratives.[126]

All these cases of Portuguesism or Portuguese influence bring us to the conclusion that the writer of the first text of the Narratives was a Portuguese and that in all probability the Narratives themselves were written in the Portuguese language.

That the writer of the Narratives of Joseph the Indian was a European and a Christian needs no other proof than the many expressions in the first person that we find in chapters 5 and 6 where the customs and the practices of the Christians of Cranganore and those of the Church of Europe are compared. We do not think it necessary to enumerate them here.

The second thing that we could affirm about the writer of the Narratives of Joseph, is that he wrote the Narratives basing himself on what he heard from Joseph. We find in Chapter 2 such expressions as "a iudicio de chi quello ha uisto & cum lui parlado" (according to the judgement of those who have seen him and spoken with him) [127], "dal quale se ha hauto" ("this has been learnt from him"). [128] Reading these expression one would be led to conclude that the writer had only second hand knowledge of the things. But, in the Latin and Dutch texts we find more positive affirmations. Speaking of Joseph and his brother Mathias the Latin text says: "ex his vero fratribus Indis

---

120. Italian Text, ch. 5, in Part IV.
121. Italian Text, ch. 12, in Part IV.
122. Italian Text, ch. 11, in Part IV.
123. Italian Text, ch. 5, in Part IV.
124. Italian Text, ch. 3, in Part IV.
125. Italian Text, ch. 3, in Part IV.
126. *Paesi* 1507, ch. cxxx.
127. Italian Text, ch. 2, in Part IV.
128. *ibid.*

quorum iam memini" ("of these Indian brothers whom I still remember")[129] and describing the person of Joseph in Chapter 2 it says: "quantum colligere ex eius consuetudine quiuimus" ("as far as we could learn from our dealings with him.")[130]

The Dutch text too has the words "In al onse gemeensaamheyd met hem knoden wy niet anders vermerken als een sonderlinge vriendlijkheyd en een onvevlekt Geloof" ("In our acquaintance with him we could not notice anything other than remarkable friendliness and blemishless faith.")[131] In Chapter 7, speaking about the construction of ships, the writer tells us: "This I have diligently learned (sciscitatus sum) from the said Joseph. For I showed him (ostendi illi) once how we construct our ships and asked..."[132] The Dutch text has almost the same expression: "They build their ships firmly with iron nails. I tell it here because some think that they use only wooden nails, over which I diligently asked Joseph who witnessed the contrary."[133]

From the Narratives one could gather that the writer was an honest man with a great deal of scientific information especilly about voyages and navigations. The variety of subjects treated from Cabral's voyage to theology of the papacy, from geography to commerce and astronomy which he discusses makes us feel that he was a man of varied interests and pursuits and of a scientific mind. We see in the Narratives the details of Cabral's voyage, his friendship and fight with the Zamorin, the description of the kingdom and port of Cochin and its commerce, the geography, flora and fauna of Cranganore, the social setup and the religious life of the Hindus, the ecclesiastical system of the St Thomas Christians, their liturgical and sacramental life, theology of the papacy, commerce, numismatics, astronomy and navigation etc., all of which show the interests of the writer, who put the questions to Joseph. For, we have to assume that his method was one of asking questions, and the range of questions he might have asked reveals his inquisitive mind and

---

129. Latin Text, ch. 1, in Part IV.
130. Latin Text, ch. 2, in Part IV.
131. Dutch Text, ch. 2, in Part IV.
132. Latin Text, ch. 7, in Part IV.
133. Dutch Text, ch. 7, in Part IV.

its extent. We see him quote from Strabo's geography[134] and the travels of Marco Polo. [135] All through his work his knowledge of things connected with navigation, spices and theology is revealed.

The Narratives reveal the scientific honesty on the part of the writer. We read almost towards the end of the Narratives, in the Italian text, the following:

> "Many things might be said concerning spices and other merchandise, pertaining to India and other parts of which we have written in the course of our discussion, but because they are not pertain to the narrative of Priest Joseph, but rather an addition... we have decided to put an end to the present subject." [136]

The Latin text has another formulation:

> "Beyond this is China... of which we do not mean to speak, for we did not hear much from the said Joseph the Indian. Nor have we gone to those remote parts of the world. We could however make further investigation about the places of gems and precious stones about the nature of pearls as well as of the many different kinds of spices, for India in the first place produces them. But, since they do not pertain to what the said Joseph narrated we abstain from making additions to it." [137]

Further, speaking of the sacrifices of the Hindus of Cranganore he is not afraid to confess that he "could hardly understand him", which show his scientific honesty and formation.

---

134. Latin Text, ch. 10, in Part IV.
135. Latin Text, ch. 5, in Part IV.
136. Italian Text, ch. 14, in Part IV.
137. Latin Text, ch. 14, in Part IV.

2.4.0. The contents of the Narratives of Joseph the Indian

The Narratives of Joseph contain a description of the India in 1500 AD. For what is contained in them were narrated by Joseph the Indian and recorded by a European writer. Joseph set sail from Cranganore on 10th January 1501. The India that he described was the India he knew before he set sail from Cranganore. Hence his description is the description of India in 1500 AD.

The Malabar Coast in 1500 AD, with its three ports of Calicut, Cochin and Cranganore, is well presented in the Narratives of Joseph the Indian. In them we find also a very valuable account of the St. Thomas Christians of Kerala in 1500 AD.

2.4.1. The voyage of Cabral and the travels of Joseph the Indian

The Narratives of Joseph the Indian begin with a description of the voyage of Cabral, his friendship and later his fight with the Zamorin of Calicut, which forced him to betake himself to Cochin. In Cochin, Joseph and his brother approached Cabral and revealed to him their desire to go to the western countries, especially to Rome and Jerusalem. In the Narratives we have a description of Joseph's voyage in Cabral's ship to Portugal and of his being received by the King of Portugal. We learn from them that Joseph along with a companion provided by the king went to Rome and Venice and (according to the Latin and Dutch texts) back to Lisbon.

2.4.2. The person of Joseph

The brief description of the voyage of Joseph is followed by a very fascinating description of the person of Joseph with his physical appearance and the inner qualities of his personality. We are told by the writer of the Narratives that Joseph at the time of his visit to Europe was forty years of age. According to him Joseph was dark coloured and medium size and was an ingenious man of very high integrity and truthfulness, a man of exemplary life, blesmishless faith and remarkable friendliness.

2.4.3. Description of the city of Cranganore: A description of Kerala in 1500 AD

The description of the city of Cranganore, the native place of Joseph, follows next. Actually, the Narratives of Joseph the Indian, that is, the narration of what Joseph the Indian recounted begins with the description of Cranganore. This description of Cranganore forms the major part of the Narratives of Joseph the Indian. It begins at the middle of Chapter 2 and ends with Chapter 10. In fact this is not merely a description of Cranganore alone. We can say that it is the description of Kerala For, in this extensive description of Cranganore we can see a picture of Kerala in 1500 AD with its people, their faith and religion, their social classes, customs and manners, the climate, navigation, monetary system, flora and fauna, especially, the spices, rice and palm trees, and the process of making toddy, vinegar, saccharin and oil from the palms. This picture of Cranganore, in fact, is a cross section of Kerala.

The description of Cranganore begins with a brief description of the location of the city of Cranganore, the people who inhabit it and the merchants who come there for trade. Then follows a description of the structure of the society and the social classes. This is followed by a discussion of the life and faith of the Hindus, their temples, and their manner of worship. The customs and manners of the king and of the people described include the marriage and other celebrations of the king, the royal succession, the practice of Sati, where women burn themselves after the death of their husbands, the apparel of the king and the people. What is actually described is the life and traditions of the Hindus in Cranganore. But it is a cross section. It depicts the life of an average Hindu in Kerala at that time.

Then follows a description of the life of Christians of Cranganore. As in the case of the Hindu community what is described is the ecclesial and ecclesiastical system, liturgical and sacrament life, the fasts, feasts and celebrations, customs and manners of the Christians of Cranganore. But actually this is the cross section of the life of the community of the St. Thomas Christians of Malabar. It is a mine of information about the Church of the St. Thomas Christians.

2.4.4. The city of Cranganore

The Narratives of Joseph the Indian tell us that the city of Cranganore was some 90 miles far from the city of Calicut and some 20 miles from Cochin. It lay some 15 miles landwards from the seashore. The city has no walls. There were many rivers flowing into the city. The houses were built at some distance from each other, often on the banks of the rivers. We are told that there were Hindus, Christians and some Jews in the city. Jews were said to be much despised. The king of the city was a Hindu.

2.4.5. The Structure of the society, social classes of the Hindus, their temples and their worship

A description of the structure of the Hindu society follows. We are told that there were three classes among the Hindus. The highest class was that of the Nairs. Then came the proletariate called "dogs" in their local language. The third and the last class was that of the fishermen, called by the name "Nuirinam" or "Nuiram" or "Nuieras". This last class was often molested by the highest class.

Each of these classes had its separate temples. Women too had their separate temples where men were not allowed to enter. The Hindus offered the first fruits of the land in their temples. They had statues of animals but they did not adore them. They believed in one god, whom they called 'Tambram'. They depicted 'Tambram' with three faces and folded hands.

We are told that the Hindus offered many sacrifices or rituals in their temples. We have an interesting accounts of one of their rituals recounted in detail by Joseph the Indian. This is a description of 'Velichapadu Thullal'. But Joseph did not give the name.

2.4.6. The customs and manners of the king and people of Cranganore

The description of the social classes and the religious life of the Hindus is followed by a description of the customs and manners of the king and of the people. We learn from the Narratives that the king of Cranganore had many wives. When a king died his wife lived only eight days more. Then she burnt herself alive in memory of her husband. In the royal succession it was not the sons who inherited the kingdom, but the nearest relatives other than the sons. As regards dress, the king wore a golden cap, and important men wore caps of velvet or silk. The others wore no caps. They moved about half naked, covering their private parts with very clean cotton cloth. They wore ornaments beautifully decorated with precious stones on their arms and legs. They wrote on the leaves of trees using an iron stylus. They had their own Indian language called 'Malanar', which stands for Malayalam.

2.4.7. The St Thomas Christians of Cranganore

The chapter 4 of the Narratives of Joseph the Indian speaks of the existence of Christians in Cranganore. The chapters 5 and 6 give an extensive description of the life of the Christians of Cranganore. Joseph the Indian was one among them. They are known in history as St. Thomas Christians. We are told that from the river Indus upto the Island of Ormus there were Christians. In no other place Christians are found except in Cranganore. The Christians of Cranganore were great in number. Joseph also narrated that there existed Christians in China. There were also kings in India who believed in Christ.

Chapter 5 begins with the furnishing of the church building. We are told that the churches were vaulted, and that there were no statues, but only a cross was seen inside the church. On the courtyard of the church is seen a cross. We are told that there were no bells in these churches.

Then follows the discussion of the ecclesiastical system of the Church. We are told that the Church of Cranganore was under the Catholicos of Babylon, under whom there were two Patriarchs, one in India and the other in China. The Catholicos also called Catholica consecrated and sent Bishops to different parts of his Church when and where it was needed.

In this chapter we are told that Joseph himself was ordained priest by the Catholicos of Babylon when he went there in the delegation sent by the people of Kerala.

98   INDIA IN 1500 AD

We are told in this chapter of Joseph's audience with Pope Alexander VI who discussed the affairs of the Church of India with Joseph. It is in this context that the Pope discussed with him about the authority of the Catholica of the East, and then shone out the theologian in Joseph. We see here how Joseph the Indian explained to Pope Alexander VI his theology of the Papacy and of the right of the Catholica of the East. For Joseph the Catholica of Babylon is also *"vicem gerens Petri"* just like the Pope of Rome.

Then follows the description of the sacramental life, the feasts and fasts, and customs and manners of the St. Thomas Christians in chapter 6. We are told that priests did not wear tonsure, instead they kept a tuft of hair on their head. We are also told that children were not baptised before 40 days except in danger of death. We are told that these Christians had both the sacraments of confession and communion. They consecrated the body and blood of Christ, and they communicated thrice a year. According to the report of the writer of the Narratives these Christians did not have extreme unction, in its place they blessed the body. (This statement is not correct). The Christians of Cranganore buried the body. When someone dies many came together for eight following days, they ate together and prayed together for the dead. They made the will and the will of the dead was respected much. The wife after the death of her husband went to her paternal house taking the dowery with her. But she cannot marry for one year. They had monks who lived in perfect continence and poverty; their priest live very chastely. Divorce was not known among these Christians.

After the description of the traditons or customs, follows the description of the feasts and fasts. We gather from the Narratives that the Christians of Cranganore observed the Fast of Advent and the Great Fast. From Good Friday until Easter-Sunday they abstained from all food. They celebrated the feast of Resurrection with the following two days. The octave of Easter was celebrated with very great solemnity, for they believed that on that day St. Thomas, to whom they have very great veneration, put the hand on the side of Christ. Among the feasts they celebrated were Ascension, Nativity and Epiphany of Our Lord, and Assumption, Nativity and Purification of Our Lady.

With great solemnity, the great annual Feast of St. Thomas was celeberated both by the gentiles and Christians alike in July.

We receive information from the Narratives that the St. Thomas Christians venerated the four Gospels and accepted the four evangelists. The study of sacred Scriptures thrived among them and they had many learned doctors who interpreted the Bible with authority.

In general we can say that from the Narratives of Joseph the Indian we get very valuable information about the St. Thomas Christians of Malabar before the coming of the Portuguese. Coming as it does from the lips of a member of the community, especially a priest and important personality of the community, they are very valuable. They provide information which none of the contemporary documents could give.

2.4.8. Climate at Cranganore, ships, navigation

Then follows the description of the climate, ships, and navigation. We find in the Narratives a description of the astronomical position of Cranganore, the monsoon, different climatic changes and seasons. This discussion of the climate leads to an account of the times of navigation, the ships used and the countries to which ships go from Cranganore for trade. We can find in them a comparison of the mode of construction of ships in India and Europe.

2.4.9. The monetary system and the flora and fauna

Then follows an analysis of the monetary system of Cranganore. We are told that there are three sorts of coins. The first is gold coin. It is called *Sarapho* or *Zaraph*; the second is silver coin. Its name is *Parante* and the third is called *Tare*. The value of each coin in relation to the Venetian ducats is also given.

This is followed by a description of the flora and fauna and the spices that abound in and around Cranganore. We are told in chapter 9 about the animals and plants especially about pepper. We are told that the region of Cranganore produces large quantities of rice and sugar. Joseph enumerated the trees that grow there. He said that apples, peaches and grapes do not grow there.

What is especially interesting for the reader is the discussion about the palm trees which the Narratives qualifies as the trees that produces the *'Indian Nuts'*. It is presented as the most perfect tree. One reads with great interest the description of the process of making toddy, vinegar, country sugar, and oil from the palm trees.

2.4.10. The city of Calicut

Chapter 11 gives us an interesting description of the city of Calicut. It contains information about the religion, customs and manners of the king of Calicut. It speaks of the different people that come to Calicut from all over the world for trade. We are told also how the Chinese who were Christians, who used to trade with Calicut, broke the relations with Calicut and went to the port of Mylapore in the kingom of Narsindo in the eastern Coast of India, because they were maltreated by the king of Calicut. The Narratives of Joseph tell us about the imports and exports at the port of Calicut and of the countries to which things were exported and from which merchandise were brought to Calicut. We learn also of the annual international fare at Calicut.

2.4.11. The West Coast of India and the islands and cities in the Arabian sea. Gujarat, Ormus and Cambay

Then follows a description of the important lands and cities on the West Coast of India Also the islands and towns in the Arabian sea like, the island of Ormus, the cities Sobobec, Semath, and Chismii are described in the Narratives. The faith and religion, customs and manners of the king and of the people are described. Very interesting are the information about the celibates, conjurers and the vegitarians of Gujarat. Gujarat was the abode of the veteran tradesmen.

The chapter 13 is the description of Cambay located on the gulf of Gujarat. It was a very civilised city, large and populous. It was the most excellent of all the Indian cities, that it was called the "Cairo of India". We are told also of the Cape of Diongul, the Cape of Ely and the island of Maya. Diongul is some 300 miles from Calicut while the Cape of Ely is 600 miles from Calicut.

2.4.12. The King of Narsindo and the Body of St Thomas in the Church of Mylapore

The description of the cities and islands west of Cranganore is followed by a descriptions of the cities, islands and the Capes east of Cranganore. There mention is made of the following: the city of Cochin in the kingdom of Cochin, the Cape of Comirin, Oriza in the gulf of Oriza and the islands like Saylam (Ceylon), Sumotra (Sumatra) called Taprobana. Mention is made also of China which is called 'the island with many islands.' Other two cities of the king Narasindus or the king of Narsindo (Narasinga) are described. They are Besenegal (Bisnagar) and Mylapore.

Bisnagar was situated three hundred miles towards the mountains from the sea. It was a great city with three rounds of walls. The king of Narasinga, according to Joseph, was a very powerful king who took hundreds of elephants, thousands of horses and innumerable foot soldiers in war.

In the same kingdom of Narasinga was the city of Milapar (Mylapore) where the church of St Thomas was built. In this church was found the body of St Thomas which was venerated by Christians and non-Christians alike. Many miracles occured there.

PART III

The Texts of the Narratives of Joseph the Indian

The Three Texts

In Part I we made a search into the sources of the Narratives of Joseph the Indian. There we analysed and studied the different sources and the various texts that originated from them. We stated there that we know today 25 different editions and versions of the text of the Narratives of Joseph the Indian in seven different languages. They originated from three main sources, *Paesi* (Italian), *Itinerarium* (Latin), and *Sonderlinge Reysen* (Dutch). There are seven Italian editions of the text. They are different editions of the text in *Paesi*. The six French editions that we know are editions of the translation of the text in *Paesi*. The four re-editions of the Latin text through *Novus Orbis* depend on *Itinerarium*. The English text is the translation of the text in *Paesi* and the Portuguese text is the translation of the English. However, the German and Dutch texts do not originate from one single source. We have two different German texts. The first is the translation of the Italian text in *Paesi* (1507), while the other is the translation of the Latin text in *Novus Orbis* (1532 Basel edition). There are three different texts in Dutch. One is the translation of the German translation of the text in *Paesi*. The second is the Dutch version of the German translation of the text in *Novus Orbis*. The third is the text in *Sonderlinge Reysen van Joseph*. According to the title page it was translated from Portuguese. All the three Dutch texts differ among themselves.

In Part I we also proposed the hypothesis of the interrelation of the texts and the sources.[1] We showed there that the common opinion that *Itinerarium* was the translation of *Paesi* is untenable, and that the text of the Narratives of Joseph the Indian in *Itinerarium* does not directly depend on the text in *Paesi*.[2] We also proposed the hypothesis of different immediate sources and one common source for *Paesi* and *Itinerarium* and hence also for the texts of the Narratives of Joseph the Indian contained in them.[3] The Dutch text claims that it was translated from Portuguese. But it has more affinity to the Latin text than to the Italian text. At the present state of research we cannot say a final word about its source. We cannot say for certain, whether it depends on the original Portuguese text, or on the Latin text of *Fasciculus Temporum* or on the source common to *Paesi* and *Itinerarium*, or on some later Portuguese translation of the Latin text of *Fasciculus Temporum*, or *Itinerarium*. So far we have not been able to identify the Latin text in *Fasciculus Temporum* and the original Portuguese text. Our hypothesis is that all the known texts depend on the original text in Portuguese (or in some Italian dialect). The Latin text of *Fasciculus Temporum* and the common source of *Paesi* and *Itinerarium* depend on this original text. The text in *Sonderlinge Reysen* might have originated from the original Portuguese or from the common source, or from the Latin text of *Fasciculus Temporum* or *Itinerarium*.

In this Part III we propose to make a detailed study of the three texts of the Narratives of Joseph the Indian originating from *Paesi*, *Itinerarium* and *Sonderlinge Reysen*. We will discuss here the history of the texts and make a comparative study of the three texts. We will consider the internal differences and similarities of the three texts and the interpolation, additions and ommissions in each of the texts. This will be followed by a detailed comparative study of the Italian and Latin texts.

---

1. Cf. 1.3.6., 1.6.0.
2. Cf. 1.3.6., 1.6.0.
3. Cf. 1.3.6., 1.6.0.

3.1.0. History of the three texts

We said above that all the known texts of the Narratives of Joseph the Indian depend on three texts: the Italian text of *Paesi*, the Latin text of *Itinerarium* and the Dutch text of *Sonderlinge Reysen*.

The Italian text was first published in 1507 in *Paesi*. Between 1507 and 1522 it was re-edited five times. The 1508 edition was reprinted in 1916, thus giving 7 editions of the text. In 1508 it was translated into German and Dutch. The first French translation appeared in 1515 and had five successive re-editions. The English translation appeared in 1937 and it was further translated into Portuguese in 1966 giving a total of 17 editions and versions of the text of the Narratives of Joseph the Indian originating from *Paesi*.

The Latin text of *Itinerarium* appeared in 1508. We are told that there were more than one re-editions. But we were not able to identify any of them. The first re-edition that we know was in 1532 in *Novus Orbis* which incorporated the materials in *Itinerarium*. *Novus Orbis* had four re-editions. The text of *Novus Orbis* of 1532 was translated into German in 1534 and into Dutch in 1563. Thus we have 7 editions and versions of the Latin texts of the Narratives of Joseph the Indian originating from *Itinerarium*.

Sonderlinge Reysen van Joseph gives us the third text of the Narratives of Joseph the Indian. Chronologically it was the last re-edition of the text.

3.1.1. The Italian Text of Paesi

The earliest known text of the Narratives of Joseph the Indian is found in *Paesi Nouamente Retrouati* of 1507. It was printed on 3rd November 1507, and is found on the last 19 pages of the work (folios 116^r – 125^r unnumbered) beginning on the folio marked Bii. This forms the last 14 chapters of the work, numbered cxxix-cxlii. Each of the chapters has its specific title, which is slightly different from the title given in the table of contents at the beginning of the work. The titles of the chapters do not always represent fully what is included in those chapters.

The language is the Italian of the 16th century. The printing is not very perfect. There are many mistakes and inconsistencies in the printing. Each chapter is given as one single piece without division into paragraphs. There are many abbreviations used, especially for the case-endings and relative pronouns which make the reading and translation difficult. The system of punctuation also makes it difficult to determine the meaning of phrases and sentences. There are many inconsistencies in the use of the names of places, which are often spelled differently. For example, Calicut is spelled as Callichut or Calichut, Ormuz as Ormus or Ornus, Cambay as Cambaia or Cambait, etc.

This Italian text is different from the Latin text of *Itinerarium* and the Dutch text of *Sonderlinge Reysen*. However, the subject-matter contained in this text is the same as that of the other texts. In the organization and division into chapters it is similar to the text of *Itinerarium*. There are instances where it agrees with both the other texts and other instances where it agrees with the Latin alone.

One thing important about the Italian text is that it gives us certain information that was not found in the other texts. For example, the exact dates and duration of time of Joseph's stay in Lisbon, and his visit to Venice. We know from the Italian text alone that there were Moors in considerable numbers in Cranganore. The other two texts do not give the name of the coin "Tare" nor the name of the language of the people of Cranganore. Though the chapters, 1 and 2, of the Italian texts are subject to considerable amount of editorial manipulation, this text is free of interpolation. Though it agrees with the other texts in many aspects it is also different from them. There does not seem to be any direct dependence of the other texts on the Italian texts of *Paesi*.

3.1.2. The Latin text of Itinerarium

The second known text of the Narratives of Joseph the Indian is the Latin text of *Itinerarium* published from Milan on 1st June 1508. Just like the text in *Paesi*, it also appears on the last folios of *Itinerarium* numbered lxxxii–lxx(x)viii wrongly numbered lxxviii. The folios are numbered wrongly in the last few folios. The text forms the last 14 chapters of *Itinerarium* numbered cxxix–cxlii as in *Paesi*. The titles of the chapters are slightly different from the titles given in the table of contents of the work. They were also different from the corresponding titles of the Italian text.

The Latin text in the *Itinerarium* was reproduced in *Novus Orbis*. In all the Latin editions of *Novus Orbis*, the text of the Narratives of Joseph the Indian occurs in the 14 chapters numbered in the same way as in *Itinerarium*, i. e. cxxix–cxlii. In the 1532 and 1537 editions of *Novus Orbis* from Basel it is found on pages 142-153 both inclusive, beginning at the middle of page 142. In the Paris edition of 1532 it appears on pages 125-134, with the same chapter numbers and the titles of the chapter as in *Itinerarium*. In the 1555 edition from Basel it occurs on pages 202-210 with the same chapter numbers and titles as in the other editions.

The organization and the sequence of the themes of the chapters are the same as that of the text in the *Paesi*. There is no division into paragraphs. The titles of the chapters in certain cases are different from those of the *Paesi* though in many aspects they are similar. There are instances where the Latin texts agree with the Dutch. The Dutch text has more affinity to this text.

The first chapter of the Latin text is marked by expressions with personal pronouns in the first person, standing for the Portuguese. The Dutch text follows this in the second half of the chapter, whereas in the Italian we see an editorial handling where they are changed into third person.

3.1.3. The Dutch text of Sonderlinge Reysen van Joseph

The third text of the Narratives of Joseph has come down to us through the booklet *Sonderlinge Reysen van Joseph*. We have already stated that this was published in a collection of voyages by Vander Aa in the year 1704. The title page of the booklet tells us that this was translated from Portuguese. From certain remarks in the texts it seems that Vander Aa had also before him some other text of the Narratives of Joseph the Indian. Most probably this was the text of the Narratives contained in the Dutch translation of the *Novus Orbis* of 1563.

This text is very different from the other two texts in the organization and division of the chapters. The subject matter treated in it is the same as in the other two. The sequence of the narration is also the same. However, the division of the chapters is different. The titles of the chapters are very different from those of the other two texts. When the texts of the Narratives in *Paesi* and *Itinerarium* have 14 chapters, the Dutch text of *Sonderlinge Reysen* has only 11 chapters and a Foreword. The chapter cxxix of the other texts is presented as Foreword (Voorberight) and the three chapters cxxxv-cxxxviii were put together as chapter VI. Even the numbering of chapters is different. While the other two texts keep the chapter number of the work, in *Sonderlinge Reysen* new numbering system is introduced. The titles of the chapters are very different from those of the other two texts. Unlike the other two, each chapter is divided into different paragraphs.

In certain areas it is similar to the other two, but in general we can say that it is closer to the Latin text. There are certain interpolations and additions in this text. It does not give us anymore information than what is contained in the other two. However, as regard the date of the arrival of Cabral's ships in Cochin it gives the correct date.

3.2.0. Comparative study of the three texts

The three texts of the Narratives of Joseph the Indian have one and the same subject matter in common, but they are nevertheless different from one another. As we have said above, the contents and the sequence of the themes in general are the same. However, we see differences in the division of the chapters, the titles of the chapters and in certain other respects. In the following pages we will discuss the differences and similarities amongs the texts. We will analyse in detail the division and titles of the chapters, the interpolations and additions.

3.2.1. The division of the chapters

In the division of the chapters the Italian and Latin texts agree, while the Dutch text has a different scheme of division. As we said earlier, both Italian and Latin texts have 14 chapters while the Dutch has a Foreword and 11 chapters (Voorberight and XI Hoofdstuk). The first chapter in the Italian and Latin become the Voorberight in Dutch. Actually the subject matter of the chapters are the same in all the three. However the numbering is different.

Here below we give the table showing the relation between the chapters of the three texts.

Italian	*Latin*	*Dutch*
Chapter 1 (cxxix)	Chapter 1 (cxxix)	Foreword
Chapter 2 (cxxx)	Chapter 2 (cxxx)	Chapter I
Chapter 3 (cxxxi)	Chapter 3 (cxxxi)	Chapter II
Chapter 4 (cxxxii)	Chapter 4 (cxxxii)	Chapter III
Chapter 5 (cxxxiii)	Chapter 5 (cxxxiii)	Chapter IV
Chapter 6 (cxxxiiii)	Chapter 6 (cxxxiiii)	Chapter V
Chapter 7 (cxxxv)	Chapter 7 (cxxxv)	
Chapter 8 (cxxxvi)	Chapter 8 (cxxxvi)	Chapter VI
Chapter 9 (cxxxvii)	Chapter 9 (cxxxvii)	
Chapter 10 (cxxxviii)	Chapter 10 (cxxxviii)	Chapter VII
Chapter 11 (cxxxix)	Chapter 11 (cxxxix)	Chapter VIII
Chapter 12 (cxl)	Chapter 12 (cxl)	Chapter IX
Chapter 13 (cxli)	Chapter 13 (cxli)	Chapter X
Chapter 14 (cxlii)	Chapter 14 (cxlii)	Chapter XI

For convenience we introduce a new number system for the chapters. We count the 14 chapters 1 – 14. However, we keep up the division of the chapters as found in *Paesi* and *Itinerarium*. The first number given for chapters in the first and second column for Italian and Latin texts in the table denote our system. The numbers in brackets are those in *Paesi* and *Itinerarium*. Here after we will follow our new system of numbers. With this we start our analysis of the table.

The first chapter of the Italian and Latin texts, is called Foreword in the Dutch text. Chapter 2 of Italian and Latin becomes chapter 1 in Dutch. Chapter 3, becomes 2, etc. The real difference occurs in the case of the chapters 7, 8, 9 of the Italian and Latin which are given as one chapter in Dutch. The rest of the chapters are the same in all three, but the numbering is different. Chapter 10 of Italian and Latin automatically becomes chapter 7 and so on. Thus chapter 14 of the Italian and Latin becomes chapter 11 in Dutch.

Another difference we note in the Dutch text is the division of each chapter into paragraphs. The Italian and Latin texts do not have paragraph division. Each chapter is a paragraph. It is an innovation in Dutch and most probably it has happened as a result of editorial work. However, we cannot say anything for certain.

3.2.2. The titles of the chapters

Another difference that is external and obvious in the three texts is the difference in the titles of the chapters. Here all the three texts are different. Though there is a closer similarity between the titles of the Italian and Latin texts, the titles of the chapters of these two texts are not always indicative of what is really contained in the chapters. The Dutch text, on the other hand has very detailed titles which are totally different from the other two.

Here below we give the titles of the three texts for comparison. We give the new numbering of the chapters as described on page 111. The title of the chapters of the three texts are given together according to chapters. The Italian and Latin titles are given in two columns side by side, the Italian on the left and the Latin on the right. The Dutch title (where ever there is one) is given below the other two for each chapter as follows.

Chapter 1

How Joseph the Indian approached our carvels and came to Portugal and the king made him to be accompanied to Rome and to Venice.	How Joseph the Indian came to Lisbon and was received by the king with honour, and how he went to Rome and Venice in our company.
ch. cxxix	ch. cxxix

Foreword (no title in Dutch)

Chapter 2

The quality of Joseph, his native place and the gentiles.	The native place of Joseph and his physical appearence.
ch. cxxx	ch. cxxx

The native place of Joseph the Indian. News from the city of Caranganor. The trade there. ch. I.

Chapter 3

The inhabitants of Carangonor, their temples and sacrifices.	The inhabitants of the city of Caranganora and their temples as well as their customs.
ch. cxxxi	ch. cxxxi

Continuation of the description of the city of Caranganor, the Inhabitants, Temples, Divine Worship and the rarities about them. ch. II.

Chapter 4

The customs of the king and the inhabitants. Where there are many Christians.	On the customs of the kings and the natives and that there are certain Christians there.
ch. cxxxii	ch. cxxxii

The manners and customs of the kings of Caranganor and other inhabitants, Dress, Ablution, Script. The Christians in this city. ch. III.

Chapter 5

Their houses and how their Pontiffs govern the Church.	About their houses and how their Pontiffs rule their Churches.
ch. cxxxiii	ch. cxxxiii

More extensive news about the Christians of Caranganor. High Priest, Archbishops, Cardinals, Patriarchs, Nestorians, Jacobites &c. Discourse on their Pope. ch. IV.

Chapter 6

How they consecrate and bury the dead, their feasts.	The manner of consecrating their churches and the customs they follow for the burial of the body.
ch. cxxxiiii	ch. cxxxiiii

Priests of these Christians, Baptism, Confessions, Holy Water, Last Supper (Eucharist), Special wine in scarcity. What they use in the place of wine. Burial of the dead, Gospels, Fasts, Sacred days, Monasteries, Chastity of the Priests, Learned men, Division of the year. ch. V.

Chapter 7

Caranganor during the winter, and their ships.	At what time is the winter in Caranganora and about their ships.
ch. cxxxv	ch. cxxxv

The site of Caranganor. Winter, Navigation and ships dragged to the sea by elephants. The different coins, the earth and its fruits. Longevity of the inhabitants, without loosing a tooth. Animals, Cheap Chickens, Rice. ch. VI.

Chapter 8

Concerning their money and the things which grow there plentifully.	About their money and the things that grow there.
ch. cxxxvi	ch. cxxxvi

(No title in Dutch)

Chapter 9

Rice bread, and palms which produce the Indian nuts.	About rice, palms and the Indian nuts.
ch. cxxxvii	ch. cxxxvii

Chapter 10

How they make wine, vinegar, country sugar and oil from the palm tree.	How wine, oil, vinegar and country sugar are produced from the palm trees.
ch. cxxxviii	ch. cxxxviii

Information about the Indian palm trees from which wine vinegar, oil and sugar are made. Besides more things. Pepper Ginger and Spices. ch. VII.

Chapter 11

Concerning Calichut and its king, with his usages and the merchandise.	About the city of Calechut and its king and the customs as well as the merchandise.
ch. cxxxix	ch. cxxxix

Description of the city of Calicuth. Its king an idolator, the merchants who come there for trade. Among them Malasines. Royal court. Pagan inhabitants never dare to eat on the sea. Medals. ch. VIII.

Chapter 12

Concerning the kingdoms of Cambaia, Ormus, and Guzerat.	About the kingdoms of Cambaia, Ormus and Guzerat.
ch. cxl	ch. cxl

The news about the kingdoms of Cambaya, Ormus, and Guzuratte in general, the head of cape of Mangolisthan, cities of moors Sobobek, Semath, Chesimy. The city of Cambaya. The river of Guzurath, the worship of the idols and other customs of these gentiles. ch. IX.

Chapter 13

The site of Cambaia, and other places, also about the king and about the spices.	About the site of the city of Cambaia and about its king and some other places as well as about the spices.
ch. cxli	ch. cxli

The site of the city of Cambaya the most excellent of all the Indian cities. Its king, trade, religion and other things. ch. X.

Chapter 14

Concerning the king Narasindo and a Church of St. Thomas.	About the king Narasindus and a certain Church of St. Thomas.
ch. cxlii	ch. cxlii

News about the kingdom of Narsinga. The city of Bisnagar, Cochin, Comara, Oriza, Maliapur. The Church of St. Thomas, China. ch. Xl.

3.2.3. Interpolations and additions

Another striking difference among the three texts is the interpolations and additions introduced in the Latin and Dutch texts. The Dutch text is more interpolated than the Latin.

We distinguish three sorts of interpolations or additions, long interpolations, short interpolations, and word interpolations. The first is the interpolation of a comparatively longer passage, while the second is of a sentence or phrase, and the third is the interpolation of a word.

We find four long interpolations. One is common to the Latin and Dutch texts. The others occur only in Dutch. The first interpolation occurs in chapter 5 of the Narratives. The context is the description of the audience Joseph had with Pope Alexander VI. After the description of the audience and Joseph's theological explanation for the authority of the Catholicos of the Orient to ordain priests and to appoint bishops, the Latin text introduces an intropolation. This is a defence of the authority of the Pope of Rome against the theological standpoint of Joseph.

We cite the interpolated passage from the Latin Text.

> "There is no one who does not know that this is false. For, there is only one spouce of Christ and this is the Roman Church. Outside her there is no salvation. All that is said about the other Churches is only fiction and is worthy of on faith. I will say this, let no one think that he should whithdraw from the rock of Christ. There is only one God, there is only one faith and one is the holy Roman Church."[4]

This is nothing but an affirmation of the theological thinking of the time, to which the thinking of Joseph the Indian did not conform. The view of Joseph irritated the editor of the Latin text of *Itinerarium* (or the editor or scribe of the some immediate source of *Itinerarium*). The Italian text does not reveal such irritation. It does not have this interpolation. In the Dutch text the editor introduces this interpolation with the words, "Here about this the Roman Catholic writer makes this comment."[5]

This interpolation is very important from the point of view of the discussion of the theological standpoint of Joseph the Indian vis-a-vis the Roman theology of Papacy, and the authority of the Catholicos of the East and the Roman Pontiff. This reveals the general attitude of the European Church to the individual Churches other than the Roman Church. In the Dutch translation we can see the influence of the Protestant theology also.

It is also important for textual criticism. The question that arises is, did Archangelo Madrignanus introduce this interpolation or did it belong to the source he used? Did the source of *Sonderlinge Reysen* have this interpolation? It is not given in the Italian text. And it is clear that this cannot belong to the things Joseph narrated.

---

4. Latin Text, ch. 5, in Part IV.
5. Dutch Text, ch. 5, in Part IV.

The Dutch text has another interpolation in the same chapter. This is, however, a short citation from Marco Polo, about which mention is made in the text. The citation is introduced with the words: "The words of Marco Polo are." Then the passage from Marco Polo is cited as given below: "The Christians are Nestorians and Jacobites. These have a great Patriarch called by them Jacelich."[6] After this citation the editor reveals the source. "We follow the Antwerp edition of 1563". This Antwerp edition is the translation of *Novus Orbis* by Cornelius Ablijn

The longest interpolation in the text occurs in the Dutch text. In Chapter 10 (Hoofdstuk VII). Speaking about the palm trees the Dutch text introduces the interpolation. This is a quotation from some source explaining the use of the palm trees and the different purpose it serves. This is found neither in the Latin text nor in the Italian text.

The next long interpolation also occurs in the Dutch text. This comes in the description of Cambay in chapter 13. We are provided more information about Cambay from some other source. This is a very long passages. It is as long as the original chapter itself. It appears only in the Dutch text.

The short interpolations and word interpolations occur in Dutch text. Short interpolations are qualifications or more information about the things described. Thus in Chapter 11 qualification of the city of Calicut is given in brackets. In Chapter 2 a second spelling is given in bracket for Cranganore. Word interpolations are equivalents of the names of places. Sometimes the Dutch equivalents are given in view of the Dutch readers to make the things more intelligible. For example, speaking of the social classes in Chapter 3, after the name of the third class of people the word "Pulayas" is given in brackets. Sometimes it is the names of the cities that are given. e. g. Masulipatam is given in bracket after Meilopetam, Gedrosia, for Betrosia, Golconda for Oriza. Other instances are: for names of Zodiac the Dutch equivalents are given in brackets.

---

6. *ibid.*

3.2.4. Internal differences

We have discussed above three types of external differences. Now we come to the internal differences of the three texts. There are some cases where all the three differ among themselves. There are others where the two agree. Sometimes one text provides information that the other texts do not have.

The first difference that we note is the difference in the mode of writing of proper nouns and names of places, especially of the countries, cities or islands. For example, in the first chapter we find that the very name of the king of Portugal is spelled in two different ways. Hemanuel in Italian, Emanuel in Latin and Emanuel in Dutch. The name of Pedro Alvares Cabral is seen in three ways, Pedro Aliares, Petrus Aliares and Peter Aliares. Calicut is spelled as Calichut (and Colochut) in Italian, Calechut in Latin, and Calicuth in Dutch. Cranganor is written, Caranga(o)nor, Caranganora and Caranganor, respectively in Italian, Latin and Dutch. Italian keeps the forms Cuchi and Cochi, Latin has Cuchinum and Cuchina, Dutch has Cochin. Cambay is named Cambaia or Cambait in Italian, Cambaia in Latin and Cambaya in Dutch. Ceylon becomes Failan, Faylla and Failla in the three texts in one place, while in another context two texts keep the form Sayla while the other keeps the form Saylam, Mylapore is called Mailapet in Italian and Mailapetem in Latin and Dutch. The king Narsindo of Italian becomes Narasindus or Narsindi in Latin and Narsindus or Narsinga in Dutch. We can adduce certain other names as examples.

We find differences in the names of the social classes of Cranganore, like Nuirnam, Nuiram and Nuieras. The names of the coins used in Cranganor are given differently in the three texts. Gold coin is named Serapho in Italian, Saraphum in Latin and Zaraph in Dutch. Silver coin is named, Parente, Parent and Paran respectively.[7]

Another thing that we note is the difference in the phrases the three texts use to describe the qualities of Joseph

---

7. Cf. Italian Text, ch. 3, Latin Text, ch. 3, Dutch Text. ch. 3, in Part IV
Cf Italian Text, ch. 8, Latin Text, ch. 8, Dutch Text, ch. 8, in Part IV..

in chapter 2. We find also differences between the three texts when they describe the same things. For example, in chapter 4 we see certain differences when the three texts describe the retuals in the Hindu temples.[8] Similarly, we see differences in the details or in the mode of description in the preparation of the four products of the palm tree in chapter 10. The differences in the expressions used when speaking about, the succession of the kings of Cranganore in chapter 3, the Christians in Cranganore and other places, discussed in chapter 4, the details about houses in chapter 5, and the differences we find when the three texts talk about the traders that come in Cranganore and Calicut (chapter 2, and chapter 11), the places to which the ships from Cranganore go (chapter 7), the things the Chinese merchants used to bring and take from Calicut (chapter 11) are good examples of what we are discussing.[9] There are also a few other instances where we find certain degrees of difference which we do not cite here.

3.2.5. Similarities of the three texts

We have enumerated above the external and internal differences among the three texts. However, the three texts have many things in common.

First of all it is to be noted that the subject matter of the Narratives of Joseph is the same in all the three texts. This agreements as regards the internal contents of the Narratives in general is another sign of the genuineness of the Narratives. The second thing that we mentioned above is that the order or sequence in which the subject matter is treated in all the three texts is significantly the same. In many cases the words, phrases, and expressions and even the sequence of formulation of the sentences are the same. There are certain striking similarities even in the structures of the sentences and phrases. The very opening sentence of the Narratives itself is a very good example. In all the three texts the sentence begins with a temporal clause and the structure itself leads to a kind of lack of clarity in the sentence. We could cite other instances from the text, where we observe word by word similarity.

---

9. Cf. The corresponding chapters in the Italian, Latin and Dutch Text in Part IV.

If we take the texts in pairs, we find that sometimes Italian and Latin agree, while Latin and Dutch agree in other cases. Take the case of the date of the arrival of the ships at Cochin. Latin and Italian agree. But the date is a mistake, and Dutch corrects this mistake. On the other hand, when the place to which the ships of Cranganore sail, or the names of the merchants who come to Cranganore or Calicut are enumerated, Latin and Dutch agree where as Italian has a different formulation. The Italian and Latin are closer to each other in the description of the four products of the palm tree in chapter 10, while Dutch and Latin are close to each other in the description of the Chinese merchants which is given in chapter 11.

3.2.6. Value of the three texts

Of the three texts the Dutch text is the most manupulated. Italian and Latin texts seem to be closer to the original than the Dutch, though they themselves are contaminated by editorial manipulations, additions and omissions. Compared with the Dutch they are purer.

The Dutch text shows more affinity to the Latin text This affinity makes us think that the Dutch text might have originated from the same source as the Latin text. But we cannot say a final word without identifying the sources of the texts in *Paesi*, *Itinerarium*, and *Fasciculus Temporum*. We feel that we cannot ascribe to the Dutch text a value equivalent to that of the Latin and Italian texts. However, the Dutch text does not lose its value from the stand point of a historian.

3.3.0. The Italian and Latin texts: a comparative analysis

In the foregoing pages we made a comparative study of the three texts of the Narratives of Joseph the Indian. We analysed the differences and similarities of the three texts. That study led us to the conclusion that the Dutch text does not have a value equivalent to that of the Italian and Latin texts. Here arises a question. Is the Italian which was first published a better text than the Latin ? Which of the two is closer to the original ?

In part I we have discussed at length the question of the interdependence of *Paesi* and *Itinerarium*. Against the common current of opinions we showed that *Itinerarium* does not depend on *Paesi*. It was the differences in the texts of the Narratives of Joseph the Indian in *Paesi* and *Itinerarium*, that led us to the comparative study of the two works. As we have not been able to identify the text in *Fasciculus Temporum* and the original text, it is important for us to make a comparative study of the Italian and Latin texts so that we may be able to identify the layers in the two texts which actually came from Joseph the Indian and the writer and also to find out the alterations made by the editors and scribes. In the following pages we attempt such a comparative analysis of the two texts.

3.3.1. Internal differences

The Italian and Latin texts agree between themselves in the division of chapters. The titles of chapters are different as already indicated above.[12] Though the subject matter, the order and sequence of narration are the same there are differences between the two texts in the manner and mode of description and in the use of the expressions. One can detect differences in the presentation of the ideas and in the constructions of the sentences even when the two texts describe the same thing. The two texts differ in certain qualificative expressions, clauses and even sentences. In some cases such instances occur in both the texts. In some cases only one text has such expressions. Differences in the mode of writing the names of places and persons was already indicated earlier[13]. Another interesting area of difference is the Latin expressions, words and sentences found in the Italian text which are not found in the same way in the Latin text. Even in the quotation from Strabo a slight difference is found. Above all there are certain factual differences One text has certain information which the other does not have. The Italian text thus gives us more information in certain areas. In the following pages we analyse these differences, chapter by chapter.

---

12. Cf. 3.2.2. pp. 114–116.
13. Cf .3.2 4. p. 119.

3.3.2. Chapter 1

The very first chapter reveals clear similarity and difference between the Italian and Latin texts. The content of chapter 1 and the order of the presentation of the subject matter is same. We find similarity and affiinity even in the construction of the first sentence. Similar expressions and similar temporal and circumstantial clauses are found in that sentence in both the texts. This points to the common source from which the Italian and Latin texts originated.

However, there are striking difference between the chapters of the two texts. As already indicated elsewhere[14], the first difference that we notice is in the spelling of the names of persons and places. Such difference is not the unique prerogative of the first chapter. Almost all the chapters have them. The second area where the Latin and the Italian texts differ is in the editorial and scribal alterations in the texts. As already shown elsewhere[15] the Latin text uses more direct expressions and is profuse in the use of personal pronouns and possessive adjectives in the first person used to denote the Portuguese. In such cases the Italian text uses indirect expressions, pronouns and possessive adjectives in the third person. Only one instance of the use of first person is found in Italian. As we have seen earlier this one single instance reveals that the original was in the first person. In this respect the Latin seems to be closer to the original.

Another difference that we find in the first chapter is in the occurence of the name of Joseph in the text. Joseph and his brother, or Joseph alone is mentioned thrice in the first chapter. However, only once the name of Joseph is given in the Latin text whereas in the Italian text it is mentioned twice. In Italian we have, "Of those two brothers one died on the way, the other named Joseph lived". The Latin puts it differently, "Of these two Indian brothers whom I still remember now, one is alive and the other died as we proceeded to Lisbon". Here the

---

14. Cf. 3.2.4. p. 119.
15. Cf. 2.3.4. pp. 88–90.

Latin text does not give the name. However, it seems to be an omission. For, in the place where the name is mentioned it is given with the supposition that the name was already mentioned. For we read: "And when we landed there the said Joseph was received by the King". Here the expression "the said Joseph" implies that the name was mentioned earlier. But in truth, we do not find the name earlier in the Latin text.

The date of arrival of Joseph in Lisbon is more specified in Italian than in Latin. In Italian we have the expression "at the end of June, 1501", while in Latin it is "sometime in June, 1501". Only the Italian text gives the duration of Joseph's stay in Lisbon upto January, 1502 and the time of his arrival in Venice in June, 1502. However, it does not mention anything about his return to Lisbon from Venice. It is from the Latin and the Dutch texts that we know of Joseph's return to Lisbon.

3.3.3. Chapter 2

In chapter 2 there is the description of the person Joseph and his native place, Cranganore. The two texts agree in the contents and in many details. However, there are differences. Speaking of Joseph's stature the Italian text uses the expression, "according to the judgement of those who have seen and spoken with him", while the Latin text says, "as those who have the experience of observing people would qualify". Speaking about Joseph, the Latin text says that he is an "Indian by nationality" which is not found in Italian. About his personality the Italian text says "He was truthful" and of "highest integrity", while the Latin has a qualification to the expression "truthful", namely, "who detested nothing so much as telling lies"; it is not found in Italian. Again when the Latin text uses the expression, "as far as we could learn of him", the Italian has "as far as could be understood of him". When we have such clear expressions in Latin as "he was a man, of whom we will never feel sorry to have made our acquaintance", there is nothing equivalent in Italian. We are struck by the fact that both in Italian and Latin texts, we find the same words of description when they describe the person of Joseph, like, "40 years of age" "medium size", "ingenious man", "ash (black) coloured", "truthful", "of high integrity", "of exemplary life", "of great faith".

The description of Cranganore is similar in both the texts. But we find differences when the names of the places from where the merchants who come to Cranganore are enumerated.

3.3.4. Chapters 3 and 4

In chapter 3, differences are found in the description of the three social classes. The name of the third social class is given in two different ways. The description of the temple rituals differs considerably, as far as certain terminologies and mode of expressions are concerned. However, the contents and the sequence of narration are same. A striking difference is in the statements which we have quoted earlier "ne hauer la lingua" (he did not have the language) and "because we could hardly understand him" which makes a big difference in the expression.[16]

In chapter 4 we find differences in the explanation of conjugal purity of the wives of the kings of Cranganore. In Italian we find the Latin expression "nec est castitas seu pudicitia inter eos". The Latin has a different expression, "quibus nullus est pudor, nullaque pudicitia". If the Latin was the translation of the Italian text there was no need to change it. Latin has more explanation about it: "Indiscriminately they give their bodies to prostitution". This sentence is not found in Italian in equivalent form. Describing the mode of inheritance there are differences in details and expressions. The name of the language 'Malanar' is given only by the Italian text. There is difference in the case of the places where there are Christians. The statement in the text "let it be known that from the river Indus where India begins, toward the west to the Island of Ormus which is not far from the Persian Gulf they obey Christ" has no equivalent in Italian. In Italian in this context there is no mention of Christianity.

3.3.5. Chapters 5 and 6

In chapter 5 the description of the mode of building the houses are given differently. According to the Italian text a cross is seen at the top of the church building. In Latin this can be interpreted also as on the top or on the foundation, meaning, in the courtyard. We cannot say which is correct. There is clear difference in the discussion of the Catholica and his rights

When they discuss how Marco Polo mentions the question of Catholica the two texts are very different in the adapted citation of Marco Polo in relation to the rights of Catholica. Speaking of the audience with the Pope of Rome the Italian text does not clearly say that the Pope was Alexander VI. It gives only the name Alexander. It is from the Latin text that we know that it was Pope Alexander VI. We have already spoken of the interpolation introduced in the Latin text which is not found in the Italian. We do not discuss it here.

In chapter 5 there are many differences of facts which we did not find in the preceding chapters, except when speaking of the ability of Joseph to speak the language. When Italian specifies 'deacons' Latin uses the word 'levite' which is imprecise. Speaking of communion and confession the Italian says "se confessano: se communicano: como nui:" (they confess, they communicate as we do). The Latin says, "Confitentur ut nos, eucharistiam sacram sumunt" (they confess as we do, they receive the Eucharist sacredly). Here the Italian is clearer. The meaning of the Latin text would change as we put the coma before or after the "ut nos" (as we do) which could be joined with "they confess" or "they communicate", as well. Speaking of the four Gospels Italian uses the expression "four Gospels of Passion" which is not found in Latin. Speaking of Good Friday night the Italian text clearly says that they preach all the night. Latin expression is not completely clear. Real scientific probelm occurs in the difference found with regard to the description of the feasts of St. Thomas. The Italian text mentions the feast of St. Thomas twice, besides the mention of St. Thomas in relation to the Octave of Easter which is similar in both. When the Latin text speaks of the feasts of Ascension, Trinity, Assumption and Nativity of our Lady, the Nativity of our Lord and Epiphany, the Italian also follows the sequence with the exception that it introduces "la festa de San Thomaso" (the feast of St. Thomas") after Ascension. We do not know which feast the Italian text speaks about. Both the texts speak of the commemoration of St. Thomas in July. There both of them have their own different ways of putting it. The Italian reads: "They celebrate two feasts the first of July in honour of St Thomas because both Christians and gentiles have great veneration (to him)". The Latin text reads: "And the first day of July is celebrated with very great solmnity by the Christians as well as the gentiles in memory of St. Thomas". We cannot explain the words "two feasts" of the Italian text in relation to the commemoration of St. Thomas in July. Nor can we explain the first feast of St. Thomas mentioned immediately after Ascension.

3.3.6. Chapters 7-10

In chapter 7, which describes the climate at Cranganore and the ships, certain differences are found in the names of places and in the mode expression of certain ideas. One difference that we note is in the specification of the names of places to which the ships from Cranganore sail. The Latin text is different here. But the information about the bombards that the people of Cranganore use, we get only from the Italian text.

In chapter 8 there are certain differences with regard to the names of the coins of Cranganore. As regards the gold and silver coins the two texts differ in their names. Only the Italian text gives the name of the third coin as "Tare". So also, we find differences in the expressions used to describe the armaments they use.

In chapter 9 we see the differences in the description of the baking of bread. Here Italian is not as clear as the Latin. Again slight differences are also noticed in the descriptions of the trees, which are mentioned in this chapter. The Italian is longer in its description of the fig trees. It reads: "and these have larger fruits than ours so much so that whatever is written about them would be incredible". This comment is not found in the Latin text. There is a difference of a word between the texts in the citation from Strabo.

In chapter 10 we can find differences in the modes of description and in the use of some expressions in describing the process of making the four products of the palm trees.

3.3.7. Chapter 11

In chapter 11 we find that the Italian speaks only of the Moorish merchants who come to Calicut for trade. The Latin text has something more to say: "many business men like Persians, Moors, Hindus, Medes, Assyrians, Syrians, Egyptians, and almost the whole world". But the Latin text does not specify the things in which these men trade as does the Italian. Both the texts mention the Gujarathis. There are certain differences in the description of the Chinese and of the customs and manners of the king of Calicut. Both Italian and Latin mentions the Book XV of Strabo. However only the Italian clearly presents the context. It reads "where he treats about the legates and ambassadors of India sent from Porro the king of that country to Caesar Augustus". This passage is lacking in Latin.

When Latin text describes the international fair at Calicut, it gives more names of the nations that come to Calicut. When the texts speak about the coins of Venice that Joseph brought with him from India; the Italian specifies it as the "ducats of the Doge of the House of Sten", where the Latin says "on which there were images of the Lord of Venice which was a very ancient one." In general the 11th chapter reveals more descriptional difference, besides the few factual differences mentioned above.

3.3.8 Chapters 12, 13, 14

In chapter 12 there is not much traceable difference between the two texts. But different modes of expressions and constructions of sentences are noted. There are differences in the names of places. The ancient name of Gujarat is Betrosia in Latin and Bedrosia in Italian. The three places Sobelch, Semanaht and Chsimii are spelled differently. While Italian calls them lands (terre), Latin calls them cities. When Italian says that the people of Gujarat 'do not drink wine', the Latin says they 'do not drink white wine'. The Italian says that the Gujarathis are "powerful people and great merchants" while Latin says Gujarat is "thickly populated by people of the place and by the merchants". However, something very interesting is that we know of the celibates of Gujarat only from the Latin text.

Coming to chapter 13 we find more similarity than differences. Slight differences are found in the mode of description and certain expressions, just like the names of places to which the ships voyage. One specific difference, but not very much important is that the Italian text mentions lac and incence as the products of the place while Latin mentions only lac.

In Chapter fourteen the Italian includes Cochin as among the places already mentioned. Though Latin says, "It remains now to speak of the kingdom of Cochin and especially some regions ...", in the course of the narration no description of Cochin is made. We can point out certain differences in the details and modes of description of the armies of king Narsindo (Narsindus). So too we can say that in the Italian the location Oriza is not clear, while Latin specifies it better.

Differences in the titles of chapters in the tables of contents

The analysis we have made above reveals that the Italian and Latin texts are different in many things, eventhough there is basic unity in the subject matter, order and sequence of narration and in the division of chapters. External difference are noted in the titles of the chapters and in certain interpolations. Internally analysed the two texts showed differences with regard to certain facts, the mode and details of description, variations of expressions, qualificative sentences, clauses, phrases and words, names of places and persons. All these show that the Italian and the Latin text originated from different immediate sources with a remote common source. The differences we see in the titles of the chapters given in the tables of contents of *Paesi* and *Itinerarium* confirms the facts. Hence in the following section we make a comparative study of the titles in the tables of the contents of Paesi and Itinerarium.

We have already given the table of comparison of the titles of the chapters in the texts. There we gave only the English translation of the titles as the complete texts will be given in Part IV. Since the titles in the tables of contents are different from those of the texts and are different from each other we give both the Italian and Latin original and their corresponding translations in parallel columns. On one page the Italian and its translation will be given and the Latin and its translations will be on the following page with proper indication of chapter numbers.

Italian	Translation

Chapter 1

Come Ioseph so uno de quelli Christiani che de poi la occisione in Calichut al Regno de Cuchin ascese nostre Caravelle per Portogallo & Roma. Cap. cxxix	How Joseph one of these Christians, who, after the killing at Calichut approached our caravel at the kingdom of Cuchin to go to Portugal and Rome. ch. cxxix

Chapter 2

La descriptione de la qualita & statura de Ioseph com la sua cita Carangonor laqual altri scriue Carangollo & que cosa sia Gentili. Cap. cxxx	Description of the quality and physical appearance of Joseph, together with his city of Carangonor which is written otherwise as Carangollo & the things about the gentiles. ch. cxxx

Chapter 3

Letre parte de gentil in Carangonor con le ghiesie & modo de sacrificare. Cap. cxxxi	The three divisions of the gentiles in Carangonor with the temples and the manner of worship. ch. cxxxi

Chapter 4

Costumi de Re de Carangonor & il principali con le sue donne & ornamenti & doue commenza India & doue sonno molti christiani. Cap. cxxxii	The customs of the King of Carangonor & the nobles with their wives & ornaments & where India begins and that there are many Christians. ch. cxxxii

Chapter 5

Case del Carangonor & Pontifice, Cardinali, Vescoui & altri sacerdoti al gouerno de loro ecclesia. Cap. cxxxiii	Houses at Carangonor & Pontiff, Cardinals, Bishops & other priests. The governing of their Church. ch. cxxxiii

Latin	Translation

Chapter 1

| Quomodo Ioseph Indus post stragem Christianorum apud urbem Calechut nostras naves conscendit & venit Vlysbonam & inde Romam.   Cap. cxxix | How Joseph the Indian after the slaughter by the christians at the city of Calechut, boarded on our ships and came to Lisbon and from there to Rome.   ch. cxxix |

Chapter 2

| De forma corporis Ioseph & de eius urbe Caranganora: quam alii Garangollam dicunt & quid sint gentiles.   Cap. cxxx | About the shape of the body of Joseph and about his city of Caranganora, which is otherwise called Garangolla and who the gentiles are.   ch. cxxx |

Chapter 3

| De triplici hominum genere gentilium Caranganorae: deque delubris & ritu eorum sacrificandi.   Cap. cxxxi | About the three groups of gentiles in Carnganora and about their temples and their rites of the sacrifices.   ch. cxxxi |

Chapter 4

| De moribus regis Caranganorae ac optimatum deque moribus & cultu suarum uxorum & ubi India auspicatur & inibi sunt complures Christiani.   Cap. cxxxii | About the customs of the king of Coranganora and of the aristocrates, and about the customs and manners of their wives and where India begins and that there are many christians, there.   ch. cxxxii |

Chapter 5

| De domibus Caranganorae deque Pontifice eorum maximo ac Cardinalibus, Episcopis ac reliquis sacerdotibus: Qui ecclesiis inibi moderantar.   Cap. cxxxiii | About the houses in Caranganora and about their supreme Pontiff and the Cardinals, Bishops and other the priests. Who govern the churches?   ch. cxxxiii |

Italian	Translation

Chapter 6

Sacerdoti con li soi habiti & con la consecratione. El sepellire del morti festa loro & li valenti homini che hanno. Cap. cxxxiiii	The Priests with their habit & with the consecration. Burial of the dead; Their feasts & the great men they have. ch. cxxxiv

Chapter 7

Sotto que parte del cielo sia Carangonor & quando hanno lo Inuerno. Item le naue como sonno fate ac in que paesi nauigano. Cap. cxxxv	Beneath what part of the sky is Crangonor & when they have winter. Similarly, how the ships are made and the countries to which they voyage. ch. cxxxv

Chapter 8

Le lor monete donde ven lo oro la qualita de li homini con la longa vita. Item la fertilita del Paese le arme che usano, li animali che hanno. Cap. cxxxvi	Their money; from where gold comes. The quality of the men with their long life. Similarly the fertility of the land. The armaments that they use. The animals that they have. ch. cxxxvi

Chapter 9

Pane, herbe & arbori uno delli quali chiamano Palma che produce iiii cose marauigliose videlicet Vino, Aceto, Zuccaro & Olio. Cap. cxxxvii	Bread, herbs & trees, one of which called palm tree which produces the iiii wonderful things, namely toddy, venegar sercharum and oil. ch. cxxxvii

Chapter 10

El modo de facere le iiii supra scripte cose con le speciarie che li nascono. Cap. cxxviii	The manner of making the above said iiii things with the spices that grow these. ch. cxxxviii

THE THREE TEXTS 133

Latin	*Translation*

Chapter 6

De habitu sacerdotum: de consacratione & modo humant corpora: deque eorum celebritatibus & ibi sunt viri eruditissimi. Cap. cxxxiv	About the dress of the priests, about the consecration and how they bury the bodies and about their feasts and that there are men of great erudition. ch. cxxxiv

Chapter 7

Sub qua parte caeli sit urbs Caranganorae & quando est eis hyems & quomodo naves fabricantur & quas regiones lustrant. Cap. cxxxv	Under what sky the city of Caranganora is situated and when is the winter there and how they make the ships and into what parts do they travel with their ships. ch. cxxxv

Chapter 8

De eorum moneta & unde aureum deque hominum moribus & eorum longiora vita & de ferecitate regionis & quibus armis utuntur quae ve animalia habeant. Cap. cxxxvi	About their money and from where comes gold and about the customs of the people and their long lives, the fertility of the region and the weapons they use and the animals they have. ch. cxxxvi

Chapter 9

De pane & herbis ac arboribus eorum & imprimis de palma: quae producit quadrigeninos fructus videlicet vinum, acetum sacharum & oleum. Cap. cxxxvii	About their bread, and herbs and about their trees especially the palms which gives four sorts of products namely, wine, acid, sugar and oil. ch. cxxxvii

Chapter 10

De modo conficiendi praedicta & de aromatibus quae inibi nascuntur. Cap. cxxxviii	How the above mentioned things are made and about the spices that grow there. ch. cxxxviii

Italian	*Translation*
Chapter 11	
De la cita de Calichut & Re con li habitanti. Item deli soi costumi & mercantie & nostri paesi la nominati. Cap. cxxix	About the city of Calichut & the king with the inhabitants. Similarly about their customs & the merchandise & our countries named there. ch. cxxxix
Chapter 12	
La descriptione del Regno de Cambaie & de la Isola Ormus com molti paesi & lor costumi presertim de guzeratti. Cap. cxl	The description of the kingdom of Cambait & of the island Ormus with many countries with their customs, especially about the Gujaratis. ch. cxl
Chapter 13	
Sito de la cita de Cambait con molti altri loci maritimi & el Re de dicta cita con sue speciarie & mercantie. Cap. cxli	The site of the city of Cambait with many other maritime places & the king the said city with its spices and merchandise. ch. cxli
Chapter 14	
De Re Narasindo & de Cumari con alcuni altri capi doue e una chiesia de san Thomaso. Item de ii celebratissime Insole Saylam & Taprobane. Cap. cxlii	The King Narsindo and about the (Cape of) Cumari with some other Capes where there is a church of St. Thomas. Similarly about two very famous islands. Saylam and Taprobane. ch. cxlii

Latin	Translation

Chapter 11

De urbe calechut deque eius habitatoribus necnon de moribus ac mercibus eorum & regionibus nostris inibi nominatis. Cap. cxxxix	About the city of Calicut and its inhabitants as well as the customs and about their wages, and our countries which are known in that place. ch. cxxxix

Chapter 12

De descriptione regni Cambaiae deque insula Ormus cum pluribus aliis regionibus & presertim de Guzerat regione. Cap. cxl	Description of the kingdom of Cambaia and of the island of Ormus with many other regions and especially the region of Guzerat. ch. cxl

Chapter 13

De situ urbis Cambaiae cum aliis locis maritimis & de rege euis deque aromatibus & mercibus eorum. Cap. cxli	About the site of the city of Cambaia together with other maitime places and about its king and about the spices and their prices. ch. cxli

Chapter 14

De rege Narsindae & Cumari cum quibusdam aliis capitibus & deque ibi ecclsia est Sancti Thomae deque duabus insulis celeberrimis videlicet Saylam & Taprobana. Cap. cxlii	About the king Narasinda and about (Cape of) Cumari together with someother capes and that theres is a church of St. Thomas and the two very important islands, namely, Saylam and Taprobana. ch. cxlii

PART IV

India in 1500 AD as described by Joseph the Indian

The Narratives of Joseph the Indian

In Part I we discussed in detail the sources of the Narratives of Joseph the Indian. There we enumerated the various editions and versions of the texts of the Narratives and their sources, and showed the interrelation of the different sources. In Part II we made a study on the person of Joseph and his Narratives delineating the origins, importance and the contents of the Narratives. In Part III we made a detailed comparative study of the three texts of the Narratives of Joseph the Indian, especially of the Italian and the Latin texts.

In this Part IV we present the Narratives of Joseph the Indian which contains the description of India in 1500 A. D. Here we present the Italian, Latin and Dutch texts and their corresponding English translations with notes and comments.

4.1.0. Presenting the three texts.

We have not attempted a critical text. On the contrary, we decided to present all the three texts originating from the three known sources. There are different reasons that made us to take such a procedure. In the first place, we have not succeeded in tracing out the original text[1] and the text in

---
1. Cf. 1.6.0. pp. 52–54, 1.1.5. p. 10.

Fasciculus Temporum.[2] A critical text without consulting these texts would be meaningless. Secondly, the present state of research in Thomas Christian and Kerala Studies does not give us enough tools and documentation on the preportuguese Christianity in India, without which a critical text is almost impossible. Thirdly, and this is the main reason why we have adopted the method of presenting all the three known texts, the differences in the texts often gives the (specialists of different subjects contained in the Narratives of Joseph the Indian) insights into the subjects in which they research. This is specially so as far as the historians are concerned. This would be so also for other fields. From our experience in research we have learned that the differences in texts very often give us new insights into certain areas of research. Moreover the Narratives of Joseph the Indian discuss problems of the traditions of the Hindus and Christians of Kerala. They handle theology and astronomy alike; they speak of social customs and religious festivals; they treat geography and navigation, trade and commerce. A critical text of the Narratives of Joseph the Indian needs deeper study in ehese fields. This is beyond over possibilities for the moment. Hence we have decided to present all the three texts with their translation, and notes and comments.

We present the Italian and Latin texts and their translation in parallel columns for easy comparative study, We do so because, they are similar, in the division into chapters, and are closer to each other in their titles of the chapters. This is so because they both originate from a remote common source and different immediate sources. They seem to be closer to the original than the Dutch text. Comparative study of these texts would be fecilitated by presenting them together.

We present the three textsdescribed in part III in the following manner. The Italian and Latin texts together with corresponging English translations first. This will be followed by the Dutch text and its English Translation. Then follows the notes and comments. The Italian and Latin texts and their

---

2. Cf. 1.1.4. pp. 7–9.

translations are given in four columns. The Italian and its translation in two columns on the left hand side page and the Latin text and its translation in two columns on th fol.owing page, following the sequence of the chapters. This is given under 4. 2. 0. with the sub-title The Narratives of Joseph the Indian, Italian and Latin texts and Translations. This will be followed by the Dutch text and its translation in 4. 3. 0. under the sub-title, The Narratives of Joseph the Indian, Dutch text and translation. Here the Dutch text will be given on left hand side page and the transation on the right hand page. This will be followed by Notes and Comments in 4. 2. 0. Reference numbers are given in the translations of the Italian, Latin and Dutch texts. Same sequence is followed in all the three texts, i. a. if the reference t number for a particular word in the Italian text is three, the same word will be indicated by the same number in all the other two texts. Some numbers will be given only in one text, when the w corresponding word or concept is absent in the other texts. The explanations given in Notes and comments are common to all the three texts.

4.1.1. The Italian and Latin Texts

We have explained above that we give the Italian and the Latin texts in parallel columns together with their translations We reproduce the Italian text as it is found in *Paesi* of 1507[3] and the Latin text as it is found in the Basel edition of *Novus Orbis* of 1532[4], which is a reproduction of the text in *Itinerarium*. We have compared the text of *Novus Orbis* with the text in the copy of *Itinerarium*[5] kept in the National Library of Paris.

We have taken the Italian text as it is given on the last $9\frac{1}{2}$ folios (folios 116^r–125^r unnumbered) beginning on the folio marked Bii of *Paesi* 1507 contained in chapters cxxix – cxlii. The Latin text we reproduce from chapters cxxix – cxlii of the Basel edition of *Novus Orbis* of 1532, given on

---

3. Cf. 3.1.1. pp. 107–108, 1.2.3. p. 15, 1.1.1. p. 5.
4. Cf. 3.1.2. pp. 108–109, 1.4.4. p. 48, 1.1.2. p. 6.
5. Cf. 3.1.2. pp. 108–109, 1.3.3. p. 128, 1.1.2. p. 6.

folios 142–153 which reproduced the text in *Itinerarium* on folios lxxxii – lxx(x)viii wrongly numbered as lxxviii with the same chapter number as in *Novus Orbis*.

We follow the division of chapters as given in *Paesi*, *Itinerarium* and *Novus Orbis*. But we give new chapter number as indicated earlier[6]. So the chapter cxxix in *Paesi*, *Itinerarium* and *Novus Orbis* becomes chapter 1 in our text and the last chapter cxlii in the sources becomes chapter 14 in our text. The Dutch text will follow the division of the chapters and the chapter numbers of the Italian and Latin texts.

We have taken care to give the titles of each chapter of the Italian and Latin texts side by side. However, always the texts could not be given side by side. Footnotes are given to each chapter under the chapter titles indicated by letters of the alphabet to indicate the corresponding chapter numbers in *Paesi* and *Itinerarium*. Footnotes are also given for certain words, to indicate the changes we have introduced, and also for explanations, indicating also corresponding references to our study.

4.1.2. The Dutch Text

The Dutch text and translation follows the Italian and Latin texts. The Dutch text is reproduced as it is found on pages 1–23 of *Sonderlinge Reysen van Joseph* published in 1706[7] However, we have divided the Dutch text into 14 chapters following the division of chapters of the Italian and Latin texts, as already indicated in Part III[8]. The difference occurs in the case of Chapter cxxix of Italian and Latin which is given as Foreword in Dutch and in the case of three chapters given as one chapter in Dutch (VI Hoofdstuk or Chapter VI). We divide this chapter into three chapters as in the other texts and we number them as chapters 6,7,8.

---

6. Cf. 3.2.1. pp. 111–112.
7. Cf. 3.1.3. pp. 109–110, 3.2.1. pp. 111–112, 1.5.0. pp. 50–51, 1.1.3. p. 7.
8. Cf. 3.2.1. pp. 111–112.

THE THREE TEXTS 143

Marginal headings in the Dutch text are omitted as they do not belong to the original text. Reference numbers are given in the translation as in the case of the Italian and Latin texts for notes and comments, which will be common to all the texts.

Footnotes are given to each chapter heading to indicate the corresponding chapters in *Sonderlinge Reysen*, indicated by letters of the alphabets as in the case of the Italian and Latin texts. Footnotes are also given for the imporatant interpolations especially those not explained in the notes and comments. The division of the VI Hoofdstuk (Chapter VI) of the *Sonderlinge Resysen* is specially indicated.

4.1.3. Organisation of the texts, notes and comments

    4.2.0. Italian and Latin texts and translations, pp. 145–217.

    4.3 0. Dutch text and translation, pp. 219–259.

    4.4.0. Notes and Comments, pp. 261–294.

4.2.0. **The Narratives of Joseph the Indian**
**The Italian and Latin Texts
and
Translations**

CHAPTER 1

Como Ioseph Indiano asceso le nostre caravelle uenne Portonigallo & lo Re lo fece acompagnare a Roma & a Venetia.[a]

How Joseph the Indian[1] approached our[2] Caravels,[3] came to Portugal[4] and the king[5] made him to be accompanied to Rome and to Venice.[6]

Hauendo altre uolte el Re de Portogal inteso per sui Nauili & altri Portogalesi per le parte australi andar a le parte de India; anderendosi ad alcuni soi uenuti de quelle parte ne li tempi preteriti delibero nel anno Mcccccel re sopra nominado[b] Hemanuel mandar xii tra naue & carauelle. Capitaneo de quelle Pedro Aliares: quale hauto el standardo del suo capitaniato a di viii del mese de Marzo del dicto millesimo se parti de Portogal & nauigando cum grandissime fortune & pericholi a di xiii del mese de Septembre pur del dicto millesimo zonseno a Calichut cum carauelle vii. iiii de quelle per fortuna erano perse & una ando a Zoffal. nel qual loco de Calichut steteno per mesi iii tandem a lultima per certe defferentie ueneno ale mano cum quelli de terra & morti

The King of Portugal[5] after, having learned at other times, through his ships and other Portuguese, to go to the regions of India through the southern parts[7] called together some who have come from those parts in the former times.[9] Taking their counsel the above said king Hemanuel[10] decided in the year 1500[11] to send out twelve ships and caravels.[12] The captain of which (was) Pedro Aliares.[13] Having received the standard of his captancy, on 8th March[14] of the same year, he set out from Portugal. Travelling under great stormes and perils he reached Calichut[15] on the 13th of the month of September of the same year, with 7 caravels. 4 ships were lost in the tempest and one went to Zoffal[16]. They tarried in the place called Calichut for three months. But because of certain

---

a. In *Paesi* the chapter number is given after the title. This is Chapter cxxxix in *Paesi* which we number as Chapter 1. Cf. 3.2.1. pp. 111–112.

Chapter 1

Qumodo Iosephus Indus venit Vlisbonam, et exceptus a rege honorifice; contendit Romam & Venetias, a nostris sociatus.[a]

How Joseph the Indian[1] came to Lisbon[4] and was received by the king[5] with honour and how he went to Rome and Venice[6] in our[2] company.

Quum igitur alias suis celocibus & liburnicis rex noster[b] regiones australissimas peragrauisset, dum ea irent in Indiam, haerendo suorum sententiae, qui easdem partes retroactis temporibus lustrauerant, decreuit eo anno quod est in ordine M. D. rex Emanuel memoratus rursum eo mittere classem xii nauium, cui praefecit Petrum Aliares, que suscepto de manu praefecti sui trophaeo, octauo mensis Martij, eius anni, soluit Vlisbona, qui inter nauigandum innumeras passus est anxietates & discrimina. Tandem annueutibus superis decima tertia Septembris eiusdem anni deueniunt ad urbem Calechut cum septem tantum celocibus: nam ex classe perierant quatuor, obrutae tempestatibus saeuissimis: alia uero Zaphalam concesserat. Steterunt igitur in portu urbis Calechut

Our[2] King Emanuel.[10] mentioned above, after having traversed the southernmost parts[7], with his fast moving Liburnian vessels[8], and having gone to India relying on the words of those who had travelled in those regions in the foregone days[9], decreed, in the year 1500[11], to send out again a fleet of 12 ships[12]. Peter Aliares[13], was the Captain. After having received the Royal standard from his Lord, on the 8th March[14] of the same year, he set out from Lisbon. On the way he had to undergo the strain of terrible anxiety and danger. At last, by the grace of God, they arrived at the city of Calechut[15] on 13th September of the same year with only seven of the ships. Four ships of the fleet perished, sunk by hard tempest, the other one sailed to Zaphala.[16] For almost three

---

a. In *Itinerarium* the chapter number is given after the title. This is Chapter cxxxix in *Itinerarium* which we number as Chapter 1. Cf. 3.2.1. pp. 111-112.

148 INDIA IN 1500 AD

Italian	Translation
alcuni de le carauelle & etiam molti del loco predicto se leuerno a di xxiiii Nouembre del dicto millesimo & zonseno dicte naue & carauelle a Cuchi loco distante da Calichut miglia cx el qual loco de Cuchi e posto sopra el mare & e signor de quello uno Re Idolatro: de la setta de quel de Colochut dal re de quel loco foreno recepatate le carauelle predicte & facto li bona compagnia: le qual stando in dicto loco & contractando diuerse mercantie come ne le nauigation antescripte appere del iii libro. Cap. lxxviii ueneno da una cita chiamata Caranganor lutan^c dal dicto loco de Cuchi per spacio de milia xx. ii fratelli Christiani quelli desideracao uenire ale parte de ponente per poter andar a Roma & Iherusalem li qual montadi sopra le Carauelle & essendo uenuti de le parte de Calichut circha lxxx uele per intrometer dicte carauelle quelle se leuono & insieme cum dicti. ii Christani & altri del regno de Cochi: li quali erano sta dati per osta si per lo contractar lassando in terra altritanti de li soi Portogalesi. Tolseno el camino^d loro uerso Portogal. De iquali do fratelli uno ne mori per camino laltro si	differences they came to fight[17] with those on the land. A few from the caravels and many from the said place, were killed. Then they set out on 24th November[18] of the same year and the said ships and caravels arrived at Cuchi[19] a place 90 miles away from Calichut. This place of Cuchi was on the sea-shore and its lord was an idolatrous king of the same sect as the king of Colochut.[15] The king of this place received the said caravels and made a good welcome. As the ships remained at the said place and engaged in diverse trades, as it appears in Chapter 78 of the third book[20] of the navigation written above, two brothers,[21] Christians, came from a city called Caranganor,[22] 20 miles distant from the said place Cuchi. They wished to go to the western countries so that they could go to Rome and Jerusalem[23]. They came on board the caravels. Then about 80 sails came from the regions of Calichut to intersect the said caravels[24] which set sail together with the said two christians and others of the kingdom of Cochi[19] who were given as hostage by agreement in the place of some of the Portuguese left on land. They

THE NARRATIVES OF JOSEPH THE INDIAN 149

Latin

mensibus fere tribus : & demum orta inter nostros & urbis incolas controuersia, occisisque hinc inde hominibus nonnullis, nostrae celoces Cuchinum profectae sunt vigesima quarta Nouembris, anni supradicti: nam Cuchinum distat ab urbe Calechut miliaribus fere centum & decem. Id regnum mari adiacet, cui dominatur rex gentilis, eius sectae cuius est rex Calechut. Is igitur rex Cuchini nostras celoces perbenigne excepit & dum illic commoramur commercia exercentes uti in superoribus retulimus libro tertio capite lxxviii duo germani fratres Indi Christianique uenerunt ex urbe quadam dicta Caranghanora, quae abest ab urbe Cuchina miliaribus fere uiginti qui aiebant se in votis gerere plurimum, ut occidentalem uiserent plagam supra autem uota gerere, ut Romam & demum sanctam ciuitatem Hierusalem inuiserent qui nostras celoces ingressi, nobiscum ultronei ibant : & ecce per id tempus ingens classis soluit ab urbe Calechut, ut nostram classem pessime acciperet : quod ut nobis compertum fuit, mox uela uentis dedimus altum petentes euntibus nobiscum dictis fratribus & nonnullis obsidibus

Translation

months they tarried at the port of Calechut. By this time there arose some dispute[17] between our people[2] and the inhabitants of the city and many were killed. Then our ships[2] proceeded on 24th November[18] of the same year to Cuchin[19], for Cuchin is about 110 miles from Calechut. This kingdom is situated on the sea-shore and is ruled by a gentile king of the same religious sect as the king of Calechut. This king of Cuchin received our ships[2] very kindly. And as we tarried there doing our trade, as already mentioned in Chapter 78 of book three,[20] two brothers,[21] Indians as well as Christians, came from a town called Caranghanora,[22] about twenty miles from Cuchin. They said that they greatly desired to visit the western countries, above all they had vowed to visit Rome and then the holy city of Jerusalem.[23] Therefore, they came aboard our ships[2] and travelled with us voluntarily. By this time, behold, an enormous fleet of ships set out from the city of Calechut to attack our[2] fleet.[24] As soon as we noticed this we set sail for the deep sea together with the said brothers and the hostages who were given in

Italian

uiuere nominato Joseph: dapoi ale fine de Zugno Mccccci ariuorono a Lisbona: zonti che foreno in dicto loco Ioseph predicto stete fino al mese de Zener & partendesi de dicto loco per la maiesta de qual S. Re, li fu dato uno per sua compagnia, quale lo acompagnasse a Roma: Venetia & Iherusalem & cosi essendo stato a Roma uene poi a Venetia ne lanno Mcccccii nel mese Zugno & dimoro per molti zorni nel qual tempo se hebbe notitia dal dicto Ioseph de le cose inferius scriptae.

Translation

took their route toward Portugal. Of these two brothers one died on the way and the other named Joseph is alive.[25] And then at the end of June, 1501 [26] they arrived at Lisbon. When the said Joseph was in that place he remained there upto the end of January[27] and as he departed from the said place, he was given by the majesty the most Serene King[28] one as a companion to accompany him to Rome, Venice and Jerusalem. Having been at Rome, he then came to Venice, in June, 1502[30], and remained there many days. During that time information has been gathered from the said Joseph about the things written below.

---

b. "sopra nominado" – This is the first instance of the occurence of the Portuguese form of past participle mentioned in 2.3.4. pp. 90-91. In the 1508 edition of *Paesi* it is corrected into sopranominato.

c. In 1508 edition it is lontan.

d. In the original text it reads as camin. We have corrected it into camino. In 1508 edition of *Paesi* it is camio.

Latin	Translation
qui loco & compensatione nostrorum dati fuerant, eorum inquam qui in urbe Cuchina negotiaturi remanserant. His igitur conspectis uersus Vlisbonam iter cepimus. Ex his uero fratribus Indis, quorum iam memini, alter uiuit, alter uero uita functus est, dum in Lusitaniam proficisceremur. Tandem aliquando mense Iunij M.D.I. Vlisbonam deuenimus: quo ubi applicuimus, dictus Ioseph commeatu a rege habito socioque, Romam & demum Venetias contendit & rursum redijt Vlisbonam & per id tempus complura scitu non indigna accepimus referente eodem Ioseph Indo, quorum latius meminisse animus est in sequentibus.	compensation, in the place of those who remained in the town of Cuchin for the purpose of trade. Under these circumstances we set out for Lisbon. Of these two Indian brothers, whom I still remember one is alive [25] and the other died as we proceeded to Portugal. At last sometime in the month of June, 1501 [26], we came to Lisbon. When we landed there, the said Joseph was received by the king. Together with a companion he travelled to Rome and Venice and then returned back to Lisbon.[29] By this time we learned many things worthy of knowing, from the same Joseph, which we propose to narrate in the following pages. [31]

---

b. "our king". Chapter 1 in Latin is a narration in the first person. We can notice the expressions in the first person as mentioned in part II, 2. 3. 4. pp. 88-90. In this it is different from the Italian text where the description is in the third person.

c. "On the eighth of the month of March." We have translated "on 8th March." Similarly, "13th September," "24th November".

d. "Two brothers born of the same parents" germanus means born of the same parents. We have translated as two brothers.

Chapter 2

La qualita de Joseph con la sua patri & genteli.[a]

Ioseph sopradicto e homo de eta de anni xl. sciuto[b] de natura beretino & de comune statura a iudicio de chi quello ha uisto & cum lui parlado:[c] e homo ingenioso ueridico & de summa integrita in tanto che per quello se potuto compren_der[d] est[e] uita exemplaris ha& possi dir de amplissima fede: dal quelle se ha hauto & primo lui esser de Carangonor la qual e posta lutan[f] de Calichut miglia xc in quodam sinut dicto Milibar & e lutan dal Mar miglia xv & in continenti. Dice esser la cita senza mure & esser molto longa per spatio de miglia xxx ma habitata separatamente uno daltro in modo de uille. Per la qual cita discore molte fiumare quasi tute le case zaseno sopra lacqua. Habitano in la dicta cita do[h] sorte de persone: cioe Christiani & zentili & azo cadauno fia noto questo nome de zentili: gentili se chiamano quelli che erano al tempo anticho che adorauano

The quality of Joseph, his native place and the gentiles.

The above said Joseph is a man of forty years of age[34] and black coloured.[35] According to the judgement of those who have seen him and spoken with him,[36] he is a man of medium stature. He is an ingenious man, truthful, and of high integrity. In so far as we could understand him, he is a man of exemplary life and one could say, of very great faith. We have learned this from him. First of all, he is from Caranganore. This place is 90 miles distant from Calichut, in a certain bay called Milibar[38] & is on land 15 miles distant from the sea. It is said to be without walls. It is very long, thirty miles in length.[39] However it is inhabited only here and there, in the manner of villas.[40] Through this city flow many rivers that the houses appear to be built on water. Two sorts of people live in the said city: namely, Christians and gentiles. In order that the term gentile be clear

---

a. This is Chapter cxxx in *Paesi*. Cf. 3.2.1. pp. 111–112.

Chapter 2

De patria Ioseph & habitudine corporis[a]

Igitur Ioseph praedictus natione Indus, patria Caraganorensis, annum agens quadragessimum, coloris subcinericij staturae fuit mediae, hoc est, inter proceriores & breues medius : id asseuerant, qui saepenumero hominem contemplati sunt. Vir erat ingenio non mediocri, uerax admodum, utpote qui nihil magis oderat quam mendacia : uirque abstemius, & integritatis non uulgaris & reuera quantum colligere ex eius consuetudine quiuimus uir erat non poenitendus, & in primis fidei inconcussae illibataeque. Vrbs igitur, unde oriundus est uir memoratus, abest ab urbe Calechut fere miliaribus nonaginta quae est in sinu quodam dicto Milibar, introrsus terras ad quintum decimum lapidem : muro haud ambitur : longitudine uero miliarium triginta : quoniam domus ut apud nos haudquaquam sunt contiguae, sed inuicem distant,

The native place of Joseph and his physical appearence.[32]

Joseph mentioned above, Indian by nationality, native of Caranganora,[33] is forty years old[34], dark-coloured[35] and of medium size, that is, neither tall nor short, as those who have experience of observing people would qualify.[36] He was a man not of mediocre intelligence and a truthful man who detested nothing so much as telling lies, a sober[37] man of unusual integrity. As far as we could learn of him, he was a man of whom we will never feel sorry to have made acquaintance; above all unwavering and unimpaired in faith. The town from which this man mentioned above, hails is about ninety miles from Calechut which is in the bay called Milibar[38], some 15 milestones from the sea-shore. The city is not surrounded by walls, thirty miles in length[39]; because houses close to one another as in our place are rare, but are far apart from one another so that it would

---

a. This is Chapter cxxx in *Itinerarium*. Cf. 3.2.1. pp. 111–112.

154 INDIA IN 1500 AD

| *Italian* | *Translation* |

li Idoli & diuerse sorte de animali: come nel processo se narrera. El re de la cita antenominada[i] e Idolatro. Anchora se ritrouano Iudei mediocre numero: ma sonno molto despresiadi & Mori assai mercadanti: liqual nauigano dal Caiero, Soria & Persia & altri lochi per mercadantar. Perche in questo loco ne nasceno diuerse sotre de mercantie.

to every one (we explain). Those who adored the idols and many sorts of animals in ancient times are called gentils, as we will narrate later. The king of the above said city is an idol worshiper. Also a small number of Jews[41] is found there. But they are very much despised. Also a considerable number of Moors[42] too are found there. They come there for trade from Cairo, Syria, Persia and other places. For, in this place grow different kinds of merchandise.[43]

---

b. In 1508 edition of *Paesi* it is suto.
c. It is the Portuguese from of past participle. In 1508 edition it is corrected into the Italian form parlato. In chapter 3 also we see it corrected. Cf. f. under ch. 3, 2.3.4. p. 90.
d. In 1508 edition it is comprendere.
e. Here it is 'e' in the original, we have corrected it into est.
f. In 1508 edition it is lontano.
g. Cf. f.
h. In 1508 edition it is doe.
i. In 1508 it is changed into 'auante nominato.'

Latin

adeo ut uideant uicatim habitare: eamque interfluunt complura flumina: & plerunque eorum aedes adiacent fluminibus. Hanc urbem incolit hominum duplex genus: alterum Christianorm, gentilium alterum. Et ut uobis cunctisque colliquescat qui sint gentiles, scitote itaque, eos esse populos qui olim pro dijs colebant idola, necnon animalia multijuga, uti in sequentibus denarrabitur. Rex eorum seruit idolis. Inibi etiam sunt complures Iudaei uerum uilipenduntur plurimum. Eo etiamnum contendunt negociatores fere innumeri commercij causa, ut sunt Syri, Aegyptij, Persae, Arabes, Medi, & id genus complusculi: quoniam illic comportantur fere omnia aromatum genera fertque plaga huiusmodi multa humano generi non ingrata.[d]

Translation

seem that they live in villas.[40] Many rivers flow through it and their houses are situated on the banks of the rivers. This town is inhabited by two groups of people, namely, Christian and gentile. You and others may ask who the gentiles are. Know that they are the people who once adored the idols and many sorts of animals as gods as will be narrated later. Their king also adores the idols. There are also many Jews[41], there; But they are very much despised. Even now many merchants come there for trade, like the Syrians, Egyptians, Persians, Arabs, Medes and many other races. For, from this place are exported almost all sorts of spices[43] and this region produces many things which are useful to mankind.

---

b. 'subcinericij'– in the Paris edition of 1532 it is subcinerii: "ash-coloured", we have translated it as "dark coloured".
c. 'sinu quodam' we have translated it as 'certain bay.'
d. The Latin text has certain qualification not found in the Italian text in this chapter.

Chapter 3

Li habitanti de Carangonor, cum le ghiesie & sacrificii.[a]

The inhabitants of Carangonor their temples[44] *and sacrifices.*

La terra per quanto aspecta a li gentilli e diuisa in iii parte. Prima sonno li gentil homini, li quali se chiamano in lingua loro Naires. Secunda sonno li rustici, qual se chiamano canes. Tertia sonno li peschatori qual se chiamano[b] Nuirinam & quaesta generation de pescador[c] e la pezor che sia & molestada da cadauno[d] quando uanno per la terra & si se incontrano in qualche zentilhomo glie necessario fuzirli dauanti: altramenti sariano mal menati. Hanno li soi templi cadauno separati: le donne etiam hanno li suo templi separati dali homini & offerischono a li templi loro de le primitie de la terra, come sonno rose, fichi & altre cose. Questi gentil adorano uno solo dio creator de tute le cose & dicano esser uno & tre & etiam ad similitudinem ipsius hanno facto una statua cum iii teste qual sta cum le mane zonte & epsi la chiamano Tambram dauanti de

The gentiles in the land are divided into three groups. The first group is the gentle men. They are called Naires[45] in their language. The second group is the rustic people. They are called dogs.[46] The third group consists of fishermen who are called Nuirinam.[47] This generation of fishermen is the lowest of all the three classes. They are molested by everyone. When they come on the land, if they meet any gentle man, they should flee from his presence. Otherwise they will be badly beaten. Each group has their own separate temples. Women have temples separated from those of the men. They offer at their temples the first fruits of the earth like rose, figs and other things. These gentiles adore only one God creator of all things, who is said to be one and three. They have made statues with three heads and folded hands as his likeness.

---

a. This is Chapter cxxxi in *Paesi*. Cf. 3.2.1. pp. 111–112.

Chapter 3

De Incolis urbis Caranganorae deque eorum delubris &moribus [a]

Vrbs trifariam diuiditur.[b] Primores, id est patritij ac primae classis uiri, sua linqua Naires dicunntur. Secuudo loco, homines census fere nullius, ut proletarij succedunt, ut sunt apud nos gregarij, canes suo idiomate appellantur. Postremo tertiam partem absoluunt capite censi, uiri nullius census & classis postremae. Hi piscatu uictum quaeritant, suntque deteriores caeteris, Nuiram eorum linqua appellantur: hos adeo odit nobilitas, ut si forte eos obuios habuerit, ni fuga sibi condicto consulant, paesime accipiat. Priue tribus priua habent delubra.[c] Mulieres uero alia templa habent, quae non adeunt uiri. Dant deo bonorum suorum, locoprimitiarum, fruges multijugas. Adorant deum coeli eumque trinum credunt: propterea trifontem pingunt in statuis complicatis manibus' Tambram nuncupant. Ante eorum statuas trahuntur plagae,

The inhabitants of the city of Caranganora their temples[44] as well as their customs.

The city has three sets of people. First, the patricians, or the men of the first class, called Naires[45] in their language. In the second class comes people who are almost of little value, like the proletariat similar to our gregarii who are called dogs[46] in their language. Lastly, to the third group of the city belong those people counted by their heads, men who have no property, and are of the last class of the society. These last mentioned earn their livelihood by fishing and are inferior to all others and are called Nuiram[47] in their language. The nobility hate them, so much so that if by chance they come across them, and if these people do not flee, they will be badly punished. Each of these three groups have their own separate temples. Women have their own separate temples where men cannot enter. They offer to the gods many fruits,

---

a. This is Chapter cxxxi in *Itinerarium*. Cf. 3.2.1. pp. 111–112.

158 INDIA IN 1500 AD

| *Italian* | *Translation* |

la qual statua e tirado una cortina la qual se auerze nel tempo deli sui sacrificii como qui deremo: hanno diuerse altre statue animali ma quelle non adorano & quando intrano in le lor ghiesi, alcuni togliano de la terra & si meteno sopra el fronte: alcuni togliano de lacqua & uano tre uolte al zorno ala ghiesia e la matina, mezodi & la sera. Fanno poi loro certi sacrificii generali inhunc modum.ᵉ Hanno certi sui deputate cum trombe corni & tamburli chiamano a la lor hora a le sua ghiesie & conuocato el sacerdote uestito de uno certo gran uestimento sta aposta al altar & comenza acantar diuerse oratione sue & unaltro si responde: poi el populo responde ad alta uoce & cosi fanno iii uolte: poi esce da una porta un sacerdote nudo cum una grande corona de rose in testa & ochi grandi & ii corne fictiue porta in mane due spade nude & corre uerso qual suo idio & tira tutta la cortina deuanti da una de le spede ne le man del sacerdote existente a lo altare poi cum laltra epso nudo se perchote de molte ferite & cosi sanguinolent corre in uno foco accesso li nel tempio saltando per quello dentro & fora tandem

They call it Tambram.[48] In front of the statue they put a curtain which they remove at the time of their sacrifice as I shall tell later. They have various other statues of animals, but they do not adore them. When they enter their temples some take the earth and smear it on the forehead, others take water. They go to the temple three times a day, that is, in the morning, at noon and in the evening. Then they perform certain general rituals in this manner.[49] There are certain people deputed, equipped with trumpets, horns and flutes. They call the people at the hours to their temple. When they are called together, the priest, vested in a certain big vestament stands before the altar and begins to sing different prayers. Another priest responds. Then the people respond in loud voice. They do so three times. Then a priest totally naked comes through a door with a crown of rose on his head and with two drawn swords and two fictitious horns. He runs toward his God and draws the curtain from before the statue. Then he gives one of the two swords to the priest who stands before the alter and

Latin

nos cortinas appellamus, ex lino candidissimo: hae referantur dum sacrificant sicuti latius in sequentibus referemus. Habent etiamnum statuas animalium varias, verum eas minime colunt. Quando delubra adeunt alij frontem terra cooperiunt aqua alij aspergunt: ter in die uisunt templa, mane, meridie & Uesperi. Sacrificant^d hoc modo: convocant plebem buccinatores cornicinae & choraulae nonnulli ut nos campano aere & tantisper concentum efficiunt, donec magnus eorum sacerdos aduentaverit, qui indutus ueste nescio qua sacerdotali astat altari & canere quaedam incipit ad cultum diuinum pertinentia, orationes nos appellamus. Mox subsequitur alius sacerdos cantans & ipse nonnulla. His populus respondent omnis, usque tertio haec fiunt. Demum peractis his egreditur sacerdos quadam porta nudus totus, habens pro corona sertum rosarum in capite, duoque magna lumina, totidemque cornua fictitia. In manibus gerit enses duos denudatos & gradu citato ueluti lymphatus quispiam uersus eorum deum currit, cortinamque mox referat & ensem alterum magno sacerdoti porrigit, altero uero seipsum complusculis consauciat

Translation

of their goods as the first fruits. They adore the god of heaven and believe him to be triune. Therefore they represent him in their statues as three-faced with folded hands. They call him Tambram.[48] Before their statues they put curtains which we call 'cortina' made of cloths of shining colours. They remove these curtains at the time of the sacrifice, which will be described in detail later. Even though they have statues of many animals, they do not venerate them. When they come into the temple some smear their forehead with earth, others sprinkle themselves with water. Three times a day they go to the temple, morning, at noon and in the evening. They celebrate their sacrifice as follows[49] trumpeters, hornblowers and flute players call the people together, as in our villages. And as they start singing together in symphony, the high priest comes dressed in, I do not know what sacerdotal vestament, and approaches the altar and begins to sing certain songs pertaining to the divine worship, which we call prayers. Generally, another priest accompanies him, who also sings certain songs, to which all the

Italian

cum li ochi reuoltadi dicesi hauer parlato[f] cum el suo Idio qual ordina che se debiamo far le tal cose & insegna al populo como i hanno a gouernaresi: sonno molte altre sorte de sacrificii liquale epso Ioseph per non hauer lalingua ne hauer gran practicha cum gentilli non se ha fa puto explicare el tutto. De suis templis & religione satis dictum est.[g]

Translation

with the other drawn one he cuts himself with many wounds. When he bleeds, he runs to a burning pire dancing and jumps into the fire. Then he comes out with revolving eyes and says that he has spoken with his God and that he has ordered that they should do such and such things. He teaches the people how they should govern. There are many other kinds of sacrifices which this Joseph, because he did not have the language[50] and he had not had many dealings with the gentiles, has not been able to explain entirely. About their temples and religion enough has been said.

---

b. In the original text it is chiano, we have corrected it to chiamano.
c. It is Portuguese form. In the 1508 edition it is pescadori. Cf. 2.3.4. p. 91. foot note 124–125.
d. "Molestada da cadauno"–this is a Portuguese expression. Cf. 2.3.4. p. 90.
e. This is a latin expression. Cf. 3.3.1. p. 122.
f. In ch. 2 we come across the form parlado. Cf. 2.3.4. p. 90.
g. This is one of the latin expression about which we have spoken in Part III. Cf. 3.3.1. p. 122.

THE NARRATIVES OF JOSEPH THE INDIAN   161

Latin | *Translation*

uulneribus & ubi se prope confecit plagis innumeris, illic prosilit in rogum ardentissimum, ibi ex composito paratum, inque eo saltat more tripudiantium & chorizantium euadit tendem rogum, tortuosissimisque occulis dicit se esse loquutum cum deo suo, taliaque mandauisse: & tunc quasi a deo accepta persona incipit docere populum. Sunt & alia complura sacrificia, quorum non meminit Ioseph, tum quia uix eum intelligere quiuimus, tum uel maxime quia is Ioseph cum gentilibus uix diuersatus fuerat, utpote qui eius sectae minime erat. Satis itaque ac super de delubris ac sacrificijs horum dictum arbitror.

people respond. They do so three times. When this is over a priest comes through a door, totally naked, having a crown of roses, two lights and two fictitious horns on his head and holding in his hands two drawn-out swords. With very speedy steps he runs to their god, as it were in a lunatic frenzy, then removes the curtain and gives the sword to the high priest. With the other he wounds himself. When he almost collapses with these many wounds, he drags himself to a blazing pyre, prearranged, on which he dances like the dancers and choral dancers. He then comes out of the pyre, with very tortuous eyes, and says, that he spoke to his god and that he commanded such and such things and then begins to teach the people as a person acceptable to god. There are many other sacrifices of which Joseph did not narrate much, because, on the one hand, we could hardly understand him[50] and more than that, this Joseph himself did not have much acquaintance with the gentiles, as he was not of the sect. Therefore, we deem that enough has been said of their temples and their sacrifices.

---

b. Literally "the city is divided into three". We have translated it as "the city has three sets of people".
c. Delubra and Templum are used equelautly.
d. Is the ritual described here a real sacrifice?

Chapter 4

Costumi de Re & habitanti & doue sonno molti Christiani.[a]

El Re gentil o uero Idolatro ha diuerse moglier e similiter tuti li altri gentil: nec est castitas seu pudicitia inter eos.[b] *Quando ueramente more el suo re: o uero cadauno*[c] *de li altri gentil li corpi loro se brusano le moglier ueramente sonno in faculta sua viii zorni dapoi morto el marito uolendose se brusar uiue & de questo dicto Ioseph dice hauerne uisto propriis oculis. Li fioli ueramente del Re dapoi la morte del padre non hereditano el regno ma li piu propinqui oltra li fioli la causa est questa che la moglier de li re hanno questa consuetudine che usano cum diuerse persone & per questo iudicano non meritano el regno sui fioli & nel sepelir di loro re usano grandissime ceremonie li gentil uanno uestiti a questo modo in testa portano una bereta cioe el re: una bareta doro & altri gran maistri ueludade: o de brocato: li altri uanno senza, sono nudi: se*

The customs of the king and the inhabitants[51] and where there are many Christians.

The gentile or idolatrous king has many wives, like all other gentiles. There is no chastity or modesty among them.[52] When their king or any one of the other gentiles dies their bodies are burned. In fact, the wives, in perfect possession of their faculty, burn themselves alive voluntarily, eight days after the death of their husbands,[53] and of this the said Joseph said that he had seen it with his own eyes. The real sons of the king do not inherit the kingdom after the death of the father but the nearest relative other than the sons.[54] The reason is this, that the wives of the king have relation with different persons. For this reason the sons of the king are not considered worthy of the kingdom. For the burial of the king, they have very grand ceremonies. The gentiles are dressed like this; that is they wear a cap on their head.

---

a. This is Chapter cxxii in *Paesi*.

Chapter 4

De regum moribus & indigenarum, & quod ibi sunt quidam Christiani.[a]

Rex gentilium colit idola, & complures habet coniuges, quibus nullus est pudor, nullaque pudicitia. Passim prostituunt corpora.[b] Ubi functi sunt uita concremantur, at eorum mulieres per octiduum tantum supeuiuunt, demum ut in memoriam uirorum & ipsae concrementur uiuae, sunt suae spontis. Haec referebat Joseph coram uidisse. Filij regum regni haudquaquam sunt haeredes, uerum qui secundo gradu succedunt in stemmate; argumentum sumunt ex incontinentia conjugum, quod uidelicet filij sunt nothi, propterea regno priuantur. Quum humant corpora, uarijs utunt ceremonijs. Gentiles hoc modo induuntur. Rex apicem aureum atalici panni gerit in capite, at urbis primores birretum ex serico contextum, caeteri aperto capite prodeunt, nudi incedunt, pudorem contegunt sindone mundissima;

On the customs of the kings and the natives[51] *and that there are certain Christians there.*

The king of the gentiles worships the idols and has many wives, among whom there is no feeling of shame nor of chastity. Indiscriminately, they give their bodies to prostitution.[52] When they are dead, the bodies are cremated as such, and their wives, live for only eight more days (after the death of the husband) and then, in memory of their husbands, they are cremated alive, of their own accord.[53] Joseph said that he had seen it with his own eyes. The sons of the king are not the heirs of the kingdom, but those of the second grade of the geneological tree, succeed the king.[54] The reason for that is the incontinence of the wives, namely, that sons are born of illegal relations and therefore are deprived of the kingdom. They hold various ceremonies when they bury the body. The mode of dressing of the gentiles is as follows: the king

---

a. This is Chapter cxxxii in *Itinerarium*.

Italian	*Translation*
couerzeno solamente le parte-pudibunde cum uno drapo di lino: portano a le braze alcuni brazaliti cum diuerse pietre preciose laurati benissimo similiter a la gambe portano anelli ne lideti cum piere preciose astissime le quel a posto loro sonno ingran precio. Se lauano el corpo ii & iii uolte al zorno & hanno molti lochi deputadi a lauerse: el populo & moglier loro sonno bellissime: portano conzada la testa a uno polito modo portano sopra epso capo assai zolie: li zentil prenominati quando scriuano in scoraza de albori cum una ponta ferrea. La lingua loro e India seu Malanar & circa hoc satis. Per che de sopra habiamo dicto in questo loco de Caranganor esser de molti Christiani de li quelli nel presente capitulio a notitia de cadaun se fera mentione & acioche a tuti sia noto dal indo flume che fa el principio del India uerso occidente la isola de Ormus:[d] che e nel principio del sino Persico: non se atroua altri christiani saulo nel dicto loco de Caranganor ma nel India ne sonno Re potentissimi christiani de Caranganor: similiter al Cataio questi christiani de Caranganor sonno in grandissima quantita: toglino casa loro per uno certo	The king has a cap of gold, other noble men wear caps of velvet or brocade. The others go about without a cap. They are nude.[55] They cover only their privy parts with a sheet of cloth. They wear on their arms bracelets beautifully worked in with various precious stones; and similarly for the feet. They wear on their fingers rings with very fine precious stones which in their place are of great value.[58] They wash their bodies two or three times a day and they have many places set apart for bathing. Men and women are very beautiful. They comb their hair very elegantly and on their heads they wear many jewels. When the gentiles above mentioned write, they scratch on the leaves of trees with an iron point.[59] Their language is Indian or Malanar.[60] And enough is said about this. Since we have said above that there are many Christians in this place of Caranganor[61] of whom some mention has been made, more will be said concerning each in this chapter. Therefore it should be known that from the river Indus, where India begins, towards the west is the island of Ormus[62] which is at the beginning of

Latin

brachia condecorant armis preciosissimis omne genus gemmarum faberrime excultis; in pedibus condalia ferunt magni precij, uidelicet annulos omnifariam insignitos lapidibus preciosis, qui inibi magni penduntur. Bis & iterum lauantur in die, locaque ad id deputata habent complura, Viri & foeminae in uniuersum sunt formosi, pulchritudine eximia honestantur: comunt capita mirum in modum uti decet muliebrem mundum; caput exornant gemmis & margaritis. Gentiles non aliter scribunt quam stylo ferreo in libris arborum: linguam habent Indam.[c] Et de his hactenus. Verum quia in superioribus commeminimus Christiani nominis, diximusque complures esse in urbe Caranganora Christianos, non ab re erit si eorum mentionem in hoc capite fecerimus. Nouerint igitur omnes ab Indo flumine, ubi auspicatur India occidentem uersus insulam Ormus,[d] quae est non longe a sinu Persico, Christo tatum parere: alibi non sunt Christiani, praeterquam in Caranganora urbe. In India uero sunt multiplices reges, qui Christum norunt. Qui uero incolunt Caranganoram urbem, Christiani complusculi sunt, penduntque

Translation

wears on his head a golden crown of atalice cloth. The elders of the city, wear turbans made of silk, while others go around with uncovered heads; they go half naked.[55] They cover their nakedness with very clean cotton cloth. They adorn the hands with precious armrings very skilfully set with all sorts of gems! On the feet they wear rings of great value, namely, rings of different sorts set with very precious diamonds. They wash themselves twice a day and they have many places set apart for this. Men and women are handsome, graced with extraordinary beauty. Women comb their hair in a wonderful way, as it befits chaste women and they adorn their heads with gems and pearls. The gentiles write with an iron stylus on leaves of trees.[59] They have their Indian language.[60] Enough about these things. As we have mentioned the name of Christians above and said that there are many Christians in Caranganora,[61] it will not be out of place to make a mention of them in this chapter. Let it be known to all, therefore, that from the river Indus where India begins, toward the west to the island of Ormus[62], which

Italian	Translation
precio dal re gentille del qual superius festemo mentione & pagano ogni anno loro censo & a questo modo habitano li.	the Persian Gulf. No other christians are found except in Caranganor.[63] But in India there are very powerful Christian kings of Caranganor like those of China.[65] These Christians of Cranganor are of very great number.[66] They take their house for a certain price from the gentile king, about whom we have made mention. Every year they pay the rent and in that way they live.

b. This is another case of use of Latin expressions in the Italian text.
c. This is a Portuguese word.
d. In the text it is Ornus, we have corrected it into Ormus. Cf. Notes and Comments, No. 61.

Chpater 5

Case loro & come li sui Pontifici regeno la ecclesia.[a]	*Their houses and how their pontiffs govern the church.*
Le case loro sonno facte de muro de tauolo in diuersi solari, similiter quelli de Gentilli; coperte de tauole daltre sorte legnami. Li templi ueramente de Christiani sonno facti consimili a li nostri excepto che ne le loro ghiesie tengono solo la crose & nela sumita etiam de epsi templi similiter una crose: non hanno campane & quando chiamano a la gesia seruano el Rito grecho. Questi christiani predicti in rebus divinis hanno	Their houses are made of wooden walls in different floors, as those of the gentiles. They are covered with boards of other sorts of wood. In fact the temples[69] of the christians are made like ours except that in their church they have only the cross and on the top of these churches there is also a cross.[70] They have no bells and when they want call the people they use the rite of the Greeks. These above said christians, in divine matters, have

a. This is Chapter cxxxiii in *Paesi*.

THE NARRATIVES OF JOSEPH THE INDIAN   167

Latin

uectigal regi genitilium: nam conducunt aere annuo eorum aedes, praeterquam quod tributa soluunt, ut latius dictum est.

---

b. This sentence is lacking in the Italian text.
c. Here the Latin text does not specify the name.
d. In the 1532 Basel edition of *Novus Orbis* a varience of the name as Ornus is given on the margin of the page.

Translation

is not far from the Persian Gulf, they obey only Christ. There are no Christians anywhere other than in the city of Caranganora.[63] In India, however, there are many kings who know Christ. Among the inhabitants of the city of Caranganora there are many Christians and they pay tax to the gentile king. For, they hire their houses on annual rent, besides which they pay tribute as is described in greater detail above.[67]

CHAPTER 5

De domibus eorum, & quod eorum pontifices moderantur ecclesias.[a]

Eorum aedes parietibus fulciunt, habentque uarias contignationes: at gentiles suas domos tegunt assamentis & lignis id genus. Christiani uero ibi delubra habent nostris non absimilia: uerum solas cruces inibi uidebis: nullas habent sanctorum imagines, concamerata sunt ut nostra, inque eorum crepidine crux uisitur pergrandis, ut est uidere apud nos: tintinabula habent nulla. quando uocant populum ad diuina,

About their houses and how their Pontiffs rule their Churches.

Their houses are supported by walls and have different floors. But the gentiles thatch their houses with leaves and wooden planks.[68] The Christians have their churches,[69] which are not different from ours, but inside only a cross will be seen. They have no statues of the saints. The churches are vaulted like ours. On the foundation is seen a big cross[70] just as in our place. They have not any bells. To

---

a. This is Chapter cxxxiii in *Itinerarium*.

Italian

per capo loro uno Pontifice: Cardinali xii Patriarchi ii Veschoui & Archiueschoui. Referrise el predicto Joseph lui esser partito cum uno suo patrone Veschouo de la dicta cita de Caranganor & montado in naue ando uerso la insula de Ormus laqual e lutan dal dicto loco de Caranganor miglia Mccccc & de li passo in terra ferma per mesi iii de zornate: se ne uenne insieme cum dicto Veschou fino in Armenia a trouar el suo Pontifice: dal qual esto Veschouo fo consechrado & pre Ioseph predicto ordinato da messa: el simile fanno tutti li Christiani de India & del Cataio. Questo suo Pontifice se chiama Catholicha & ha la testa rasa ad formam crucis: fa sui patriarchi ut superius dictum est, uno videlicet nel India: laltro al Cataio: li altri Veschoui & Archiueschoui: come e dicto de sopra, manda a le sue prouincie: come a lui pare. De questo Catholicha[b] ne e facto mentione in Marcho Polo doue tracta de larmenia: in quel loco dice esser due generation de Christiani una de la qual se chiama, Iacopiti laltra Nestorni & dice loro hauer uno Papa el qual se chiama Iacolita: che e questo Catholicha: che dice pre

Translation

as their head a Pontiff,[71] twelve Cardinels,[72] two Patriarchs,[73] Bishops and Archbishops.[74] The said Joseph explained that with the Bishop of Caranganora, one of his patrons, he set out on board a ship and went toward the island of Ormus which is 1500 miles distant from the said place of Caranganora. From there he travelled on land for three months together with the said Bishop and arrived at Armania[75] to meet his Pontiff by whom the said Bishop was consecrated and the said priest Joseph was ordained priest.[76] All the Christians of India and China do the same way. This Pontiff of theirs is called Catholica[77] and he has his head shaven in the likeness of a cross. He appoints his Patriarches[78] as said above, namely one in India and one in China. And he sends Bishops and Archbishops as said above to the provinces as he deems good of this Catholica[79] mention is made by Marco Polo when he treats of Armania where he wrote that there are two groups of Christians one called Jacobites and the other Nestorini[80] and that they have a pope who is called Jacolita, who is this Catholica about whom the above said

Latin	Translation
seruant morem Graecorum. Hi populi habent magnum antistitem, cui adstant Cardinales duodecim, Patriarchae duo, Archiepiscopi uero & Episcopi complures. Referebat propterea dictus Ioseph cum quodam Episcopo soluisse ab urbe Caranganora & conscensis ratibus iuisse ad insulam Ormum, quae est a Caranganora miliaribus fere mille & quingentis. Et inde petijt mediterranea itinere trium mensium, una cum Episcopo memorato, peruenit in Armeniam majorem ut consalutarent reuerentissime suum magnum Pontificem, a quo Episcopus dictus initiatus sacris, Josephque memoratus ad sacerdotij gradum promotus est. Itidem agunt Christiani omnes Indi, & regni Cataij Eorum Pontifex Catholica dicitur, fertque tonsuram instar crucis: praeficit Patriarchas suos, ut dictum est, alterum in India, in Cataio alterum: alios uero Episcopos alio mittit, prout expedire uisum fuerit, ut ad suas prouincias moderandas stransmittantur. Huius Catholicae commeminit Marcus Paulus in tractatu Armeniae, & ibi dicit duo esse genera Christianorum, Iacobitarumu idelicet, & Nestorianorum quorum papa dicitur Iacobita, qui est hic Catholica, de	call the people to the divine service, they use the system of the Greek. These people have a great Pontiff[71] under whom are twelve Cardinals[72], two Patriarchs[73], and many Archbishops and Bishops.[74] The said Joseph mentioned that, with a certain Bishop, he had set out from the city of Caranganore and on board the ship had gone to the island of Ormus which is 1500 miles away from Caranganora. From there he travelled on land together with the said Bishop for three months and came to the great Armenia[75], to greet their most reverend great Pontiff, by whom the said Bishop was initiated into the sacred orders, and the said Joseph was ordained priest.[76] So do all the Christians of India and of the kingdom of China. Their Pontiff is called Catholica[77] and wears a tonsure in the likeness of a cross. He appoints his Patriarchs[78], as we have already said, one in India and another in China. He sends other Bishops, as required, to govern their provinces. Marco Polo had made mention of this Catholica in his treatise on Armenia[79], where he says that there are two kinds of Christians, Jacobites and Nestorians,[80] whose pope is called Iacobita,

Italian

Ioseph prenominato dice insuper el dicto Papa far Veschoui: Arciueschoui & Patriarchi & mandano nel India potriano esser alcuni che diranno che auctorita hauesse questo Pontifice el Pontifice nostro Alexandro: essendo pre Ioseph predicto a Roma & parlando cum sua sanctita de le parte de India el Pontifice demando chi haueua dato quaesta auctorita al suo Catholica: & pre Ioseph li respose: che al tempo de Simon Mago Sancto Pietro era Pontifice in Antiochia & essendo ne le parte de Roma molestadi li Christiani per larte de questo Simon Mago non hauendo niuno li potesse obstar: fu mandato a suplicar a San Pietro: che se uolesse transferir fino a Roma: qual lassando uno suo Vicario: uene a Roma & questo e quello che al presente chiama Catholica & gerit vicem Petri. Cerca el far del dicto Pontifice o uer Catholica li xii Cardinali predicti se reducano ne la prouincia de Armania: doue fanno el pontifice loro qual auctorita diceno hauer dal Pontifice Romano.

Translation

priest Joseph relates. He says in addition that the said Pope creates Bishops, Archbishops and Patriarchs and send them to India.[81] There may be some who would ask what authority this Pontiff has? When Joseph was in Rome and was speaking with his Holiness Pope Alexander, the Pontiff asked him who had given this authority to the Catholica. And priest Joseph replied him that saint Peter was the Pontiff in Antioch at the time of Simon Magus[83] and the Christians in the region of Rome where molested by the art of Simon Magus. Because there was no one who could oppose him they send to suplicate saint Peter to allow him to be transferred to Rome. Leaving a vicar of his (in Antioch) he came to Rome. And this is the one who is now called Catholica and he acts as the vicar of Peter. As regards how this Pontiff or Catholica is made, the twelve cardinals mentioned above gather in the province of Armania where they elect their Pontiff. This authority, they say they have from the Roman Pontiff.[84]

---

b. The word Catholicha is spelled in two ways we have kept both forms.

THE NARRATIVES OF JOSEPH THE INDIAN

Latin	*Translation*

quo est sermo, cuiuspue meminit Ioseph saepe dictus. Et quum dictus papa uarios homines promoueat ad gradus huiusmodi, efficiatque multiplices antistites, posset non ab re ambigere quispiam, unde ei haec sit autoritas, autorandi homines cum sancta Romana ecclesia, quae est unica, & unicam habet fidem, unumque Romanum Pontificem recipit. Sciant igitur tempore quo Alexander VI, sceptra moderabatur ecclesiae uniuersalis, dictum Ioseph Romam contendisse: hunc Alexander Maximus Pontifex percunctatus est, a quo Catholica praefatus habuisset facultatem antistandi in Oriente: huic respondit Ioseph his uerbis, Olim diuum Petrum apostolum Antiochiae praefectum fuisse: & quum sancta Romana ecclesia schismate laboraret atroci, duce Simone mago, qui sui nominis monumenta reliquit sanctus Petrus accersitus est Romam, ut Simonem confunderet, & laborantibus Christianis non deesset. Hic itaque Petrus non prius soluit Antiochia, concessurus Romam, quam uicarium Antiochiae praefecerit, & is est qui Orientalem plagam moderatur, & dicitur Catholica, geritque Petri uices: hunc uero

who is the Catholica in question about whom the said Joseph speaks. And because the said Pope promotes different people to such grades and appoints many bishops, it may not be irrelevant to ask, from where he has this authority of ordaining people, when the Holy Roman Church, which is one and has one faith, accepts only one Roman Pontiff.[82] Let them know this. When Alexander VI was holding the sceptre of the universal Church, the said Joseph went to Rome and the supreme Pontiff, Alexander asked him, from whom the said Catholica had got the authority to consecrate Bishops in the East. To this question Joseph replied in the following words: Once St. Peter, the apostle, was prefect in Antioch and when the holy Roman Church was troubled by great schism under the leadership of Simon the magus[83], who has left monuments in his name, St. Peter was sent to Rome to confound Simon and to comfort those suffering from the trouble. Here, Peter, before leaving Antioch for Rome, deputed his vicar in Antioch and it is he who governs the oriental parts and is called Catholica and is

[*This blank space is due to an interpolation in the Latin text about which we have spoken in Part III, 3.2.3. The last paragraph in the Latin text is the interpolated passage. There is no Italian equivallent as the Italian text does not have this interpolation. Therefore the Italian text is shorter. Cf. 3.1.1. pp. 116-117, No. 85 in Notes and Comments in Part IV.*]

CHAPTER 6

Como consacrano & sepelliscono li morti cum le sue feste.[a]

How they consecrate[86] and bury the dead, their feasts.

Hanno insuper Sacerdoti Diaconi & Subdiaconi. Li Sacerdoti ueramente non portano chierecha, ma ne la summita del capo portano uno poco de capilli: se batizano li puti xl zorni dapoi nasciuti salvo sel non occurresse caso de necessita: se confessano: se communicano como nui ma non hanno lultima

Above all they have priests, deacons and sub-deacons.[87] In fact the priests do not have tonsure, but at the top of their heads they keep a little hair[88], children are baptized 40 days after birth, if a case of necessity does not occur.[89] They confess,[90] they receive communion as we do. They do not have extreme

---

a. This is Chapter cxxxiiii in *Pæsi*.

Latin

Catholicam praeficiunt Cardinales duodecim in Armenia, & id iactant autoritate Romani Pontificis facere.

Quod esse falsum nemo est qui nesciat quandoquidem una est sponsa Christi quae unam figurat ecclesiam Romanam, extra quam salus est nulla: quae uero dicuntur de alijs, commenta sunt omnia & fidei nullius. Haec dixerim ne quis putet a soliditate petrae Christi esse recedendum. Vnus deus igitur, una fides, una est sancta Romana ecclesia.

Translation

the vicar of Peter. This Catholica is elected by twelve Cardinals in Armenia. They say that they do this with the authority of the Roman Pontiff.[84]

There is no one who does not know that this is false. For, there is only one spouse of Christ and this is the Roman Church, out-side her there is no salvation. All that is said about other Churches is only fiction and is worthy of no faith. I will say this: Let no one think he should withdraw from the rock of Christ. There is one God, there is one faith and one is the Holy Roman Church.[85]

Chapter 6

De modo consecrandi eorum ecclsias & de moribus quos seruant dum humant corpora.[a]

The manner of consecrating their churches[86] *and the customs they follow for the burial of the body.*

Itaque hi habent sacerdotes, leuitas, & hypodiaconos. Sacerdotes uero non ferunt tonsuram, sed nonnihil capillorum in summa parte capitis habent. Infantes non baptizantur ante quadragesimum diem sui ortus, nisi morte ingruente. Confitentur ut nos, eucharistiam sacram sumunt: extremam autem

Thus they have priests, levites and subdeacons.[87] The priests, however, do not have tonsure, but they have a little hair on the top of their heads.[88] The children are not baptised before forty days, except in danger of death.[89] They confess as we do[90] and they receive the Eucharist

---
a. This is Chapter cxxxiiii in *Itinerarium*.

Italian	Translation
untione & in loco di quella benedicano el corpo. Hanno aqua sancta ne lo intrar de le ghiesie. Consachrano[b] el Corpo el Sangue del nostro Signore como nui in azimo & dice che quando non hanno uino perche in quelle parte non nasce uua tolgeno de lua passa de la qual ne vien grandissima quantita dal Cataio & quella mentano in acqua & la strenzeno & ne cauano certo sucho & cum quello consacrano. Sepeliscono[c] li sui corpi morti como nui hanno questa consuetudine che quando alcuno more molti Christiani se reducano insieme & manzano per viii zorni & da poi pregano per el morto: fanno testamento & non faciando; li ben sui uanno a li piu propinqui. Le moglier loro morti le mariti se pagano de dote sui & poi se parteno & sonno in faculta loro post annum maritarsi & hanno iiii euangelista & iiii euangeli de passion; obseruano la quadragesima & Aduento, al di del Venere sancto & Sabbato sancto non manzano fino le di de Pasqua:[d] predicano la nocte del uenare sancto & tra anno hanno le infrascripte feste la Resurection[e] cum doe festa sequente: la octaua de Pasqua ne la qual fanno mazor festa che le altre de tuto lanno: dicono questo farsi: per che in quel	unction,[92] in its place they bless the body. They have holy water at the entrance of the church. They consecrates the Body and Blood of our Lord, as we do, with unleavened bread.[93] And he says that since they have no wine, because grapes do not grow in those regions, they use dried grapes which come from China in very great quantities. They put them in water and squeeze and from it certain juice is produced with which they consecrate. They bury the body of the dead as we do. They have this custom that when someone dies, many Christians come together and eat together for eight days and then they pray for the dead.[95] They make their last will and testament and when they do not leave one, the property goes to the closest relatives. The wives after the death of their husbands are paid the dowry and then they leave and they have the right to marry after one year. They have 4 evangelists and 4 gospels of passion.[96] They observe the lent and the Advent.[97] On Good Friday and Holy Saturday until the Easter day,[98] they abstain from food and they preach in the night of Good Friday. During the

Latin

unctionem non habent, sed loco eius corpora benedicunt: quum ingrediuntur eorum delubra, latice benedicto corpora aspergunt ut nos: consecrant Corpus Christi & Sanguinem[b] si tamen id consequi possunt, in azymis, hoc est, in pane non fermentato, more nostro: & ubi non habent uinum, quoniam eo regio uitium est impatiens, uuas passas immergunt aqua, & demum succum exprimunt, eoque uice uini utuntur: nam eo ex Cataio comportantur uuae passae complures: humanat humana corpora more nostro, quumque quispiam uitam exhalauerit, mox conueniunt multi, & diebus octo continuis simul commessant. Peractis uero epulis, fundunt pro defuncto preces, testantur, supremaque colitur uoluntas: & ubi intestati decesserint, qui arctiore gradu defuncto est proximior, is est haeres. Eorum coniuges uiris uita functis, cum dotalitio abeunt in paternas aedes: ita tamen, ut intra annum luctus non nubant. Quatuor euangelistas habent, totidemque euangelia colunt: obseruant quadragessmam, & aduentum ieiunijs & orationibus perquam diligentissime: inter caetera a die parasceues usque in diem paschae omni cibo abstinent, nocte sancti

Translation

sacredly.[91] They do not have extreme unction,[92] but, in its place they bless the body. When they enter the churches, they sprinkle their body with blessed water as we do. They consecrate the Body and Blood of Christ, if possible, in azymis i. e. with unleavened bread, as we do.[93] And there they do not have wine, because vine do not grow in those regions; they immerse raisins in water and then squeeze the juice which they use for wine, for many raisins are brought there from China.[94] They bury the human bodies as we do. When someone dies, many gather together. For eight continuous days they come together and eat together and after the meals they pray for the dead.[95] They generally make their last will and testament. The testament of the dead is honoured with much devotion. When somebody dies without executing the will, the one who is closest to the dead is the heir. Their wives, at the death of the husbands, go back to their paternal house taking the dowry with her. But, she cannot marry again for one year. They have four Evangelists and they venerate the same number of Gospels.[96] They observe the

Italian

zorno San Thomasoᶠ pose la man nel costado de Christo & cognoscere quello non esser fantasma. La festa de la Ascension: la festa de San Thomaso: la Trinita: de la Assontion de la Beata Vergine Maria, la Natiuita & la Purification: la festa de la Natiuita del nostro Signor: & la Epiphania: fanno la feste de li Apostoli & le Domenicha & fanno due feste el primo di de Zuio in honor de San Thomaso: per che si Christiani como gentil hanno in grandissima ueneration. Hanno monici uestiti de negro liquali uiueno in grandissima pouerta & castita: similiter moneche: li Sacerdoti uiueno in castita & si susteno trouadi in qualche manchamento perdeno la messa. Li Christiani non ponno far diuortio. Tutto el populo se comunica iii uolte a lanno: hanno doctori excellentissimi & studio de lettreᵍ hanno de propheti como nui c dice preterea pre Ioseph sopra dicto esser molti libri de doctori quali hanno parlato sopra la Biblia & propheti: uesteno li Christiani como Mori cioe de panno de lino hanno lanno diuiso in mesi xii

Translation

year they celebrate the following feasts, the feast of Resurrection with the two feast days following.[99] On the octave of Easter they have a greater feast than the others in the whole year,[100] for they say that they do so because on that day St. Thomas put his hand in the side of Christ and recognized that he was not a phantom, the feast of Asension,[101] the feast of St. Thomas,[102] of the Trinity, of the Assumption of the blessed Virgin Mary, her Nativity and Purification,[103] the feast of the Nativity of our Lord and the Epiphany.[104] They celebrate the feast of the Apostles and Sundays. On the first day of July[105] they have two feasts in honour of St. Thomas because Christians as well as gentiles have great veneration to him. They have monks clothed in black, who live in great poverty[106] and chastity and so do the nuns. The priests live in chastity[107] and if they are found lacking in chastity they will loose the right to celebrate the mass. These Christian cannot be divorced,[108] All the people communicate 3 times a year,[109] they have excellent doctors and study of the letters thrive (among them). They have prophets, as we do.

THE NARRATIVES OF JOSEPH THE INDIAN

Latin

Veneris orationibus & concionibus sacris iugiter insistunt. Intra annum has sanctorum celebritates mire obseruant. Primo die santae Resurrectionis cum duobus sequentibus diebus. Octauum diem paschae supra omnem festiuitatem colunt. Quippe qui affirmant ea die diuum Thomam, cuius sunt ipsi perquam studiosi, in latus nostri seruatoris manum posuisse, cognouisseque non esse phantasma. Deinde diem qua Christus coelos conscendit, eximie colunt. Post haec Trinitatis, Assumptiones Beatae Virginis, Natiuitatis eiusdem & Purificationis, Natiuitatis nostri Seruatoris, Epiphaniae & omnium Apostolorum, diesque domnicos obseruant. At primam diem Iulij mirum in modum custodiunt in memoriam diui Thomae Christiani pariter ac gentiles. Coenobia habent ubi continentissime uiuunt monachi nigri, habent & sanctimoniales complures: sacerdotes uiunt castissime, & si qui comperti fuerint incontinentiae, hi mox priuantur missarum clebratione. Qui Christo parent, diuortijs minime utuntur, bonum uel malum sit matrimonium, perennat ad ultimum usque fati diem. Ter in anno populus suscipit Eucharistiam sanctissimam. Doctores

Translation

Lent and Advent [97] with fasts and prayers, with very great diligence. Among other things, from Good Friday until the day of Easter they abstain from all food.[98] In the night of Good Friday they insist on prayers and sacred gatherings without interruption. During the year they celebrate the following feasts. First, the sacred day of Resurrection[99] with the following two days. They observe the octave of Easter with more festivity than any other,[100] for they affirm that on that day St Thomas, about whom they are very zealous, put his hand in the side of our Lord and recognised that he was not a phantom. After that, the day on which Christ ascended into heaven is observed very specially.[101] After this the feast of the Trinity, of the Assumption of the Blessed Virgin, her Nativity and Purification,[103] the Nativity of our Saviour and the Epiphany[104] and of all the apostles and the Sundays. And, the first day of July[105] is celebrated with great solemnity by Christians as well as by the gentiles in memory of St Thomas. They have the hermitages where the black monks live in perfect

178 INDIA IN 1500 AD

Italian	Translation
fanno etiam el zorno intercalare: el suo zorno ueramente e diuiso in hore lx le quale hore cognoscono de zorno a la sole & la nocte a le stelle.	The above said priest Joseph also said that there are many books of the doctors who have spoken about the Bible and the Prophets.[110] The Christians dress like the Moors, namely in cotton clothes.[111] They divide the year into 12 months. They have also the intercalary days. In fact their days are divided into 60 hours.[113] During the day they know the hours from the sun and in the night by the stars.[114]

---

b. "consachrano" in the text. We have corrected it as "consacrano" as is given in the title of the chapter and in other places in the text.
c. "sepelliscono" in the title of the chapter it is spelled as "sepelliscono".
d. "Pasqua", in the text it is written with a small letter. We have changed it into capital letter.
e. "Resurrection": in the text it begins with a small letter. We have changed it into capital letter, as in the case of the names of the feasts like the "Ascension, Assontion, Natiuita, Purification, Epiphania."
f. "San Thomaso": in the text it is san Thomaso. We have corrected it.
g. "Studio de lettre" the phrase seems to be incomplete and does not have a complete sense.

Latin

habent egregios, eosque eruditissimos. Literarum studia ibi uigent plurimum. Prophetas ut nos legunt. Addebat etiam dictus Ioseph inibi esse complures sacntos doctores, qui uetus & nouum Testamentum explicarunt cordatissime: habitu utuntur Maurico, id est, lineis tunicis: diuiserunt annum ut nos in menses duodecim,&habent intercalarem diem. Verum diem partiti sunt in horas sexaginta, easque ad aspectum solis interdiu cognoscunt, noctu uero intuitu stellarum.

Translation

continence.[106] And they have also many nuns. The priests live very chastely.[107] If one is found lacking in chastity, he is deprived of the right to celebrate the Mass. Those who believe in Christ very seldom divorce, whether the marriage is good or bad, it is perennial up to the last day.[108] The people receive the most blessed Eucharist thrice a year.[109] They have very excellent and learned doctors. The study of letters thrives well there. They read the Prophets as we do. The said Joseph also added that there were many holy doctors, who interpreted very wisely the Old and New Testaments.[110] They use the dress of the Moors, i e. cotton clothes.[111] They divide the year into twelve months, as we do.[112] There are intercalary days. The day is divided into 60 parts[113] and they recognise these hours during the day from the sun and during the night looking at the stars.[114]

---

b. "Corpus Christi & Sanguinem", in the text it is written with small letters. We have corrected it.

Chapter 7

In Caranganor quando e lo inuerno & le ior naue.[a]

At what time is winter in Caranganor and their ships.

Vesti de Caranganor sopradicti sonno posti tra el circulo equinoctiale & el circulo del cancro: & secundo referisse pre Ioseph hanno xiii hore & meza: el zorno mazore che sia nel anno: el menor x intendando hore nostre & non sue: quando el sol e in segno de Tauro: hanno lombra pendicular: quando ueramente le in Cancro: fa lombra austral: quando el sole in Vergene: fa lombra pendiculare: Ma quando le in Capricorno: fa lombra septentrional: la motion ueramente de li tempi fa da mezo Mazo: fino a mezo Agosto: & in quello tempo non nauigano quelli Mari respecto[b] le grandissime fortune: sonno in quelle parte de India infinitissimi nauili: liquali nauigano in occidente: in Persia: Arabia[c] & mar rosso: in oriente: in India: Catnio: Taprobana: Faillam & molte altre insule la quale naue sonno grandissime: & portano alcune xii uele & marinari infiniti: & alcune mancho secundo le portade sue sonno alcune che hanno le uele

The people of Caranganor mentioned above are placed in the circle of Equinox and in the circle of Cancer[1,15] and as the priest Joseph related, they have 13 and a half hours for the longest day in the year and ten hours for the shortest day, speaking in terms of our hours and not theirs[116]. When the sun is in the sign of Taurus, they have perpendicular shadow, and when the sun is in Cancer the shadow falls in the south and when the sun is in Virgin its shadow is perpendicular and when in the Capricorn the shadow falls in the north.[117] The change of the seasons is from the middle of May up to the middle of August and at that time they do not navigate, because of the fact that the sea will be troubled by very great tempest.[118] In those parts of India there are innumerable ships which navigate to the west[119] to Persia, Arabia, the Red Sea, to the orient, to India[120] and China, Taprobane[122], Faillam[123] and

---

a. This is Chapter cxxxv in *Paesi*.

Chapter 7

Quando hyems est in urbe Caranganora, & de nauibus eorum.[a]

Qui Caranganoram incolunt, hi sunt inter tropicum aestiuum & aequatorem, & ut referebat dictus Ioseph, diem habent maiorem horarum tredecim cum dimidia, minorem uero decem, ita ut intelligas de nostris horis, non autem de suis, quae sunt multo minores, ut dictum est. Quum uero sol est in tauro, umbram habent perpendicularem quando est in cancro, proijcitur umbra ad Austrum: & ubi est in uirgine, rursum habent perpendicularem: quando autem est in capricorno ad Septentrionem umbra proijcit: temporis mutationem apud eos uidebis a medio mense Maij, usque ad medium Augusti: tunc temperant a nauigationibus & nullo pocto ob saeuientem per id tempus fortunam maria sulcant. Sunt etiamnum in illis Indiae partibus innumera nauigia, quae in occidentem contendunt: alia uero in Arabiam, in Persidem alia: nonnulla mare Erythreum arant: alia uastissimam lustrant Indiam ad orientem in primis, usque ad Chersonesum auream.

At what time is winter in Carangonora & about their ships.

Those who inhabit Caranganora are found between the tropical zone and the equator,[115] and, as the said Joseph narrated, there the longest day has thirteen and a half hours and the shortest ten hours. if you understand in terms of our hours and not in terms of theirs, which are much shorter than ours.[116] When the sun is in Taurus, the shadow is in perpendicular position and when it is in Cancer the shadow falls on the south and when it is in Virgin again it is perpendicular and when it is in Capricorn it casts shade to the north.[117] The change of season is visible in their place, from the middle of the month of May upto the middle of the month of August. At this time they abstain from navigation and all sorts of trade, because at this time the sea will be very rough with very severe tempests.[118] Even now there are innumerable ships in those parts of India which voyage to the west,[149] some go to

---

a. This is Chapter cxxxv in *Itinerarium*.

Italian	Translation

de stuore: queste uengano da le insule: le altre hanno le uele de gottonina: & de boni fustagni como li nostri: le naue sonno facte cum agudi de ferro: questo dico perche sonno alcuni che dicono esser fitte cum pironi de legno: & de questo uolsi diligentemente intendere dal predicto pre Ioseph: monstrando li la factura de li nostri nauili: se ne ridea dicendo che li suo erano consimili ali nostri: la pegola e facta de incenso & altra mistura: soleuano per auanti al butar de le naue in acqua meter doe elephanti uno per banda & per che alcune uolte dicti elefanti erano causa de la morte deli homini loro: non usano piu tal modo: ma fanno uegnir gran numero de zente: le quale le butano in acqua. Hanno bombarde una sorte de ferro: & una de legna da focho: ma non sonno come le nostre ne hanno quella posanza: & circha hoc plura.[d]

many other islands.[124] These ships are very large. Some of them have twelve sails and infinite number of mariners and others less, according to their load. There are some which have the sail of mat, they come from the islands;[125] others have the sail of cotton and of good endurance like ours. The ships are made of nails of iron. I say[126] this, because there are some who say that it is made of nails of wood and I wanted to know this exactly from the said Joseph and when I showed him the construction of our ship he laughed and said that theirs were similar to ours. The pitch is made of frankensence and other mixtures. Formerly for launching the ships into water they had the custom of using two elephants one at each side and because sometimes the said elephants were the cause of the death of their men they no longer use

---

b. In the 1508 edition it is "rispecto".
c. Some names are spelled with small letters in the text, we have corrected them.
d. This is one of the cases of the use of Latin expressions in the Italian text about which we have spoken in 3.3 1., p. 122.

THE NARRATIVES OF JOSEPH THE INDIAN 183

Latin

& deinceps ad extrema Indiae, praetereuntes Cataium & Taprobanam insulam Fayllamque, & complures alias. Naues itaque huiusmodi quibus sulcant, sunt praegrandes, adeo ut circa duodecim uela habeant, remiges innumeros, nonnullae uero minus, aliae autem pro uelis tegetes, id est, storias habent, & huiusmodi ab insulis proficiscunt, aliae uero ex cotonina omne genus uela conficiunt. Naues fabricant clauis ferreis: & propterea id dixerim, quoniam falso arbitrati sunt quidam clauis ligneis eorum naues consolidari. Haec enim non indiligenter sciscitatus sum a Ioseph praedicto. Ostendi illi aliquando formam conficiendi nostra nauigia, ratus longe alium esse eorum morem: at ille subridens, ait itidem Indos quoad fabricandas naues seruare, eas etiam feruminant thure admixtis nonnullis alijs. Quum autem in mare fabrefactas naues proijciunt, elephantos hinc & hinc ponunt, qui non sine hominum strage molem trahunt in mare. Coeperunt ob tot hominum cladem ab hoc more temperare, & dimissis beluis, quibus utebantur ad nauandam hanc operam,

Translation

Arabia and Persia, others to the Erythrean Sea and still others voyage round the vast Indian Ocean, especially to the east[120] upto the golden Chersonesum[121] and then passing the extreme limits of India they go up to China, to Taparbane[122] and to the island of Faylla[123] and many other islands.[124] These ships,[125] which they use for voyage, are very large and have up to twelve sails and innumerable sailors, but some have less. Some others, however, have sails of mat i. e. rush mats. Such kind come from the islands. Some others make the sails from cotton of every sort. They use iron nails in making ships, and I mention this specially,[126] because there are people who falsely think that they join together the planks of the ship with wooden pegs. This I have learned very diligently from the said Joseph. For, I showed him once how we construct our ships and asked if their ways of constructing the ships were different. He said laughing that the Indians used the same methods in constructing the ships. They also used a kind of cement with frankincense and some other mixtures. When they

Italian

them in this manner, but they call great number of people who put it in water. They have bombards, one sort made of iron and the other of wood. They are not like ours but less powerful.[127] Much is said about it.

Translation

CHAPTER 8

De le loro monete: & le cose che li nascano in copia.[a]

Tre sonno le generation de le sue monete: una chiamano Sarapho doro: la qual e de peso del nostro ducato: laltra e darzento: la qual chiamao Parante: laqual uale soldi vi a la terza chiamata Tare: tre de lequale fa uno de li nostri soldi tutte queste monete hanno scolpite lettre del suo Re: ne le parte sopradicte non se troua oro ne metallo de sorte alcuna ma se ritroua in certe montagne li propinque per spacio de miglia ccl in ccc la prouincia doue e posto el loco de Caranganor e tuta

Concerning their money, and the things which grow there plentifully.

There are three kinds of money.[128] One is called Sarapho[129] of gold, which is of the weight of our ducat, the second, of silver, which is called Parante,[130] is equivalent to six soldi, the third is called Tare[131] three of which make one of our soldi. All these coins have the letters of their king[132] engraved on them. Neither gold nor any other metal is found in those regions, but are found in a certain mountain in the neighbourhood, at a distance of 250 to 300 miles.[133] The province

---
a. This is Chapter cxxxvi in *Paesi*.

Latin	Translation
numerosiorem hominum coetum addunt donec moles in pelagus trahatur.	launch the constructed ships into the sea they place elephants here and there which, together with men in line, carry the ship to the sea. The elephants thus used often caused the death of men. Therefore, they have discontinued the system of using the elephants to move ships. Now, therefore, large number of men lined together carry the ship to the sea.

Chapter 8

De moneta illorum, & de rebus quae ibi nascunt.[a]	*About their money and about the things that grow there.*
Triplex est genus monetae illic. Saraphum appellant suum aureum nummum ualoris & ponderis nostri ducati. Aliam uero appellant Parantem argenteam, & ea est ualoris solidorum sex e nostris. Habent & aliam ualoris solidi unius: & hae omnes habent imaginem subscripionemque sui regis: ibi aurum neque alia metalla inueniuntur, illuc comportantur aliunde uidelicet ab montibus quibusdam, qui absunt miliaribus fere ccc. Plaga Caranganorae est soli patentis eiusdemque aprici, & feracis:	There are three kinds of money there.[128] First is their gold coin which they call Saraphum[129], equivalent to our ducat in value and weight. The other is a silver coin, which they call silver Parant[130] and is equivalent to six solidi in value. They have another coin which has the value of one solidum.[131] All these have the image and the inscription of their king.[132] Neither gold nor silver is found in this place. They are brought from elsewhere, namely, from some

a. This is Chapter cxxxvi in *Itinerarium.*

Italian	Translation
piana: & ha le montagne lontano: & ha aiere caldo: & tuti sonno beretini: quelli che sonno ale montagne sonno bianchi: & uiueno per spatio grandissimo, secundo dice pre Ioseph sonno homini che hanno anni c li quale hanno tuti li sui denti. La terra de Caranganor e fertilissma excepto che non produce frumento: ne caualli: & el frumento ueramente uiene da alcune insule li propinque: & aquesta instesta condition sonno li lochi de Calichut: & Combait:& questo precede per esser lochi arenosi li caualli uengono da Ormus & de le montagne loro: non li adoperano saluo che in portar mercantie de loco ad locum: ne etiam in combater: ma combateno a predi: le arme loro sonno archi & freze: spade & targhe in modo de rodelle hanno lanze & sonno gran zugadori de spade sonno alcuni che se fanno arme de dosso de cerra pelle de pesse: la quale e durissima: & alcuni le fanno de ferro. Hanno molte sorte de animali: Bo: Vache Castroni: Bufali: Pecore: & altre molte sorte li qual tuti animali manzano per uiuer lor excepto li Bo li qualli li Gentile adorano: hanno Elephanti in grandissima copia: hanno animalli	in which this place of Caranganor is situated is completely flat and has mountains at a distance and has a warm climate and all the people are dark coloured. Those in the mountains are white. They live for a very long time. As the priest Joseph narrated, there are people who are 100 years old who have all their teeth. The land of Caranganor is very fertile except that it does not produce wheat and horses. Wheat, in fact, comes from some islands closeby. And of the same conditions are the places of Calichut and Combait.[134] This is so because they are sandy places. Horses come from Ormus and from their mountains, they do not adopt them except to carry the merchandise from place to place and not in wars. They fight on foot. Their weapons are bow and arrow, swords and bucklers like rodelle. They have lances and they are great sword jugglers. There are some who make weapons for themselves from the back of the skin of certain fish which are very hard. Some make them of iron. They have many kinds of animals, oxen, cows, herses, buffallows, sheep and many other sorts, they eat all these for food except the

Latin

longe absunt montes: coeli est perquam clementis: uiri sunt subscinericij: qui uero montes incolunt, hi sunt albicantis coloris, & nonnisi annosi pereunt. Referebat Ioseph mihi uiros centenarios esse, qui adhuc dentium ordinem illaesum habebant. Regio est admodum ferax, licet triticum non gignat, neque equos: eo triticum comportatur a quibusdam insulis eiusdem naturae, cuius est regio Calechut, & Cambaiae, & id efficit arenosa plaga: equos mittunt Ormus & montes quidam, eis minime utuntur nisi ad gerulam operam quum ultro citroque compartantur merces, ad bella non utuntur: pedites praeliantur arcubus & sagittis, necnon machaeris & clypeis obrotundis, hastis nonnullis is utunt in praelio, digladiatores sunt eximij, alij se loricant piscium pellibus, quae sunt ad quoscunque ictus prope impenetrabiles, alij loricas & thoraces ferro fabricantur. Animalia omnifariam habent, ut sunt boues, arietes, bubali, precora, id genus compluscula & ea vice numinis gentiles colunt. Regio etiam fert elephantos uberrime, minutiora etiam habent animalia, ut sunt gallinae, anseres: sues non habent. Percunctati sumus etiam precium

Transalation

mountains about 300 miles away.[133] The Caranganora region is a plain land, sunlit and fertile and is far remote from the mountains. The sky is very clement. Men are dark-coloured. Those who live in the mountains are white. The people there live very long. And Joseph said that there are men there who are hundred years old who still have all their teeth. The land is very fertile. though it does not produce grain and horses. Grain is brought from some islands which are of the same nature as the region of Calechut and Cambaia,[134] and it is sandy soil. Horses are sent from Ormus and some mountains. They are not used much except for work, to carry merchandise from place to place. They are not used for wars. They fight on foot, with bows and arrows, sword and round shields. They use also lances for war. They are very excellent sword jugglers. Some wear breast-plates made of hard skin of fishes which are almost impenetrable. Others make breast-plates and corselets of iron. They have many kinds of animals, like oxen, sheep, buffaloes, and many other kinds; the gentiles worship them as

Italian

menuti como sonno Galline & Oche in grandissima copia: non hanno Porci: & per uoler particularmente intendere la ualuta de alchune cose: fo mostrato a pre Joseph predicto le Galine & uno ducato: rispose che cento Galine per uno ducato se haueua.

Translation

oxen which the gentiles worship. They have elephants in very great number. They have small animals like hens and geese in great number. They do not have pigs. And wishing particularly to know the value of some things, the priest Joseph was shown hens and a ducat. He replied that a hundred hens could be bought for a ducat.

CHPTER 9

Pan de Riso: & Palme che produce le noce de India.[a]

Questa prouincia produce maxima quantita de Risi: & similitar de zuchari: iqual risi usen per maxenadi & in sieme cum zucharo & oglio maxenado: epsi risi fanno pan perfectissimo: & questo manzano in loco de pane. Hanno etiam xx sorte de herbe: & tute sonno nutritiue: de le qual se passeno & precipue de alcune radice de herbe: non hanno rosmarin: ne bussi: ne etiam perseghi ne pomi: ne uite: perche tute le predicte cose sonno mostrate al dicto Joseph el qual ne disse non esser in la religione sua tal

Rice bread and the palms which produce the Indian nuts [135]

This region produces great quantity of rice and similarly of sugar. This rice they use by mixing it together with sugar and oil. From this rice they make very good bread which they use in the place of our bread.[136] They have also 20 sorts of herbs which are nutricious. These they eat and especially some (sorts) of roots[137] of herbs. They do not have rosemary nor boxwood, likewise they have no peaches nor apples, nor vine. All these things were shown to the said Joseph, and he said such sorts

---

a. This is Chapter cxxxvii in *Paesi*.

Latin	Translation
rerum & ostensis gallinis ipsi Iosph Indo, dixit apud suos se centum gallinas aureo uno consequi quire.	divine numinous. In this place there are many elephants. They have also small animals like hens and geese. They have no pigs. We wanted to know the price of things. When we showed Joseph the Indian hens he said that in his place a hundred of them could be bought for a gold coin.

Chapter 9

De oriza, palmis, & nucibus Indiae.[a]	About Rice, Palm trees and the Indian Nuts.[135]
Haec plaga fert orizam eximie; & saccarum tritum, utrunque emittit, ac oleo conditum oriza panem conficiunt non insuauem; habent herbarum genera uiginti quae hominem alunt plurimum, radicibus in primis oblectant. Rosmarinum non habent, neque bussum, poma, uites, nec persica: haec momnia ostendimus illi quae dixit haud esse in regione sua: ficus habent complures, adeo ut uix sit credibile, quantum scateat regio fructibus huiusmodi: habent & aliam arborem quae fert Indas nuces: & hae	Much rice grows in this region and also ordinary sugar. They mix them together, and bake with oil, and thus make delicious bread.[136] They have twenty different kinds of vegetables, which are very nutritious. They eat roots especially.[137] They have on rosemary bussum, apples, vine nor peaches. We showed all these trees to Joseph and he said that they do not grow in his place. They have many fig trees, and it would be incredible when we say that the region is full of this sort of fruits.[138] They have another

a. This is Chapter cxxxvii in *Itinerarium*.

Italian

sorte de arbori: ma altri infinitissimi: & maxime Figari: de li qual ne hanno grandissima quantita: & fanno mazor Fichi de li nostri: in tanto che cui scriuesse seria piu cose incredibile che altramente. Hanno uno altro arboro: che chiamano Palma: quel arboro a modo nostro produee le noce de India: & de epse como habiamo inteso dal dicto pre Ioseph: se trazeno quatro cose: uidelicet uino: aceto: zucharo: & olio: & perche el pareria cosa noua ad molti: como de uno arboro escono tante cose: non uoglio in hoc capitulo pretermetter el testo de strabon in libro XVI quando loquitur de palma quale e consimile al dicto de epso pre Ioseph: poi se dechiarita el modo li servano in far le cose sopracripte. Capitulum uero sic incipit: Cetera uero ex palma prebet: ex ea enim panis & mel & uinum & acetum fit & testilia uaria, nuncleis pro carbonibus fabri ferrari utuntur, qui in aqua macerati bobos & ouibus in pabulum dantur.

Translation

of trees do not grow in his region, but there are infinite number of other trees especially fig trees in very great quantity. They produce figs larger than ours, such a way that whatever be written about them would appear incredible than otherwise.[138] They have another sort of tree which they call palms, which produce what we call the Indian nuts.[139] And as we have learned from the said priest Joseph, they give four things, namely, wine, vinegar, sugar and oil.[140] And since it would appear as something strange to many, how a single tree gives so many things, I wish to add in this chapter nothing other than the testimony of Strabo in his Book XVI, where he speaks about the palm tree which is similar to what the said Joseph narrated. Later we will describe the methods they use in making the things said above. The chapter begins as follows: "Other things are furnished by the palms, from it bread and honey, wine and vinegar are produced, and many kinds of textiles. The pith is used by blacksmith instead of charcoal, steeped in water, it is given to oxen and sheep for fooder."[142]

Latin

arbores, ut referebat Ioseph, quadrigeminos gignunt fructus, uidelicet, oleum, uinum, acetum, & saccarum qui uero his fidem non adhibent, legant Strabonem in XVI suae Geogaphiae & adstipulabuntur Ioseph Indo uera narranti. Sic enim Strabonis caput incipit: "Caetera uero ex palma praebet, ex ea enim panis, mel, acetum, & oleum fit, & testilia uaria: nucleis pro carbonibus fabri ferrarij utuntur, qui in aqua macerati bobus & ouibus in pabulum dantur.[b]

Translation

tree that produces Indian nuts.[139] These trees, as Joseph narrated, produce four things,[140] namely, oil, wine, vinegar and sugar. Those who cannot believe this, let them read Book XVI of Strabo's Geography[141] and they will find that what Joseph narrated is true. The chapter in Strabo begins: "Other things are obtained from palms, from them are made, bread, honey, vinegar and oil, and various textiles. Blacksmiths use the pith instead of charcoal; steeped in water, it is given as fodder for oxen and sheep."[142]

---

b. Note the differences in the citation from Strabo's Geography. The simularity points to a remote common source and the differences point to different immediate sources. Cf. Notes and Comments no. 142.

Chapter 10

Como se fa Vino: Aceto: Zuccaro & Olio de la Palma.[a]

How wine, vinegar sugar and oil are produced from the palm.

El far de le quatro cose soprascripte e in questo modo dice el predicto che el mese de Agosto quelli incoli uanno & tagliano li rami dele dicte palme: come se fa apresso nui el cerpir de le uide: che a questo se iudica esser la primauera aposto loro: perche li arbori uano in amore: & butano como le uite aposto nui: liqual rami tagliadi dal arboro butano certa acqua biancha: sotto la qual poneno uasi: & quella arcoglieno: li primi tre zorni de lacqua predicta colta chi ne beue e como uino. Passati li tre zorni: se conuertisse in acceto: a uoler ueramente far el zucharo: o uer miel seu uin cocto a modo nostro: toglino quel acqua de li tre primi zorni: & quella meteno al foco in alcuni uasi: & per forza de foco lacqua se reduce in pocha quantita & fasse dolce: ut superius dictum est:[b] a forza de foco: & sopra de quello meteno de lacqua & messedano ogni zorno per fina zorni xx. Poi la poneno a colar & de quello usano in loco de uino quel per quanto dicano e

The making of the four things mentioned above is in this manner.[143] The above said person narrated that in the month of August the inhabitants go and cut the branches of the said palms, as we do among us when we trim the branches of the vine, Since this season is considered to be spring in their place; and the trees are in sap, they are cut them like vines in our place and when the branches are cut, certain white liquid flow from them. Under they put vases, where it is collected. The first three days, the above said liquid thus collected they drink like wine. After three days, it will be changed into vinegar. When they really want to make sugar or honey or boiled wine like ours, they take from the liquid of the first three days and put on fire in some vase and by the force of the fire, the water is reduced to small quantity and it becomes sweet, as said above by force of the fire. And to it they add water and mix every day for twenty days.

---

a. This is Chapter cxxxviii in *Paesi*

Chapter 10

Quomodo ex palma fit uinum, oleum, acetum, & faccarum.[a]

How wine, oil, vinegar and sugar are produced from the palm trees.[143]

Ex palma igitur hoc modo quatuor fiunt fructus in mense Augusti, id enim est eis primum uer: palmam putant, ut nos uites: & quoniam tunc arbores potissimum luxuriant, gemunt incisae, lachrymasque instar consauciatae uitis emittunt:[b] has uasis excipiunt, tribus solum diebus ab arbore sauciata, ea pro uino utuntur albicante aqua. Elapso triduo ex latice fit acetum suapte natura. Qui uero saccarum efficere uoluerit, is aquam hiusmodi sumat emanantem intra triduum, & ahenis impositam tantisper coquat donec uix tertia pars supersit, tunc sic decocta mel efficitur suauissimum. Vbi uero mel est effectum, id rursum aquis immergunt, & compurgant subinde usque ad uigesimum diem & quum diligenter defecauerint, eo utuntur pro uino, & quidem ut aiunt, suauissime. E nucleis uero frucutus palmae exprimunt oleum. Habes igitur ex una arbore fructus complures: ex liginis etiam semicombustis carbones fiunt, ex libro arboris

The four things are produced from the palm in this way. In the month of August, which for them is spring, they prune the palms as we do with the vine, for, then these trees are very luxuriant and when they are cut they give out immediately like the vine, the tears of the wound which they collect in pots. Taken from the tree this white liquid is used as wine for the first three days. After three days it normally changes into vinegar. Those who want to make sugar take this kind of water that emanates within three days and boil it, putting it into vessels so much so that its quantity is reduced to one third; and, thus they make very sweet cooked honey. When this honey is extracted, they again treat it for twenty days adding water and mixing it every day. When they have thus diligently purified it, they use it as wine which, as already said, is very delicious. From the kernel of the fruits of the palms oil is

---

a. This is Chapter cxxxviii in *Itinerarium*.

Italian

in summa perficion del fructo ueramente de larboro predicto chiamado Palma toglino quello & dentro le noce ne fanno oglio & cuzi particular sonno dechiarite le quatro cose & ulterius del legno ne fanno carbon & de la scorza corde: & zanie: concludendo che le el piu perfecto arboro si atroua a nostra cognition: in quelle parte ne nasce grandissima quantita de peuere: el qual come e facto per el grande calor del sol se secha: & li arbori soi sonno de mediocre qualita: & piu ne nasce in quello ioco che in tute le altre parte de India, similiter Zenzeti, Mirabolani, Cassie & altre speciarie: le qual sonno comprate: & mercadantade per Mori che pratichano in quella region: & qulle conducano al Cairo: & in Alexandria: & Damasco: & Persia: & etiam per quanto dice dicto pre Ioseph: ne uano mazor quantita ala uolta de le montagne & ala uolta del Cataio: che non uano a queste nostre parte: como nel processo nostro diremo. Poi che habiamo dicto de la cita de Caranganor: costumi: religione: & modi & etiam la fertilita sua: hora ritorneremo a la cita de Calichut.

Translation

Then they put it through a strainer and use it in the place of wine. This, as many reported, is of highest quality. From the kernal of the said tree called palms they make oil.[144] Thus the four things are explained clearly. Further, from its wood they make charcoal and rope and baskets from its bark.[145] In conclusion this is the most perfect tree that is found, to our knowledge. In this region very large quantity of pepper[147] grows which dries because of the heat of the sun. Its tree is of mediocre quality. It grows here in greater quantity than in any other place in India. Similarly, ginger mirabolin, cassia and other spices which grow there are bought and marketed by the Moors, who trade in that region. They carry them to Cairo, Alexandria, Damascus and Persia. The priest Joseph mentioned above also narrated that greater quantity of them goes to the mountains and to China. And they do not come to our regions as will be said shortly. Since we have said enough about the religion, customs and manners of Caranganor and about its fertility, now we turn to the city of Calichut.

Latin

funes. Haec itaque summa sit nullam esse aliam arborem quae magis humanis usibus conducat. Ibi etiam ubertim piper nascitur, quod torret ad calorem folis, ne forte satum alibi germinet in damnum eorum. Arbores ibi non sunt magnae proceritatis, nusquam tamen sunt frequntiores, praesertim in India. Ibi etiamnum copia est ingens zinziberis, myrobolani,[c] cassiae, & aromatum fere omne genus. Haec omnia praestinant Mauri negociatores, & ea Babyloniam. Cayrum nunc appellant, urbe Niloticam comportant, inde Alexandriam, Damascum, & demum ad Persas. Conuehunt haec etiam uersus montes, & ad Cataium, quae regiones plurimum a nobis absunt, prout latius referemus in sequentibus. Verum postque satis ac super de urbe Caranganora dictum est, aequum censeo ut rursum ad urbem Calechut redeamus.

Translation

sqeezed out.[144] Thus one tree has many products; half burned wood of the palm is used as charcoal and from the bark of the tree cord is made.[145] Thus it is the most perfect tree; there is no other tree which is of so much use for men. There grows a large quantity of pepper[147], which dries with the heat of the sun. Perhaps no where else it sprouts enough to their own damage. These trees are not very tall, nowhere are they so abundant, especially in India. They have also much ginger, myrbolin, cassias and almost all sorts of spices. All these are bought by the Moors who transport them to Babylon, and the Nilotic city now called Cairo, and from there to Alexandria, Damascus and also Persia. They carry these also to the mountains and to China, which are regions very distant from us, as will be narrated in the following. Now that we have spoken more than sufficiently about Caranganora, I consider it right that we again go back to the city of Calechut.

---

b. What is meant here by the lachrymis is the sap of the tree, which is compared to the tears of a wounded tree.
c. In the Italian text it is "Mirabolani"

Chapter 11

De Calichut & Re con sue usanze & mercantie.[a]

About Calichut, its king and his customs, and the merchandise.

La cita de Calichut e posta uerso occidente lutan da Caranganor miglia xc sopra la ripa del mare & li ha porto perfectissimo: la qual cita e grande piu de Caranganor: & el Signor suo e Idolatro de secta de quel che e Signor de Caranganor non distante alcuna cosa de costumi de dicto Re: si in religione come in tute[b] altre cose de lequal per hauer, sopradicto satis difuse: non se extenderemo piu oltra: in questa cita ne praticano infinitissimi mercadanti Mori: li quali conducono Corali: Zanbeloti: Tapedi: & altre mercantie gli sonno etiam alcuni mercadanti che se chiamano Guzerati liquali etiam fanno diuerse mercantie ne laqual cita ue concorre quasi tuta la India: & piu era anchora per auanti quando quelli dal Cataio soleuano praticare[c] questi populj da Cataio sonno Christiani: & sonno bianchi como nui & ualentissimi homini: li qualli teniuano uno fontego in Calichut & pol esser cerca anni lxxx, in.

The city of Calichut is located on the sea-shore 90 miles westward[148] from Caranganore and has a very good port. This city is greater than Caranganor and its king is an idol-worshiper of the same sect as the king of Caranganor, who does not differ from the aforesaid king in anything of the customs as far as religion and other things are concerned. Since we have said above enough about them, we shall not go into further details. In the said city countless Moorish[150] merchants engage in trade dealing in corals, zanbeloti, carpets and other merchandise. There are also some merchants called the Guzerathis,[151] who trade in different commodities. In this city almost all India comes together and it was much more so formerly when those from China used to trade there. These people of China are Christians[152] and they are white like us and are very valiant people. Some 80 or 90 years ago, they had

---

a. This is Chapter cxxxix in *Paesi*

Chapter 11

De urbe Calechut, deque eius rege & moribus, necnon mercibus.[a]

About the city of Calechut, its king, the customs and merchandise.

Urbs itaque Calechut, occidentem respicit, abestque ab urbe Caranganora miliaribus prope xc. mari adiacet & portum habet non incelebrem, maior est Caranganora, cuius dominus est idolorum cultor & eius sectae, cuius est dominus Caranganorae: in nullo prope differunt, si cultum deorum si mores, si superstions spectaueris, uti latius commeminimus in superioribus: propterea parcamus iusto uolumini, parcius in praesentia de hac re loquemur. Illud tamen non praeteribo, illic esse prope innumeros negociatores, Persas uidelicet Mauros, Indos, Medos, Assyrios, Syros, Arabas, Aegyptios, & fere ex omni orbe conuenas: alij alias ducunt merces, adeo ut ibi fere nihil quod ad humanum cultum spectet desideres. Sunt inter caeteros illic nonnulli qui Guzerati appellantur, qui multijuga tractant mercimonia. Eo itaque quasi tota India merces comportat uberrimas: frequentior

Therefore, the city of Calechut is towards the west[148] and is distant by about ninety miles from the city of Caranganora. It is close to the sea and has a port which is not unimportant. It is greater than Caranganora. Its chieftain is an idol worshiper and is of the same sect as the chieftain of Caranganora. They do not differ much if we consider their divine worship, customs, and superstitions as we have said at length in the previous pages. Therefore, lest it should become much voluminous, we will speak very sparingly in the present chapter about the matter. However, I cannot leave out in silence that there are many businessmen there, like Persians, Moors, Hindus, Medos, Assyrians, Syrians, Arabs, Aegyptians and almost from the whole world.[150] Each one brings his proper goods so much so that there is nothing lacking which is conducive to human culture. Among other people, there are some

---

a. This is Chapter cxxxix in *Itinerarium*.

Italian	Translation
xc & essendoli facti oltrezeti[d] per quel Re del dicto loco: se leuorono: & facta grandissima armada: ueneno a la cita de Calichut: la qual destrusseno: & da quel tempo sino al presente non sonno piu uenuti a merchadantar in dicto loco: ma sonno andati ad una cita de uno Re Narsindo: laqual se chiama Mailapet uerso oriente ala uia del Indo fiume circa miglia dcccc. Questi populi sonno chiamati Malasines:[e] portano diuerse merchantie: cioe panni de seda de v sorte: Rami: Piombi: Stagni: Procelane Muschio: & questi sonno quelli che leuano li Corali: & leuano bona quantita de Specie: se dice esser da Calichut fino ne la region sua miglia. vi M. portano sesse in testa de grande ualuta: & sonno richisimi merchadanti. Tornamo ala cita de Calichut: el Re dela cita predicta se chiama Baufer: & ha uno grande palazo: in el quale tien per custodia dela persona sua. vii M. homini: la nocte fa andar le guardie atorno le case per non esser la cita murato & a tal guardie sonno deputadi. ccc. homini: ha preterea un palazo grandissimo: nel qual ha iiii audientie separate: una per Gentil una per Mori: & una per Iudei: & una per Christiani & quando occorre che qualche una de queste quatro natione	a factory in Calichut. Having been outraged by the king of that place, they rebelled and gathering a large army came to the city of Calichut and destroyed it. From that time up to the present day they have never come to trade in the said place, but they go to a city of a king Naisindo which is called Milapet[153] about 90 miles toward the east by way of the Indus river. These people are called Malasenes[155] and they carry diverse merchandise, that is silk cloth of five kinds, copper, lead, tin, porceline and musk. These are the ones who trade in corals and good quantity of spices. It is said to be six thousand miles from Calicut to the frontiers of their regions,. They wear on their heads fezzes of great value and are very rich merchants. To return to the city of Calichut, the king of the said city is named Baufer and has a big palace, in which there are, seven thousand men for the protection of his person: During the night he makes the guard to go around among the houses because the city is not fortified. Three hundred men are assigned for his guard. In addition, they have

Latin

etiam inibi negociatorum numerus erat, quum incolae Cataij illo proficiscebantur. Hi igitur Cataij populi colunt Christum, & coloris sunt albicantis ut nos, uiri sunt perquam strenui, qui olim in urbe Calechut eximie negociabantur. Verum quum rex Calechut male eos accepisset, soluere illinc, & paulopost reuertentes, stragem non mediocrem incolis urbis Calechut intulerunt, & deinceps non sunt regressi. Post haec adiuere urbem Mailapetam, quae urbs paret regi Narsindo: regio respicit orientem, & distat ab Indo flumine miliaribus xc ibi nunc sua exercent mercimonia: populi dicuntur Malasines, multijuga ferunt mercimonia, uidelicet serica omne genus, aera, plumba, stagna, ac castorium, & id genus innumeros odores, haec sunt quae eo ipsi comportant. Quae uero exportant illinc, haec sunt uidelicet coralli omnium generum & aromata. Aiunt eorum regionem abesse ab urbe Calechut milaribus sex mille: in capite ferunt ornamenta quaedam ingentissimi precij, locupletes sunt in uniuersum. Redeamus ergo ad urbem Calechut, cuius rex dicitur Baufer, qui magnam regiam habet

Translation

called Gujarathies[151] who are people specialized in every kind of trade. From this city therefore, the whole of India takes goods abundantly. There were more business men there when the people of China used to go there for trade. These people of China are Christians[152] and are white-coloured as we are. They are very dynamic people who at one time were having much trade in Calechut. But once it happened that the king of Calechut badly received them. So they went off from there, but shortly returned and killed many of the inhabitants of the town of Calechut and afterwards they have never returned. Then they went to Mailaperam[153], which town is under king Narsindus.[154] The region is towards the East and is distant by about 90 miles from the river Indus. Here they carry on their trade. These people are called Malasines.[155] They trade in many goods, namely silk of every kind, copper, zink, lead, aromatics and several perfumes. Things which they export from the place are the following namely, corals of all varieties and aromatics. They say that

Italian	Translation

uol audientia ua nel loco suo deputado: & li dal Re sonno alditi: ma prima sonno obligati lauarsi perche altramente el Re non li parleria: hanno preterea dicti Gentili una consuetudine: che quando entrano in mare no mangeriano per conditione alcuna: perche manzando seriano priui de ueder piu el suo Re: non restaremo de dire: anchora che di sopra habiamo scripto le femine dapoi la morte deli mariti: hanno per consuetudine de brusarse uiue & perche porria esser che de zo se ne marauigliaria: non e cosa marauigliosa: perche sempre li Indi hanno habuto questa consideatione: non solum le femine: ma etiam li homini: li pareno a questo modo conseguir certa immortalita: come dice Strabo nel Libro. XV due le tracta de li legati: uer. Ambasiadori del India mandati da Porro Re de quella a Cesare Augusto: el Capitulo e tale refert enim Nicolaus Damascenus se Antiochie &c. Preterea ne la cita de Calichut prenominada se fanno grandissime merchantie: como de sopra ho dicto & a certi tempi de lanno se fanno alcune fere doue ne concorreno tuti li populi dal Cataio: India: Persia: & Soria: & domandando

a very great palace which has four separate chambers for audience: one for the gentiles, one for the Moors, one for the Jews and one for the Christians; and when one of these four groups wishes to have an audience, they go the place alotted to them. And they are received by the king and are heard. But they are obliged to wash themselves first, becauses, otherwise the king will not speak to them. These gentiles have a custom that when they travel on sea, under whatever circumstance, they will not eat, for if they do so they will lose their right to see the king. We will not hesitate space to discuss again what we have written above: according to their custom the women burn themselves alive after the death of their husbands.[156] Because one might wonder thereat it, is not strange because the Indians always had this custom, not only for women, but also for men. They think that in this manner they can attain certain immortailty, as Strabo says in Book XV[157] where he treats of the legates and Ambassoders of India send from Porro, the king of that country, to Caesar Augustus. The Chapter begins thus: "Nicolas Damascenus says

Latin

instar theatri, cuiusque latera stipant septem milia hominum, qui pro salute principis uigilant. Hi noctu urbem lustrant quoniam uasta est & patens absque moenijs. Per uices propterea uigiliae disponuntur ne quid inopinatum accidat dum dant membra quieti. Hanc curam uiri ccc habent. In theatro uisuntur aulae siue coenacula magna quatuor, quae singula singulis patent nationibus, alia Indis, Mauris alia, alia Iudaeis, Christianis alia patent: unaquaeque natio nouit suum auditorium in alieno non admittitur. Priui priua loca audientiae habent & ibi expediuntur: uerum eo prius non accedunt quam loti fuerint, alioquin ad regem minime admitterentur, illoti uidelicet, utpote immundi ac foedi. Gentiles hunc morem seruant, in mare nunquam comedunt quoniam si id agerent, nunquam regem uiderent deinceps: neque ommittemus quin & rursum de hac re mentionem faciemus, licet in superioribus commeminirimus, nam retulimus paulo supra, mulieres Indas hunc morem habere quod uidelicet nihil ducunt honorificentius, quam cum uiris simul occumbere. Comburi propterea cum coniugibus iam fato functis

Translation

their region is distant from the city of Calechut by about 6000 miles. They wear on their heads ornaments of great value. In general they are very rich. Now we will return to Calechut whose king is called Baufer. He has a great palace which is like a theatre. About 7000 men are stationed on the boundaries to keep vigil to protect the king. In the night they patrol the city because it is very vast and there are no fortifications. They therefore in turn keep vigil lest anythig unexpected happen and in order to give peace to the members of the family. About 300 men are employed for this service. In the theatre there are 4 halls or big dining halls, each of which is destined for particular people of the kingdom, namely, Hindus, Moors, Jews and Christians. Each set know their proper auditorium and are not admitted in a different one. There are also private rooms for special audiences and the people are sent there only after they have washed themselves. Unless washed they are not granted audience with the king. Those who have not washed themselves are considered unclean and dirty. The gentiles observe this custom. They never

Italian

a pre Ioseph se in quel loco e facto mentione de le parte nostre: dice deli non se far mentione saluo che di Roma: Fraza: & Venetia: & esser facta grandissima existimatione dele monete Venetiane: el qual pre Ioseph essendo stato mandato dauanti la nostra Illustrissima signoria monstro alcuni ducati del doge da Ca Sten: che lui da quelle parte haute portade.

Translation

that he in Antioch" etc. Further more in the city named above much merchandise is handled as we have said above. And at certain times of the year they hold a certain fair to which people from China, India, Persia and Syria come.[158] When we asked priest Joseph about our places mentioned in his place, he said that they do not mention any place except Rome, France and Venice, and that the money of Venice is held in very great esteem among them. The said Joseph when he was ordered to appear before our most Illustrious Signoria showed them some ducats of Doge of Ca Sten which he brought from his country.[159]

---

b. In *Paesi* 1507 it is "tutte", which was corrected in the 1508 edition. We have corrected it accordingly.

c. In *Paesi* 1507 it is "praticarre" which was corrected into "praticare" in the 1508 edition. We follow the correction.

d. "facti oltrazeti": in the 1508 edition of *Paesi* it reads "facto oltrazato", we keep it as in the 1507 edition.

e. "Malasines": both in the 1507 and 1508 editions of *Paesi* it begins with a small letter. We have corrected it.

Latin

summe apperunt nec id mirum. Putant enim non posse aliter sibi parere immortalitatem. Huius rei commeminit Strabo XV suae Geographiae eius, caput sic auspicatur: Refert enim Nicolaus Damascenus se Antiochiae & c quae sequuntur. Sicuti igitur praefeci, in urbe Calechut magna fiunt commrcia & statis annis temporibus fiunt nundinae non incelebres, eoque undequaque cateruatim populi confluunt, ex Cataio in primis, demum Indi omne genus, Persae, Medi, Syri, Turcae, Assyrij, Arabes, Egyptij, & hi presertim qui Babylonem, id est Cayrum incolunt, urbem Aegytiam quae Nilo adacet amni famigerato multarumque gentium ac regionum termino. Percunctati sumus etiam Ioseph praedictum Indum, an illi nostrae huius regiones cognitione habent quampiam. Referebat Romanam urbem & Venetias, necnon Galliam, quae Francia dicitur, esse apud eos nonnihil in precio,

Translation

eat on the sea. If they do so they will not see the king again. We will not omit, rather will mention this matter again although we have spoken something above. We mentioned above that the Hindu women have the custom[156] that they do not consider anything more noble and anything worthy of honour than to die with their husbands. Therefore, they greatly desire to be cremated with their dead husbands. This is nothing strange because they believe that otherwise they cannot gain immortality. Strabo makes mention of this in chapter XV[157] of his Geography. The chapter bigins so: Nicholaus Damascenus says that he in Antioch etc. As said above, much business is done there in the city of Calechut and on fixed dates of the year there are markets which are well known everywhere People from every place come together on such days, namely from China especially and Hindus of all castes Persians, Syrians, Turks, Assyrians, Arabs, Aegyptians and especially those who inhabit Babylon, namely Cairo the town of Egypt adjacent to the river Nile and many people from the border areas.[158] We

Chapter 12

Del Regno de Cambaia: de Ormus & Guzerat.[a]

Dicto che habiamo de Calichut: andaremo uerso occidente uerso el Regno de Combait: el qual e luntan da Calichut miglia xii M. & da Combait[b] pur uerso occidente fino ala insula de Ormus sonno miglia ccc la qual e posta nel principio del sino Persico: & lutan dala terra ferma miglia xx che se chiama el Capo de Mogolistam: che e principio del Colfo. Questa insula colze miglia cl el signor de

About the kingdom of Cambaia,[160] Ormus[161] and Guzerat.[162]

After having talked about Calichut, we now turn westward towards the kingdom of Cambait. It is 12000 miles[163] away from Calichut. And from Cambait toward the west up to the island of Ormus, which is located in the beginning of the Persian gulf, it is 300 miles. And 20 miles distant from the mainland is what is called the Cape of Mogolistan which is at the beginning of the gulf.

---

a. This is chapter cxl in *Pœsi*

Latin	Translation

& in primis aurum Venetorum signatum argentumque illic esse eximio in precio. Is ergo Ioseph adiuit illustrissimos dominos Venetos & eis ostendit nonnullos antiquissimos aureos in quibus erat expressa Veneti ducis perquam vetus imago.

inquired of the said Joseph if he had any previous information about our region. He said that the city of Rome, Venice and Gaul which is called France are held in great esteem among them. He further said that Venetian gold coins and silver are very much valued among them. Therefore the said Joseph visited the illustrious Lords of Venice and showed them some ancient gold coins on which there was the image of the Lord of Venice, which was very ancient.[159]

CHAPTER 12

De Regnis Cambaiae, Ormus & Guzerat.[a]

About the kingdom of Cambaia[160] *Ormus*[161] *and Guzerat.*[162]

Postque satis ac super de urbe Calechut dictum remur, de rebus occiduis fiet sermo, & in primis de regno Cambaiae, quod abest ab urbe Calechut miliaribus prope mille & deinde ad insulam Ormus miliaria ccc & ea est in principio sinus Persici introrsus terras miliaria xx & id loci dicit caput Mogolistanum, ubi auspicat sinus haec insula circuitu patet miliaribus fere cl eius dominus seruit Mahumeti, urbs

After having spoken sufficiently and more about the city of Calechut, let the discussion be about the things of the west. First of all, about the kingdom of Cambaia, which is about a thousand miles[163] from Calechut. From there, it is 300 miles to the island of Ormus, which is in the Persian Gulf, twenty miles away from the mainland. This place is called Cape of Mogolistan, and it

---

[a] This is chapter cxl in *Itinerarium*

Italian

quella Machometan: & ha una cita grandissima: populatissima produse infinite^c cose: & merchantie: in questo loco se fano Veri como li nostri qui se cattano le perle produse caualli in grande quantita li quali conduseno poi per lindia per condur le merchantie: da questo Capo de Mogolistam: che e per mezo dela insula de Ormus uerso la cita de Combait: se trouano de molte terre habitade da Mori: la prima se chiama Sobelch, la secunda Semanaht, la terza Chesimii, poi infra terra la cita de Guzerat^d da poi fu la riua del mar e posta Combait: laqual pol esser lontan dal capo de Mogolistam como habiamo predicto miglia ccc questa cita de Combait e incolfada molto: & el colfo doue posta la cita chiama el colfo de Guzerat: & la prouincia al presente se chiama Guzerat: ma antiquitus era chiamada Bedrosia: & perche in questo loco habiamo facto mentione de Guzerat:^e de chiararemo la condition sua. Questa prouincia ha molte cita & castelle: sonno populi potentissimi e grandissimi mercatanti: sonno Idolatri: adorano el Sol & la Luna: & le Vache: & se uno amazasse una Vacha: lo amazeriano lui: non manzano de

Translation

It is 300 miles around and its Lord is a Mohammedan. It has a very large city thickly populated which produces countless things and merchandise. In this place glasses like ours are produced, pearls are gathered, and horses are raised in great number. These they take through out India to carry the merchandise. From this cape of Mogolistan, which is opposite of the islalnd of Ormus, up to the city of Cambait, there are many lands inhabited by the moors; the first is called Sobelch, the second Semanaht and the third Chesimii.[164] And then in land is the city of Guzerat and Cambait is located on the seashore. As we have already said this is 300 miles distant from the cape of Mogolistan. The city of Cambait is much engulfed and the gulf where the city is located is called the gulf of Guzerath and this region at present is called Guzearth. But in antiquity it was called Bedrosia.[165] Because we have mentioned Guzerat in this context, we will speak about its condition.[166] This region has many cities and castles. They are very powerful people and are great merchants. They are idol worshipers, they adore the sun,

Latin

est uasta admodum & habitators frequentissima, ac prope omnium rerum ferax mercimonia emittit quasi innumera ibi & uitrea fiunt uasa elegantissime. Legunt illic unionum copiam maximam equos fert eximios quos in Indiam uenales mittunt, eis etiam merces comportant suas hinc igitur id est ab hoc capite Mogolistano, quod est in umbilico insulae Ormus usque ad urbem Cambaiam intercedunt innumerae Maurorum urbes, inter quas hae minime sunt obscurae, uidelicet Sobobec, Semath, & Chesimii. Introrsus uero est urbs Guzerat. Secus autem littus urbs Cambaiae uisit, quae, ut prefecimus, potest abesse a capite Mogolisteno mil quasi ccc haec urbs Cambaiae plurimum sinuat & ubi est sita urbs, dicitur sinus Guzerat uerum olim dicebat Betrosia. Et quam meminimus huius loci Guzerat, non nulla de eo referemus. Eius itaque plaga habet urbes complures uicos & oppida, frequentissimis est habitatoribus, ʿeisdemque negociatoribus idola colunt necnon solem & lunam bouesque foeminas adeo ut apud eos capitale sit bouem foeminam occidisse. Morticina non comedunt uinum non bibunt album uiri

Translation

is here that the gulf begins. This island is 150 miles in circumference. Its lord worships Muhamed. The city is very large and populous. It yields almost everything, it sends much merchandise. There they make very elegant glass, collect pearls in abundance. Horses are bred in large numbers, which they send to India for sale, and they transport their merchandise. From here, that is, from the Cape of Mogolistan, which is at the centre of the island of Ormus, up to the city of Cambaia, there are many cities of the Moors among which the following are to be mentioned, namely, Sobobec, Semath and Chesimii.[164] Into the land is the city of Guzerat. Against the shore is seen the city of Cambaia, which, as said above, is some 300 miles distant from the Cape of Mogolistan. Cambaia is a much winding city and the place where the city is situated is called the Gulf of Guzerat. This city was once known as Betrosia.[165] Because we have mentioned Guzerat we shall speak something about it.[166] This region has many cities, castles and towns, very thickly populated by the people of the place and by the

Italian	Translation
alcuna cosa che receue morte: non beueno uino: Sonno homini piu bianchi che li naturali de Calichut: Sonno mazori incanta-tori del mondo: portano capelli molto politi & barba: & quelli inuoltano como fanno le femene: togliono una moglier sola: sonno molte caste: el uiuer suo e de legumi & herbe che produse la terra: secundo la opinion de Pitagora: habiamo dicto de Guzerat: mo diremo dela cita de Cambaia.	the moon and the cow. If some one kills a cow they will kill him. They will not eat anything that meets death. They do not drink wine. They are whiter than the natives of Calichut. They are the greatest magicians of the world. They keep their hair and beard elegantly. They arrange their hair as women do. They are monogamous and are very chaste. They live on vegitables and herbs in accordance with the principles of Pythagoras. Having spoken about the Guzerathis we now will speak about the city of Cambaia.

b. The name Cambaia is seen in two other forms in *Paesi* 1507, Cambait and Combait.
c. In *Paesi* 1507 it is "infenite", we have corrected it.
d. In *Paesi* 1507 it is "Guzirat", we have corrected it.
e. In *Paesi* 1507 it is "Guzerati", we have corrected it to Guzerat.

Latin	Translation
sunt albicantis coloris superantque albedine incolas Calechut fascinatores sunt eximij comunt capillum & barbam & cincinnos ut mulieres ciruciunferunt, torqueque ex capillo facto caput mire exornant mulieres uni uiro solum nubunt & rursus uiri unam ducunt coniugem. Post quam uitam celibem agunt, in uniuersum sunt continentissimi, nec in Venerem facile ruunt ut reliqui falaces. Legumine uiuunt, & oleribus, quae parens mittit terra ut autor est Pithagoras. Abunde dictum arbitror de urbe Guzerat, superest ut nonnihil de urbe Cambaiae disseramus.	merchants. They worship idols, the sun, the moon and the cows, so that to kill a cow would incur capital punishment among them. They do not eat anything that is dead. They do not drink white wine. The men are whiter than the inhabitants of Calechut. They are great conjurers. They comb their hair and beard, and they tie up their hair as women do and adorn their head making a wreath of hair. The women marry only one man and the men take only one wife. When they live a celibate life, generally in a very chaste way they do not commit sexual faults as like the other immoral people. They eat vegetables and herbs, which the land produces, in accordance with the ideal of Pythagoras. We think enough has been said of the city of Guzerat, and it remains that we say something about the city of Cambaia.

Chapter 13

Sito de Cambaia: & altri lochi. Item de Re, speciarie.[a]

The site of Cambaia[167] and other places, also about the king and the spices.

La cita de Cambaia e posta nel colfo Guzerati la qual e grandissima & populatissima: & secundo la uulgar opinione e la piu nobil cita che sia in tuta la India la qual chiamano Cairo del India: e murata: ha dentro dignissime habitation. Soleua antiquamente el signor suo esser gentile & Idolatro: al presente e Machometano: la causa e questa: che per esser accresuto piu el numero de Machometani che de gentili: li Machometani hanno tolto lo imperio de la prouincia: la qual e quasi tuta piena de gentili: & fimiliter la terra. In questo loco nasce lacha, incenso in mazor copia che in tute le altre parte del mondo. Sonno grandissimi Mercadanti: & hanno assaissime naue: cum le qual nauigano in Ethiopia, Mare Rosso, Sino Persicho: & India. De questa cita de Cambaia fino al capo del colfo: el qual se chiama Diongul sonno migla ccc. Se trouano in questo colfo molte cita: che e longo anarrarle.

The city of Cambaia is situated at the gulf of Guzerat.[168] It is very large and thickly populated. According to the common opinion, it is the noblest city in all India. and is called the Cairo of India It is walled and has very excellent buildings in it. Formerly its Lord was a gentile, and a worshiper of idols, but at present is a Mohammedan.[169] The reason is this, when the number of the Mohammedans became greater than that of the gentiles the Mohammedans took over the government of the region, which is almost totally of gentiles as also the land. In this place grow lac and frankincense[170] in greater quantity than in any other place in the world. They are very great merchants and they have many ships with which they sail to Ethiopia, Red Sea, the Persian Gulf and India.[171] From this city of Cambaia to the Cape of Gulf which is called Diongul: it is 300 miles. In this gulf are found

---

a. This is Chapter cxli in *Paesi*.

Chapter 13

De situ urbis Cambaiae, deque eius rege & nonnullis aliis locis, ac de aromatibus.[a]

About the site of the city of Cambaia[167], its king and about some other places and about the spices.

Vrbs Cambaiae sita est in sinu Guzerat, ea est maxime culta, eximiaque uastitate & uirorum frequentia ac fere omnium est Indiae urbium excellentior. Cayrum propterea Indiae appellatur muro ambit & pulcherrimas habet aedes. Olim eius dominus erat gentilis & idolis seruiebat, nunc sectae est Mahumetanae, id efficit numerosior coetus Mahummetanorum qui urbem incolunt, eamque moderandam suscepere, quae scatet gentilibus. Ibi lacha nascitur uberius quam alibi gentium negaciatores sunt non incelebres, naues habent innumeras quibus sulcant maria & in primis Aethiopicum, Erythraeum, Persicum, nec non Indicum. Abest haec urbs a capite quod dicitur Diongul miliaribus ccc. In eius sinu sunt complusculae urbes quas percensere longum foret. Inque ea insula quae Maya dicitur & post id caput Diongul orientem uersus

The city of Cambaia is located in the gulf of Guzerat.[168] It is a very civilised city, very large and thickly populated and is almost the most excellent of all the Indian cities. It is therefore called the Cairo of India. It is circumscribed by a wall and has very beautiful houses. Once its lord was a gentile and adored the idols but now is one of the sect of the Mohammedans.[169] It happened so when the population of the Mohammedans increased they took over the government of the place which abounds in gentiles. In this place grows lac[170] more than anywhere in the world. The merchants of this place are well known. They have ships with which they voyage on the sea especially to the Ethiopean and Erythrean Seas, the Persian Gulf and the Indian Ocean.[171] The city is 300 miles away from the Cape called Diongul. In its gulf there are many cities, but it would take

---

a. This is Chapter cxli in *Itinerarium*.

Italian	Translation
Sopra questo Capo de Diongul se atroua una insula chiamata Maya: & da questo capo de Diongul sequndo uerso oriente: se atroua uno capo chiamato Ely distante uno da laltro miglia ccl. & da capo dali fino a Calichut sonno piu de miglia dc.	many cities, which it would take long time to describe. Above this Cape Diongul is found an island called Maya.[172] From this Cape of Diongul going toward the east, is found the Cape called Ely,[173] 250 miles distant from each other. From this Cape up to Calichut it is 600 miles.

Chapter 14

De Re Narsindo & de una ecclesia de San Thomaso.[a]	About the king Narisindo[175] and a church of St Thomas.[176]
Perfino qui habiamo dicto tuto el paese che si troua ale marine comenzando da Ormus fino in Caranganor: & el regno de Cuchin:[b] diremo dele parte fra terra: se atroua uerso le montagne: circha milia. ccc. lontan dale marine uno Re potentissimo el qual se chiama Re Narsindo & ha una grandissima cita cum. iii. cente de mure: le qual se chiama Besenegal: questo Re: secundo referisse pre Ioseph: lui hauere uisto cum li ochi: quando el ua cum exercito contra li sui inimici: mena cum si Elephanti. dccc. Caualli iiii M. & una infinita de pedoni: & dice chel campo	Up to this point, we have described all the countries which are found along the sea, beginning from Ormus up to Caranganor and the kingdom of Cuchin.[177] We shall now speak about the region inland. About 300 miles from the sea, towards the mountain, is found a very powerful king called Narisindo. He has a very large city called Besenegal[183] with three circuits of walls. This king, as the priest Joseph who had seen it with his own eyes narrated, when he goes in battle against his enemies takes with him 800 elephants, 400 horses and

---

a. This is chapter cxlii in *Paesi*.

Latin

aliud capud occurrit, quod appellatur Ely, ad miliaria fere cl & inde ad urbem Calechut miliaria DC.

Translation

long to describe them all. Among them there is an island called Maya[172] and after the Cape of Diongul towards the east there is another Cape called Ely[173] some 150 miles away from it and from there to Calechut it is 600 miles distance.

Chapter 14

De rege Narsindo & quadam ecclesia Sancti Thomae[a]

About the king Narasindo[175] and a certain church of St. Thoms.[176]

Hucusque littoralia omnia percurrimus, uidelicet ab urbe Caraganora usque ad insulam Ormus. Superest ut de regno Cuchini praesertim de mediterraneis nonnihil exaremus. Est igitur introrsus ad miliaria fere ccc. non longe a montibus rex quidam nimium potens Narsindi. Is quum sit ualde potens urbem habet triplici cirumdatam muro, ea dicitur Besenegal. Is rex, ut retulit Ioseph Indus, quum ad bella proficiscitur, secum ducit elephantos dccc. equites iiii mille, pedites uero innumeros adeoque magnum innumerumque, quum exit ad bella, secum trahit

Up to now we have traversed all the cities along the sea-shore namely from Caranganora up to the island of Ormus. It remains now to speak of the kingdom of Cuchin[177] and especially some regions in the interior of the land. About 300 miles from the sea-shore, not distant from the mountains, there is a powerful king called Narasindus.[182] Since he is a very powerful king he has a city which has three circuits of walls. It is called Besenegal.[183] This king, as Joseph the Indian narrated, takes with him, when he goes to war, 800 elephants, 4000 horses and innumerable foot

---

a. This is Chapter cxlii in *Itinerarium*

Italian	Translation

suo per ostro & tramontana tenia per miglia. xxx. & per ponente: & leuante altro tanto in tanto se pol coniecturar el suo regno esser grandissimo: & per quanto piu dice pre Ioseph el circunda miglia. iii.M. La fede sua e idolatra: hora torniamo a le parte finitime al mare: & prima comencemo da Cuchin uerso loriente & India partendosi da Cuchin per andar uerso oriente miglia c. se atroua uno capo che se chiama Cumari: da questo capo de Cumari fino al fiume Indo sonno miglia. ccccc. doue che in questo spacio se atroua uno colfo grandissimo: el qual se chiama colfo de Oriza: & ha una cita grandissima dicta Oriza apresso laqual passa lo fiume Indo: & in questo proprio Colfo e sita una cita sopra una ponta in mare: la qual se chiama Milapar: ne la qual cita e una ghiesia de San Thomaso grande: come quella de San Zuanne & Paulo in Venetia: ne la qual e posto el corpo de San Thomaso: el qual fa de molti miraculi: & gentili & Christiani hanno in suma reuerentia. Se atroua insuper in questo mar Indico de molte isole. Tra le qual ne sonno ii. degne de memoria: la prima e Saylam distante dal Capo Comari miglia. cc. ne la qual nasceno

innumerable foot soliders. And he said that his camp from south to north is 30 miles long and west to east is of equel breadth, so much so that it is possible to conjuncture how large his kingdom is. As priest Joseph said, its circumference is 3,000 miles. His religion is idol worship. Now we turn to the regions closer to the sea. First we begin with Cuchin towards the east and to India. Starting from Cuchin and coming 100 miles towards the east is found the cape called Cumari. From the cape of Cumari up to the river Indus,[186] it is 500 miles, in which space is found a very great gulf called Oriza. It has a very great city called Oriza near which the river Indus flows. In this same gulf is situated a city called Milapar, on a promontary extending in to the sea. In this city is found a Church of St Thomas,[189] as big as St John's and St Paul's in Venice. In this church is placed the body of St Thomas, who works many miracles. Both gentiles and Christians have great devotion to him. Moreover, in this Indian sea are found many islands. Two of them are worthy of mention. The first is Saylam 200 miles distant from

Latin

exercitum, ut spacio xxx milia rium ad quamcumque orbis partem minime contineri possit, id est, quadrata acie tantundem terrarum uersus orientem & occidentem & rursum itidem uersus Aquilonem & meridiem exercitus occupat. Res prope incredibilis, licet uera addebatque dictus Ioseph reqnum huiusce regis patere circuitu trium milium miliarium. Is rex colit idola. Verum reuertamur ad littoralia & primo loco auspicabimur ab Cuchina, quae respicit orientem & praetenta est Indiae. Dum igitur [soluis ab urbe Cuchina, tendisque ad ortum solis, ad miliaria fere centum, caput comperies quod appellant Cumar & inde usque ad Indum fluuium, ubi auspicatur India intercedunt miliaria quingenta. Inque eo itinere sinus uisitur non incelebris, cui nomen est Orizae & ibi famigerata urbs de nomine sinus Oriza dicta, eam praeterfluit Indus. Et in eodem sinu est urbs alia, quae instar promontorij in mare prominet, ea dicitur Milapar, in qua diui Thomae Apostoli delubrum celebre colit eximie, idque templum refert ecclesiam santorum Ioannis & Pauli Venetiarum. In eo igitur delubto corpus diui Thomae quiescit, quod claret innumeris miraculis. Colitur

Translation

·soldiers. So great and innumerable an army he takes with him to war that a space of thirty miles to every side would not contain them; that is, the army occupies an area of thirty miles to the east and west to the north and south. Somethig almost incredible, but true. And the said Joseph added that the kingdom of this king has a circumference of three thousand miles. The king worships idols. Now, we turn to the regions next to the sea. First we will begin with the city of Cuchin, which extends to the east[184] and projects India. Now leaving Cuchina and travelling towards the east, about 100 miles, we come to the Cape called Cumar[185] and from there, to the river Indus[186], where India begins, it is 500 miles. And on journeying we come to a famous Gulf called Oriza[187] and there is a famous city of the name Gulf of Oriza beyond which the Indus flows· In the same Gulf there is another city, on a promontory extending into the sea, which is called Milapar.[188] In that city there is the much venerated Church of St Thomas the Apostle[189], and this Church is comparable with the Church of St John and Paul in Venice. In it rests the body

Italian	Translation

le Caualle: dapoi questa uerso oriente e la insula de Samotra: o uer Taprobana: la qual e distante da Calichut per mesi· iii. de zornate: poi piu in la se atroua el Cataio & altre regione: dele quale non scriueremo altro per non hauer potuto piu sapere da pre Ioseph superius notado. Molte cose se poteria dir si de Specie como de altre mercantie apertinente ala India: & ale parte che habiamo scripto in questo nostro progresso: ma per non esser cose pertinete. Immo superuacante dela narration facta per Ioseph: & per non uoler azonzer altro: ma dir la pura uerita: habiamo uoluto meter fine a la presente materia.

    Finis atque soli Deo honor & gloria.

the Cape of Cumari, where horses are raised. After this, toward the east is the Island Samotra[193] or Taprobana which is three months journey from Calichut. And much further is found China and other regions. I shall not write anything about them because I could not learn more from priest Joseph mentioned above. Many things might be said cancerning spices and other merchandise pertaining to India and other parts of which we have written in the course of our discussion but because they do not pertain to the narratives of priest Joseph and since we do not want to add other things but only to tell the simple truth we have decided to put an end to the present subject.

    End and to God alone be honour and thanksgiving.

Latin

propterea eximie ab omnibus licet infidelibus. Praeterea in hoc mari Indico complures insulae uisuntur & inter alias duae sunt, quae caeteras omni rerum celebritate praestant, altera Sayla dicitur quae abset a dicto capite Comar miliaribus prope cc ea est quae mittit equos. Post hanc ad orientem altera uisitur, quae dicitur Samotra, nos Taprobanam appellamus, quae abest ab urbe Calechut itinere trium mensium. Vltra eam est Cataium feracissima, ut dictum est insula cum alijs compluribus, quarum haudquaquam meminisse est animus, quandoquidem ab dicto Ioseph Indo plura non aceepimus, neque nos eas remotiores orbis partes adiuimus. Potuissemus quidem longiore subsellio gemmarum ae lapidum, margaritarumque naturam indagere, necnon de aromatum generibus differere complura, quum haec in primis ferat India. Verum qnum minime pertineant ad id quod retulit Ioseph praedictus, ex composito temperabimus, tum ut praeter uerum nihil relatum putetis, tum uel maxime, ut tandem aliquando coeptum ſopus ad umbilicum deueniat. Finis.

Translation

of St Thomas[190], which is evident from the countless miracles there. It is very much venerated by all, including the gentiles. Farther, in this Indian Ocean there are many islands, among which two are very important. One is called Sayla[191] which is about 200 miles from the Cape of Comar mentioned above. It is from there that horses are sent. Beyond that, towards the east is seen the other, called Sumatra[192], which we call Taprabana[193], which is three months, journey from Calechut. Beyond this is China, the most fertile, as already said; it is an island with many islands, of which we do not mean to speak, for we did not hear much about it from the said Joseph the Indian. Nor have we gone to those remote parts of the world. We could, however, make further investigation about the place of gems, and precious stones, about the nature of pearls as well as of the many different kinds of spices, for, India in the first place produces them. But, since they do not pertain to what the said Joseph narrated, we abstain from making additions to it, lest you should think that we narrate anything other than the truth and that the work begun may come to conclusion. End.

4.3.0. **The Narratives of Joseph the Indian Dutch Text and Translation**

Chapter 1

(There is no title in Dutch Text for this Chapter)[a]

Na dat Koning Emanuel van Portugal eenige Jagten en Galeyen had uytgesonden, welke de Zuyder-Gewesten doorvoeren, en door dien wegh in Indien waren gekomen, volgens d'aanwijsingh der geene, die in voorige Jaren deese Landen hadden ontdeckt, heest defelve Majesteyt Anno 1500 een andere Scheepsvloot doen uyt-rusten, bestaande in twaalf Scheepen, om sigh derwaarts te begeven. Den Oversten op deselve was Petrus Aliares, die op den aghtsten Martius van Lisbona af-voer. Na veel uytgestane gevaren quam by eyndlijk den derthienden September des selven Jaars te Calicuth aan, alleen met seven sijner Kielen; want van d'overige vijf waren'er vier door een seer vervaarlijk Onweer, na den afgrond gesonken; 't vijfde had den wegh na Sofala genomen.

Drie Maanden langh bleven de gemelde Scheepen in de Haven van Calicuth leggen. Maar vermits doe een groote twift ontstond tusschen d'Inwooners der genoemde Stad en deese Portugeezen, waar door veele Menschen om 't leven quamen, soo vertrocken de laetstgenoemde na Cochin op den vier-en-twintighsten December.

Dit Koninghrijk Cochin leght over de 110 Mijilen van Calicuth, aan de Zee; en heeft een Heydenscher Koningh, van even deselve secte als dien van Calicuth is. Deesen Koningh van Cochin ontfingh onse scheepen (wy spreken nu met de woorden der Portugeezen)[b] seer vriendlijk; en terwijl wy hier onsen Koophandel dreven, quamen'er twee Broeders aan, sijnde Indiaansche Christenen, geboortigh uyt de Stad Caranganor, ontrent twintigh Mijlen van Cochin afgeleegen. Deese verklaarden, een seer groote begeerte te bebben, om de Westersche Landen te besightigen. Hadden ook een Belofte gedaan, om een Beedevaart na Romen en Jerusalem te verrighten. Sy gingen vrywilligh in onse Scheepen, en voeren met ons af.

Ter selver tijd quam een sterke Vloot van Calicuth na ons toe, om onse Scheepen te verderven. Maar als wy haar voorneemen

---

a. This Chapter appears as Foreword (Voorberight) in *Sonderlinge Reysen* on pp. 3–4.

Chapter 1

(The is no title in the Dutch text for this Chapter.)

The King Emanuel[5] had sent out some yautches and galleys which traversed the southern regions[7] and through that way had finally gone to India. Following the counsel of some who in the foregoing years[9] had discovered these lands, the same Majesty[10] equipped in the year 1500[11] another fleet consisting of twelve ships[12] to go to those regions. The Captain of this fleet was Peter Aliares[13], who on 8th March[14] set out from Lisbon. After having faced many dangers, at last he arrived at Calicuth[15] on 13th September of the same year with only seven of his ships. Of the five others, four were sunk in the deep sea by very severe tempest and the fifth sailed off to Sofala[16].

For three months the above mentioned ships remained at the port of Calicuth. But, there arose a big dispute[17] between the inhabitants of the siad city and these Portuguese, in which many were killed. Therefore the last mentioned set out to Cochin on 24th December[18].

This kingdom of Cochin[19] lies over 110 miles away from Calicuth on the sea-shore. Its king is a gentile, of the some sect as the king of Calicuth. This king of Cochin received our ships (we speak now in the words of the Portuguese)[b] in a very friendly way. When we[2] were engaged in trade, there came two brothers[21], who were Indian Christians, born in the city of Caranganor[22], which is about twenty miles away from Cochin. They said that they had a great desire to visit the western countries and that they had made vows also to make a pilgrimage to Rome and Jerusalem.[23] Of their own accord they entered our ships[2] and sailed off with us.[2]

At the time there came a very strong fleet[24] from Calicuth against us to destroy our ships.[2] But, as we became aware of it, we gave ourselves[2] to the deep sea as quickly as we could. With us[2] came the said two brothers besides

---

b. This is one of the interpolations in the Dutch text of which we have spoken earlier. Cf. 3.2.3. pp. 116–118. This corroborates our hypothesis in 2.3.4. pp. 88–90.

gewaar wierden, begaven wy ons, ten snelsten dat wy konden, op de Hooge Zee; by ons hebbende de gemelde twee Gebroederen, nevens eenige Pandsmannen, ons gegeven tegens de geene, welke wy tot Borgen gelaten hadden binnen Cochin, om daar haren handel te drijven. Dus zeylden wy na Lisbona, en onderwegen stierf eenen der Indiaansche Broederen. Den anderen leefd noch. Eyndlijk quamen wy in Junius Anno 1501 te Lisbona aan; van waar Joseph den Indiaan, met bewilligingh des Koninghs, na Romen trock; van daar sigh na Venetien begaf, en weer te Lisbona quam. Van den selven hebben wy veele seer aanmerklijke dingen vernomen; welke wy den Leeser hier sullen voordragen.

Chapter 2

't Vaderland van Joseph den Indiaan. Berigt van de Stad Caranganor Koophandel aldaar.[a]

Joseph den Indiaan had tot sijne Geboorte-plaats de Stad Caranganor, by andere gespeld Cranganor. Ter tijd by sigh te Lisbona bevond telde hy ontrent veertigh Iaren sijns ouderdoms. Sijne couleur was aschverwigh; sijne lenghte middelmatigh; een verstandigh en seer geloofwaardigh Man; nergens grooter vyand van dan van leugenen. Noyt dronk hy Wijn. In al sijn bedrijf toonde hy sigh gantsch reedelijk. In al onse gemeensaamheyd met hem konden wy niet anders vermerken als een sonderlinge vriendlijkheyd en een onbevlekt Geloof.

Sijne Geboort-Stad Caranganor leght over de tnegentigh Mijlen van Calicuth, aan een Rivier genoemd Milibaer, ontrent vijfthien mijlen binnen in 't Land. Deese Stad heeft geen Mueren en strekt sig in de lenghte uyt tot veele Mijlen; doch hier by heeftmen aan te merken dat de Huisen niet soo by malkander gebouwd sijn glijk in andere Steeden; maar verre d'een van d'andere sulker wijs dat yeder als in een bysonder Dorp schijnd te woonen. Veele Wateren vlieten'er door heenen; en de huysen staan gemeenlijk aan 't Water.

Tweederley Volckeren woonen in de gemelde Stad, Christenen, en Heydenen. Doortijds hebbense gesamentlijk

---

a. This Chapter appears as I. Hoofdstuk (Chapter I) on p. 4–5 in *Sonderlinge Reysen*.

some who were given to us² as guarantee against those whom, we² left in Cochin as caution to carry out business there. Thus we² set sail to Lisbon, and on the way one of these two Indian brothers died.²⁵ The other still lives.²⁶ Finally, we² came to Lisbon in June 1501²⁷, from where Joseph the Indian, with the consent of the king, went to Rome and from there to Venice and then came back to Lisbon.²⁹ From the same Joseph we have learned very interesting things which we will now present to the reader.³¹

Chapter 2

The native place of Joseph the Indian. News from the city of Caranganor, the trade there.[b]

Joseph the Indian has as his birthplace the city of Caranganor which is spelled also as Cranganor.³³ At the time he was in Lisbon he was forty years of age.³⁴ He was ash-coloured³⁵ and was medium size in height; he was an intelligent and highly trustworthy man, who was a great enemy of lies. He drank no wine.³⁷ In all his enterprises he showed himself to be completely reasonable. In all our acquaintance with him we could not find in him anything other than remarkable friendliness and blemishless faith.

His native place, Caranganor, lies more than ninety miles away from Calicuth, in a bay called Milibaer³⁸, about fifteen miles inside the land. This city has no walls and stretches many miles in length.³⁹ It should be remarked here, that the houses are not built close to one another as in other cities, but are far apart one from the other, in such a way that each one seems to be living as in a separate village.⁴⁰ Many rivers flow through the place. And the houses generally stand on the bank of the rivers.

Two sorts of people live in the above said city: Christians and pagans. In former times they generally adored idols and

---

b. Compare this title with the corresponding titles in the Italian and Latin texts. Cf. 4.2.0. pp. 152, 153; 3.2.2. p. 113.

d'Afgoden en meenigerley slagh van Dieren aangebeden. Haren Koningh is noch heden Afgodisch. Daar-en-boven sijn hier veele Joden maar seer veraght. Den groot getal kooplieden komen derwaarts uyt Syrien, Egypten, Persien, Arabien en Meden, om haren Handel hier te drijven; want byna alle *Speceryen* werden daar heenen gebraght; ook wassen hier veele dingen welke de Menschen tot nut en gesondheyd dienen.

Chapter 3

Vervolg van de Beschrijvingh der Stad Caranganor. Inwooners, Tempelen, Godsdienst en seldsaamheden daar ontrent.[a]

D'Inwooners deeser Stad sijn verdeeld in driederley soorten. De voornaamste en agtbaarst onder deselve werden in haare Spraak genoemd Naires. D'andere niet van soo grooten Aansien en Rijkdom: Hond. De derd Nuieras (of Polyas)[b] geheeten sijn 't gemeense en arme Volck sigh geneerdende van Pisschery. Deese sijn veel snooder en boosaardiger dan de voorgemelde werden van d'Eedele of Naires seer veraght en gehaat. Indien eenen van deese eenen der Naires te gemoet koomd en niet terstond van hem wijkt so heeft desen 't reght om hem te mogen doorsteken.

Deese driederley Standen hebben yeder hare bysodere Tempelen; de Vrouwspersoonen ook de hare afsonderlijk waar in geenen van 't Manlijk Geslagt sig magh vervoegen. Haar Afgoden offerense veele Vrughten. Ook biddense eenen God in den Hemel aan deinse Tambram noemen en hem afbeelden met drie Aangesigten en t'saamgevouwene handen; even als ofse eenhge Besessing van de H. Drievuldigheyd hadden.

Haare Beelden sijn omhangen met suyver sijn lijnwaad. Wanneerse offeren willen ontdeckense deselve gelijk hier na geseght sal werden. Daar-en-boven hebbense beelden van sommige Gedierten; doch deselve eerense niet meer. Alsse in hare Tempelen gaan soo bedecken sommigh haar Aangesighten met Aarde; andere besyrengen sigh met Water. Driemal yeder dagh begevense sigh in deselve 's morgens, 's middaghs en' 's avonds; en verrighten

---

a. This Chapter appears as II. Hoofdstuk (Chapter II) on pp. 5-7 in *Sonderlinge Reysen.*

many kinds of animals. Its king still is an idol-worshipper. Besides, there are many Jews here, but they are much despised. Merchants in great numbers come there from Syria, Egypt, Persia, Arabia, and Media for trade. For, all sorts of spices are brought there and also there grow many things that are useful to men and to their health.[43]

Chapter 3

Continuation of the description of the city of Caranganor. The inhabitants, the temples[44], worship[45] and the rarities about them[c]

The inhabitants of this city are divided into three groups. The first and the most honourable among them are named Naires in their language. The second which is not of so high status and riches are called dog(s).[46] The third, named Nuieras[47] (or Polyas),[b] are poor people nourishing themselves from fishing. They are more lowly and abject than the above-mentioned, and are much despised and hated by the nobles or Naires. If some of these meet one of the Naires and do not immediately stand aloof from him, then the Nair has the right to pierce him through.

These three classes have their own separate temples. The women have their own temples separately, which no men are allowed to enter. To their idols they offer many fruits. Also they adore one God in heaven, whom they name Tambram[48] and they depict him with three faces and folded hands, as if they had some notion of the Holy Trinity.

In front of their statues they hang a curtain of pure fine linen which they remove when they wish to offer up a sacrifice as will be said later. Besides, they have statues of some animals. But, they do not adore them. When they enter their temples some smear their face with earth, others sprinkle themselves with water. Three times every day they go to the temple, morning, midday

---

b. This is a 'word interpolation' mentioned in 3.2.3. pp. 116-118.
c. Compare this title with those of the Italian and Latin texts. Cf. 4.2.0. pp. 156; 157; 3.2.2. p. 113.

haar Offerhanden. Door een Hoorn of eenigh ander Instrumenten-geluyd roepense 't Volk by een gelijk de Christenen met hare Klocken doen. Dan singense soo lang tot dat haren Grooten Priester koomd aangedaan met een Priesterlijck Kleed. Die dan vervolgens aan den Altaar gaat staan; en een Gesangh begind, ter eeren van sijnen God, in plaats van een Gebed. Stark daar na koomd eenen anderen Priester; die desgelijks yets singhd; en van de Vergaderingh beantwoord werd. Dit werd dus driemaal hervat.

Na deese verrightingen gaat de Priester geheel naakt uyt eene der Poorten des Tempels dragende een Roosen-krans op sijn Hoofd nevens twee Kaarssen en twee gemaakte Hoornen. In de handen houd by twee bloote Swaarden. Dus toegesteld, looptijy ten snelsten even als een onsinnig Mensch na sijnen God; doet den Omhangh open, en reyckt 't een Swaard den Grooten Priester: met 't andere geest by sigh veele wonden; tot soo verre toe, dat by byna ont 't leven is geraakt Voorts springhd hy, even als of hy ten Dans gingh, in een brandende Hout-hoop hier toe bereyd. Eyndlijk koomd hy weer daar uyt met een eser vervaarlijk gelaat, en seght met sijnen God gesproken te hebben, die hem dit of dat heeft aanbevoolen. Daar na begind by 't Volck te leeren, als eenen die van God de Magt daar toe heeft ontfangen. Meer andere Offerhanden hebbense, doch van Joseph den Indiaan niet vermeld.

Chapter 4

Manieren en gewoonten des Konings van Caranganor, en der anderer Ingesetene. Kleeding. Wasschingen. Schrift. Christenen in dese Stad.[a]

De Koning van Caranganor is een Heyden, eerende d'Afgoden. Heeft veele Vrouwen al t'samen sonder schaamte en eer; bedrijvende Ontugt met elk.

Als de Mannen sterven, soo werdense verbrand. Hare Wijven leven niet langer dan agt dagen daar na; dan verbrand

---

a. This appears as III Hoofdstuk (Chapter III) on pp. 7-8 in *Sonderlinge Reysen.*

and evening and make their offering. Through a horn or by the sound of some other instruments they call together the people like the Christians do with their bells. Then they sing some song as their high priest comes, vested in a sacerdotal vestament. He then goes and stands at the altar and begins a song in honour of his god, instead of a prayer. Immediately after that another priest comes. He also sings something similar and is answered by the gathering. This they repeat three times.

After that a priest comes out of one of the doors of the temple completely naked wearing a crown of roses on his head together with two torches and two fake horns. In his hands he holds two drawn swords. So arrayed he runs very speedily to his god, as if in a frenzy and removes the curtain. Then he gives one of the swords to the great priest, and with the other he cuts himself to many wounds so that he nearly collapses. After that he springs, as if he goes to dance, into a burning pyre prepared in advance. Finally, he comes out of it, with a very terrifying face and says to have spoken with his god who commanded him this and that. With that he begins to instruct the people, as one who got the authority from god.[49] They have other offerings too. But, they were not mentioned by Joseph the Indian.[50]

Chapter 4

The manners and customs of the kings of Caranganor and the other inhabitants,[51] Dress, Ablution, Script. The Christians in this city.[b]

The king of Caranganor is a pagan worshipping the idols. He has many wives and has no sense of shame and honour in having unchaste relation with each.[52]

When men die they are cremated. Their wives do not live longer than eight days and after that, they also

---

b. Compare the title with those of the Italian and Latin texts. Cf. 4.2.0. pp. 162, 163; 3.2.2. p. 113.

men deselve ook, met haren wille; waar van by andere breeder berigt te vinden is.

De Soonen des Konings erven 't Rijk niet, maar de geene die sijnen Nabestaanden is in den tweeden Graad. D'onkuysheyd sijner Wijven veroorsaakt datmen sijne Kinderen voor Bastaarden houd; en even hierom werdense tot de Heerschappy niet toegelaten.

By de Begraafnis der Lijkken makense veele seldsame gebeerden. Belangende de Kleeding der Heydenen, de Koning heeft een spitsen Hoed op 't Hoofd van Attalisch Laken. De voornaamste der Stad dragen Bonnetten van Sijde. D' andere gaan bloots hoofds; en voorts al t' samen naakt; alleenlijk de Schaamte bedeckt hebbende met een schoonen Dock van Lijnwaad. Haar Armen vercierense met treslijke Eedele Gesteenten. Ook hebbense seer kostlijke Schoensoolen om hare voeten aardig gemaakt, met Ringen waar in dierbare Besteenten sijn geset. Dese sijn seer hoog by haar geagt.

Yeder dag wasschense sich drie maal; waar toe sy eygene afgesonderde Plaatsen hebben. Soo wel de Mans als Vrouwspersoonen sijn in 't gemeen seer schoon van gedaante. Vercieren 't Hoofd met Eedele Gesreent en Paarlen. De Heydenen schrijven met Ysere Griffien op Schorssen van Bomen, en gebruyken d'Indiaansche Spraak.

Vermits wy hier boven gewach gemaakt hebben dat in dese Stad sig ook Christenen bevinden soo sal 't niet ondiensrig sijn, een weynig breeder bericht hier van te geven. Men weete dan dat by dei Rivier Indus, daar Indien van 't Westen begind, een Eyland is niet verre van den Persischen Stroom, ganoemd Ormus, daar Christenen sijn en anders nergens in dit Gewest dan in de Stad Caranganor (Men moet aanmerken den tijd, waar in dit geschreven is).[c] Anderssins sijn in Indien veele Koningen die den Heere Christus belijden.

are burnt of their own accord. About which more news can be found⁵³ elsewhere.

The sons of the king do not inherit the kingdom, but the one who is his closest relative in the second degree.⁵⁴ Because of the unchastity of the wives their children are considered as bastards. And for that reason they are not admitted to the Lordship.

For the burial of the bodies they hold special ceremonies. Concerning the dress of the pagans: the king has a pointed cap on his head made of attalic linen. The noble men of the city wear bonnets made of silk. The others go bare-headed, and in general are naked⁵⁵, only their shame being covered with a piece of cotton cloth. They adorn their arms with attractive precious stones. Also they have very costly shoesoles⁵⁶ for their feet, very nicely set with rings in which precious stones are set. They are much priced⁵⁷.

Everyday they wash themselves three times, for which they have some special places. Men and women in general are very beautiful in their aspect. They adorn their heads with precious stones and pearls.⁵⁸ The pagans write with iron stylus on the bark of trees⁵⁹ and they use an Indian language.⁶⁰

Since we have mentioned that there are also Christians in this city (of Caranganor)⁶¹, it may not be irrelevant to give some further information about them. Let it be known that at the river Indus where India begins from the West, there is an island, not far from the Persian gulf, named Ormus.⁶² There are Christians there and in no other places in this region than in the city of Caranganor.⁶³ (One should have in mind the time when it was written)ᶜ. Otherwise there are in India many kings who serve the Lord Christ.⁶⁴

---

c. This is an interpolation about which we have spoken in 3.2.2. pp. 116–118.

Chapter 5

Breeder beright van de Christenen te Caranganor. Hoogen Priester. Aarts–bisschoppen. Cardinalen. Patriarchen. Nestorianen. Jacobyten, &c Discours over desen Paus.[a]

De Christenen te Caranganor bouwen hare Huysen met Wanden en hebben aan deselve veelerley Spar-werk; doch de Heydenen dekken hare Huysen met houte Planken. De Kerken deeser Christenen hebben met d'onse eenige gelijckheyd; doch alleenlijk Kruyssen sijn'er in; maar geene Beelden van Heyligen. Sy sijn verwelft gelijk d'onse en op 't bovenste staat een Kruys; gelijk op de Kerken in Europa. Noch Klokken noch Schellen hebbense; en wanneerse 't Volk tot den Godsdienst t'samen roepen soo houdense hier in de gelwoonte der Grieksche Christenen.

't Volk heeft eenen Grooten of Hoogen Priester (Paus)[b]; en deesen ontrent hem twaalf Cardinalen, twee Patriarchen, nevens veele Aarts-bisschoppen en Bischoppen.

Joseph den Indiaan verhaalde ook bat hy met eenen Bischop der stad Caranganor was gevaren na 't Eyland Ormus over de vijfthien-hondered Mijlen wegs. Daar na hy drie Maanden lang te lande tot in Groot Armenien, om aldaar haren Grooten Bischop aan te spreeken: die den gedagten Bischop ten Bischop Maakte (of bevefrigde)[c] en Joseph den Indiaan ten Priester wijdde. Dus handelen alle Indiaansche Christenen, en die van 't Koningrijk Cathay. Haren Over-bischop noemense Catholica. Hy heeft een kruyn geschooren op de manier van een Kruys. Hy steld de Patriarchen aan; den eenen in Indien te Cathay den anderen. De Bischoppen send hy heenen daar 't hem goed dunkt om dese of die Provintic te regeeren.

Van deesen Catholica schrijft Marcus Paulus Venetus in sijn beright van Armenien; en segt dat'er tweederley Christenen

---

a. This appears as IV. Hoofdstuk (Chapter IV) on pp. 8–10 in *Sonderlinge Reysen*.
b. This is an instance of the interpolation mentioned in 3.2.3., pp. 116–118.

THE NARRATIVES OF JOSEPH THE INDIAN 231

Chapter 5

More extensive news about the Christians of Caranganor. High Priest, Archibishops, Cardinals, Patriarch, Nestorians, Jacobites &c. Discourse about their Pope.[d]

The Christians of Caranganore build their houses with walls and have on them a lot of woodwork.[68] The pagans cover their houses with wooden planks. The Churches of these Christians are similar to ours [69], but only a cross is seen in them and no statues of saints. They are vaulted like ours and on the top stands a cross,[70] like that of the churches of Europe. Neither bells nor hand bells have they. When they want to call the people to the services in the church they do it in the manner of the Greek Christians.

These people have a Great or High Priest[71] and around him are twelve Cardinals,[72] two Patriarchs,[73] and many Archbishops and Bishops.[74]

Joseph the Indian said that with one of the Bishops of the city of Caranganor he had travelled to the island of Ormus more than 1500 miles distant and journeyed three months on land upto the great Armania[75] in order to speak to their great Bishop who made (consecrated)[c] the said Bishop and ordained Joseph the Indian as priest.[76] So do all the Christians of India and those of the kingdom of China. They call their overbishop Catholica.[77] He has a tonsure in the likeness of a cross. He appoints the Patriarchs,[78] one in India and the other in China. He sends Bishops whereever he thinks good, to govern the Province.

Marco Polo,[79] the Venetian, speaks of this Catholica in his treatise on Armania and says that there are two kinds of Christians, the Jacobites and the Nestorians,[80] whose Pope is called Jacobita. This is the Catholica about whom we are speaking

---

c. This is another interpolation mentioned in 3.2.3. pp. 116–118.
d. Compare this life with those of the Italian and Latin texts. Cf. 4.2.0. pp. 166, 167; 3.2.2. p. 114.

sijn genoemd Jacobiten en Nestorianen; welker Paus den Naam van Jacobita draagd. Dit is dien Catholica, van wien wy hier spreeken. (De woorden van Marcus Paulus sijn: De Christienen sijn Nestorianen en Jacobyten. Dese hebben eenen grooten Patriarch, van haar genoemd Jacelich. Wy volgen den Antwerpschen druk van 't Jaar 1563.)[e]

Maar vermits deesen Paus aan veele de Waardigheyd van Geestlijke Bedieningen geeft, en veele Bischoppen maakt soo sou men mogen vragen van wien hem dese Magt koomd alsoo de H. Roomsche Kerck die eenigh is in 't Geloof met meer dan eenen Roomschen Bischop heeft? Hier op staat te berigten dat Joseph den Indiaan na Romen is getrokken doe Paus Alexander de VI. regeerde; die Joseph vraagde waar van daan dien Catholica de Magt had, om Bischoppen te maken in de Landen van 't Oosten? Deesen gaf hem tot antwoord: S. Petrus was Bischop 't Antiochien geweest. Doe nu ontrent dien tijd te Romen een groote Tweedragt was ontstaan veroorsaakt door Simon den Toveraar, wiens Naam sig aldaar een geheugems heeft nagelaten soo wierd Petrus na Romen geroepen om Simon te schande te maken en d'aangevogtene Christenen te hulp te komen. Eer nu S. Pieter sig van Antiochien na Romen begaf stelde hy in sijne Plaats eenen Stadhouder; wiens Nasaat (in een vervolgende Successie)[e] even den selven is die in de Morgen-landen regeerd en den Naam van Catholica voerd; tot dit hooge Ampt verkooren werdende door de twaalf Cardinalen in Armenien &c.

Hier op nu maakt de Roomsch-Catholijke Schrijver deese Aanmerkingh: Yeder kan wel bemerken, dit valsch te sijn. Want Christus heeft maar eene Bruyd, welker Figuer is de Christlijke Kerk. Buyten deselve is geen saligheyd te hoopen. Al wat men van andere seght, is Fabel-werck. Dit segge ik daarom, op dat niemand sigh ondersta af te wijcken van de sterkte des Steens, die Christus is. Een God 'is' er; een Geloof, en een Heylige Christlijke Kerk.[f]

here. (The words of Marco Polo are: The Christians are Nestorians and Jacobites. These have a Patriarch called by them Jacelich. We follow the Antwerp edition of the year 1563).[81]

But since this Pope confers the dignity of spiritual offices on many and creates many Bishops one could ask from whom he gets this authority since the holy Roman Church which is unique in faith has no more than one Roman Bishop.[82] Here we have to say that Joseph the Indian had gone to Rome when Pope Alexander VI was Pope. He asked Joseph from where this Catholica had the authority for making Bishops in the countries of the East. The latter answered him that St. Peter to had been Bishop in Antioch. Around that time there arose a great discord in Rome caused by Simon the Magus[83], whose name has left for himself reputation. Then Peter was called to Rome put Simon to shame and to help the incriminated Christians. Before Peter went from Antioch to Rome he installed in his place a vicar whose descendent (in a following succession) is precisely the same who rules in the Eastern regions, and bears the name of Catholica. He is elected to the high office by the twelve cardinals in Armenia.[84]

Here, about this the Roman Catholic writer makes this remark[85]: Anybody can see that this is false. For Christ has only one Spouse, whose Figure is the Christian Church. Outside of this there is no salvation. All other things that any one says is fable work. I say therefore, in order that nobody should dare deviate from the strength of the stone that is Christ. There is one God, one faith and one Holy Christian Church.[f]

---

e. This is another interpolation about which we have spoken in 3.2.3. pp. 116–118.
f. This is another interpolation of which we have spoken in 3.2.3. pp. 116–118.

Chapter 6

Priester deeser Christenen. Doop. Biecht. Wijwater. Avondmal, sonder Wijn, by gebrek. Watse gebruyken in plaats van Wijn. Dooden-begraving. Euangelien. Vastern. Heilyge dagen. Kloosteren. Der priesteren Kuysheyd. Geleerde. Jaar-verdeeling.[a]

Sy hebben Priesters, Leviten, en Onder-helpers. De Priesteren drangen geen Kruyn op haar Hoofd maar eenig hayr boven op 't selve. Die Kindernen doopense niet voor datse veertig daagen oud sijn ten ware datse in doods-gevaar geraakten. Sy Biechten gelijk de Roomschgesinde; en ontfangen ook alsoo 't Sacrament. Geen Heiylige Oly hebbense; maar in plaats van deselve zeegenen sy de Ligchamen. Wanneerse in haare Kerken gaan soo besprengense sig met gewijd Water gelijk by de Roomsch-Catholilijke gebruyklijk is.

't Ligchaam en Bloed Christi zegenen sy; en bedienen 't Sacrament des Avondmaals met ongedeessemd Brood. Sy hebben geenen Wijn vermits dit Land geen Wijndruyven heeft en derhalven weykense Rosijnen in Water; parssense dan uyt en gebruyken dit Sap in plaats van Wijn. Deese Rosijnen werden haar uyt Cathay toegevoerd.

Sy begraven hare Dooden gelijk wy. (De Schrjver is een Portugeezsche.)[b] Soo hast yemand gestorven is koomen harer veele by een en brassen dan agt dagen long met malkander. Als nu dit Slempen een eynde heeft genomen soo biddense voor den Dooden. Ook is by haar gebruyklijk Testamenten te maken; en der selver Inhoud werd seer precys uytgevoerd.

Wanneer yemand sterft sonder Testament na te laten soo is den geenen die hem 't aldernaast bestaat sijnen Erfgenaam. De Weduw des overledenen neemd haar ingebragte Houwlijks-goed na haar en gaat weer by haar Ouders woonen. Mag oock in een Jaar tijds geenen anderen ten Man neemen.

---

a. This appears in V. Hoofdstuk (Chapter V) on p. 16 in *Sonderlinge Reysen*.
b. This is another interpolation referred to 3.2.3. pp. 116-118.

THE NARRATIVES OF JOSEPH THE INDIAN 235

Chapter 6

The Priests of these Christians, Baptism, Confession, Holy Water, Last Supper (Eucharist), special wine, in scarsity. What they use in the place of wine. Burial of the dead. Gospels, Fasts, Sacred days. Hermitages, Chastity of the priests, Learned men. Division of the year.[c]

They have priests, levites and underhelpers.[87] The priests do not have tonsure but a little hair is kept on the top of their head, as a tuft.[88] They do not baptise the children before they are forty days of age except when they are in danger of death.[89] They confess like those faithful to Rome[90] and receive also the Sacrament.[91] They do not have (the sacrament of) sacred oil,[92] but instead they bless the body. When they enter the churches they sprinkle themselves with holy water as is done among the Roman catholics.

They consecrate the Body and Blood of Christ, and they celeberate the Sacrament of Last Supper with unleavened bread.[93] They have no wine. Since no vine grows in that country, they soak raisins in water and squeeze them and use this sap instead of wine. These raisins are imported from China.[94]

They bury their dead as we do. (The writer is a Portuguese)[c] When somebody dies many of his relatives come together and eat together for eight days together. When the banquet is over they pray for the dead. It is a custom among them to make the last will and testament and the content of the testament is very precisely executed.[95]

If somebody dies without leaving a testament, then he who is the nearest relative to him is his heir. The widow of the dead takes the dowry she brought and returns to stay in house of her parents'. She is not allowed to marry anothsr man within a year.

---

c. Compare the title with those of the Italian and Latin texts of 4.2.0. pp. 172, 173, 3.2.2. p. 114.

Sy hebben de vier Euangelien der vier Euangelisten. De Vasten en Advent onderhoudense seer streng; ter dier tijd vastende en biddende. Danden Goeden Vrydag af tot Paasschen toe nuttigense geenerley Spijs. De Nagt des Goeden Vrydags brengense door met Predicatien te hooren en te bidden. De jaarlijksche Heylige Dagen vierense seer nauw; te weeren voor eerst den Heyligen Paaschdag met twee volgende dagen. D' Octave van Paaschdag agtense hooger van eeneigen anderen dag; vermits volgens haar voorgeben S. Thomas op den selven sijne handen in Christi zijde leydde en daar by ondervond dat hy geenen Geest was. Daar na vierense den dag van Christi Hemmelvaart. Desgelijks dien de H. Drievuldiheyd; Mariae Geboorte, Reyniging en Hemelvaart d'openbaaring Christi de Dagen van al d'Apostelen. Ook onderhoudense de Sondagen met een sondelinge viijt. Den eersten dag der Maand Julius vieren sy seer hoog (gelijk ook de Heydenen doen) om S. Thomas will. Hebben Kloosters, waar in Swarte Monicken leven in een sonderlinge Kuysheyd; gelijk ook hare Priesters, en de Maagden in de Vrouven Kloosteren doen. Indien eenigen Priester in onkuysheyd bevonden werd soo mag hy geen Mis meer verrigten.

By deese Christenen valt geen Echtscheyding. 't Sy een der getrouwde goed of quaad is beyde moetense tot hare dood toe by malkander blijven. Driemal jaarlijks ontfangense 't Heylige Sacrament Hebben veele geleerde Lieden en goede Predikanten; desgelijks goede Schoolen. De Leeraars leggen haar gelijk Joseph seyde den Byble heerlijk uyt. 't Leesen der Propheeten is by haar gebruyklijk.

Haare kleeder-dragt is als die van de Moorn; bestaande in Roken van Lijnwaad. 't Jaar verdeelense in twaalf Maanden, gelijk als wy; en hebben ook om 't vierde Jaar een Schrickeljaar van drie honder ses-en-tsesting dagen. Haren dag werd verdeeld (niet in vier-en-twintigh uyren als by ons maar)[d] in tsestigh deelen. Deese deelen onderscheydense by daah aan de Son; by nagt aan de Starren.

They have four gospels of the four evangelists.[96] They observe very strictly the Lent and the Advent[97], with fast and prayer. They do not take any food from Good Friday until Easter day.[98] They spend the night of Good Friday hearing sermons and in prayer. They observe very strictly the annual sacred days namely: First of all the Holy Resurrection with the following two days.[99] They celebrate the octave of the day of Easter with greater solemnity than any other day[100]. For according to their opinion, on the same day St. Thomas put his hand in the side of Christ and thereby found that he was not a ghost. After that they clebrate the Ascension of Christ.[101] Likewise they celebrate the feasts of the Holy Trinity, the Nativity of Mary, her Purification[103] and Assumption, the day of the Transfiguration (Revelation) of Christ[104], the day of all the Apostles and also the Sundays with exceptional zeal. They celebrate very solemnly (so also the pagans do) the first day of the month of July in memory of St. Thomas.[105] They have hermitages where black monks live in exceptional chastity[106], like their priests and the virgins of the hermitages of women. If any priest is found in unchastity, he is no longer allowed to celebrate Mass.[107] Among these Christians no divorce occurs. Whether one of the married is good or bad both must remain together until their death.[108] Three times a year they receive the Holy Sacrament.[109] They have many learned men and good preachers and also good schools. These teachers, as Joseph said, explain very magnificently the Bible. The reading of the Prophets is a custom among them.[110]

Their (mode of) dress is like that of the Moors consisting of frocks of linen.[111] They divide the year into twelve months like us and they have also every fourth year a leap year of three hundred and sixty five days.[112] Their day is divided (not into twenty four hours as among us but) into sixty parts.[113] These parts they distinguish at day time from the sun and at night from the stars.[114]

---

d. This is another interpolation mentioned in 3.2.3. pp. 116–118.

238 INDIA IN 1500 AD

CHAPTER 7

Legging van Caranganor, Winter, Schipvaart en Scheepen, van Elephanten na de Zee getrokken.[a]

D'inwooner van Caranganor leggen volgens 't beright van Joseph den Indiaan, tusschen de Somer-Sonnen wende (Solstitium Aestivum),[b] en den Aequator, of Evenar.[b] Haren langesten dag is van derthien en een half uyr den kortesten van thien uyren na onse uyren te reekenen niet na de hare die veel korter sijn gelijk in 't veorige Hoofdstuk getoond is.

Wanneer de Son in 't Teeken van Taurus, of de Stier[b] is soo valt de Schaduw haar lijn-regt op 't hoofd. Als de Son sich in Cancer of de Kreeft bevind soo werpt deselve haar Schaduw tegen 't Zuyden, of in Virgo (de Maagd),[b] so hebbense de Schaduw wederon lijn-regt. Maar in Capricornus of de Steenbok valt de Schadouw ten Noorden.

De Jaar-tijd veranderd sig van 't midden der May-maand, tot in 't midden van Augustus. Beduerende deese drie Maanden sullense om geenerley oorsaken wil sig met hare Scheepen op zee begeven. Veele van deese Scheepen in Indien varen na 't Westen; andere na Arabien sommige na Persien, na de Pontus Euxinus, of Roode Zee; na de hooge Indische Zee tot in de Morgenlanden aan Chersonesus Aurea, en ook tot aan 't eynd van Indien voorby Cathay, 't Eyland Taprobana, Faylla, en veele meer andere.

De Scheepen welkese tot hare Vaardten gebruyken sijn seer groot soo datse meer dan twaalf Zeylen voeren en een meenigte van Roeyers hebben. Dese komen uyt d'Eylanden. Andere bereyden allerley Zeylen en Touwwerk van Cottoen.

---

a. This appears as VI Hoofdstuk (Chapter VI) in *Sonderlinge Reysen* beginning on p. 12. As we have a indicated in 3.2.1. pp. 111–112. the VI Hoofdstuk (Chapter VI) is equivalent to Chapters 7,8,9, of the Italian and Latin texts. We have divided this Chapter VI of the Dutch text into three chapters corresponding to the Chapters 7,8,9, of the Italian and Latin texts, as indicated in 3.2.1. Hence we have divided also the title of this Chapter accordingly.

THE NARRATIVES OF JOSEPH THE INDIAN 239

CHAPTER 7

Site of Caranganor, Winter, Navigation and ships dragged to the sea by elephants.[c]

The inhabitants of Caranganor, according to the reports Joseph, are situated between the Summer Solstice (Solistitium Aestivum) and the equator or 'Evenaar'.[115] Its longest day is of thirteen and a half hours, the shortest is of ten hours, according to the calculation of our hours and not according to theirs, which are much shorter as said in the foregoing chapter.[116]

When the sun is in the sign of Taurus or the 'Stier', the shadow falls perpendicular upon their head. When the sun is in Cancer or 'Kreeft' it casts its shadow towards the south, and in the Virgin, the 'Maagd', they have again the shadow in perpendicular, but when it is in Capricorn or in 'Steenbok' the shadow falls in the north.[117]

The seasons of the year change from the middle of the month of May, up to the middle of August. During these three months, no for reasons will they sail with their ships in the sea. Many of those ships in India sail to the West[119], others to Arabia, some to Persia, to the Pontus Euxinus, Red Sea, to the high Indian Ocean[120] unto the Orient up to the 'Chersonesus Aurea'[121] and also up to the end of India, beyond China, the island of Taparbane[122], Failla[123] and many others.

The ships[125] which they use for their travels are very big so as to have more than twelve sails and lots of rowers. These come from the islands.[124] Others prepare various sails and cordage of cotton. They build their ships firmly with iron

---

b. We find in the Dutch text interpolation of Latin and Dutch equivalents for the sign of the Zodiac, which are not fouend in the Latin and Italian texts.
c. Compare this title with those of the Italian and Latin texts in 4.2.0. pp. 180,181 and 3.2.0. p. 114.

Hare Scheepen bouwense wel vast met ysere Nagelen. Dit verhaal ik hier om dat sommige voorgeven datse alleenlijk houte Nagelen gebruyken; waar over ik Joseph vlijtig ondervraagd heb die 't tegendeel getuygde en my ook berigtte dat d'Indianen hare Kielen toerusten gelijk als wy d'onse welkense versorgen met Pek vermengd met Wierook en andere dingen, Wanneerse hare Scheepen in Zee willen brengen soo pleegnese Elephanten daar voor te spannen doch vermits hier door veeele Lieden om 't leven geaakten so hebbense deese manier van doen nagelaten en spannen soo veel meer Menschen in om dien swaren last in Zeen te trecken.

Chapter 8

Verscheydene Munten. Aardbodem en Vrugten. Hoogen ouderdom der Inwooners, sonder eenen Tand verlooren te hebben. Dieren. Goed koop Hoenderen.[a]

Driederley Munten gaan by die van Caranganor in swang. Hare Goudene Munt niemense Zaraph, sijnde in waarde soo veel als een Ducaat. Een anderee van Silver draagd den Naam Paran; doende soo veel als ses Schellingen na onse waardeering. Dan is 'er noch een van onterent eene Schelling. Al deese Munten sijn gettekend met des Konings Afbeelding en onderschrift. In haar Land hebbense noch Goud noch andere Metallen; maar 't werd haar van elders gebragt uyt sommige Bergen wel drie honderd Mijlen van daar.

't Gewest rondom Caranganor heeft een vlacken Aardbodem sijnde groen en vrugtbaar. In een groote streek wegs verneemd men geene Gebergten. Heeft een goeden milden Hemel. De Mannen sijn Aschverwig van couleur doch die in de Gebergten woonen sijn blanker en sterven eerst in een goeden ouderdon. Joseph verhaalde ons dat er Lieden waren over de honderd jaren oud welke noch noyt eenen Tand uyt den mond gevallen was.

---

a. This Chapter formed part of the VI Hoofdstuk (Chapter VI) in *Sonderlinge Reysen*, appearing on pp. 13–14. We have reorganised this part into a new chapter corresponding to the chapter division of the Italian and Latin texts as indicated in 3.2.1. pp. 111–112.

nails. I tell it here, because some think that they use only wooden pegs. I diligently asked Joseph about this and he witnessed the contrary.[126] He also told me that the Indians fit out the ship with pitch mixed with incense and other things. When they want to bring the ship to the sea they use elephants to move it. But since many persons were often killed when elephants were used they abandoned this manner of doing and put many men to draw such a heavy burden into the sea.

Chapter 8

Different coins, soil and fruits. Longevity of the inhabitants without loosing a teeth, Animals, cheap chicken.[b]

Three kinds of money are in use among the people of Caranganor.[128] Their gold coin, they call Zaraph,[129] has the value of a ducat. The second of silver, bears the name Paran,[130] having a value of six shillings[131] according to our estimation. There is still another, of about one shilling with the figure of the king and underscript.[132] In their country they have neither gold nor other metals, but they are brought there from elsewhere from some mountains around three hundred miles from there.[133]

The region around Caranganor has a flat land, being green and fertile. In a long stretch of the country one sees no mountains; it has a good mild climate. The men are ash coloured but those who live in the mountains are white and they die only at a very old age. Joseph told us that there are persons who are more than hundred years old who have lost not even a tooth.

The country as we have already said is very fertile, although wheat does not grow there. Also they have no horses.

---

b. Corresponding to the division of the chapter indicated in a, we have also divided the title of Chapter VI of *Sonderlinge Reysen*. Compare this title with the corresponding titles of the Italian and Latin texts. Cf. 4.2.0. pp. 184,185, 3.2.2. p. 114.

't Land gelijk alreeds gesegt is toond sig seer vrugtvaar alhoewel 't geen Tarwe draagd. Ook heeft men hier geene Paarden, 't Koorn brenghdmen van andere Eylanden derwaarts. De Paarden kommen van Ormus, en uyt sommige Geberghten. D'inwooners gebruyken deselve niet dan alleen om lasten te dragen wanneerse eenige Waren na een andere Plaats willen vervoeren. Selfs gebruykense die niet in den Oorlog.

't Voetvolk begeeft sig ten Strijde gewapend met Boogen Pijlen Swaarden en Rondassen. Ook begruykense somtijds wel Spiessen. Seer goede Schermers en Vegters sijnse. Eenige maken Pantzieren van Visch-huyden voor alle Beschut schootvry. Andere neemen Yser daar toe.

Allerley Gedierten vindemen hier als Runderen, Hamelen. Schapen, Buffels en meer andere soorten; van de Heydenen geeerd als Goden. Meenigte van Elephanten sijn'er daar-en-boven veel Darkens Hoenderen, Gassen en ander Gevogelte. Honderd Hoenderen kammen hier kopen voor eene gulden.

Chapter 9

Rijs.[a]

Seer schoone Rijs wast in dit Land waar van d'Inwooners seer goed Brood bereyden. Twintigderley slag van Kruyden vindmen hier welke de Meschen tot goed Voedsel verstrecken. Groote lust hebbebse tot Wortelen. 't Ontbreekt haar niet aan Oly en Suyker; maar wel aan Granaat-Appelen, Wijnstocken, Persicken en diergelijke Gewassen. Daar tegens hebbense een ongelooflijke meerighte van Vrijgen van welke Vrugten 't Land vol is. Noch heeft men hier eenen anderen Boom dragenede Indiaansche Noten; van welke men bekoomd Oly, Wijn, Azijn en Syuker; waar van ook Strabo heeft gesprooken. Breeder sal hier van gehandeld werden in 't volgende Hoofdstuk.

---

a. This Chapter originally formed part of the VI. Hoofdstuk (Chapter VI) in *Sonderlinge Reysen*, We have divided the chapter corresponding to the chapter division of the Italian and Latin texts. Cf. 3.2.1. pp. 111-112. We have also divided the title of Chapter VI of *Sonderlinge Reysen* correspondingly. See b.

They bring the coin from some islands. The horses come from Ormus and from some mountains. The inhabitants do not use them except for carrying burdens when they transport some merchandise from one place to another. They do not use them in war.

Foot soldiers go to battle armed with arrows and bows, swords and bucklers. Sometimes they use lances also. They are good sword jugglers and fighters. Some make cuirras from the skin of fishes, safe against every shot. Some use iron for that.

One finds here various animals like cattle, camels, sheep and buffalos and many other sorts, revered by the pagans as gods. There are great many elephants. Besides, there are many pigs, chickens and geese and other fowls. One can buy a hundred chickens for one gulden.

Chapter 9

Rice. [b]

Very beautiful rice grows in this land from which the inhabitants prepare very good bread.[136] One finds here, twenty kinds of herbs, which serve as good food for the inhabitants. They like very much the roots.[137] There is no scarcity for oil and sugar, but they do not have pomegranates, vine, peaches and similar plants. On the contrary, they have an incredible number of figs,[138] of which the country is full. Here there is also another tree bearing Indian nuts from which[139] are made oil, wine, vinegar and sugar of which also Strabo[141] has spoken. More about which will be spoken in the following chapter.[142]

---

b. Compare this title with the corresponding titles of the Italian and Latin texts. Cf. 4.2.0. pp. 188, 189; 3.2.2. p. 114. See a.

Chapter 10

Berigt van den Indiaanschen Palmboom, van welke men Wijn, Asijn, Oly en Suyker maak, nevens meer andere dingen. Peper, Gingebar, Speceryen.[a]

In de Maand van Augustus maaktmen van den Indiaanschen Palmboom insonderheyd vierderley voor de Menschen seer dienstige dingen op de volgende wijse. De gedagte Maande Augustus is der Inwoonderen Lentetijd. Dan snoeyense de Palmbomen gelijk men de Wijnranken doet; en vermitsse in die jaartijd 't meeste Sap hebben soo loopt'er een vogt uyt gelijk uyt de gesneedene Wijnranken.

Dit Nat een wit Water gelijk vergaderense en drinken 't voor Wijn. Dit duurd dus drie dagen na dat dien Boom gewond is geworden. Dan werd dit Water van sig selven tot Edick. De geene welke Suyken of Honigh willen maken neemen 't Water 't welk in d'eerste drie dagen uytgedruppeld is en sieden 't in een Ketel tot dat'er niet meer dan 't derd deel van overig blijft. Na diese kooking werd het tot een seer soeten Hoonigh. Dan gietens'er weer Water op en schuymen 't gedurig tot op den twintigsten dag. Dus gereynigd sijnde werd het voor seer goeden Wijn gebruykt. Dande komen der Vrught parssense Oly. Dus veele nuttigheden trektemen van dien eenen Boom. Van 't half-verbrandde Hout des Booms makense Houts-koolen ten brand. Van de Schorssen weetense Touw-werk te bereyden. Als men de Kornen der Nooten laat droog werden sijnse een goede Spijs voor Menschen. Deselve dan in Water geweykt geven Voeder voor Runderen en Schaapen.[c]

[De Portugeezen weeten'er oock Brandewijn van te maken. De Stam van de Cocos-boom diend d'Indianen om'er een Schuyt van te bereyden sonder dat'er een eenige ysere Nagel ontrent koomd. Zeylen en Touwen komen al t'samen van deesen Boom. Men bereyd'er Hoofd-hoeden of Deksels van tegens den Regen; desgelijks Matten tot Deksels over de Palankyns, waar in de Vrouwen sig laten dragen. De Schaal der Noot verstrekt voor

---

a. This Chapter appears as VII Hoofdstuk (Chapter VII) on pp. 15-16 in *Sonderlinge Reysen*.

Chapter 10

Information about the Indian palm tree from which wine, vinegar, oil and sugar are made.[143] *Besides more things, pepper, ginger, spices.*[b]

In the month of August they make four kinds of things, very useful to mankind from the Indian palm trees in the following way. Forenamed month of August is the spring time for the inhabitants. They trim the palm trees as we do with the vine branches, and in that time of the year the trees have the highest quantity of sap, which flows out as from a trimmed vinebranch.

This white liquid they collect and drink for wine. It remains so for three days after this tree has been cut. Then this water becomes vinegar by itself. Those who want to make sugar or honey take the water, which has trickled down in the first three days and cook it in a kettle till there remains only one third of it. After this cooking, it becomes very sweet honey. Then they pour again water and scum continually up to twenty days. Thus being purified it is used as a very good wine. From the kernel of the fruit, they press oil.[144] Thus they draw many useful things from this tree alone. From the half-burned wood of the tree they get charcoal for burning. From the barks they know how to prepare cords.[145] When the kernel of the nuts is dried they are good for food for men.[146] This then soaked in water gives good fodder for the cattle and sheep.[c]

[The Portuguese know also how to make Brandewine from it. The trunk of the coco-nut trees serves the Indians for preparing a (small) boat without using any iron nail for it. Sails and cords also are made from this tree. From it men prepare hats for the head or covering against the rain. Similarly mats for covering over the palanquin wherein ladies let themselves to be carried. The shell of the nut serves as cup for drinking. The

---

b. Compare this title with the corresponding titles in the Italian and Latin texts. Cf. 4.2.0. pp. 192,193; 3.2.2. p. 115.
c. What follows in Dutch text is an interpolation about which we have spoken elsewhere. Cf. 3.2.3. pp. 116–118. We have give it in brackets.

een Drink-becker. De buytenste ruyge Schel voor Werk, om de reeten der Scheepen dar meede te stoppen. Dan de binnenste maaktmen behalven de Drink-vaten ook Leepels, en Koppen om uyt t'eeten of Water mee te scheppen. Met de Melk uyt de Cocos-noot kookense hare Rijs. Uyt 't Sap werd een treslijk Zuyker bereyd. D,Oly is goed om tot hare Spijsen te gebruyken of om in Lampen te branden. Diend daar-en-boven tegens veelerley gebreeken. Kortlijks een geheel Schip met alles wat'er aan is bestaat enkelijk van den Cocos-boom. De Menschen met alles watse behoeven tot Dekesel en Voedsel konnen van den selven genoeg tot haar onderhoud trecken; en men kan seggen datse selfs wegens 't gebruyk tot Spijs en Drank meer dan de helft uyt Cocos bestaan.]

Ontrent Caranganor wast veel Peper welkese in de Son droogen op dat deselve elders gezaayd werdende niet mogt opkomen tot haare schade. De Peeper-boomen sijn nergens in Indien soo meernigvuldig als hier; doch met groot. Overvloedig veen Gengebar werd hier gewonnen. Ook heeft men 'er Mirabolanen, Cassie, en byna allerley soorten van Speceryen. Hier mee drijven de Mooren een grooten handel vermits deese dingen vervoerd werden na Babylonien, of Alcair, een Stad aan de Rivier de Nyl; van daar na Alexandria, Damascus en eyndlijk in Persien. Brengense ook over 't Gebergte na Cathay. Dit nu sal genoeg sijn van de Stad Caranganor keeren derhalven weer na Calicuth.

Chapter 11

Beschrijving der Stad Calicuth Haren Koning een Afgodendienaar. Kooplieden, welke in deese Stad komen, tot haren Handel. Onder deselve Malasines. Koninglijk Hof. Lijfwagten. De Heydensche Inwooners derven noyt op de Zee eeten. Medalien.[a]

Die Stad Calicuth legt tegen 't Westen van de Stad Caranganor over de tnegentig Mijlen aan de Zee en heeft een vermaarde Haven. Is ook grooter van de Stad Caranganor. (Is

---

a. This Chapter appears as VIII Hoofdstuk (Chapter VIII) on pp. 17–19 in *Sonderlinge Reysen*.

outer rough skin is used to fill the crevices of the ships. Besides vessels for drinking out of it they make also spoons for eating and cups for taking water. With the milk of the coconut they cook their food. From the sap good sugar is prepared The oil is good for using with their food, or for burning in their lamps. It serves moreover manifold purposes. In short the whole ship with all that is on it consists only from the coconut tree. For all they need for food and shelter people can draw from the tree sufficiently enough for their subsistence One can say that more than half of what they need for food and drink comes form the coconut trees.]

Around Caranganor grows much pepper which they dry in the sun[147]; because the same planted elsewhere does not grow to its own discredit. The pepper trees are nowhere in India as numerous as here, but they are not high. A great lot of ginger is grown here, Also they have Mirabolens Cassias, and other manifold spices. The Moors trade with these. Since these things are transported to Babylonia, or Alcair, a city on the river Nile, and from there to Alexandria, Damascus and finally to Persia. They carry it also over the mountains to China. This now will be enough about the city of Caranganor and therefore we go back to Calicuth.

Chapter 11

Description of the city of Calicuth. Its king an idolator. Merchants, who come there for trade. Among them Malasenes. Royal Court. The pagan inhabitants never dare to eat on the sea. Medals.[b]

The city of Calicuth lies more than ninety miles, west of the city of Caranganor[148], [and is up to now a famous commercial city, the most important of a great kingdom in the south-west part of East Indies, with a very important harbour on the

---

b. Compare this title with the corresponding titles in the Italian and Latin texts. Cf. 4 2.0. pp. 196,197: 3.2.2. p. 115.

noch hedensdaags een vermaarde Koopstad en de voornaamste van een groot Koningrijk in 't Westerdeel ten Zuyden van Oost-Indien, met een redelijke Haven op de Kust van Malabar, byna halfweegen tusschen Cananor en Caranganor). Haaren Heer of Koning is een Afgodendienaar van deselve Secte als dien van Caranganor is. In haren Godsdienst Ongeloof en manieren kammen geen onderscheyd bermerken. Derhalven behoeven wy niet verder hier van te spreeken.

Hier sijn en komen veele Kooplieden Persianen, Mooren, Indianen; Meders, Syriers, Assyriers, Arabiers, Egyptenaren, en voorts uyt byna alle Gewesten der Weereld. Yeder derselve brengd hier wat; soo dat hier werd gevonden alles wat tot der Menschen onderhoud noodig is.

Onder deese Kooplieden sijn'er eenige welke men Guzuratters noemd en met meenigerley Koopmanschappen handel drijven. Geheel Indien brengd hier kostlijke Waren. 't Getal der Kooplieden was hier aldergrootst doe die van Cathay derwaarts quamen. Deese Cathayers geloven in Christum, en sijn blanke Lieden gelijk d'Europianen. Pleegen sterk op Calicuth te handelen met kostlijke Waren. Maar als deesen Koning haar begon qualijk te tracteren, trockense van daar weg; quamen na eenige tijd weer derwaarts en sloegen seer veele der Inwooners van Calicuth dood; na welken tijd sy sig niet weer daar heenen begaven; maar trocken na Meliopetam (Masulipatam) welke Stad staat onder den Koning van Narsinga. Dit Land siet tegens 't Osten en legt tnegentig Mijlen van de Rivier Indus. Hier drijvense nu haren Koophandel.

Seekere Natie, genoemd Malasines, brengen hier veelerley Waren als Sijde, Koper, Lood, Tin, Muscus en andere welriekende dingen. Daar tegens vermangelense en voeren met haar weg Coralen en allerley Specieryen. Seggen dat haar Land ses duysend Mijlen wegs van Calicuth legt. Boven maten kostlijke cieraden dragense op hare hoofden; vermitsse seer rijk sijn.

Der Koning van Calicuth werd van sijne Onderdanen genoemd Baufer. Hy heeft een groot Koninglijk Hof, gelijk een Amphitheater; en altijd ontrent hem tot sijne Lijfwagt seven duysend Mannen om hem te bewaren. Deese gaan by nagt door

Malabar Coast, about half way between Cananor and Caranganor[149]. Its lord or king is an idol worshiper of the same sect as that of the king of Caranganor. In their Religion, belief and manners one cannot see any distinction. Therefore we ought not speak any further about that.

Here there are many merchants and many come there, Persians, Moors, Indians, Medians, Syrians, Assyrians, Arabs, Egyptians and from almsot all the regions of the world.[150] Each of them bring here something so much so that one can find here all that is necessary for the subsistence of mankind.

Among these merchants there are some called Guzurathis[151] and they engage in manifold trades. All India brings here precious merchandise. The number of merchants was at its greatest when those of China came there. These Chinese believe in Christ[152] and they are as white as the Europeans. They used to transact commerce very intensively at Calicuth with costly merchandise. But, when this king started to treat them badly they went away from there, came back after some time and killed very many inhabitants of Calicuth after which time they have never come there, instead they went to Meilopetam, (Masilupatam)[153] which is under the king of Narasinga.[154] This country looks towards the East and lies ninety miles from the river Indus. Now they transact their commerce there. These people named Malasines[155] bring here manifold things like silk, copper, lead, tin, musk, and other sweet-smelling things. Against that they carry corals and different spices. They say that their country lies six thousand miles away from Calicuth. They wear ornaments, since they are very rich.

The king of Calicuth is called Baufer by his subjects. He has a great royal court like an amphitheatre. There are seven thousand men always close to him like body guards to protect him. In the night they go round through the city, which is big and open, having no walls. Therefore there are squads of guards, three hundred strong, to avoid that something harm should happen to the people while they are asleep.

In this court there are four halls, one for the Moors, the other for the Indians, the third for the Jews, and the fourth for

de Stad om welke groot en open is geenen Muur hebbende. Ter dier oorsaak sijn'er Rotten van Wachters drie honderd sterk om te verhoeden dat'er niet yets terwijl 't volk in slaap is ontstaan mogt t'harer schaade.

In dit Hof sijn vier groote Salen d'eene voor de Mooren d'andere, voor d'Indianen, de derde voor de Jooden, de vierde voor de Christenen. Elk deser Natien weet waar sy verhoord sullen werden; 't welk haer anderweegen niet toe gelaten werd. Eerse derwaarts gaan moetense sig wasschen; anders soudemen haar als vuyle en onreyne niet voor den Koning laten verschijnen.

De Heydenen te Calicuth hebben deese gewoonte: Nimmermeer eetense op de Zee: want indiense sulks deeden soo soudense noyt den Koning derven aanschouwen. Noch eens moet ik herhalen 't geen alreeds hier boven gesegd is te weeten dat d'Indiaansche Vrouwen niets eerlijker en roemwaardiger achten dan met hare gestorvene Mannen te sterven; en derhalven met der selver Lijken begeeren verbrand te werden. Men behoefd sig hier over niet te verwonderen wijl haar sterk ingeprent is datse anders geen geluksalige onsterflijkheyd souden konnen erlangen. Hier van spreekt ook Strabo in sijne Geographia lib. 15 in 't Capittel beginnende, Nicolaus Damascenus segt, dat hy 't Antiochien &c.

Te Calicuth is in yeder jaar op seekeren bestemden tijd een seer voortreflijke Jaarmarkt. Derwaarts komen dan meenigten van Menschen uyt verce Landen insonderheyd uyt Cathay; dan noch uyt Indien, Persien, Meden, Assyrien, Syrien, Turkyen, Arabien en uyt Egypten aan de vermaarde Rivier de Nyl, maar voornamentlijk van Babylon, of Alcair.

Wy vraagden Joseph den Indiaan of men hier ook wist te spreeken van onse Landen in Europa? Waar op hy antwoordde dat Romen, Venetien en Frankrijk hy haar in een groote agting waren. Dat insonderheyd de Venetiaansche Ducaten en Silvere Munt hier in groote waarde was. Deselve Joseph te Venetien gekomen sijnde toonde aldaar de Venetiaansche Signoria eenige seer oude Ducaten, waar op stond d'Afbeelding van een seer ouden Hertog van Venetien.

the Christians. Each of these nationals knows, the place where he will be heard, into which otherwise he is not allowed to enter. Before going there they must wash themselves. Otherwise they will not be allow to appear before the king, as dirty and unclean.

The pagans of Calicuth have this custom: they will never eat upon the sea, for if they do so they would never dare to appear before their king. Once more I should repeat, what is already said before,[156] namely, that Indian women esteem nothing more honest and praiseworthy than to die with their husbands and therefore like to be burned with the bodies of their dead husbands. One must not wonder about that since it is very strongly impressed in them that otherwise they cannot get to the blessed immortality. About this also Strabo speaks in Book XV of his Geogrphy. The chapter beginning: Nicolaus Damascenus says that he in Antioch etc.[157]

In Calicuth at a certain time every year there is an excellent annual fair, to which come multitudes of people from far off countries especially from Cathay, far from India, Persia, Media, Assyria, Syria, Turkey, Arabia and from Egypt on the famous river Nile but, mainly from Babylon and Cairo.[158]

When we asked Joseph the Indian if they know about our countries in Europe, he answered that Rome, Venice and France were greatly esteemed among them and that the Venetian ducats and silver coins have great value among them. The same Joseph, having come to Venice showed the Venetian Signoria some very old ducats upon which was the figure of a very ancient duke of Venice.[159]

Chapter 12

Berigt van de Koningrijken Cambaya, Ormus en Guzuratte in 't gemeen. t'Hoofd, of Caap Mogolistan. Moorsche Steeden Sobobek, Semath, Chesimy. De Stad Cambaya. Rivier Guzurath. Afgodendienst en andere Gewoonten deeser Heydenen.[a]

Vermits wy nu genoegsaam berigt gegeven, soo sullen wy nu ook yets seggen van de Landen tegens den Nedergang of 't Westen, en voor eerst van 't Koningrijk Cambaya, overde duysend Mijlen van Calicuth, gelegen. Van daar tot 't Eyland Ormus sign drie honderd Mijlen.

Dit Eyland legt by den aanvang der Persische Rivier, ontrent twintig Mijlen landwaars in. De Plaats daar deese Rivier begind werd genoemd 't Hoofd Mogolistan. 't Eyland begrijpt in 't ronde ontrent ander-half-honderd Mijlen. Den Heer van 't selve is een Mahometaan. De Stad is seer groot en heeft veel Inwooners, en 't Land is vrugtbaar van alles. Veele Koopmans Waren komen derwaarts en weer andere werden van daar vervoerd. Seer schoon Glas-work werd hier gemaakt, ja selfs 't alder schoonste. Paarlen vindmen hier in veelheyd. Ook een groot getal Paarden welke in Indien verkogt werden, en haar dienen om hare Waren op te vervoeren.

Van 't Hoofd Mogolistan, gelegen in 't midden van 't Eyland Ormus, tot aan de Stad Cambaya sietmen veele Steeden der Mooren, onder welke de treflijkste sijn Sobobek, Semath en Chesimy. Binnenwarts legt de Stad Guzurath, maar aan den de Over de Stad Cambaya ontrent drie honderd Mijlen [van 't Hoofd Mogolistan.

De Stad Cambaya legt seer krom en hier werd de Rivier geheeten Guzurath. Voortijds was de Stad Guzurath genoemd Betrosia (Gedrosia)[c] Dit Gewest heeft veele Steeden, Vlecken, en Dorpen al 't samen wel bewoond. D'inwooners geneeren sig van allerley Handwerken en Koophandel. Sy eeren d'Afgoden de Son en de Mann, ook de Koeyen, welke by haar in sulk een agting

---

a. This appears as IX Hoofdstuk (Chapter IX) on pp. 19-20, in *Sonderlinge Reysen*.

Chapter 12

The news of the Kingdoms of Cambaya,[160] Ormus,[161] and Guzuratte,[162] in general. The Head or Cape of Mogolistan, cities of the Moors, Sobobek, Semath, Chesimy. The city of Cambaya. The Gulf of Guzurath. Idolatry and other customs of these gentiles.[b]

Since we gave sufficient news about the city of Calicuth, we will now say also something of the cities towards the setting sun or the west. First of all the kingdom of Cambaya, situated over thousand miles from Calicuth.[163] From there to the island Ormus there are three hundred miles.

This island lies at the beginning of the Persian Gulf about twenty miles inland. The place where this Gulf begins is named the Cape Mogolistan. This island is about 150 miles around. The Lord of it is a Mohamedan. The city is very big and has many inhabitants and the country is very fertile. Much merchandise comes there and others are carried from there. Very fine glass is made here, indeed the most beautiful. One can find here pearls in plenty. Also there are great numbers of horses which are sold in India and are used for carrying their things.

From the Cape of Mogolistan, situated in the midst of the island Ormus upto the city of Cambaya, one sees many cities of the Moors, among which the most remarkable are Sobobek, Semath and Chesimy.[164] Toward the inland lies the city of Guzurath. But, on the sea-shore is the city of Cambaya about three hundred miles from Cape Mogolistan.

The city of Cambaya lies very curved and here the gulf is called Guzurath. Formerly the city of Guzurath was named Betrosia[165] (Gedrosia).[c] This region[166] has many cities, boroughs and villages, altogether well inhabited. The inhabitants live by hand work and trade. They adore the idols, the sun and the moon, also cows which are held in such esteem among them that he who kills the cow must also die, immediately. They

---

b. Compare this title with the corresponding titles of the Italian and Latin texts in 4.2.0. pp. 204, 205; 3.2.2. p. 115.
c. This is another example of the interpolation mentioned earlier. Cf. 3.2.3. pp. 116–118.

sijn dat de geene die een Koe dood terstond ook sterven moet. Sy dooden geen Beesten, en eeten ook geene Gedierten welke van andere gedood sijn. Drinken geenen witten Wijn.

De Manspersoonen sijn blank veel meer dan d'Inwooners der Stad Calicuth. Maar daar nevens Toveraars. Laten haar Hoofdhayr en Baard wassen. Soo datse Lokken of Tuyten hebben gelijk de Vrouwen. Dit Hayr windense wonderlijk om haar hoof. Niet meer dan eene Vrouw neemense en de Vrouwen maar eenen Man. Die ongetrouwd sijn leven in een sonderling-groote Kuysheyd. Sy eeten Moes van allerley kruyden welke d'algemeene Moeder, 't Aardrijk (gelijk Pithagoroas 't selve noemed) daar voortbrengd. Dit sy nu genoeg gesegt van de Stad Guzurath. Wy willen nu ook eenig berigt geben van de Stad Cambaya.

Chapter 13

Gelegenheyd der Stad Cambaya, de voortreflijkste onder al d'Indiaansche Steeden. Haren Koning. Koophandel. Religion. Andere Saken.[a]

Te Stad Cambaya legt in de Rivier Guzurath. Is seer wel gebouwd, groot en vol volk so datse werd geagt te sijn de voortreflijkste onder al d'Indiaansche Steeden; en derhalven heeft bekomen den Naam van 't Indiaansch Cair. Van binnen isse verciered met seer schoone Huysen van buyten heesftse rondom een goede Muur.

Voortijds was den Heer een Heyden, dienende d'Afgoden; maar nu is hy van Mahomets Secte gelijk ook de Regenten der Stad deese Religie hebben aangenomen welker voorbeeld de meeste Inwooners sijn gevolgd. Ebenwel sign'er noch Heydenen.

Lak vindmen hier meer dan ergens elders. Vermaarde Kooplieden sijn'er die veele Scheepen hebben bevarende tot haren Koophandel d'Ethiopische, de Roode, de Persische, en d'Indische Zee. Deese Stad legt van 't Hoofd Diongaal ontrent

---

a. This Chapter appears as X. Hoofdstuk (Chapter X) on pp. 21–22 in *Sonderlinge Reysen*.

do not kill beasts and also do not eat animals which are killed by others. They do not drink white wine.

The men are white much more than the inhabitants of the city of Calicuth. Moreover (there are) magicians. They let grow their hair and beard, so that they have lock or nozzles like the women. They tie up their hair wonderfully around their heads. Their men do not marry more than one wife and the women marry only one husband. Those who are not married live in remarkably great chastity. They eat all the herbs which the general mother earth (as Pythagoras says) brings forth for them. We have said enough about the city of Guzurath. We will now give also some news about the city of Cambaya.

Chapter 13

The site of the city of Cambaya,[167] the most excellent of all Indian cities. Its King, Trade, Religion, Other things.[b]

The city of Cambaya lies in the gulf of Guzurath.[168] It is very well built, large and very thickly populated, so that among all the Indian cities it is esteemed to be the most excellent, and therefore it has the name, the Cairo of India. Interiorly it is decorated with very beautiful houses and exteriorly it has a very good wall around it. Formerly its Lord was a pagan serving the idols. But now he is of the sect of Mohammed.[169] So as the regents of the city have accepted this religion, most of the inhabitants followed the example although still there are pagans.

One finds here more lac than anywhere else.[170] There are famous merchants who have many ships sailing for their trade to the Ethiopian Sea, Red Sea and the Indian Ocean.[171] This city lies about three hundred miles from the Cape Diongaal. In this gulf are many cities whose description would be too long here.

---

b. Compare this title with the corresponding titles in the Italian and Latin texts. Cf. 4.2.0. pp. 210, 211. 3.2.2.p. 116

256 INDIA IN 1500 AD

drie honderd Mijlen. Op de Rivier leggen veele Steeden, waar van 't verhaal hier te lang sou vallen.

In 't Eyland genoemd Maia, en agter 't Hoofd Diongaal tegen 't Oosten heeftmen een ander Hoofd of Caap, geheeten Ely ter wijdte van anderhalf-honderd Mijlen. Van daar tot de Stad Calicuth rekendmen ses-honderd Mijlen.

[De Stadt Cambaya heet aldereerst van de Portuguesen dien Naam bekomen met verbastering van 't eygentlijk woord Cambewath, of Cambebath. In onse Taal so veel als de Stad Cambe. Sy legt op een seer lustige Vlakte in de binnenste Kaken eens grooten Inhams na deese Stad genoemd de Golf van Cambaya aan den Oever van de Rivier Meli, of May, anders Guandari; ter plaats daar deselve haar Water in de gedagte Zeeboesem uytstort. De Stad Cambaya is noch eens soo groot als de Stad Guzuratte of Suratte, van twee uyren gaans in den omvang of rondte. 't Voornaamste verciersel deser Stad bestaat in hare groote Voor-Steeden. De Straten sijn regt en breed; welke yeder nagt werden afgesloten door een seer sterke Poort even als een Stads-Poort. De huysen sijn pragtig ten deelen van gebakkene ten deelen van gehouwene Steenen; doch seer vogtig en onder-aardsch. Varsch Water ontbreekt hier; doch vermits in de drie Winter-maanden ongemeen-sterke regenen vallen soo versorgen 'd Inwooners sig van dit Water 't welk bewaard word in groote Regen-bakken. D'Ebb' en Vloed der Zee is ontrent Cambaya geweldig fel en snel. In minder dan 't vierde deel eener uyr rijsd hier de Zee tot haare gewoone hoogte; met sulk een snelheyd en storting dat'er nauwlijks 't oog op te houden is; ja sneller daan een Paard soukommen lopen.][c]

CHAPTER 14

Berigt van den Koning van Narsinga. De Stad Bisnagar. Cochin. Comara, Oriza, Maliapar. Kerk van S. Thomas. Cathay.[a]

Tot hier toe hebben wy doorlopen al d'Oevers van de Stad Caranganor af tot in 't Eyland Ormus. Nu is overig noch yets te sggen van 't Koningrijk Cuchin (Cochin)[b] en deese Landstreek.

---
c. This is a long interpolation in the Dutch text. Cf. 3.2.3. pp. 116–118.
a. This appears as XI Hoofdstuk (Chapter XI) on pp. 22–23 in *Sonderlinge Reysen*.

In the island named Maia[172] and behind the Cape Diongaal toward the east one finds another head or Cape named Ely[173] of the breadth of hundred and fifty miles. From there to the city of Calicuth there are six hundred miles.

[The city of Cambaya[174] has for the first time got this name from the Portuguese with the degeneration of the real name Cambewath or Cambebath in our language as much as 'the city of Cambe'. It lies upon a very even plane between the inner cheeks of a great bay called after the city, the Gulf of Cambaya, on the shore of the river Meli or May, otherwise called Guandari, in the place where the same river pours its water into the bosom of the said sea. The city of Cambaya is still as large as the city of Guzurath or Souratte, of two hours' walk in circumference or around. The principal ornaments of the city are its great suburbs. The streets are straight and broad, which every night are closed by a very strong door, like a city door. The houses are magnificent of partly baked stones and partly of cut stones, but very damp and subterraneous. Fresh water does not lack there, but since in the three winter months exceptionally strong rains fall, they provide themselves with this water which is conserved in rain cistern. Low tide and high tide of the sea around Cambaya is violently strong and rapid. In less than a quarter of an hour the sea rises here up to its normal height with such rapidity and rise that it is hardly possible for you to hold the eye upon it, yes more quickly than a horse would be able to run]

Chapter 14

News about the king of Narasinga.[175] The city Bisnagar,[176] Cochin,[177] Comara,[178] Oriza,[179] Maliapur,[180] the Church of St Thomas,[181] China.[c]

Up to here we have traversed through all the shore from the city of Caranganor up to the island of Ormus. It remains

---

b. This is an instance of the interpolation about which we have spoken earlier. This chapter has many such instances. We named them short interpolation or word interpolation. Cf. 3.2.3. pp. 116–118

c. Compare this title with the corresponding titles of the Italian and Latin texts. Cf. 4.2.0. pp. 212, 213; 3.2.2. p. 116.

Ontrent drie-honderd Mijlen binnens Lands niet verre van 't Gebergt is een Koning Narsindus (volgens een andere Vertaling regeerd de Koning van Narsinga) seer magtig. Hy heeft een Stad omvangen van drie dubbele Muuren genoemd Besenegaal (Bisnagar). Wanneer hy ten strijde uyttrekt soo voerd hy met hem volgens 't verhaal van Joseph den Indiaan, agt-honderd Elephanten vier-duysand Ruyters en Voetvokl in sulk een meenigte daar-door een ruymte van dertig Mijlen sou konnen beslagen worden; 't welk wel ongeloofijk te hooren maar evenwel waaragtig is, waar by Joseph voegde dat dit Koningrijk over de drie duysend Mijlen wijd is. Deesen Koning diend d'Afgoden.

Wy keeren weer na de Kusten en beginnen met de Stad Cuchina (Cochin) gelegen tegen 't Oosten. Alsmen van Cochin honderd Mijlen Oostwaarts vaart koomdemen aan een Hoofd of Caap genoemd Cumaar (Comori) en vaan daar aan de Rivier Indus alwaar Indien begind sijnde vijf-honderd Mijlen.

Op deesen weg vindmen de vermaarde Rivier Oriza, waar ontremt een beroemde Stad is na deese Rivier ook genoemd Oriza (veellight Orixa, anders Golconda) waar voorby de Vloed Indus loopt. Noch een andere Stad is 'er sig uytstrekkende in de Zee gelijk Voor-haven genoemd Milapaar (Maliapur). Hier heeftmen een heerlijke Kerk S. Thomas toegeeygend. Deese is gelijk de S. Johannis en Pauli Kerk te Venetien; en S. Thomas Ligchaam rust in deselve; doende veel Wonder-teekenen; derhalven hy ook van yeder geerd word schoon d'Inwooners Hedenen sijn.

Voorts sietmen veel Eylanden in d'Indiaansche Zee, onder welke de twee vermaardste sijn Sayla en Samotra. Sayla legt twee-honderd Mijlen van Capo Comori en van daar vervoerdmen Marrie-paarden. Samotra legt tegen 't Osten drie Maanden Reysen van Calicuth; en werd van ons genoemd Taprobana.

Hier na is Cathay 't aldervrugtbaarste Eyland onder veel andere; waar van wy voorbedagtlijk niet spreeken willen, vermits wy van den meergemelden Joseph niets meer hebben konnen verneemen.

EYNDE

now to say something about the kingdom of Cuchin (Cochin) in this region.

About three hundred miles inland, not far from the mountain there is a very powerful king Narasindus[182] (according to another translation, reigns the king of Narasinga). He has a city, named Besenegaal[183] (Bisnagar) surrounded by three double walls. When he goes on battle he takes with him, according to the narration of Joseph the Indian, eight hundred elephants, four thousand cavalry, and infantry in such plenty that with it a space of thirty miles could be covered, which is incredible to hear, but, still is true. To which Joseph added that his kingdom is three thousand miles in extent. This king serves the idols.

We turn back to the coasts and begin with the city of Cuchin (Cochin) lying against the East.[184] As one sails from Cochin a hundred miles eastwards he comes to the Cape named Cumar (Comori)[185], from there to the river Indus[186] where India begins it is five hundred miles.

On this route one finds the famous river Oriza near which there is a famous city called also Oriza, named after this river,[187] (Perhaps Orixa otherwise Golconda) where the flood of Indus passes. There is still another city, stretching itself into the sea like an outpost named Milapar (Maliapur).[188] Here is a splendid church dedicated to St Thomas.[189] It is like the Church of St John and Paul in Venice and the body of St Thomas rests in this church,[190] working many miracles for which he is honoured by everyone although the inhabitants are pagans.

Besides, one can see many islands in the Indian Sea among which the two most famous are Sayla[191] and Samotra.[192] Sayla lies two hundred miles from Cape of Comari and from there men transport she-horses. Samotra lies against the east three months' travel from Calicuth and is called by us Taprobana.[193] After this China is the most fertile island among many others, about which we will not speak deliberately, since from the often-mentioned Joseph we have learned nothing more.

THE END

4.4.0. Notes and Comments

The Notes and Comments on the following pages are given with reference to the Italian, Latin and Dutch texts of the Narratives of Joseph the Indian given on the preceeding pages. They are not exhaustive, but only aids for understanding the texts. More research and study is required for many of the points referred to there.

The numbers refer to the reference numbers given in the English translations of the Italian and Latin texts on pp. 146-217 and the Dutch text on pp. 220-259. For facility of reference the numbers under each chapter are given with the indication to the corresponding chapters.

We use certain abbreviations in this section. I: stands for the Italian text (and sometimes its translation); L: stands for the Latin text (and sometimes its translation) and D: stands for the Dutch text (and sometimes its translation). Other References are indicated in the context, wherever complete titles are not found they are to be sought in the Bibliography.

Chapter 1

1. *Joseph the Indian.* I: gives the form "Ioseph Indiano", L: gives the form "Iosephus Indus", D: has no equivalent here in Chapter 1 as it has no title. But D has the form "Joseph den Indiaan" in the text and on top of the pages of the text. In the title of the booklet it is "Joseph den geboorenen Indiaan". I: has another form "pre Ioseph". *Novus Orbis* has the form "Ioseph Indus". The French translation of *Paesi* follows I and has the form "Ioseph Indian", German translation of *Novus Orbis* has "Joseph der Indiaaner", its Dutch translation has "Ioseph der Indiaaner". Assemanus uses the expression "Iosephus Indus", Germann, "Joseph der Inder". W.B. Greenlee following *Paesi*, uses two forms "Joseph the Indian" and "priest Joseph". Banha de Andrade who follows Greenlee and Doria uses the form "Padre José" in Portuguese. P. J. Podipara, Schurhammer, Nagam Aiya and A. M. Mundadan use the form, "Joseph the Indian". We establish the form "Joseph the Indian" as the standard form.

2. *"our"*, the possessive adjectives and pronouns in the first person occur very frequently in the first chapter of the three texts, in the combinations like "our ships", "our king", "our people", "our fleet", "with us", etc. In all these cases the pronoun or possessive adjective in the first person stands for the Portuguese. L: has many such expressions, D: has them from the middle of Chapter 1 and has an interpolation "now we speak in the words of the Portuguese" (Cf. pp. 220-221). I has only one instance "nostre Caravelle": our Caravels. We have discussed it in detail elsewhere. Cf. 2. 3. 4. pp. 88-90.

3. Caravels. see below no. 8.

4. The king referred to here is King Manuel or Emanuel I (1495-1521) who succeeded King John II of Portugal. It was during his reign that Vasco da Gama first set out to India Contemporary documents refer to him as the Serene King. See also No. 10.

5. I: to Portugal, L: to Lisbon, D: has no equivalent.

THE NARRATIVES OF JOSEPH THE INDIAN 263

6. *Rome and Venice.* The title of this chapter mentions only Rome and Venice as the targets of the travels of Joseph. All the three texts mention Jerusalem when they speak of the plans of Joseph at Cochin. But only I mentions Jerusalem, when it speaks of the person to accompany Joseph. For details Cf. 2. 2. 4. pp 79-81. Did Joseph go to Jerusalem and Babylon.

7. I: *"parte australi"* i. e. southern parts. Greenlee wrongly translated it as *"northern parts"*. L: *"regiones australissimas"* – the southernmost parts. D: *Zuyder Gewesten"* – southern provinces. Probably it refers to the Portuguese discoveries around Africa, especially the discovery of the Cape of Good Hope.

8. L: uses *"celocibus ac liburnicis"*; celox is a ship, the adjective "liburnicus" signifies "liburnian". Here it is used as an adjectival substantive. However, we translate the two nouns together as "liburnian vessels" implying fast moving ships. The Liburnians are known for their fast moving ships. I: uses the words 'navilli', 'nave' and 'caravels'. W. B. Greenlee, says: "A Venetian would naturally think of the Portuguese ship as a caravel. Prior to the voyage of Vasco da Gama (1497) the Portuguese had caravels on their voyage and established a well-deserved reputation on the Atlantic. Venetians used galleys both in the Mediterranean and in their fleet to Flanders". D: "Jagten en Galayen"- yachts and galleys. Cf W.B. Greenlee, *The Voyage of Pedro Alvares Cabral to India and Brazil from Contemporary Documents*, London, 1937.

9. This seems to refer to Vasco da Gama's first voyage to India from 9th July 1497 to 10th July 1499. Vasco da Gama landed on the shores of Malabar in 1498. It can also mean the expedition of the discoveries of the African Cost. Cf. no 7 above.

10. I: has the name Hemanuel while the others use Emanuel. Cf. sup. no. 4.

11. The date given in D is 1550, which evidently is wrong as is clear from D itself. I and L give 1500 and hence we corrected D.

12. All the three texts tell us that the fleet of Cabral comprised 12 ships: I, "xii nave et carauelle", L, "classem duodecim navium", D, "in twaalf scheepen". The *Anonymous Narrative* says the same: "In the year 1500 the most Serene King of Portugal sent ⋯ in which Armada there were twelve large and small ships". (W B. Greenlee, *op. cit.* p. 56.) Castanheda says that there were 13 ships: "des naos & tres navios redõdos". The letter of a certan Cretan written on 27th June, 1501 gives the number 13: "⋯but thirteen of which went seven were lost on the voyage." (W.B. Greenlee, *op. cit.*, p. 120.) But, a letter of Giovanni Francisco de Affetadi to Domenico Pisani dated 26th June 1501 mentions 12 ships. (W.B. Greenlee, *op.cit.*, p. 126) The Encyclopaedias mention 13 ships. This problem perhaps would be resolved if we take into account the fact that those who speak of 12 do not include the small ship of Gasper de Lemos. *Anonymous Narrative* informs us: "And the said captain promptly dispatched a small supply ship which they had with them, in addition to the twelve ships aforesaid." (W.B. Greenlee, *op. cit.*, p. 60).

13. I: Pedro Aliares, L & D: Petrus Aliares, both stand for Pedro Alvares Cabral. This form "Aliares" is not Portuguese. Pedro Alvares Cabral (1467/8-1520) is credited with the discovery of Brazil and was one of the foremost of the Portuguese navigators who brought fame to his country in the age of discovery. Born in Belmonte, Portugal, son of Fernao Cabral and Isabel de Gouveia, he enjoyed the esteem of King Manuel I of Portugal from whom he received many privileges in 1497. In 1500, as the Narratives tell us, he was entrusted with the command of the second major expedition to India. The king's esteem is clear from his own words: "expressing the great confidence we have in Pedralvares de Gouveia, noble man of our household." On April 22, 1500 Cabral discovered Brazil and on 13th September arrived at the port of Calicut. Cabral came back to Lisbon in June, 1501. He died in 1520 in Santarem, Portugal, where his tomb was identified in 1848 by the Brazilian historian Francisco Adolfo Varnhagen. For more details about Cabral's travels Cf. Part II, 2.2.1 and 2.2.2. pp. 71,74.

14. The date given in L and D appears to imply that Cabral set out from Lisbon on 8th March. I: on the other hand could be interpreted to mean that he received the standard of captancy on 8th March, the date of the departure being not specified. According to the *Anonymous Narrative* the king officially gave the standard to Cabral on 8th March after a liturgical celebration at the church of Belem, which then was outside the city of Lisbon. So in fact the ship set out from a spot two miles from the old city. And actually, it was on the 9th that he set sail from there. (W.B. Greenlee, *op. cit.*, p. 57.) *Navegação* also says the same thing but does not specify the date and day as Monday 9th March like *Anonymous Narrative*. It says that the royal standard was given on the 8th and on the following day "levantamos ancoras com vento prospero." (*Navegação, da Pedro Alvares Cabral*, Lisbon, 1812, p. 100.) Almost all the encyclopaedias give the date 9th March. According to A. M. Mundadan, (*St Thomas Christians* Bangalore, 1967 p. 54, hereafter, Mundadan, STC) Cabral set out from Lisbon on 19th March. He mentions also that the date given by Correa (25th March) as not reliable. We feel that the dates given by the *Anonymous Narratives* probably are the correct ones: "And on the 8th of the month of March of the said year they were ready and on that day, which was Sunday, they went a distance of two miles from this city to a place called Rastello, where there is a church called Sancta Maria de Baller (Belem, this place today inside the city of Lisbon). To this place the most Serene King went in person to consign to the captain the rayal standard for the said armada. Monday, which was the 9th day of March, the said armada departed on its voyage with good weather." (W.B. Greenlee, *op. cit.*, p. 57).

15. *The city of Calicut.* The name of the city is given by the three texts differently. I has two forms, Calichut and Colochut. L: Calechut. D: Calicuth. In the translation we keep the forms as they appear in the respective texts. We find that in the 16th century each author followed his own spelling of the city. They are reproductions of the Malayalam name of the city: Kozhikode. Kozhi, in

Malayalam, is a cock or rather a fowl and 'kod' means port. It was the most important port in coast of Malabar when the Portuguese came to India. It was the capital city of the mightiest of the princes of Kerala. In Chapter 11 of the Narratives of Joseph the Indian we find a good description of the city. Cf. also W.B. Greenlee, *op. cit.*, pp. 78-83., *Navegação,* pp. 126-129, *Novs Orbis*, 1537, pp. 79-82, Mundadan, STC p. 12. The date given by all the three texts for the arrival of the Portuguese in Calicut is 13th September, though the second edition of *Paesi* gives it as 14th September. The *Anonymous Narrative* gives the date 13th September. Mundadan gives the date 30th August. *Navegação* has 13th September.

16. I: Zaffal, L: Zaphala, D: Sofala. The *Anonymous Narrative*: Zaffalle. (Greenlee, *op. cit.*, p. 61.). *Navegação*: Cofala (p. 107).

17. About the quarrels between the inhabitants of Calicut and the Portuguese, Cf. *Anonymous Narrative* (W.B. Greenlee, *op. cit.*, p. 61.), *Novus Orbis*, 1537, pp. 82-84.

18. I and L give 24th November, while D gives 24th December *Anonymous Narrative* gives 24th December, "And we reached Cuchin the 24th of December". (Greenlee *op. cit.* p. 61). Mundadan gives 24th December. 24th December seems to be is the correct date and agrees better with the statement that they remained there for three months.

19. I: gives Cuchi and Cuchin L: Cuchinum and Cuchina, where it seems to be used as an adjective as Regnum Cuchinum, urbs Cuchina, rex Cuchinus. D: has three forms: Cochin, Cuchina, Cuchin. It is the present city of Cochin. All these forms are adapted translation of the Malayalam name "Kochi". It was a port to the south of Calicut, and the capital of the kingdom of Cochin. Today it is the only port in Kerala. Perhaps the first instance "Cuchi" in *Paesi* can be read also as "Cuchin". Cf. also no. 177.

20. Here the reference is to Chapter 78 of Book III of *Paesi* and *Itinerarium* (Cf. *Novus Orbis*, 1537, p. 85.) It is part of the *Anonymous Narrative*. We cite the English translation of the text in the *Paesi* from W.B. Greenlee: "And thus

we were twelve or fifteen days loading the ships at a
distance from Cucchin, at a place called Carangallo
(Cranganore). In this place there are Christians, Jews...
and from there two other Christians came with us; they
said they wished to go to Rome and Jerusalem. The captain
had great pleasure with these two men." (W.B. Greenlee,
op. cit., p. 86.). The Latin text we cite from *Novus Orbis*,
1537, Book III, Chapter 78,: "Igitur illic commorati sumus
circiter dies xv naves exonerantes non longe ab urbe
Cuchina, ubi portus est, qui dicitur Carnagallo... duo
Christiani qui asseuerabant se profecturos Hierosolymas
& inde Romam, quod profect perquam *gratum* profecto
nostro fuit." (p. 85). *Navegação* also gives the same
idea, in ch. xix, p. 134. Evidently this reference does not
occur in D as it is a booklet by itself. Though the
Narratives of Joseph the Indian tell us that Joseph and
his brother approached Cabral in Cochin, from the above
citations of the different editions of the *Anonymous
Narrative* and from other sources it appears that they
approached Cabral in Cranganore. We have discussed this
in Part II, 2.2.1 p. 73, 2.2.2. p. 74 where we have quoted
also other sources

21. I: doi fratelli christiani = two christian brothers, L: Duo
germani fratres Indi Christianique = two brothers of the
same parents Indians as well as Christians, D: Twee
broeders Indiadnsche Christen = two brothers Indian
Christians. The Narratives of Joseph the Indian do not
give the name of Joseph's brother, but from other
sources we know that his name was Mathias. For
further details, Cf. Part II, 2.2.1. pp 71–74.

22. I: Caranganor, L: Caranganora, and Caranganorensis, D:
Caranganor. The *Anonymous Narrative* has Carangallo,
Novus Orbis 1537 has Carnagallo. All these are attempted
equivalents of the Malayalam name Kodungallor, which
today we call Cranganore in English. Cranganore was an
ancient Christian centre. According to tradition, St Thomas
the Apostle landed at the port of Cranganore in 52 A.D.
The see of the Metropolitan of India was at Cranganore.
Cranganore is said to be 20 miles away from Cochin and
90 miles south of Calicut. Osorius says: "Distat Cranganor

Cochino ad Septentriones decem & sex millibus passuum... Erat urbs sane magna & a multis nationibus, propter admodum celebre emporium, frequentata," (*op. cit.*, col. 725 see Bibliography). Cf. Mundadan, STC, p. 12, See also infra no. 33.

23. All the three texts mention Jerusalem when they mention the intentions of Joseph and his brother when they approached Cabral. I: mentions it also when it speaks about the companion given by the king (see inf. no. 29). However, it is not clear from the Narratives or any other documents we know of, if Joseph went to Jerusalem or not. For details Cf. Part II, 2.2.4. Did Joseph go to Jerusalem and Babylon? pp. 79-81.

24. All the three texts have slightly different formulations I: specifies the number of ships as "eighty sails", while L says: ingens classis "an enormous fleet:", and D uses the expression "een sterke Vloot: a strong fleet." The *Anonymous Narrative* says, "When we were nearly loaded, there came an armada from Calichut in which there were some eightyfive sails, among which were twentyfive very large ones." (W.B. Greenlee, *op. cit.*, p. 87). Dom Manuel in his letter to the Spanish Sovereign and Goes say 15,000 men. De Barros says 70 ships, of which twentyfive were large. Goes and Osorius say twenty large ships.

25. According to the three texts Joseph's brother died on the way, but De Barros and Gouvea say that Mathias, Joseph's brother, died in Lisbon. For further details Cf. Part II, 2 2.2. pp. 74-78.

26. I: one named Joseph is alive. L & D: the other is alive. Here I mentions the name of Joseph. L does not give the name in this context. It first mentions the name later when it says "the said Joseph." Hence we have to think that there is an omission of the name in L which is given in I. D also omits the name here but gives it later as Joseph the Indian.

27. I: at the end of June. L: some time in the month of June, D: in the month of June. The questions of the different

THE NARRATIVES OF JOSEPH THE INDIAN 269

dates of the arrival of Cabral's ships in Lisbon we have discussed in the Part II, 2.2.2. pp. 76-77.

28. The date of arrival of Joseph in Lisbon and of his departure we get only from I.

29. Only L and D give this information. Cf. Part II, 2.2.2. p. 78.

30. This is also a valuable piece of information for which we are indebted to I. No other source we know tells us about the date of Joseph's stay in any of the places. We do not know exactly how long Joseph was in Venice. What I says is "many days."

31. Chapter 1, in fact, is an introduction to the Narratives of Joseph the Indian. It is in the Chapter 2 onwards that what Joseph narrated is reported by the European writer.

CHAPTER 2

32. L: 'de habitudine corporis', we have translated it as 'physical appearances'. But actually the description contains also the inner qualities of the person of Joseph. I: uses the expression "la qualita de Joseph: the quality of Joseph." D: does not mention it in the title. The person of Joseph and his native place Cranganore are the subjects treated here.

33. I: does not mention Caranganore in this context as the native place of Joseph. L: which uses the form Caranganora elsewhere has a new form "Carangonrensis". D gives another spelling 'Cranganor'. Cf. Sup. no. 22. In the tables of contents of *Paesi* and *Itinerarium* other spellings are given. One reads: "Description of the quality and stature of Ioseph together with city of Caranganor which is written otherwise as Carangolo."

34. I and L simply say that Joseph was forty years. D says "At the time he was in Lisbon he was forty years of age." W.B. Greenlee in a footnote says that it was at the time of his visit. But the problem remains: was he forty years of age when he was in Lisbon or in Venice? Between his arrival in Lisbon and his visit to Venice, there is a gap of one year. Or was he forty years of

age when he returned to Lisbon after his visit to Venice and Rome?

35. I: nature beretino: dark by nature, L: coloris subcinerii: dark coloured: D: sein couleur was aschenverwigh: his colour was of ashes. We have translated it as black-coloured, dark-coloured and ash-coloured.

36. I: ".... of ordinary stature, according to the judgement of those who have seen and spoken with him." W.B. Greenlee associates the phrase "according..." to the sentence "He was an ingenious man." We feel that in Italian it better goes with the first part. L: qualifies it as "neither tall nor short." D: medium size in height.

37. L: virque abstemius: a sober man. D: he drank no wine, I does not have this piece of information.

38. I: sinut dicto Milibar. L: sinu quododam dicto Milibar, D: Rivier genoemd Milibar. W.B. Greenlee has translated sinut as bay. We follow him. Dutch has 'River called Milibar.' Milibar seems to stand for Malabar. The coast is called Malabar. The city of Cranganore is located on the mouth of the river Periyar. We do not know if Periyar had this name some time before. The expressions remain unclear.

39. I and L say thirty miles, D: many miles.

40. I: in modo de uilla, "in the manner of a villa" L: vicatim, D: dat yeder als in een bysondere Dorf scheint te woonen. All these three expression are not easy to translate to bring at the full sense.

41. I: A small number of Jews are also found here. L & D. there are (also) many Jews. It is historically known that there were Jews on the Malabar Coast from very ancient times onwards.

42. I: says that there are Moors who come here from Syria, Persia and Cairo. L & D do not have this specification as regards Moors. They say, Syrians, Eyptians, Persians, Arabs and Medes come.

43. I: for this place is the source of diverse sorts of merchandise. L & D: this region produces (there grow) many

things that are helpful (useful) to mankind (men and health). L: mentions spices very specially.

Chapter 3

44. I: 'Ghiesie' actually means church but in this case it means a Hindu temple. I uses templi also for temple. L: delubra or templum. D: has Tempelen.
45. *Naires*: All the three texts agree in the spelling. The word seems to denote "Nairs".
46. *Canes* (I & L), *Hondt* (D) which means dog(s). We do not know what Malayalam equivalent they used. I: says that they are farmers. L says they are poor people like the proletariate similar to the Roman gregarii. D says poor people, not of high status
47. I: Nuirinam, L: Nuiram, D: Nuieras (Nueiran). We cannot make out the Malayalam equivalent. D: Gives in brackets Polyas. We cannot say anything for certain about this. They seem to be the untouchables.
48. 'Tambram' stands for the Malayalam word for 'Tambran' or 'Tampuran' which means Lord. God is called 'Tampuran' and a landlord is called Tambran. In Christian prayers we use the expressions like "Bhava Tampuran: God the Father," "Puthran Tampuran: God the Son" &c. where "Tampuran" means God.
49. I: Sacrificii generali; L: Sacrificant. They are temple rituals. Are they real sacrifices? The description given here seems to be that of "Velichapaduthullal". In the Dutch text there is a picture of a temple and the service described here.
50. I: ne haver la lingua, L: uix eum intelligere quivimus. This does not necessarily mean that Joseph did not know the language. We have discussed the question at length elsewhere. Cf. 2.3.3. p. 84. What language did Joseph speak?

Chapter 4

51. For the customs of the people of Cranganore Cf. Correa, *Lendas da India*, ch. 14, The manner of the living of the people.

52. The translation of I by W. B. Greenlee does not seem to be correct. He translated 'ne est castitas seu pudicitia inter eos" as "Nor in their chastity is there modesty among them." L: "quibus nullus est pudor, nullaque pudicitia, passim prostituuntur corpora."

53. This practice is called Sati. More about this is said in Chapter 11. Cf. inf. no. 156, 157.

54. I: the nearest relative other than the sons. L: second grade of the geneological tree. D: his relative in the second grade. It seems to denote the "Marumakkathayam", i. e. matrilinear system, where nephews follow the uncles. Matrilinear systems of inheritance, came into vogue in Kerala in the 11th century. Friar Jordanus of Severic who came to Quilon in 1324 is the first traveller to mention the existence of the matrilinear system of inheritance in Kerala. For further details Cf. Sreedhara Menon, *A Survey of Kerala History*, Kottayam, 1967, pp. 2, 154, 377-79.

55. Does this mean that they had loin cloths only to cover their private part, or does it mean that they were half-naked wearing only a cotton dhoti.

56. D: Schoensoolen: literally means shoe-soles but it is not clear what is meant here. I and L seem to be clearer.

57. L: does not have this.

58. We do not what ornament is meant here.

59. I: on leaves of trees with an iron point L: with iron stylus on leaves of trees. D: met Ysere Griffien of Schorssen van Bomen: with iron stylus on barks of trees. The custom in Kerala was to write on palm leaves with an iron stylus, that is what Joseph mentions here.

60. L & D omits the name. I gives the name "Malanar", which stands for Malayalam.

61. I: there are many Christians. But in the title of the chapter in L it has the expression: "ibi sunt quidam christiani." : There are some Christians there.

THE NARRATIVES OF JOSEPH THE INDIAN 273

62. I has Ornus here and in other places Ormus. L and D give Ormus. *Novus Orbis* gives Ormus and Ornus as a variant reading. It is also written as Ormuz. More details about Ormus are given in the Narratives of Joseph the Indian in Chapter 12. Cf. inf. no. 161, 167.

63. The idea is not clear in I, L seems to be clearer.

64. This is a remark by the editor of the *Sonderlinge Reysen*.

65. L & D omit this. Cataio is China. In the description of Calicut in chapter 11 of the Narratives of Joseph the Indian we are told that the merchants from China, who were Christians used to come to the port of Calicut (Cf. 4.2.0.). That there were Christians in China is known from other sources. John Monte Corvino (1505) writes of the Christians of China. Jordan Catalani saw Christians in Thana and Guzerat. Cf. P. J. Podipara, *The Hierarchy of the Syro-Malabar Church;* Saeki, P. Y., *The Nestorian documents in China*, Tokyo, 1937.

66. These two sentences are omitted in D.

67. "ut latius dictum est" does not seem to be correct. For there is no mention of the taxes etc. before.

CHAPTER 5

68. It is not easy to translate this passage in Latin.

69. The word used in L is delubra, which we translate here as church. Above in no. 44 we have translated it as temple when it was used in relation to the gentiles. I here uses "templi" but in the following sentence it uses ghiesa, which means church. Also in relation to the gentiles ghiesa is used in I. Cf. supra no. 44.

70. According to I, the cross is on the top of the church. D also seems to mean top. But, L uses the words "in crepidine" which could mean also on the base or foundation. In Malabar we see even today very big granite crosses in the courtyards of many of the churches Big crosses are not found on the top of the church as the text would

274 INDIA IN 1500 AD

mean. We cannot make out from the texts where the cross actually was. Nor does the qualification "as in the churches of Europe" help us here, as we do not find big crosses on top of the Cathedrals of Europe either.

71. I: Pontifice, L: magnum antistitem, D: Grooten of hogen Priester (Paus). This is a European equivalent employed by the European writer to signify the Catholicos or Patriarch of Babylon or Chaldean Patriarch. The Church of Malabar was under the jurisdiction of the Chaldean Patriarch at the time of Joseph the Indian. Vatican Syriac Codez 22 of 1301 speaks of the Church of Malabar being under the Chaldean Patriarch. For further details Cf. inf. no. 77, 78, 79, 82, 85. Mundadan, STC, pp. 17-28. P. J. Podipara, *The Hierarchy of the Syro-Malabar Church*, Alleppey, 1976. pp. 31-63.

72. Twelve Cardinals. The term Cardinals seems to be a Roman or European term. The number 12 for the assistants of the Catholicos seems to be interesting. For we read of the twelve priests who assisted the Governador Paremakal who succeeded the late Archbishop Kariattil in the 18th century in the Malabar Church. We have the Malayalam manuscript in our personal collection coming from the Library of the late I. C. Chacko. The letter is addressed to Paremmakal and the twelve priests.

73. See under no. 78.

74. Here the reference seems to be to all the Bishops and Archbishops under the Catholica and not merely of Malabar, see under no. 78 also.

75. This is a misnomer for "Aramea" and "Arameans" which seem to be confused by the Portuguese. This region was once in the Persian Empire and was successively ruled by the Babylonians, Assyrians, and Chaldeans and has been known as Babylonia, Assyria and Chaldea. The commercial language of this place continued to be Chaldean or Aramaic even after the Persians became rulers of the Empire. And people hailing from these parts were known in Malabar as "Arameans" and their country as "Aramea." The Portuguese confused these terms with Armania and

Armenians. (Cf. A. M. Mundadan, Origins of Christianity in India, in: *Christianity in India, Ecumenical perspectives*, pp. 24-25 and also no. 79 below.

76. Perhaps this is the incident mentioned in the letter of the four Bishops which we have quoted in 2.1.0. p. 58.

77. Catholica is a Syriac word. W.B. Greenlee translated it as Catholicos. We keep the original form as in the Italian text. Cf. sup. no. 72, inf. 78, 79, 82, 85.

78. The word Patriarch used in this context needs to be studied in greater detail. Does it mean Metropolitan or Patriarch? Did Joseph really mean Patriarch? We cannot affirm either now. For, on the one hand, we know that the most important title used for the head of the Malabar Church is the title of *"The Metropolitan and the Gate of All India"*, (Cf. Podipara, *op. cit.*, pp. 31-39, esp. 32, 35.). We know that Cranganore had the title of the Metropolitan See at the time of the coming of the Portuguese. We read in history how this title was given to Goa later, and how Ros. S. J. fought to get it back in Cranganore when he was made Bishop of Cranganore. However, in the Narratives the term used is Patriarch. And we know also that just before the Coonan Cross oath of 1563, in a letter sent by Ahatalla, he designated himself as the "Patriarch of China and of All India." (Podipara, *op. cit.*, p. 124.). Does this mean that the title of Patriarch was one that was applied to the heads of China and India? If this was not a term known to the Christians of Malabar why did Ahatalla use it? Further, Podipara thinks that the Metropolitan of India had a kind of quasi-patriarchal power. (*op. cit.*, p. 32.). This needs more research.

79. This reference is to Marco Polo Book I, Chapter 15, where he actually speaks of the Kingdom of Mosul and not of Armenia. "Regnum Mosul ad orientem situm, partim confine est Armaniae Maiori, habitantque in eo Arabes Mahumetum colentes & multi Christiani, Nestoriani atque Iacobini quibus praeest patriarcha magnus, quem ipsi Iacelich vocant". (*Novus Orbis*, Basiliae 1537, p. 336). D cites the text of Marco Polo from the 1563 Dutch

translation of the *Novus Orbis*, which citation is not found in I and L. It is clear here that the reference is to the Chaldean Patriarch. The confusion is with the word Armania. Besides the reason given above in no. 75, perhaps the fact that this kingdom has the same boundary with Armania the two might have been confused. About the Catholica Osorius wrote" Summum eorum (Christians of Chaldea) antistes, in montibus qui septentriones spectant a maris dissunctissimis quam illi regionem Chaldeam nominat sedem habet", (*op. cit.*, col. 725.) Cf. Marco Polo: *The Book of Sir Marco Polo.* Translated and edited by Sir Henry Yule. 3rd ed., London, 1903, 2 vols. and Marco Polo: *Il millione di M. Polo*, ore per la prima volta pubblicato ed illustrato dal Conte G. B. Baldelli Boni, Florence, 1827; *Marci Pauli Veneti De Regionibus Orientalibus*, (Liber Primus, Liber Secundus, Liber Tertius) in *Novus Orbis* Basel, 1537, pp. 330–417. Cf. also nos. 71, 77, 78, 82, 85.

80. The concept of Nestorians here in Marco Polo is a typical Middle Ages concept of Nestorians. It needs more study and proper evaluation. It is a fact of history that the St Thomas Christians of Malabar were often qualified by the European writers, out of sheer ignorance and sometimes of malice, as Nestorians. We should remember that for the European writers of the Middle Ages and of later periods, especially of the age of the discoveries all the Christians outside the Holy Roman Empire, in Chaldea, Persia and other parts of the ancient Persian Empire were "Nestorians". Nestorians and Nestorianism are concepts which need more clarification and real research even in our times, which attach so much importance to scientific accuracy.

81. This is found neither in L nor in D. Cf. sup. no. 78.

82. Here we are face to face with two views on the Supremacy and Jurisdiction of the Pope of Rome. This is perhaps a meeting of two divergent theological positions on the question. It is very important for any theologian of the Papacy to see how a son of the Malabar Church viewed the question. Reading the three texts one

would be able to sense the theological preoccupation of the compilers of the three texts. The compiler of I probably did not have much in the way of theological preoccupation. He just gives the report. The compiler of the Latin text seems to be an adamant defender of the Roman position. We see an interpolation in L and D not found in I and which the editor of D sees as the addition made by the Roman Catholic compiler of L. The editor of D probably was approaching it from the Protestant position. His expression "Roomsch-Katholijk Schreijver" with Roomsch Katholijk in italics and with some changes in the translation of the additional text of the L makes us feel that he was a Protestant. (We do not know!) What we can detect here is the classical Roman theological position with regard to Papacy and the attitudes in the century to any position other than that of the Roman Church. We do not make any comment on the validity or non validity of the theological explanation of Joseph, nor that of the compiler of the L. However we feel that the Roman position of the universal jurisdiction really does harm to the theological polivalence and, pushed to the extreme, can even harm the real growth of the Church. The question needs more study. We can only list here some authors who can throw light on this question:

Torquemada, Juan de.   Summa de Ecclesia, 1489.

Zanarini, G.   Pope et Patriarches, Paris, 1962.

Giamil, S.   Genuinae relationes inter Sedem Apostolicam et Assyrorum Orientalium seu Chaldeorum Ecclesiam, Romae, 1902.

Vries, Wilhelm de.   Rom und die Patriarchate des Osten Freiburg, 1963.

Vries, Wilhelm de.   Orient et Occident; les structures ecclesiales vues dans l'histoire des premiers concils oecumeniques, Paris, 1974.

Vries, Wilhelm de.   Der Kirchenbegriff der von Rom getrennten Syrer, Roma, 1955.

Kane, Th. A.	The Jurisdiction of the Patriarchs of the major Sees in Antiquity and in the Middle Ages, in Catholic University of America Canon Law Studies, No. 276, Washington, 1949.
Vogel, Fr. J.	Rom und die Ostkirchen, Aschaffenburg. 1959.
Runciman, S.	The Eastern Schism, Oxford, Clarendon, 1955.
Congar, Y. M. J.	L'Ecclesiologie du haut Moyen Age, Paris, 1968.
Maclean, A. J.	The Cathalicos of the East and his people, London, 1892.

83. Acts of the Apostles.
84. This is omitted in D.
85. This is an interpolation in the Latin and Dutch texts We have discussed it in detail in 3.2.3. pp. 116-117.

Chapter 6

86. I: does not have the word "churches," as also the tables of contents of both I and L. In both the word consecration does not seem to be associated with the burial. The content of the chapter which corresponds to it is about the sacraments. There is no mention of the consecration of the churches to justify the word. D has a detailed heading. The title in the tables of contents of *Paesi* and *Itinerarium* probably is more correct. "Sacerdoti com li soi habiti & con la consecratione" and "about the dress of the priests, about consecration and how they bury the bodies...." Cf. pp.

87. I: diaconi et subdiaconi, L: Levitas & hypodiaconas and D: Leviten en Onderhelpers. The Italian diaconi and the Latin and Dutch levitas, (leviten) seem to be equivalent of the M'samsana. in Syriac. Whether there existed subdeacons in the Malabar Church is to be examined. Whether these

words, subdiacon (I), heupdaiacon (L) and onderhelpers (D), denote the Syriac expression of 'heupadiacon' is not clear. Cf. also Mundadan, *Trad.* p. 147; Vries, W. de, *Sakramental theologie bei den Nestorianern*, Roma, 1947, p. 141, Der Subdiakon.

88. The Malabar priests used to retain a tuft of hair on their head as a sign of their priesthood, as did the *Namputhiris* or Hindu priests. It is said that the Christian priests wore a cross on this tuft of hair. Osorius seems to refer to this: "Sacerdotes in capite ita sunt atonsi ut crucis imaginem in vertice summo contineant", *op. cit.*, col. 725, Cf. also Mundadan, *Trad.* p. 147.

89. Osorius confirms this, *op.. cit.*, col. 725. Mundadan, *Trad.* cities Monserrate according to whom children were baptized on the 40th day after birth at the earliest. For further information Cf. Mundadan, *Trad.* p. 168 ff.

90. On the question of the Sacrament of Confession the three texts vary slightly I: 'se confessano se communicano como nui' = 'they confess themselves they communicate as we do.' In the 1507 edition there is no "e" (and) between the two phrases. But in the 1508 edition there is an "e" between the two. Hence, in I "como nui" does not apply to 'confessano'. In L: 'confitentur ut nos eucharistiam sacram sumunt.' It depends on where we put the comma as there is no "et" between the two. But D puts it very clearly: "they confess like those faithful to Rome." We cannot pronounce a final word until we find the Portuguese text on which D was based and also some copy of the original. Though we do not know the exact form of the confession, there was some kind of general confession in practice among the St Thomas Christians. (Cf. Mundadan, *Trad.* p 172.) Penteado, who worked in Malabar in the first half of the 16th century, was told by the Christians that they had only general confession and that they confessed to God in a clear voice all together. That confession as it was known in Europe was not known in Malabar before the coming of the Portuguese is almost accepted by historians now. It is interesting to note that the term used in the canons of the Synod of Diamper

(1599) and the Statutes of Ros, S. J., (1606) to denote the sacrament of confession is *"Kumpasaram"* This is derived from the Portuguese word "Confessao" and is the only European word used in Malayalam to signify any sacrament. For Baptism and Eucharist we have Syriac words; for ordination and matrimony the words are from ancient Malayalam. For Confirmation and Extreme Unction the same Syriac word "Rusma" which means "singing", is used with prefixes "first" and "last" in Malayalam to denote Confirmation and Extreme Unction, respectively. But, for Confession the word used is of Portuguese origin, which shows that it was a Portuguese introduction. But though the canon uses the word *"Kumpasaram"* in different forms the canons of the Synod, when it refers to the act of confessing, it uses the Malayalam word *"Pizhamulal"*, which denoted some kind of sacrament of reconciliation other than confession. Further we read in the Statutes of Ros that if there are people who have not made the "confession" who come for the *"Pizhamulal"*, they should have their sins absolved before coming to it. (Scaria Zacharia, *Randu Pracheena Krithikal*, p. 132.) We feel that this is an indication that the auricular confession, which is a Portuguese introduction and *"Pizhamulal"* was the tradition of Malabar. Hence we feel that the Italian "se confessano" is independent of "como nui" and perhaps the "ut nos" of the L is to be associated with communion. Anyway, it may not be correct to say that Joseph the Indian meant to say that there was confession in the Malabar Church as it was practised in the Roman Church. Ros, S. J., attributes the introduction of confession to Mar Jacob (1498-1552) whereas Soledado attributes it to the work of the Franciscans. Mundadan, *Trad*, p. 173. Vires, Wilhelm de, *Sakramentaltheologie bei den Nestorianern*, Roma, 1947, Ch. VIII, pp. 265-280.

91. According to I: communion is 'como nui" which too is not fully correct if it refers to the mode of communion. For the Eucharist was administered in both species. (Cf. Mundadan, *Trad.*, p. 167 quotes Penteado). Osorius is also very clear on this. "Omnibus sine discrimine, cum

Eucharistiam accedunt, non solum Christi corpus in panis specie, verum & in Calacis consecrati potione porrigitur" *op. cit.*, col. 725.

92. This is one of the sacraments whose existence in Malabar is denied by the Portuguese and post-Portuguese documents. Speaking of confirmation and extreme unction Mundadan says: "as for the other two sacraments it is not impossible that the Portuguese were led to deny their existence on account of the absence of the anointing usually considered necessary at that time for their valid administration." (*Trad.* p. 176.) What Joseph reports is not that there was no Extreme unction but in its place bodies were blessed. The term used in the canons of the Synod of Diamper for Extreme Unction and confirmation as we have stated above are combinations of two prefixes to the adapted form of the Syriac word "Rusma" which in Malayalam becomes *"Oprusma"*. Rusma is the noun form that derives from the verb "rsm" = to sign, sign with the mark of the cross etc which is used in its different shades of meaning. In the common use of the word in Malayalam today, *"Oprusma"*, without the differentiating prefix, "first" or "last', normally signifies the sacrament of Extreme Unction. Perhaps this etymological fact corrobrates what Joseph the Indian said. But, this needs more study before we could say anything finally. We do not know what the rites of this blessing were. The canons of the Synod of Diamper do not tell us much about the ancient practices here. However, the question why this word was chosen for signifying Confirmation and Extreme Unction both of which imply anointing in the Portuguese tradition seems to be a very interesting one. Did the blessing of which Joseph speaks imply oiling? Cf. Also Mundadan, *Trad.*, p. 176. Vries, Wilhelm de, *op. cit.*, Ch. IX, Krankenölung, p. See also Irving, *The ceremonial use of oil-anointing among the Nestorians*, London, 1903.

93. The Malabar tradition seems to have been the use of fermented bread. Discussing this Mundadan writes: "To all probability the bread used in the liturgy was fermented bread although Joseph the Indian is reported to have told the Venetians that the asym bread was in use as in

282 INDIA IN 1500 AD

the Latin Church. No other account of the time except Goes (whose account, as it has been already pointed out earlier, tallies with the report of Joseph) concedes this but all state that the bread used was fermented bread." (*Trad.*, p. 165.). Here though I says: "como nui in azymo", and D: Ongedesemd Brood, L has the clause: "Si tamen id consequi possunt, in azymis, hoc est in pane non fermentato, more nostro." Here there seems to be an implication in the Latin text, at least when non-fermented bread was not available, fermented bread was used as we do. D does not have the expression "as we do", but says "unleavened bread". Here we need to find the original that the translator used before the final word. For more details on Malabar tradition Cf. Mundadan, *Trad.*, pp. 165-6. Vries, W. de. *op. cit*, Die Azymen Frage, p. 193 ff.

94. Barbosa says it came from Mecca and Ormus.

95. This is even now prevalent in traditional families. Cf. also Mundadan, *Trad.* p. 174.

96. It is the "Peshitha" or Syriac translation of the Bible that was in use among the St Thomas Christians. Osorius says: "Sanctis litteras, Syro sermone, quem Chaldaeum nominant, scriptas studiosissime colunt." *op. cit.*, col. 725.

97. Though the word used in I and L is "quadragessima", the fast was called in Malabar "Ampathunoympu" i. e. fifty days fast, which begins at the midnight of the 7th Sunday before Easter. The fasting during this period of advent was also in practice, as the Canons of the Synod of Diamper seem to indicate. 15 days of fasting and 3 days of fasting which were in practice are not mentioned by Joseph. The practice of the three-day fast called the fast of the Ninevites was well-known in some churches. Cf. Mundadan, *Trad.*, pp. 178-9.

98. In spite of the mitigation of these fasts under the Roman influence, traditional people even until recently were very strict about the fast of Good Friday and Holy Saturday.

99 It is very interesting to note the sequence of the feasts in the Narratives of Joseph. It begins not with the date

sequence, but following the oriental tradition, begins with the central feast of Resurrection. Two days following the feast of the Resurrection is also attested by the Synod of Diamper.

100. The octave of Resurrection is celebrated with great solemnity in special commemoration of St Thomas even today in some churches. This feast was also celebrated in the Chaldean churches as many manuscripts reveal. Cf. Vallavanthara, A, *Liturgical Year of the St Thomas Christians, a Study of the Sources,* (Manuscript) Louvam-la-Neuve 1978. See also: Hanssens, J. M., *Institutiones Liturgicae de Ritibus Orientalibus,* Rome, 1930-1932.

101. W. B. Greenlee's translation of the Narratives from *Paesi* omits this feast. In Malabar it was called the feast of the Fortieth day. Synod of Diamper uses the same word. The Syriac expression was Ascension of the Lord.

102. I mentions the feast of St Thomas, which is not found in L or D. We do not know what feast the text means.

103. Assumption, Nativity and Purification of Our Lady were celeberated among the St Thomas Christians. We have already mentioned (n. 97) that there was a 15-day fast, which was in preparation for the feast of Assumption. The Purification of Our Lady was known to the Chaldean Church at least from the 13th century. It might have come to Malabar Church from the Chaldean tradition. Cf. Vallavanthara A. *op. cit.,* p. 181. The order in which D gives the three feasts is different.

104. I and L use the word Epiphany. But D has "Openbaring Christi" which may mean the Revelation or Transfiguration of the Lord. In the Chaldean and Malabar tradition there was the feast of "Gelyane d'maran" i. e. Transfiguration of the Lord, attested by many manuscripts before the 16th century. Does D mean that or does it simply mean Epiphany? Another thing to be noted is that D omits the feast of the Nativity of our Lord.

105. This feast of St Thomas the Apostle is called Dukrana in Malayalam, which is the Syriac word for commemoration. In the oriental Syrian tradition the word feast is used only for the feasts of our Lord, those of the saints,

including our Lady, are called commemorations. I, L and D put this on the first day of the month of July. This does not agree with the living tradition according to which the feast is on third July. This date, 3rd July, cannot be a change that occurred later. For, all liturgical Manuscrip'ic traditions dating back to the 12th century specify the third July, and the rubrics say it should be celebrated on 3rd July, whatever day that may be. This statement is very important in the face of the fact that commemoration of the saints is not usually observed except on Fridays. We cannot accept that Joseph the Indian, who was well-versed in the traditons of the Church, could make mistake in this. Hence the mistake should be attributed to the compiler's lack of understanding, (Cf. also Mundadan, *Trad.*, p. 177.)

106. I: gives poverty and chastity. But, L and D do not mention poverty. On the question of chastity, I and D use he term chastity, (castita and kuysheid) wheras L uses the expression "continentissime." I and D use the word in both cases. Cf. n. 107. The monks are called black monks by L. Goes says the same: "They have monasteries of monks, who wear black dress. There are nuns too. Both monks and nuns live in great observance of honesty, chastity and poverty." (Mundadan, Trad. p. 119). This remark of Goes, adds honesty as the special virtue of the monks which is missing in our document.

107. There is no doubt that the priests were generally married. Although I and D use the same word for monks and priests L clearly distinguishes the two. For monks it uses "continentissime" and for the priests "catissime." Goes, who agrees with Joseph in many things, is clear on this. "The priests keep conjugal chastity, that is, after the death of the first wife they do not marry another." But, later under the influence of the Portuguese, celibacy came into use. Dionysio wrote in 1579: "A few years ago the priests were married. Now all keep celibacy and if some one gets married he remains suspended." (We cite Goes and Dionysio from Mundadan, *Trad.*, p. 148). But the canons of the Synod of Diamper (Canon 11 of the 5th Mautha) very clearly say that there were married priests

in Malabar and introduce new laws of celibacy, and asked them to separate and exercise the priesthood. (Scaria Zacharia, *op. cit.,* P. 60.). Osorius very clearly says: "Sacerdotes uxores ducunt. Prima tamen uxore mortua, est illis in posterum nuptiis omnibus interdictum", (*op. cit.,* col. 726). For the history of the celibacy of priests in the Church see also Gryson, R., *Les Origines du Celibat Ecclesiastique du premier au septième siècle,* Gembloux, 1968; Herman, E., *Celibat et droit Oriental,* in Dict. de Droit Canon, III, pp. 153-154.

108. L and D have the clause whether the marriage is good or bad etc. which I does not have. Joseph says nothing about the sacramentality of marriage.

109. We do not know what the occasions of these communions are? We know that the Christians of St Thomas always made proper preparations for communion, and communion does not seem to have been frequent.

110. On the question of doctors of theology, interpreters of the Bible, all the three sources agree though they are different in the order of their description. Special mention is made of the books of the prophets. Goes repeats what Joseph said: "Their doctors teach the Old and New Law, especially the prophets in public schools. Some of them are well-versed in Law." (Mundadan, *Trad.,* p. 150.)

111. The Christians of Malabar wear cotton clothes. The men and women had their own proper dresses. We do not know why the writer uses the comparison with the Moors.

112. I and L say they have intercalary days, while D says that every four years they have a leap year of three hundred and sixty-six days. The year is divided into 12 months. The era that was in use in Kerala was the Kollam Era, which started in 825 A. D. The peculiarity about the year is that in some parts of Kerala it begins on Chingam 1, the Zodiac month of Leo (August-September) while in other places it begins in Kanni 1, the month of September when the Sun enters the Zodiac sign of Virgo. Cf. Sreedhara Menon, *A Survey of Kerala History,* Kottayam, 1967, Ch. viii, p. 112ff.

286   INDIA IN 1500 AD

113. I and L call these hours, D calls them parts. The hour or part is called "Nazhika"; there are thirty Nazhikas for the day and thirty for the night. D says in brackets not twenty-four hours

114. Even today there are elderly people who can tell the time by looking at the stars.

CHAPTER 7-8

115. I: between the equinoctial circle (circulo equinoctiale) and the Tropic of Cancer (circulo cancro). L: Summer tropic (tropicum aestivum) and the equator (aequatorem). D: tusschen de Somer Sonnen wende (Solstitium Aestivum) and the equator (Aequator of Evenaar).

116. The difference between the length of the day or night in summer and winter is not so much marked as in Europe.

117. Even today the ordinary people in their everyday language use these astronomical information and express them in their own terminology derived from daily experience. The astronomical data that we have here in scientific terms, they express as "south slanting and north slanting."

118. Here mention is made of the monsoons called 'Kala Varsham,' when there are heavy rains and the west wind blows very strongly. On the coast of Kerala there are two seasons for rain. The first is Kalavarasham of which mention is made here. The other is Thulavarsham i. e. the rain of the month of Thulam (mid-September to the end of October.).

119. The names of the countries of the west to which the ships from Cranganore sail are slightly different in the three texts. I: gives Persia, Arabia and the Red Sea. L: gives Erythrian Sea and not Red Sea. D: gives Red Sea and Pontus Exinus. On the east the countries mentioned are the same, except for two. (Cf. no. 120 and 121.)

120. It is not clear what I means by this. L and D mention the Indian Ocean.

121. I does not mention this. L: Chersonesum aureum. D: Chersonesus aurea.

122. Taprobana in the Narratives of Joseph the Indian stands for Sumatra. This is well specified in the last chapter of the Narratives. The Latin text clearly says: "Post hanc (Cape Comerin) ad orientem visitur quae dicitur Samatra nos Taprobanam appellamus quae abest ab urbe Calechut itinere trium mensium." (Cf. nos. 194 and 195.) I: says there "Samotra o uer Taprobana." D: "Samotra ... en werd van ons genoemd Taprobana." We do not know from what year the name Taprobana came to be used for Sumatra. In the *Christian Topography* of Cosmas Indicopleustes of the 6th century, Cosmos uses this word for Ceylon. Cosmos writes: "This is a big island situated in the Ocean, in the Indian Sea, the island named by the Indians Sielediva and by the Greeks Taprobane." (Cosmas Indicapleustes, *Topographie Chretienne*, edited and translated (French) by W. Wolska Conus, Paris, 1973, Vol. III, p. 342, translation mine.). For more details about the name Taprobane Cf. E. O. Winsted, *The Christian Topography of Cosmas Indicapleustes*, edited with geographical notes, Cambridge, 1909; J. W. Mc Crindle, *The Christian Topography of Cosmas, an Egyptian Monk*, London, 1897, p. 363, n. 3.

123. I: Faillam, L: Faylla (m), D: Faylla. This is Ceylon or present-day Sri Lanka. In the last chapter of the Narratives it is given as Saylam or Sayla. (See inf. no. 193.)

124. Greenlee gives these islands as the Laccadiv Islands. Cf. W.B. Greenlee *op. cit.*, p. 105.

125. The three texts reveal certain differences in the description of the ships. D is briefer than the other two.

126. "questo dico pche sonno alcuni che dicono ester...& ac de questo volsi diligemente intendere dal predicto Joseph." It is very important here to note that the Italian uses the first person here; compare this with the expressions in 2 Chapter "according to the judgement of those who have seen and spoken with him," "in so far as could be understood by them, he is of exemplary life" etc. which

would make us feel that the writer of the Narratives did not have personal acquaintance with Joseph. But here the text of I is closer to the L, where we read: "id dixerim," "sciscitatus sum," and "ostendi...ratus (sum)" etc. Both I and L mention how Joseph laughed and said, which is omitted in D. Cf. Part II, 2.3.4. p. 91-92. The writer of the Narratives.

127. This information is not given in L & D.

128. For the coins of Kerala, Cf. Yule and Burnell, *Hobson-Jobson: A Glossary of Colloquial Anglo-Indian Words and Phrases and of Kindred terms. Etymological Historical, Geographical and Discursive*, London, 1903, articles "Pardao," "Xerafina," "Tara or Tare."

129. I: Sarapho, L: Saraphum, D: Zaraph. I says it is equivalent in weight to one ducat, while D says it is worth one ducat and L says it is equivalent to a ducat both in weight and value. Cf. Yule and Burnell *op. cit.*, article on Xarafina.

130. Silver coin: I: Parante, L: Parantem, D: Paran. I & L says that it is equivalent to six soldi. D says it is equivalent to six Dutch Schelling in the 18th century. Cf. Yule and Burnell *op. cit*, article on Paradao.

131. Tare. Only I gives the name. L and D mention only the value. This coin is equivalent to one soldi, or one Dutch Schelling. Greenlee says that Tare also was a silver coin. Cf. Yule and Burnell *op. cit.*, article on Tare.

132. I says: "these coins have the letters of their kings engraved." L & D say that there is the image and the "subscription" or "onderschrift."

133. The place mentioned here seems to be Mysore.

134. Cambay. I calls it here Cambait, and elsewhere Cambaia. D. does not mention it in this context. More details about it Cf. Chapters 12 and 13 in 4.2.0. pp. 204-213 and 4.3.0. pp. 252-256. inf. nos. 160, 162, 167.

135. I: Palme che produce le noce de India. (Palm which produces India (n) nuts). L: De palmis & nucibus Indiae. About palms and Indian nuts. Cf. inf. no. 139.

Chapter 9

136. As regards the preparation, D says only that the inhabitants prepare very good bread. According to L it is prepared by mixing rice (flour) and sugar. I says: "grinding with sugar and oil."

137. Probably the root meant here is tapioca (?)

138. Probably the fig tree mentioned by Joseph here is jackfruit.

139. I: nuts of India (le noce de India), L: fert Indas noces: produces Indian nuts. D: Indiaansche Noten. Indian Nuts. Here we have the echo of Karua Indika of Cosmas Indicapleustes. In Book XI of the Christian Topography Cosmas speaks about the Karuon ton Indikon. (W. Wolska-Conus, *op. cit.*, Vol. III, pp. 336–337). Perhaps this terminology of Cosmas was prevalent in Europe at the time of Joseph. For I uses the expression: "quel arboro a modo nostro produce le noce ap India." However, seeing the mention of the four products we ask ourselves, if there is not some confusion or mix up of coconuts and the other palm trees by the writer. Cf. no. 140.

140. Of the four products that Joseph mentions, sugar is prepared not from coconut trees but from palm trees. The process of the production of these things are given in detail. Cf. no. 143.

141. Strabo (64/63 BC–23 AD). The work mentioned here is *Strabonis rerum geographicorum libris XVII*. Lutentiae, Parisorum 1620.

142. I and L give the citation from Strabo here. D omits the citation here but has more additions later Cf. no. 146.

Chapter 10

143. Certain details of the prepartion of these four products are defective and show lack of knowledge of the writer of those things rather than defective narration of Joseph. For example, the author compares the process of drawing the wine with the pruning of vines etc. So too with the process of making sugar. In spite of all these defects it is very informative and close to the reality.

144. Dried kernel of the coconut is called "Copra."

145. Ropes are made from the fibres covering the outer shell of the coconuts. Baskets are made from the central stem of the leaves.

146. What is given in brackets in the Dutch text is not found in the other two texts. It seems to be an interpolation.

147. The coast of Malabar is known for its pepper. We know that to the port of Cranganore was brought much pepper from the interior of the country. We know that the St Thomas Christians were cultivators of pepper. This is clear from the letter of Mar Jacob to the King John III of Portugal. (Schurhammer, *Three Letters*, pp. 339-342.) It is the "country of pepper", "Male where pepper grows", "the Male with its five ports exporting the pepper" of which Cosmas Indicopleustes speaks in his *Christian Topography*. Cf. Wanda Wolska-Conus, *op. cit.*, pp. 344, 346.

CHAPTER 11

148. Westward. This is to be understood according to the geographical conceptions of the time. Actually Calicut lies to the north of Cranganore. They thought that the coast of Malabar lay east-west rather than north-south.

149. This is an explicatory addition by the editor of the Dutch text, which is not found in the other two texts. This is another interpolation Cf. 3. 2. 3. pp. 116-118.

150. Note the differences in the these texts in the names of the merchants who come to Calicut.

151. Guzerati. The people of Gujarat are well-known as traders.

152. Cf. sup. 65.

153. I: Mailapet, L: Mailapetam, D: Meilopetam. D give another reading: Masulipatam. Greenlee says that it is Malakka and the qualification "a city of a King Narsindo" he explains as a confusion. And he changes Indus into Ganges and then the 900 miles east of it would bring to Malakka. On the other hand if we take Indus for what it is, then

the 900 miles from there eastward according to the geographical conception of the time would bring us to the Choramandel coast. However, we cannot say with certainty that it is Mylapore since speaking about the Church of St. Thomas and the body of St Thomas the three texts mention Milapar, which in the three texts is given in the same way. Here the three texts have three different names. The Dutch text gives as a second reading Masulipatam. (Note Mailapet, Mailapetam, Masulipatam are wrongly printed in the translations on pp. 198, 247, read them as in the original texts.)

154. Cf. inf. nos. 175, 182.
155. Malasines: Greenlee thinks that they are Chinese.? I follows the description of the Chinese and begins as follows: "These people are called Malasines." L also has the same expression. However D begins as follows: "certain nations named Malisines", which would give the impression that it is not the sequence of what was being discussed but a new topic. Has it got anything to do with Maha Cina = Great China. Cf. Podipara, *op. cit.*, p. 32. (Corrigendum: read Malasenes as Malasines in I & D.)
156. The practice of Sati was mentioned above in chapter 4 of I and L and 3 of D. Cf. sup. no. 53.
157. D: confuses the two citations.
158. The names of the countries from which merchants come to the annual fair of Calicut are given differently in the three texts.
159. I: alone gives us the name of the duke whose coins Joseph brought. The coins were of Michele Steno, Venetian Doge 1400-1414. Cf. Greenlee, *op. cit.*, p. 110.

Chapter 12

160. *Cambaia.* I has two forms: Cambaia and Combait (sup. no. 134). L: Cambaia, D: Cambaia and Cambaya. The Grande Encyclopedia Portuguesa e Brasileira describes it as follows: "Golfo do oceano Indico, na costa do qual estao situado os dist. de Goa Damao e Dio da India Portuguesa. The gulf is also known by the same name: Gulf of Cambaia.

292 INDIA IN 1500 AD

161. *Ormus* (Ormuz). This is the island located where the Persian gulf begins. It always played an eminent role in the trade and commerce between the coast of Malabar and Europe. Its geographical midway position on the route gave it great importance. According to the Narratives of Joseph the Indian, Ormus is 1500 miles from Cranganore, 300 miles from Cambaia. Ormus was visited by Marco Polo and Oderic in the 13th century. Milton in his *Paradise Lost* speaks about the glory of Ormus. Cameons wrote of Ormus in the Os Lusiades II, 49.

"Vireis de Ormuz o reino poderoso
Duas vezes tomado e subjugado"

162. Guzerat. It is the present Suratte.
163. I: gives 12,000 miles which is to be understood as 12,00 miles. L & D say above thousand miles, which is more accurate. We are told in the Narratives that Ormus is 1500 miles from Cranganore and Ormus is 300 miles from Cambaia. Between Calicut and Cranganore the distance is 90 miles. Hence it should be exactly 1110 miles from Calicut.
164. We do not know exactly which cities these are.
165. I: Bedrosia, L and D: Betrosia. D gives another reading: Gedrosia.
166. This statement is not found in D.

CHAPTER 13

167. This is Cambay.
168. L: Gulf of Guzerat. D: River of Guzerat.
169. I says Mohammedan, the other two say, of the sect of Mohammed. D does not clearly tell as how the Hindu ruler was replaced. I and L describe it.
170. I alone gives incense. L and D mention only lac.
171. I: India as in no. 120, while L and D give Indian Ocean.
172. I: Maya, L: Maya, D: Maia.
173. All the three give the same name.
174. D: has some additional information about Cambaia, which is not found in the other two.

Chapter 14

175. I and L call him Narsindo. D says King of Narsinga and Narsindus. L later uses the form Narsindi. He is the Vijayanagar King. The Portuguese name Vijayanagar as Bisnaga or Narsinga. Cf. also nos. 154 and 182.
176. See inf. no. 183.
177. Cochin of today. Cf. sup. 19. From the three texts we have three different spellings of this. On the kingdom of Cochin Cf. Francis Day, *The Land of the Perumals or Cochin its past and present*, Madras, 1863.
178. Comera. It stands for Cape Comerin. See inf. no. 185.
179. Oriza. See inf. no. 187.
180. Stands for Mylapore. See inf. no. 188.
181. See inf. no. 190.
182. What Joseph says seems to be very true. The kingdom of Vijayanagar was a small kingdom in the 14th century. But, at the time of Joseph the Indian, it included a greater part of South India. Mundadan enumerates the areas included in the kingdom of Vijayanagar. We quote him: "The kingdom of Vijayanagar, which had grown from being a small state of Karnataka in the 14th century, in this period included the greater parts of South India. On the North-East it extended to Telungana, on the South-East to the Tamil speaking Malabar or Choramandel, or the country of the Cholas. Toward the West it included the coastal provinces below the Ghats consisting of N. and S. Canara. This province of the Vijayanagar ended in Cumbola, as has been pointed out earlier, at the Chandragiri river from where Malabar extended Southwards." (Mundadan STC, p. 7, Cf. also no 154 and 175.).
183. It is the famous city of Bisnagar: Vijayanagara.
184. This is to be taken in the geographical concept of Ptolemy according to which India lies East to West. Actually of the places described Cape Comerin is South of Cochin, Ceylon South-West, Sumatra is in the East, Oriza is north-east of Cochin.
185. I: Cumari, L: Cumar, D: Cumaar. The Cape is called

Kanya Kumari and in English Cape Comerin. I is closer to the Malayalam.

186. Indus. Greenlee corrects it as Ganges. This needs further study.

187. Oriza: According to Barbosa the kingdom Oriza is one of the 16th century north Indian kingdoms. The city of Oriza belongs to it. Barbosa I 228 ff., quoted by Mundadan STC, p. 7.

188. All the three texts agree on the name. It is Mylapore. For more details about this Cf. Mundadan, *Traditions*.

189. The Church of St Thomas see no. 190.

190. The question of the Church of St Thomas and the tomb of St Thomas were subjects of many studies and controversies. That St Thomas died in Malabar belongs to the living traditions of the St Thomas Christians of Malabar. The best and most recent study on the question is found in Mundadan's *The Traditions of Thomas Christians*. From there one can get all the references to other studies. After studying the question at length Mundadan makes the following remark which is worth citing.

"Whatever be the conclusion from these facts as to the certainty, or high probability, or probability, of the South Indian apostolate of St Thomas and as to the origination from the Apostle of the Christians of St Thomas, we should think that we are entitled to say at least this much: in the light of these facts the position of those who deny the South Indian apostolate of St. Thomas is much more difficult to demonstrate than that of those who assert it." *op. cit.*, p. 82.

191. Sayla. Ceylon. See sup. 123.

192. See sup. no. 122

193. This shows the scientific truthfulness of the writer.

Appendix I

Paesi Nouvamente Retrouvati

Different editions and versions

Introduction

We have said in Part I that *Paesi* was first published in 1507 and was re-edited five times in 1508, 1512, 1517, 1519 and 1521. A fascimile reprint of the 1508 edition appeared in 1916. The German and Dutch translations were made in 1508. The French translation was first published in 1515 and was re-edited in 1515-16, 1516, 1521, 1528 and 1529. Partial translation of *Paesi* into English and Portuguese appeared in 1937 and 1966 respectively.[1] In the following pages we attempt a detailed description of the *Paesi* and its various editions and translations.

First edition of the Paesi: 1507

The *Paesi* of 1507 was quarto in size and consisted of 125 folios. The title-page is followed by five folios containing table of contents, and the dedicatory letter of Montalboddo Fracan. The rest of the folios (7^r – 125^r) contain the description of the voyages. On the verso of the last folio is the colophon.

The folios are not numbered. The fascicles are numbered + a, b, c, d, e ····z P A B C D. For facility of understanding we count the folios from 1 in the normal way. There are 125 folios. We do not know if Harrisse is correct in giving the number of sheets as 126. The two copies we could consult have only 125 folios.

Folio 1^r	Title page (verso is blank)
Folios 2^r – 6^r	Table of contents
Folio 6^v	Dedicatory letter of Montalboddo Fracan
Folios 7^r – 47^r	Book I

---

1. For details Cf. 1.1.0., 1.1.1. pp. 3,5, 1.2.0. ff. pp. 11-24.

⁋ Stampato in Vicentia cū la impenſa de Mgſo
Henrico Vicentino: & diligente cura & indu
ſtria de ȝamaria ſuo fiol ad. M.ccccvii. a
di. iii. de Nouembre. Cum graua &
priuilegio p ani. x. como nella
ſua Bolla appareche p
ſo del Dominio Ve
neto nó ardiſca i
primerlo.
✠

✠ a b c d e f g h i k l m n o p q r s t v x y z ꝫ & A B C D
Tutti ſono ducmi excepto la tauola che i cerno

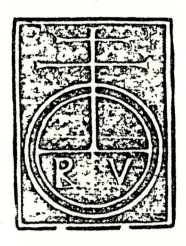

The last page (folio 125v) of *Paesi* 1507 with the colophon,
"Printed in Vicentia ...... on 3rd November 1507
(Cf. pp. 297 1.2.1. p. 12-13)

Folios 47v – 64r	Book II
Folios 64r – 77v	Book III
Folios 77v – 100v	Book IV
Folios 101r – 107v	Book V
Folios 107v – 125r	Book VI
Folio 125v	Colophon.

The Narratives of Joseph on folios 116r – 125r.

On the title page there is a rectangle in which is a globe surrounded by a scroll. On the upper edge of the rectangle is printed CUM PRIVILEGIO. On the scroll encircling the globe inside the rectangle is printed in red, and irregularly owing to the folds of the scroll the title: *Paesi Nouvamente Retrouati et Novo Mondo da Alberico Vesputio Florentino Intitulato.*[2]

The verso of the title page is blank, which is followed by five folios containing tabula communis and the dedicatory letter of Montalboddo Fracan The following folios contain the description of the voyages, which end on the recto of folio 125.

The colophon is given on the verso of folio 125 which reads: "*Stampato in Vicentia cum la impensa de Mgro Henrico Vicentino: & diligente cura & industria de Zamaria suo fiol nel M.CCCCCVII a di iii. de Novembre. Cum gratia & privilegio p āni X como nella sua Bolla appare che per sōa del Domino Venato non ardisca i primerlo.* Below that there is cross on a circle inside a small rectangle in which are the letters R. V. (See p. 296)

Book I. (Chapters 1-47)

"*In comenza el libro de la prima Navigatione per loceano a le terra de Nigri de la Bassa Ethiopia per comandamento del illustr. Signor Infante Don Hurich fratello de Don Dourth Re de Portugallo.*

Beginning of the book of the first Navigation to the "land of the Black" from "Bassa Ethiopia" by the order of Illustrious Infante Don Hurich brother of Don Dourth, king of Portugal.

---

2. Countries newly discovered and the New world of Alberic Vesputius, the Florentine.

¶ Montalboddo Fracan. al suo amicissimo Ioánimaria Anzolello Vicentino. S.

¶ Volentiere adesso io alderia la opinióe de alcuni Ioánimaria mio charissimo: liquali ardiscono imbrattarse la bocca cótra de Plinio Sūmo scriptor & recitatore deli altri grauissimi cusi greci como latini Auctori: existimante chello piu psto cose icredibile & uane: ch d alcūa ueresi. xiliitudie & uerita scriua. Et p qsto temerariamète el biasemano de mendatio: psuadendose pch loro nó hāno uisto: ne cognosciuto tal cose: ne se retrouāo inqsti nri paesi: ch ne anch altroue siāo. La opinióe dliqli qto sia futile & d niuo momēto: le pnte Nauigatióe idiuersi paesi dal nro cótinēte disiūcte: mai piu p memoria de hó cognosciute aptamēte el dechiarano. Doue o ueramēte ch tu cósideri le moltiplice spē de li Aiali: dele piāte: dele herbe: deli Metalli & pietre: o ueramēte la diuersita d li lochi: & qlita del cielo: nó meno cose admirāde: & qsi icredibile se retrouane: ch apsto della Naturale historia pliniana. Et sesostēno cusi cū pingue & florido stile latino scripte: como in rude parlar uulgare: & Portogallese lingua: forsi q!!e trapassariano. Comoch tu medesimo p la expientia de molte cose: & longa lectióe poterai iudicare: & respondere ala temerua de qlli: liquali tāto sogliano credere: qto uedeno. La ql cosa azo tu el faccie piu uolentier mio amātissimo: ho uoluto ch qsti Viaggi uengheno in luce: & sotto del tuo nome siano publicati. Si pch hauēdo tu qsi tutta la Europa: & grā parte del Asia pagrato: intanta diuersita de cose discerne: ql siano piu marauigliose. Si ancora azoch li audienti & cupidi lectiōn de cose noue intendano te da nui & meritamēte esser ben soluto: & singularmēte amato. Vale.

The dedicatory letter of Montalboddo Fracan,
on folio 6v of *Paesi* 1507.

Book II. (Chapters 48-70)

Libro secundo de la naviagatione de Lisbona a Callichut de lengua Portugallese intaliana.

The second book of the navigation from Lisbon to Callichut (translated) from Portuguese language into Italian.

Book III. (Chapters 71-83)

De la Navigatione de Lisbona a Calichut de lingua Protugallese intaliana.

Of the naviagation from Lisbon to Calichut (translated) from Portuguese language into Italian.

Book IV. (Chapters 125-142)

In comenza la navigatione del Re Castglia dele Isole & Paese nouamente retrouate. Libro quarto.

Beginning of the navigation of the King of Castiglia of the islands and countries newly discovered. Book four.

Book V. (Chapters 114-124)

El Nouo Mondo ¦de Lengue Spagnole interpretato in Idioma Ro. Libro Quinto.

"The New World (translated) from the Spanish into the Roman Language." Book five.

Book VI. (Chapters 84-113)

Libro sexto de le cose da Calichut conforme ala navigatione de Pedro Aliares nel ii & iii libro lequelle se hanno uerisseme perle copie de alcum lettre. secundo lordne de li millessimi in questo ultimo racolte.

"The sixth book of the things about Calichut which corresponds to the navigation of Peter Aliares (contained) in the 2nd and 3rd book which are proved to be true by some letters (given) according to the order of the year collected in this last (book).

TABVLA

Contra laudatia de chi uol fapere piu che nō fe coûenc.c.cxxiiii.
Copia de una littera del.D.Credico Nancio de la Illuſtriſſima Signoria de Venetia in Portogallo. Cap.cxxv.
Copia de la littera:de.D.Piero Paſqualigo Orator de la Hiuſtriſſima Signoria in Portogallo doue ſe contiene una altra. nauigatione uerſo tramontana. Cap.cxxvi.
Littera de Franceſco de la Saita Cremoneſe a.D. Pietro Paſqualigo. Cap.cxxvii.
Littera de li Mercatanti de Spagna ali ſoi côreſpondēti.c.cxxviii.
Com: Ioſeph ſo uno de quilli chriſtiani che de poi la occiſione in Calichut al Regno de Cuchin aſceſe noſtre Carauelle per Portogallo & Roma. Cap.cxxix.
La deſcriptione dela qualita & ſtatura de ioſeph cō la ſua cita Carangonor; laqual altri ſeriue Carangolo : & que coſa ſia Gentile. Cap.cxxx.
Le tre parte de gentil in Carangonor con le gluefie & modo de ſacrificare. Cap.cxxxi.
Coſtumi del Re de Carangonor & li principali con le ſue dōne & ornamenti & doue comenza la India ; & doue ſonno molti chriſtiani. Cap.cxxxii.
Caſe del Carangonor:& Pontifice:Cardinali:Veſcoui & altri ſacerdoti al gouerno de la loro eccleſia. Cap.cxxxiii.
Sacerdoti con li ſoi habiti & con la conſecratione:El ſepelire deli morti:le feſte loro:& li ualenti homini che hāno. Cap.cxxxiiii.
Sotto que parte del cielo ſia carangonor:& quando hanno lo inuerno.Item le naue como ſonno fatte: & in que paeſi nauigano. Cap.cxxxv.
Le lor monete:donde uen lo oro:la qualita deli homini con la longa uita. Item la fertilita del paeſe:le arme che uſano: & li animali che hanno. Cap.cxxxvi.
Pane herbe & arbori : uno deliquali chiamano Palma che produce.iiii.coſe marauiglioſe uidelicet Vino : Aceto : zuccaro : & Olio. Cap.cxxxvii.
El modo de fare le.iiii.ſupraſcripte coſe con le ſpeciarie che li naſcono. Cap.cxxxviii.
De la cità de Calichut & Re con li habitanti . Item deli ſoi coſtumi: arme: & noſtri paeſi la nominati. Cap.cxxxix.
La deſcriptione del Regno de Cambaie:& de la Iſola Ormus: cō molti preſenti lor coſtumi:preſertim de guzeratti. Cap.cxl.
Sito de la cita de cambaia con molti altri lochi maritimi:& el Re

The table of contents of *Paesi* 1508. (Cf. p. 305, 1.1.1. p. 5., 1.2.5. p. 16) Note the titles of the chapters of the Narratives of Joseph the Indian (Cf. pp. 130, 132, 134, 297).

Chapter cxxv (125):

Copia de uno Capitulo de lre de D. Critico de la illustrisima Signoria de Venetia in Portugallo date a di XXVII Zungo Mccccci.

Copy of a chapter of the letter of a Cretan, the correspondent of the illustrious Segnoria of Venice in Portugal, written on 27th June 1501.

Chapter cxxviii (128)

Copia de una La receuta da li Mercanti de Spangna ali soi Corespondenti in Fiorenza & in Venetia del trato de la pace intra el Re de Portugallo & el Re de Calichut.

Copy of a letter of the Spanish merchant to his correspondent in Florence and in Venice, about the treaty of peace between the king of Portugal and the king of Calichut.

Chapter cxxvi (126)

Copia de una lre de Dno Piero Pasqualigo orator dela illustrassima Signoria in Portugallo scripta a soi fratelli in Lisbona a di XIX Octobrio del Mccccci.

Copy of a letter of Peter Pasqualigo the ambasador of the illustrious Signoria to Portugal written to his brothers in Lisbon (dated) 19th October 1502.

Chapter cxxvii (127)

Copia de una Lre de Francesce de la Saita Cremone se data in Lisbona a di XVI Septembrio Mcccccii & derizata in Spagna a Domino Pietro Pisqualigo oratore de la Illustrissimi Re de Castiglia.

Copy of a letter of Francis de la Saita Cremone given in Lisbon dated 19th September 1502 written to Spain to Peter Pasqualigo, ambassador of the Most Illustrious King of Castiglia.

Chapters 129-142: The Narratives of Joseph the Indian.

As already indicated the Narratives of Joseph the Indian occurs in Chapters 129-142 contained on the last nine and a half folios of *Paesi*.

A 1.1.1. The different editions of Paesi

Paesi had been re-edited five times, within fifteen years,

SEXTO

⁋ Como Ioseph Indiano ascesso le nostre Carauelle uéne Porto nigallo & lo Re losece acópagnare a Roma & a Venetia.   c.cxxix.

Auendo altre uolte el Re de Portogal inteso p̄ sui Nauili & altri Portogalesi per le p̄te australi andar ale p̄te de India: aderendosi ad alcuni soi uenuti de q̃lle p̄te ne li tempi pteriti delibero nel áno.M.ccccc.el re sopra nomi nado H. manuel mandar.xii. tra naue & Carauelle: Capo d q̃lle Pedro aluares: q̃le hauto el Ståndardo dl suo Capitáiato a di.viii. del mese de Marzo del dcō millesimo: se parti d portogal: & nauigádo cū gradissime fortūe & pericholi adi. xiii. del mese de Septēbre pur del dcō millesimo zonseno a Calichut cū Carauelle.vii.iiii. de q̃lle psortuna erano pse & una ando a Zaflal: nel q̃l loco' de Cali. but steteno per mesi. iii. tandé a luli ma per certe desterente ueneno ale mano cum quelli de terrai & morti alcuni de le Carauelle & etiam molti del loco predicto se leuoreno adi. xxiii. Nouembre del 'dcō millesimo: & zonseno dū naue & Carauelle a Cuchi loco distáte da Calichut mugha.cx. el q̃l loco de cuchi e posto sopra el mar & e signor d q̃llo ano Re Idolatro: d la letta d q̃l d Colochut: dal re d q̃l loco soreno receptate le carauelle p̄ dcēr & factoli bona cōpagnia: le q̃l stando in dcō loco & cōtractādo diuerse mercātie: cōe nele nauigano ānscripte appere del.iu. libro.cap.lxxvii. ueneno da una cita chiamata car̄a ganor luta dal dcō loco d cuchi p spacio d milia.xx.ii. fratelli apiāi q̃li d̄siderāoāo uennte ale pte d ponēte p poter andar

B 11

Folio 116r of *Paesi* 1508
Here begins the Narratives of Joseph the Indian. (Cf. p. 297, 301 p. 15)

three in Venice and two in Milan. We know also of the facsimile edition in 1916 of the 1508 edition. Here, below we, give the details of the title, place and date of the various editions.

1. Second Edition (1508)

The second edition of *Paesi* was brought out in the year 1508. It was published from Milan under the title: *Paesi Nouamente Retrouati et Nouo Mondo da Alberico Vesputio Florentino, Intitulato*, Milan 1508. The facsimile edition of this was published in the year 1916, under the title Vespucci Reprints, texts and studies, VI, London.

2. Third Edition (1512)

The third edition of *Paesi* was again published from Milan on 27th March 1512, by Ioanne Angelo Scinzenzeler. It was entitled: *Paesi Nouvamente Retrouati & Nouo Mondo da Alberico Vesputio Florentio Intitulato*, Milan, 1512.

3. Fourth Edition (1517)

The fourth edition of *Paesi* was published from Venice. This edition shows some difference in the title: *Paesi Nouvamente Retrouati per la Navigatione in Calicut. Et da Albertutio Vesputio Fiorentino Intitulato Mondo Novo*. This was published by Zorzi Rusconi on 18th August 1517 in Venice.

5. Fifth Edition (1519).

The fifth edition of work was again published on 5th March by the same Ioanne Angelo Scinzenzeler under whose care the 1512 edition was prepared. It had the title: *Paesi Nouamente Retrouati & Nouo Mondo da Alberico Vesputio Florentino Intitulato*.

6. Sixth Edition (1521)

The sixth edition of *Paesi* again came from Milan. It has the same difference in the title as the 1517 Milan edition of Zorzi Rusconi, as this edition, was done under his guidance. The title reads: *Paesi Nouamente Retrouati per la Navigatione di Spagna in Calicut. Et da Albertutio Vesputio Fiorentino Intitulato Mondo Nouo. Nouamente impresso*. This was published on 15th February, 1521.

Paesi nouamente retrouati.& Nouo Módo da Alberico Vespu
cio Florentino intitulato.

Title page of *Paesi* 1508 (Cf. p. 303, 1.2.5. p. 16. 1.1.1. p. 5).

APPENDIX 305

The Various Translations of Paesi.[1]

Paesi was translated into German, Dutch and French. We do not know of any complete English or Portuguese translation of *Paesi*. However, some part of *Paesi* related to the voyage of Cabral was translated into English in 1937. The same was also translated into Portuguese from English. Hence we have the translation of the Narratives of Joseph the Indian contained in *Paesi*, both in English and Portuguese. We do not know any other translation of *Paesi*. There was no Latin translation of *Paesi*. We have proved elsewhere that the general view that the *Itinerarium Portugallensium* of Archangelus Madrignanus of 1508 is the translation of *Paesi* is not correct.[2]

The German Translation

The German translation of *Paesi* appeared in 1508. It was made by Jobston Ruchamer and was published from Nuremburg in Germany on 20th September, 1508. Its title was *Newe Vnbekanthe landte und ein newe weldte in kurtz verganger Zeythe erfunden*. The colophone reads as follows: "There ends this little book which has been translated from Italian into German by the most worthy and learned Jobston Ruchamer, Doctor of Arts and Medicine. It was printed and published by me George Stuechezen at Nuremburg, A. D. 1508, the Wednesday before St. Mathew's September 20th." It seems that there were different editions of this translation. Camus gives a short description of the contents of the German editions. Harrisse and Vignaud give some description.

The Dutch Translation

The Dutch translation of *Paesi* appeared in 1508 in Lübeck. It depends wholly on the German translation. Its title was; *Nye unbekande Lande unde eine nye Werldt in korter forgangener tyd gefunden*.

The French Translation:

The French translation of *Paesi* came from the pen of Mathurin de Redouer, licencé in Law. There were in all

---

1. Cf. 1.2.5. pp. 16-17.
2. Cf. 1.3.6. p. 38.

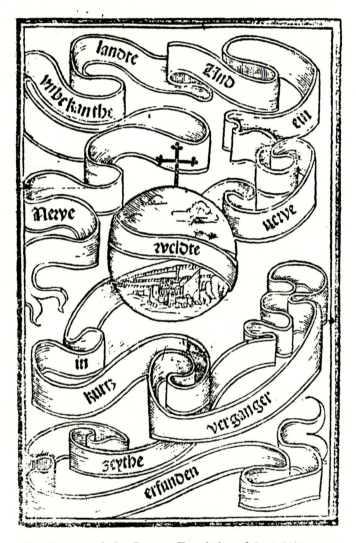

The title page of the German Translation of *Paesi* (1508). The title reads *Newe vnbeckanthe landte und ein newe weldte in kurtz verganger zeythe erfunden* (Cf. p. 307, 1.2.5. p. 16).

six editions of the French translation. The first edition, not dated, is supposed to have been published in 1515 The last edition of the French translation, also not dated is considered to have been published in 1529. The other editions appeared in 1515-16, 1516, 1521 and 1528. Here below we give more details about each edition.

First Edition (1515)

The title of the first French translation was: *Sensuyt Le Nouveau Monde & Navigationes faictes par Emeric de Vespuce Florentin. Des pays & isles nouuellement trouvez, au parāuant a nous incognez, tant en Ethiopie que Arab, Calichut et autres plusieurs regions estranges. Translat de l'Italien en langue Francoise par Mathurin du Redouer licencé en loix.*

The title could be translated into English as follows: *The New World and Navigations made by Emirie of Vespuce the Florentine. Of the countries and islands newly discovered which were unknown to us before, such as Ethiopia and Arabia, Calichut and many other foreign regions. Translated from Italian language into French by Mathurin du Redouer, licencé in Law.* It is octo in size and has 94 folios. This was printed in Paris. Harrisse says that Brunet is of the opinion that this should be the earliest edition of the French translation of *Paesi*, and ascribes it to the year 1515. Lenglet du Fresnoy thinks the date 1519.

This translation into French has corrected the mistake in the numbering of the chapters, and hence has only 141 chapters all together. The table of contents of the first edition does not indicate the division of the books. In the title of the 2nd and 3rd Books we have: *The second Book (The Third Book) of the Navigation from Lisbon to Calicut, translated from Portuguese into Italian and from Italian to French.*

Second Edition (1515-1516)

The title of the second edition is: *Sensuyt le Nouveau Monde & Navigations faictes par Emiric de Vespuce Florentin. Des Pays & isles nouvellement trouvez au pauāt a nous incognez. Tant en l'Ethiopie que Arabie, Calechut & aultres plusieurs regiõs*

The title page of the French translation of 1515–1516 (?) edition
(Cf. p. 307, 309)

estranges. XIX. Brunet says that: "This edition does not contain, neither the privilege nor the date, so that it is difficult to know if it was prior to or follows that of "Galliot du Pre" which was published in 1516. It was published from Paris.

Third Edition (1516)

The title of the third edition is: *Le Nouveau Monde et Navigation par Emeric de Vespuce florentin. Des pays et isles nouuellmet trouvez au parauant a nous incognez. Thant en lethiopie, q' arabie, Calichut & aultres plusieurs regions estranges. Translate de italien en Langue francoyse par Mathurin du Redouer, licencie es Loix.* This was published in 1516. Camus says: "La croix du Main a indique cet ouvrage comme imprimé à Paris Galiot du Prē en 1616."

Fourth Edition (1521)

The title is: *Sensuyt le Noueau Monde et Navigations faictes········ estranges* (as in the first and second editions). *Translate de ytalie en langue francoyse per Mathurin du Redouer licencie es loys.* XIX. This was published in Paris by Philip Noir.

Fifth Edition (1528)

The title is: *Sensuit le nouveau monde····* (as in the previous editions). Imprimé nouvellement en Paris, 1528.

Sixth Edition (1529)

The title is the same as above. There is no means of fixing its date. Harrissee locates it in the year 1529.

The English translation

We do not know of any complete English translation of *Paesi*. Parts of *Paesi* related to the voyage of Cabral was translated into English by W. B Greenlee and published by the Hakluyt Society in 1937. The work was entitled *"The Voyage of Pedro Alvares Cabral to Brazil and India from contemporary documents and Narratives.* It contains among other things, the *Anonymous Narratives* (i. e. What is contained in chapters 63-82 of *Paesi*) and the *Narratives of Joseph the Indian* (contained in chapters 129-142 of *Paesi*).

The Portuguese Translation

Greenlee's work was translated into Portuguese by Antonio Alvaro Doria in 1966. The title of the work is: *A Viagem de Pedro Aliares Cabral por William B. Greenlee.* It was published from Porto. The chapters 63-83 of *Paesi*, which Greenlee calls the *Anonymous Narrative* is given here as *A Relacao do Piloto Anonimo.* And the chapters 129-142 of *Paesi* which we call the Narratives of Joseph the Indian is given in Portuguese as *O relato do Padre Jose.* Doria produces some additional references not given in the English original.

Navigators and their Expeditions

Here below we give some general information about the important Navigators and their expeditions described in *Paesi* (and *Itinerarium* and *Novus Orbis*).

Ca da Mosto (1432-1488)

Louis Ca da Mosto was a Venetian explorer and trader. He was born in 1432. In 1454 he was permitted by Henry the Navigator, (king of Portugal) to go to the African Coasts. He set sail on March 22, 1455. He visited the Canary Islands and arrived at Senegal. In 1456 he voyaged again doubling Capo Blaco and discovered Cape Verde Islands. Ca da Mosto returned to Venice in 1463, where he held very high offices until his death.

Vasco da Gama

Vasco da Gama was born in 1460. He was instrumental for the discovery of the new sea routes to India. He set out from Lisbon on his historic expedition with the concent of the Portuguese King, on 8th July, 1497. He landed at Calicut in August 1498. It was on his return that King Emanuel sent Cabral.

Pedro Alvares Cabral

Cf. Notes and Comments, no. 13, p. 264, and Part II, 2.2.1. and 2.2.2. pp. 71 ff.

Christopher Columbus (1451-1512)

A great Navigator and explorer, Christopher Columbus is credited with the discovery of the new world. Born in 1451 he became a sailor at the age of 14. In 1476 he settled in Lisbon.

His suggestions did not find favour with the king of Portugal. But he won the confidence of the Spanish King and set sail from Spain on 3rd August, 1492. He discoverd El Salvador in October 1492. After his first discovery he had undertaken three more expeditions, 1493-1496, 1498-1500, and the last 1502-1504.

Amerigo Vespucci

He was an Italian merchant and navigator. The continent of America is named after him. Vespucci was born in Florence in 1454. In 1491, he was sent to Seville. There he collaborated with Berardi who prepared the ships for Christopher Columbus. In the last expedition of Columbus, Vespucci was a collaborator of Columbus. Later he became associated with the Spanish "Commercial House for the West Indies". In 1508 the house appointed him as chief navigator.

Traditionally four voyages are attributed to Vespucci First, 1497-1498, second, 1499-1500, third, 1501-1502, fourth 1503-1504. Of these the first and the last are considered uncertain by specialist, while all affirm the genuineness of the second and the third.

Besides his private letters, his letter of 4th September 1504 is important. It was written from Lisbon and was published in Florence in 1508. Two Latin versions of the letter are printed under the title *Quatuor Americi Navigationes* and *Mundus Novus* or *Epistola Alberici de Novo Mundo*. *Paesi*, *Itinserarium* and *Novus Orbis* contain these documents.

Pinzon Brothers

The Pinzon brothers are known for their association with Columbus and also for their own discoveries. Martin Alonzo Pinzon and Vincent Yanes Pinzon were brothers who commanded the "Pinta" and "Nina" of Columbus' expedition. Born at the middle of the 15th century, they associated themselves with Columbus. Vincent Yanes always remained with Columbus. Martin, on the other hand, separated from Columbus, for some time. It was at Martin's suggestion that Columbus changed his course and discovered San Salvador. Martin sailed alone and discovered Haiti in December 1462. Later he rejoined Columbus. Soon he died. Vincent made his own discoveries later. He sailed in 1499 and discovered Costa Rica, with his four caravels.

Appendix II

Itinerarium Portugallensium

In Part I we have described *Itinerarium Portugallensium* which we have designated as *Itinerarium*.[1] We have said there that it has two titles. The first title reads: *Itinerarium Portugallensium e Lusitania in Indiam & inde in occidentem & demum ad aquilonem* (The Portuguese expeditions to India and to the west and then to the north). The second title, found on the folio marked I, is slightly different as indicated earlier and this title reads as follows. *Itinerarium Portugallensium ex Vlysbona nec non in occidentem ac Septemtrionem ex Vernaculo sermone in Latinum traductum* (The Portuguese Expeditions to India and to the West and to the North. Translated from the vernacular into Latin. Translation made by Archangelus Madrignanus, of Mediolense, monk of Carevalense.)

Organisation and division of the work.

As we have indicated earlier *Itinerarium* consists of 98 folios, the first 10 of which contain the coverpage, the letter of dedication of Madrignanus and the table of contents. The following 88 folios marked I- LXX(X)VIII contain the subject matter of the work contained in six books, starting with a second title on folio 1ᵇ. Here below we give the details of the organisation of the work.

First 10 folios:	Introductory part
recto of the cover:	Title and map
verso of the cover:	Epigramme
folios Aii–A8:	Letter of dedication of Madrignanus.
Next two folios: (unnumbered)	Table of contents
Folio Iʳ:	Second title and the dedicatory letter of Montaboldus Fracanus

---

1. Cf. 1.1.2. p. 6, 1.3.1. ff. p. 26 ff.

Itinerariũ Portugallẽsiũ e Lusitania in Jndiã ꝛ in de in occidentem ꝛ demum ad aquilonem.

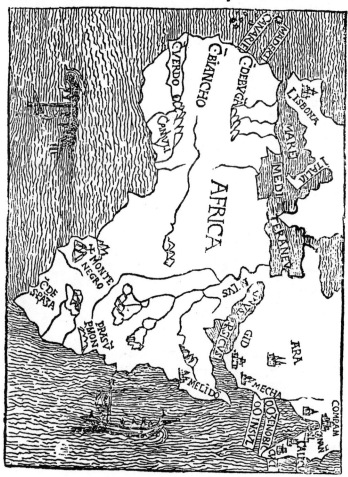

Title page of Itinerarium Portugallensium (1508)
(Cf. 1.3.1. p. 26. p. 312.)

Folios Iv–XXXr: Book I
Folios XXXr–XXXPI Book II
Folios XXXXl–LI Book III
Folios LI LXXX Book IV
Folios LXXr–LXXVr Book V
Folios LXXVr–LXX (X)VIIII: Book VI
Folios LXXXIIr–LXXXVIII v The Narratives of Joseph the Indian.

We have said earlier that *Itinerarium* is divided into six books and also indicated the division and contents of each books. Here we indicate the Latin equivalents of the titles of each book with its translation for comparative study.

Book I (No Title) **(Chapters 1–47)**

Book II (Chapters 48–70)

Liber secundus navigationis e Vlisbona usque Calechut traductus ex idiomate lusitano in italicum sermonem.

The Second Book of the Navigation from Lisbon to Calechut translated into Latin from Italian.

Book III (Chapters 71–83)

Liber Tertius navigationis factae ex Vlisbona in Calechut.

The third Book of navigation made from Lisbon to Calechut.

Book IV (Chapters 84–113)

Incipit navigatio regis Hispaniae qua multas regiones hactenus orbi incognitas invenit. Inventasque coli iussit & frequentari

Beginning of the Navigation of the King of Spain through which he discovered many regions of the world unknown upto now and ordered to inhabit to frequent the lands discovered.

Book V (Chapters 114–124)

De Novo Orbe: e lingua hispana in italicum traducta.

About the New World: translated into Italian from Spanish language.

Book VI (Chapters 125–142)

Liber sextus rerum mirabilium Calechut quae non sunt absimilis illis quas Peter Aliares secundo & altero tractatu scripsit quae rursum colliquescunt ex litteris quorandarum nobilium uirorum ut latius in sequentibus patebit.

The sixth book containing astonishing things about Calichut which are not different from what Peter Aliares wrote in the second and third books which are again collected from the letters of certain noblemen as given in the following.

This Book VI contains four letters and the Narratives of Joseph the Indian.

Here below we give the titles of the Chapters containinng these letters.

Caput. cxxv. Exemplum literarm cuiusdaum Cretici dominorum Venetorum legati apud Lusitanorum die xxvii Junii MDI.

Chapter 125. Copy of a letter of a certain Cretan legate of the Signoria of Venice to the King of Spain, written on 27th June, 1501.

Caput. cxxvi. Exemplum quarundam literarum negociatorum Collybistarum ac trapezitarum Hispaniae ad corresponsales suos in urbe Florentiae & Venetiarum de pace & foedore inter reges Portugalliae & Calichut.

Chapter 126. Copy of a letter of the Spanish merchants to their correspondents in the cities of Florence and Venice about the peace and the quarrel between the kings of Portugal and Calichut.

Caput. cxxvi: Exemplum quorundorum literarum Petri Pasqualigi oratoris Venetorum apud regem Portugalliae ad suos germanos in Vlisbona commorantes die Octobris MDI.

Chapter 126. Copy of a letter of Peter Paqualigi the legate of the Venetians to the King of Portugal to his brothers living in Lisbon.

Caput. cxxvii. Exemplum literarum Fracisci de Sagitta Cremonensis datarum Ulisbonae quarundam Septembris MDII directarum ad oratorem Venetorum Pasqualigum apud reges Castiliae agentem.

Chapter 127. Copy of a letter of Francis Sagitta Cremonis dated 16th September, 1502 written to Paqualigo the legate of the Venetians to the kings of Spain.

Chapter 129-142. Contain the Narratives of Joseph the Indian.

Appendix III

Novus Orbis

In Part I we have described the work *Novus Orbis Regionum ac Insularum* which is generally known as *Novus Orbis*[1]. We said there that the complete title of this work was *Novus Orbis Regionum ac Insularum Veteribus Incognitarum una cum tabula cosmografica & aliquot aliis consismilis argumenti libellis quorum omnium catalogus sequenti patebit pagina*. We have described *Novus Orbis* of 1532[2] and given details about the organisation division and contents of the work.[3] In Part I we have also indicated the different editions and translations of *Novus Orbis*.[4] In the following pages we give additional information about *Novus Orbis*, its editions and translations.

Table of Contents of Novus Orbis of 1532

Here below we give the table of contents of *Novus Orbis* of 1532.

Preface of Simon Grynaeus to Collimitius.
Introduction to the cosmographic map, by Sebastian Munster.
Navigation of Aloysius Cadamustos to the unknown Lands, translated by Archangelo Madrignanus.
Navigation of Christopher Columbus to many islands up to now unknown, by the order of the Spanish King translated by Archangelus Madrignanus.
Navigation of Peter Alonsus, by the same translator.
Navigation of Pinzon by the same translator.
Epitome of the Navigation of Alberic Vesputius.
Small book on the Navigation of Peter Aliares & the letter of certain merchants.

---

1. Cf. 1.1.2. p. 6, 1.4.0. ff. pp. 42–50.
2. Cf. 1.4.2. p. 44.
3. Cf. 1.4.3., 1.4.4. pp. 45, 46.
4. Cf. 1.4.5., 1.4.6. pp. 48, 49.

NOVVS ORBIS REGIO-
NVM AC INSVLARVM VETERIBVS INCOGNITARVM,
una cum tabula cosmographica, & aliquot alijs consimilis
argumenti libellis,quorum omnium catalogus
sequenti patebit pagina.

His accessit copiosas rerum memorabilium index.

ἐν ϑεῷ ἀμύ

Fata uiam inuenient

BASILEAE APVD IO. HERVAGIVM, MENSE
MARTIO, ANNO M. D. XXXII.

The title page of Novus Orbis, Basel edition (1532)
(Cf. 1.4.2. ff. pp. 44 ff.)

Navigations of Joseph the Indian.

Four Navigations of Americ Vesputius.

Letter of King Emanuel of Portugal to Pope Leo X about the victories in India and Malacha.

Navigation of Ludvic Varthemanus, the Roman Patrician, to Ethiopia, Aegypt, both the Arabias, Syria, India interior and exterior to Ganges books translated by Acrhangelus Madrignanus.

Exact description of the b places in the Holy Land, by monk Brocard.

Three Books Marco Polo about the Oriental Regions.

Book of tartar by Haithin the Armenian of the Order of Ptaemontr.

Smartia Asiana and Europeana of Mathias Michou. II Books.

Book of Delegation to Mosco by Paulus Iovius.

Book of the newly discovered islands.

Two Book of the Antiquities by Erasmus Stella of Borussia.

Division of the work

We have also divided the *Novus Orbis* into four sections and have given the details about the first section of the work which is equivalent to *Paesi* and *Itinerarium*. In the following pages we give more details about the organisation of the work. in accordance with the division we have introduced in 1.4.2. and 1.4.3. pp. 44-48, giving more details where ever found necessary.

Introductory Section	pp. i-xlviii
Section 1	pp. 1-153
Section 2	pp. 154-297
Section 3	pp. 297-584

Introductory Section

We have given the details of this section in Part 1[5].

Section 1

We have already indicated that this section contains six books and 142 chapters.[6]

They are the following.

Book I	Chapters 1-47	pp. 1-50
Book II	Chapters 48-70	pp. 51-70

---

5. Cf. 1.4.4. p. 46. 6. Cf. 1.4.4. pp. 46,48.

NOVVS ORBIS RE

GIONVM AC INSVLARVM VEteribus incognitarum, una cum tabula cofmographica, & aliquot aliis consimilis argumenti libellis, quorum
omnium catalogus fequenti patebit pagina.

His acceffit copiofus rerum memorabilium index.

PARISIIS APVD GALEOTVM A
Prato, in aula maiore regii Palatii ad primam columnam

1532

The title page of Novus Orbis Paris edition (1532).
(Cf. 1.4.6. ff. pp. 49ff)

320 INDIA IN 1500 AD

Book III	Chapters 71–83	pp. 71–89
Book IV	Chapters 84–113	pp. 90–121
Book V	Chapters 114–124	pp. 122–130
Book VI	Chapters 125–142	pp. 130–153

Here details about Books VI are to be furnished which are not indicated in 1.4.4.

Book IV (Chapters 125–142) (pp. 131–153)	Memorable things (about) Calichut, which are similar to those Peter Aliares wrote in his second and third treatises, which are collected from the letters of certain nobility.
Chapter cxxv (125) (pp. 130–133)	Copy of a letter of a certain Cretan, the legate of the Venitian nobility of the king of Portugal, written on 27th June 1501.
Chapter cxxvi (126) (pp. 133–137)	Copy of a letter of the merchants collybites and trapezites in Spain in his correspondent in Florence and Venice, about peace and treaty between the king of Portugal and the king of Calichut.
Chapter cxxvii (127) (pp. 138–140)	Copy of the letter of Peter Pasqualigi the ambassador of the Venetian nobility, as the most serene and invincible king of Portugal to his brothers in Lisbon, written on 19th October 1501.
Chapter cxxviii (128) (pp. 140–142)	Copy of a letter of Francis Sagitta of Cremonense to Peter Pasqualigus legate of the Venetians to the king of Castilia given at Lisbon on 16th September, 1502.
Chapter (129–142) (pp. 143–153)	*Josephi Indi Navigationes*. With this chapter the section ends with a definite finis (end) printed in capital letters.

Section 2

What we call the second section is contained on the pages 154–297. The first contains accounts all of four navigations of Amerigo Vespucci, the second is the smallest of the group pp. 184–187 containing the letter of king Emmanuel to Pope

APPENDIX 321

Leo and the third, the longest in the whole section, consists of all the 7 books. Ludovic Varthemanus.

pp. 154-187	*The Navigations of the Amerigo Vespucci*
pp. 154	Introduction to the Navigations of Vesputius
pp. 155-168	The first Navigation
pp. 169-175	About the course of the second Navigation
pp. 175-181	Third Navigation of Amerigo Vespucci
pp. 181-183	About the course of the fourth Navigation
pp. 184-187	*The letter of King Emmanuel of Portugal to Pope Leo X about the victories in India, Malacha etc.*
pp. 187-297	*The Navigations of Ludovic Varthemaus, 7 books.*
pp. 187-188	Preface
pp. 189-207	The first book of the Navigations of Ludovic Varthemanus, the Roman Patrician, to Ethiopia, Egypt, Arabia, Persia, Syria and India both extra Ganges and intra Ganges. *21 Chapters*
pp. 207-219	The second book of Ludovic Varthemanus the Roman Patrician, on Arabia Felix. *16 Chapters*
pp. 220-225	The third book of Ludovic Varthemanus the Roman Patrician on the things about Persia. *6 Chapters*
pp. 225-236	The fourth book of Ludovic Varthemanus the Roman Patrician on the things about India. *12 Chapters*
pp. 236-251	The fifth book of Ludovic Varthemanus the Roman Patrician on the things about India. *23 Chapters*
pp. 251-292	The sixth book of Ludovic Varthemanus the Roman Patrician on the things about India.
pp. 292-296	The seventh book of Ludovic Varthemanus the Roman Patrician on the things about Ethiopia.

The books of Varthemanus were translated and published by Archangelo Madrignanus and these are included here. The books 4, 5 and 6 of Ludovic Varthemanus are important for the

The title page of the German translation (1534), of *Novus Orbis*.
(Cf. 1.4.5. p. 48–49)

APPENDIX 323

study of Kerala and India in general. Of these books, 5 and 6 are of special interest for our study, because they talk about many of the places like Calicut, Cannanore, city of Cambaia, Bisinagar, Caicolon, Choramandal, etc. which are mentioned in the Narratives of Joseph the Indian.

Section 3

The last section of *Novus Orbis* consists of the accounts of those Navigations related on pages 297-584, containing 7 navigations. They are:

pp. 297-329	Brocard Monachus. Exact description of the Holy Land.
pp. 330-417	The three books of Marco Polo. Book I : 67 Chapters pp. 330-360 Book II : 70 Chapters pp. 361-396 Book III: 50 Chapters pp. 397-417
pp. 419-481	The book on the Tartar by Haithon
pp. 482-531	Mathia Michou: Two books of Sarmatia Asiana & Europea.
pp. 532-548	Libellus of Paul Jovus to Archiepiscope Constantine.
pp. 549-569	Peter Martyr: About the islands he discovered and about the customs of the people there.
pp. 570-581	The two books of Antiquities by Erasmus Stella.

Though the title of the book implies that it has a map the two copies of 1532 we have seen do not have the map. This was to be found, however, in the 1555 edition. The Paris edition has a map. But this is different from the one contained in the 1555 edition. Some copies of the 1532 editions are said to have the map.

Various editions of Novus Orbis

We have described the different editions of *Novus Orbis*. We said there that there were three re-editions of *Novus Orbis*, and that the first was in 1532 itself and was published from Paris. The next edition was in 1537 again from Basel. This had the addition of the Navigation of Carol Caesar. The last

NOVVS ORBIS REGIO-

NVM AC INSVLARVM VETERIBVS INCOGNITARVM
una cum tabula cosmographica,& aliquot alijs consimilis
argumenti libellis,quorum omnium catalogus
sequenti patebit pagina.

His accessit copiosus rerum memorabilium index.

Nihil arduum satis.

ADIECTA EST HVIC POSTREMAE EDITIONI
Nauigatio Caroli Cæsaris auspicio in comi-
tijs Augustanis instituta.

BASILEAE VP IO. HERVAGIVM MENSE
MARTIO ANNO M. D. XXXVII.

Title page of *Novus Orbis* 1537 (Cf. 1.4.6. p. 50.)

edition was in 1555. It had still further additions to the 1537 edition. They are the following.

1. The letter of Maximilianus Transylvanus about Molucca, pp. 524-538.
2. The Narration of the island newly discovered by Ferdinandus Cortetius to the Emperor Carolus the V. pp. 538-644.
3. Two letters about the progress of the Gospels among the Indians. p. 665
4. The letter of Bishop of Temixtian p. 666.
5. Epitome on the converting of the Indians into the faith of Christ by Nicolai Herbon.

Novus Orbis was translated into German in 1534. It was further translated into Dutch in 1563. The Dutch translation was different from the German in the organization of the work. Here below we give details about the Dutch translation.

1.4.7. The Dutch Translation 1563

The Dutch translation was the last reproduction of *Novus Orbis*. It was published from Antwerp in 1563 as we have already stated, the translation being the work of Cornelius Ablijn The title of the translation is: *Die Nieuwe Weerelt der Landtschaapen ende Eylanden die tot hie toe allen ouden Weerelt beschrijbern onbekent geweest sign. Waer nu onlac vanden Portuggalosiern en Hispaniern.* Thantwerp Jan Vander Leo.

But as far as the organization of the book is concerned, it is different from the Latin. From the title it is clear that this is a translation of the German translation. (We were not able to compare it in detail with the German and the Latin because these editions are so rare. No one Library contains all of them.) The whole book consists of vi+818 pages, the title page included.

1. pp. 1-26 Brocard's description of the Holy Land
2. pp. 27-103 Three books of Marco Polo
3. pp. 104-152 Haithon's book on Tartar
4. pp. 151-193 Mathias Michou, The two Sarmatia
5. pp. 193-205 Paulus Ivanus' two books

NOVVS ORBIS RE-
GIONVM AC INSVLARVM VETE-
RIBVS INCOGNITARVM VNA CVM TABVLA COS-
mographica, & aliquot alijs confimilis argumenti libellis, nunc no-
uis nauigationibus auctus, quorum omnium catalogus
sequenti patebit pagina.

His accessit copiosus rerum memorabilium index.

ᾧ πρῐόδῳ αἰμί.

Nihil arduum satis.

ADIECTA EST HVIC POSTREMAE EDITIONI
Nauigatio Caroli Caesaris auspicio in comi-
tijs Augustanis instituta.

BASILEAE APVD IO· HERVAGIVM.
ANNO M. D LV.

The title page of the 1555 Basel edition of *Novus Orbis*
(Cf. 1.4.6. p. 50.)

APPENDIX 327

6. pp. 206-216   Two books of the Antiquities.
7. pp. 216-219   Wonderful things about Calicut which are not unlike those which were written by Peter Aliares in the two books
8. pp. 219-226   Copies of some letters
9. pp. 226-235   *The Narratives of Joseph the Indian*
10. pp. 235-238   The letter of King Emmanuel to Pope Leo X
11. pp. 238-259   Christophorus Columbus
12. p. 259   Lands discovered by Alonso
13. pp. 260-263   The Navigation of Pinzon
14. pp. 263-301   The Navigations of Aloysius Ca da Mosto Chapters 1-47
15. pp. 301-318   Voyage from Lisbon to Calicut, 2nd book of Ca da Mosto. Chapters 48-70
16. pp. 319-333   Third book of the Navigation from Lisbon to Calicut
17. pp. 334-503   The true history of New Spain by Ferdinand Cortesius
18. pp. 504-521   History of the newly discovered islands
19. pp. 523-710   The voyages of Peter Martyr and a description of the islands
20. pp. 710-735   A short description of the Navigation of Vespucci
21. pp. 735-818   The 7 books of Ludovic Varthemanus

Here what is interesting is the fact that the first three books of *Paesi* and of *Itinerarium* come as no. 14, 15, 16; the 4th book is given here as 11, 12 and 13; the 5th book becomes no. 17 and the 4 letters of the 6th Book of *Paesi, Itinerarium and Novus Orbis* is given as no. 7 and 8. No. 9 is Joseph the Indian. The title is: *Die Reysen Josephi der Indianer*. But the table of contents gives it as the eighth and is described as *Den boecrken der Schipvaert des Josephi des Indianers van der Stadt Caranganora*, i. e. the book of the Navigation of Joseph the Indian from the city of Caranganora. This shows that the author and the editor feel that the Narratives of Joseph the Indian is a piece independent and complete by itself.

Bibliography

ABLIJN, Cornelius, *Die Nieuwe Weerelt der Landtschaapen ende Eylanden die tot hie toe allen ouden Weerelt beschrijbern ontbekent geweest zijn. Waer nu onlac vanden Partuggalosiern en Hispanien.* Antwerp, 1563.

ADAMS, H. M., *Catalogue of Books Printed on the Continent of Europe 1501–1600, in Cambridge Libraries*, 2 Vols. Cambridge, 1967.

ALMAGIA, R., *Interno a quattro codici fiorentini e ad uno ferrarese dell' erudito veneziano Allessandro Zorzi.* Firenze, 1936.

AMADOS, J. C., *Pedro Alvares Cabral*, 1968.

ANSELMO, A. J. A., *Bibliographia das obras impressas em Portugal no seculo XVI*, Lisbon, 1926.

ASSEMANUS, J. S., *Bibliotheca Orientalis Clementino – Vaticana*, 4 Vols. Rome, 1718–1728.

ASSEMANUS, J. S., *Codex Liturgicus Ecclesiae Universae*, Rome.

BADELLI–BONI, G. B., *Il Millione di Marco Polo*, Firenze, 1827.

BANHA DE ANDRADE, A. A., *Mundos Novos do Mondo.* Lisbon, 1972.

BARBOSA, Duarte, *An account of the countries boardering on the Indian Ocean and their Inhabitants, written by Duarte Barbosa and completed about the year 1518 A. D.*, English Edition by Mansel Longworth Dames, 2 Vols. London, 1918.

BARROS, Joao de, *Da Asia... dos feitos, que os Portuguezes fizeram no descubrimento e conquista dos mares e terras do Oriente. With continuation by Diogo De Couto.* 24 Vols. Lisbon, 1777, Coimbra, 1932.

BIDLE, *Memoir of Sebastian Cabot* London, 1831.

BELLO, L. A. de O., *A descorberta do Brasil por Cabral nao foi obra do acoso. A sua verdaderra data.* Rio de Janeiro, 1939.

BRION, H. de, *India Portugueza*, Lisbon, 1908.
BROWN, L. W., *The Indian Christians of St. Thomas*, Cambridge, 1956.
Bullarium Patronatus Portugaliae Regnum. 3 Vols. Lisbon, 1868-73.
BRUNET, *Manuel de Librarie et de l'amateur de Livres*, 1921.
BRUZO, G., *Di Francanzio da Montalboddo e della sua racolta di viaggi, Rivista geogr ital*, 1205, pp. 284-90.
BUHLER, C. F., *The Fasciculus Temporum and Morgan ms. 801.* Cambridge, Mass., 1952.
BUHLER, C., F., *The laying of a ghost?* Observation on the 1483 Radholt edition of the Fasciculus Temporum.
CAMOENS, *Os Lusiadas*. Lisbon, 1572.
CA DA MOSTO, L. da, As Navagacaoes in *Colleccao de noticias para a historia e geographia das naceos ultramrinas, que vivem nos dominos portuguezes*. 7 Vols. Lisbon, 1812-29.
CAMUS, A. G., *Memoir sur collection des grands et petits voyages et sur la collection des voyages de Melchisedech Thevenot*. Paris, 1902.
CASTANHEDA, F. L. de, *Historia do Descobrimento & Conquistada India pelos Portuguese*. 4 Vols. Coimbra, 1551, 1924-33.
New Edition: *Tesouros de literatura et da Historia* Porto, 1979.
Catalogo, da Livraria Duarte de Sousa Seculos XV a XVIII. Lisbon, 1974.
COELHO, *Navigateur Portugais*.
CONGAR, Y. M. J., *L'Ecclesiologie du haut Moyen Age*. Paris, 1968.
CORREIA, *Historia do Colonizacao Portuguesa na India*. 6 Vols. Agencia Geral do Ultramar, Lisbon, 1948-54.
CORREA, G, *Lendas da India*, (ed.) R. J. de Lima Felner. 4 Vols. Lisbin, 1858-64.
CORTESAO, A., *Cartografia e cartografos portugueses dos seculos XV e XVI*. 2 Vols. Lisbon, 1935.
CORTESAO, J. A., *Expedicao de Pedro Alvares Cabral e o Descobrimento do Brazil*. 1922.

CROZE. La, *Histoire du Christianism aux Indes.* Vol. I, La Haye, 1758.

COUTO, Diogo de, *De Asia.* Lisbon, 1788.

COUTO LUPI, Eduardo do, *A Empresa Portuguesa do Oriente Conquista e sustentacao do Senhorio do Mar.* (Seculo XVI). Lisbon, 1943.

DANVERS, F. ch., *The Portuguese in India, being a History of the Rise and the Decline of their Eastern Empire.* 2 Vols. London, 1894.

DAY, Francis, *The Land of the Perumals or Cochin, its past and its present.* Madras, 1863.

DIONYSIO, F., S J., *Informacão da Christiandade de São Thome que estam no Malavar. Reino da Oriental* (1578) = SRD XII 394-403.

DORIA, A A., *A Viagem de Pedro Alvares Cabral a Brasil e a India, pelos documentos et relacoes coevas.* Porto, 1966.

DVORNIK, F., *Byzance et la Primaute Romaine.* Paris, 1964.

EDEN, R, *Treatise of the New India, with other New foundlands and Islands.* E. Sutton, London, 1533.

FARIA Y SOUSA, M. de, *Asia Portuguesa.* 3 Vols Lisbon, 1666-75.

FARIA Y SOUSA, M. de, *The Portuguese Asia or History of the Discovery and Conquest of India by the Portuguese,* translated by Capt. John Stevens. London, 1695.

FUMEGALLI, G., *Bibliotheca degli scritti Italiani o stampati in Italia sopra Christoforo Colombo, la scoperto del Nuovo Mondo e i viaggi degli Italiani in America.* Roma, 1893.

FRANCESCO DE SOUSA, *Oriente Conquistado a Jesu Christo pelos padres da Campanhie de Jesu da provincia de Goa* II, Lisbon, 1710.

GERMANN, W., *Die Kirche der Thomaschristen,* Gütersloh, 1877.

GIAMIL, S., *Genuinae relationes inter Sedem Apostolicam et Assyrorum Orientalium seu Chaldeorum Ecclesiam.* Romae, 1902.

GOUVEA, A. de, *Jornada do Arcebispo de Goa Dome Frey Aleixo de Meneses Primas da India Oriental religioso da Ordem de S. Agostinho.* Coimbra, 1606.

GREENLEE, W. B., *The Voyage of Pedro Alvares Cabral to Brazil and India, from contemporary documents.* London, 1937.

GRYSON, R., *Les Origines du Celibat Ecclesiastique du premiere au septiéme siècle.* Gembloux (Belgique), 1968

HANSSENS, J. M., *Institutiones Liturgicae de ritibus Orientalibus.* Rome t. ii, 1930, t. iii, 1932.

HARRISSE, H., *Bibliotheca Americana Vetustissima. A Description of the Works related to America*, New York, 1866.

HARRISSE, H., *Additions*, Paris 1870. New edition: Madrid, 1958

HERMAN, E., *Celibat en droit Oriental in Dicti. de Droit Canon*, III. 153-154.

HERR, M., *Die New welt der landschaften unnd Insulen so bis hierher allen Altweltbeschreibern unbekant. Jungst aber von den Portuguesen unnd Hispaniern in Niedergenlishen Meer erfunden*, Strassburg, 1534.

HOSTEN, H., S J., *Antiquities from San Thome and Mylapore.* Calcutta, 1936.

HOUGH, J., *The History of Christianity in India from the commencement of Christian era.* 5 Vols. London, 1839-1860.

HUMBOLDT, A. von, *Examen critique de l'histoire de la geographie du nouveau continent et des progres de l' astronomie nautique aux quinzieme et seizieme siècles* Paris, 1836-9.

HUNTER, W., *A History of British India.* 2 Vols, London, 1899.

IRVING, *The Ceremonial use of oil anointing among the Nestorians.*, London, 1903.

JAYNE, K. G., *Vasco da Gama and his Successors 1460-1580* London, 1910.

KANE, Th. A., The Jurisdiction of the Patriarchs of the major Sees in Antiquity and in the Middle Ages. *Catholic University of America Law Studies*, Nr. 276. Washington, 1949.

KERALA, Society papers Vols. I and II, Trivandrum, 1928-38.

KLUB, *Geschichte der Entdeckungsreisen.* Mentz, 1841.

LABOURT, L., *Le Christianism dans l'Empire Perse sous la dynastie Sassanide.* Paris, 1904.

LILLIE, A., *India in Primitive Christianity.* London, 1909.

LOWENBERG, J., *Geschichte der geographischen Entdeckungsreisen.* 3 Vols. Leipzig, 1880.

LOGAN, W., *Malabar.* 3 Vols. Madras, 1887,

MACLEAN, A. J., *The Catholicos of the East and his people,* London.

MADRINGANUS, A., *Itinerarium Portugallensium e Lusitania in Indiam & Inde in occidentem ac demum ad aquilonem.* Milan, 1508.

MAFFEI, J. P., *Historiarum Indicarum Libri XVI. Opera Omnia.* Vol. I. Bergomi, 1747.

MARCI PAVLI VENETI, De Regionibus Orientalibus, Liber Primus, Libe Secundus, Liber Tertius in *Novus Orbis* Basel, 1537.

MCCLYMONT, J. R., *Pedraluarez Cabral* (Pedro Alluarez de Gouvea), *his progenitors, his life and his voyage to America and to India* London, 1914.

MEUSEL, J. G., *Bibliotheca Historica Lipsiae. Part 1*, Vol. III. 1787.

MUNDADAN, A. M. *St. Thomas Christians, 1498-1552.* Bangalore, 1967.

MUNDADAN, A. M. *Traditions of the St. Thomas Christians.* Bangalore, 1970.

NAGAM AIYA, *The Travancore State Manual,* Vol. II, Trivandrum 1906,

NAVEGACAO de Pedro Alvares Cabral in *Colleccao de noticias para a historia e geografia das nacoes ultramarinas, que vivem nos dominios portuguezes.* 7 Vols. Lisbon, 1812-29.

NIJHOFF, W., and KRONENBURG, M. E., *Nederlandse Bibliografie van 1500 tot 1540,* S-Gravenhage M. Nijhoff, 1919-80.

NILLES, N. The Syro-Chaldaische Kirchenjahr der Thomas-christen, in *Zeitschrift fur Katholische Theologie.* 1896.

NILLES, N., *Calendarium Utriusque Ecclesiae.*

Novus Orbis Regionum ac insularum Veteribus incognitarum . Basiliae, 1532.

Novus Orbis Regioaum ac insularum Veteribus incognitarum. Paris, 1532

Novus Orbis Regionum ac insularum Veteribus incognitarum. Basiliae, 1537

Novus Orbis Regionum ac insularum Veteribus incognitarum. Basiliae, 1555

Nye unbekande Lande unde eine nye Werldt in korter forgangener tyd gefunden. Lubeck, 1508.

OSORIO, J., *De Rebus Emmanuelis, Lusitanae Regis invictissimi, virtute et auspicio, annis sex ac viginti, domi forisque gestis, libri duodecim,* in *Hieronymi Osorii Lusitani episcopi Algarbiensis Opera omnia. Hieronymi Osorii nepotis canonici Eborensis diligentia.* Romae, 1592.

OSORIUS, H., *De Rebus Emmanuelis, Lusitanae Regis invictissimi, virtuti et auspicio, annis sex ac viginti, domi forisque gestis, libri duodecim.* Cologne, 1856.

PADMANABHA MENON, *A History of Kerala, written in the form of Notes on Visscher's Letters from Malabar,* Ernakulam, 1924–37.

Paesi Nouamente Retrouati et Nouo Mondo da Alberico Vesputio Florentino intitulato. Vicentia, 1507.

Paesi Nouamente Retrouati et Nouo Mondo da Alberico Vesputio Florentino intitulato. Milan, 1508.

Paesi Nouamente Retrouati et Nouo Mondo da Alberico, Vesputio Florentino intitulato, Milan, 1508.
Fascimile edition: *Vespucci Reprints, Texts and Studies VI,* Princeton. London, Oxford, 1916.

Paesi Nouamente Retrouati et Nouo Mondo da Alberico Vesputio Florentino intitulato Milan, 1512.

Paesi Nouamente Retrouati per la Navigatione in Calicut: Et da Albertutio Vesputio Florentino intitulato Mondo Nouo. Venice, 1517.

Paesi Nouamente Retrouati et Nouo Mondo da Alberico Vesputio Florentino intitulato. Milan 1519.

Paesi Nouamente Retrouati per la navigatione di Spagna in Calicut. Et da Albertutio Vesputio Fiorentino intitulato Mondo Nouo. Venice, 1521.

PANIKKAR, K. M., *Malabar and the Portuguese (1500–1663).* Bombay, 1929.

PANJIKARAN, J. C., *The Syrian Church of Malabar.* Thrichinopoly, 1914.

PANZER, *Annales Typographici, ab anno MDI ad MDXXVI continati.*

PAULINUS, A. S. B., *India Orientalis Christiana*. Roma, 1794.

PEREIRA, D. A., *Pedralvares*. 1968.

PLACID, T. O. C. D., Hindu in Culture, Christian in Religion, Oriental in Worship, *Ostchristliche Studien*, 8 (1959).

PLACID, T. O. C D., Portuguese Religious Conquests in Malabar under the Diocese of Cochin during the Sixteenth Century, the Report for 1557. *Neue Zeitschrift für Missionswissenschaft* 13 (1957).

PODIPARA, Placid, J., *The Hierarchy of the Syro-Malabar Church?* Alleppey, 1976.

POLO, M,. *The Book of Sir Marco Polo*. 2 Vols. London, 1903.

POLO, M., *Il Milione di M. Polo*. Florence, 1827.

RAMUSIO, G. B. ed. I., *Delle Navigationi et Viaggi nel si contiene la Descrittione dell' Africa, et del Paese del Prete Joanni, con varii Viagii, dal Mar Rosso a Calicut et in fin all isole Molucche, dove nascono la Spetierie, et al Navigatione attorno il Mundo*. Venice, 1550.

RAY, J., *Collections of travels and voyages*. London, 1705.

REIS, E., *Duarte Barbosa pioneiro reveledor dos costumes das Indias*. Impressa Nacional. Macau, 1948.

REDOUER, M. ed, *S'ensuyt le Nouveau Monde & Navigatiōs: faictes par Emeric de Vespuce Florentin*. Paris, 1515.

REDOUER, M. de, *S'ensuyt le Nouveau Monde & Navigations faictes par Emeric de Vespuce floretin*. Paris, 1515-16.

REDOUER, M. de, *Le Nouveau Monde et Navigacions faictes par Emeric de Vespuce florentin*. Paris, 1516.

REDOUER, M. de, *S'ensuyt le Nouveau Monde et Navigations faictes par Emeric Vespuce Florentin*. Paris, 1521.

REDOUER, M. de, *S'ensuyt le Nouveau Monde et Navigntions faictes par Emeric Vespuce Florentin*. Paris, 1528.

REDOUER, M. de, *S'ensuyt le Nouveau Monde et Navigations faictes par Emeric Vespuce Florentin*. Paris, 1929.

RICHARDERIE, B. G. de, *Bibliothèque Universelle des Voyages ou Notice complète et raisonnée de tous les differentes parties du monde, publiés tant en langue Française qu'un en langues étrangères classe par ordré de pays dans leur serie chronologique; avec des extraits plus ou mains rapides des voyages les plus estimés de chaque pays, et les jugements motivès sur relations anciennes qui ont le plus de cèlèbritè.* Paris, 1808.

RICHARDSON, D., *A general collection of voyages and discoveries made by the Portuguese and Spaniards during the fifteenth and sixteenth centuries.* London, 1789.

ROLEVINCK, W., *Fasciculus temporum, omnes antiquorum cronicas succincte complectens.* Venezia, 1480. Paris, 1512.

RUCHAMER, J., *Newe unbekanthe landte und ein newe weldte in kurtz verganger zeythe erfunden.* Nuremberg, 1508.

RUNCIMANN, S., *The Eastern Schism,* Oxford, Clarendon, 1955.

SAEKI, P. Y., *The Nestorian documents and relics in China.* Tokyo, 1937.

SCARIA ZACHARIA, *Randu Pracheena Gadhyakritikal,* Changanacherry, 1976.

SCHURHAMMER, G., *The Malabar Church and Rome during the Early Portuguese Period and Before.* Trichinopoly, 1934.

SCHURHAMMER, G., *The Malabar Church and Rome before the coming of the Portuguese,* Joseph the Indian's Testimony in *Orientalia,* Rome, 1963.

SCHURHAMMER, G, *Three Letters of Mar Jacob, Bishop of Malabar,* in *Orientalia,* Rome, 1963.

SILVA REGO, A. da, *Historia das Missoes do Padroado Portugues do Oriente, India,* Vol. I (1500-1542). Lisbon, 1949.

SOLEDADE, F. da, *Historia Seraphica da Ordem dos Fradres Menores de S. Francisco na Provincia de Portugal, Continuator da obra de Frei Manuel Esperanc, que apresenta este mesmo titulo, III Vol., que e o primeiro que escreveu.* Lisbon, 1705.

SPRENGEL, *Geschichte der wichtigsten Entdeckungen.* Halle, 1792.

THACHER, J. B., *Christopher Columbus; His Life, His Work, His Remains.* 3 Vols. New York, 1903-4.

THALIATH, J., *The Synod of Diamper.* Roma, 1958.

THOMAS, H., *English translations of Portuguese books before 1640.*

TIRABOSCHI, G., *Storia della litteratura Italiana.* 8 Vols. Venezia, 1800.

TISSERANT, E., *Eastern Christianity in India,* Authorized Adaptation from the French by E. R. Hambaye, S. J., Bombay, Calcutta, Madras, 1957,

TORQUEMADA, J. de *Summa de Ecclesia.* 1489.

VALLAVANTHARA, A., *The Litrugical Year of the St. Thomas Christians, Study of the Sources*, Louvain-la-Neuve, (Manuscript) 1978.

VAN ABKOUDE, J., *Naamregister van de bekendste en meest in gebruik zijnde Nederduitsche boeken, welke sedert het jaar 1600 to in het jaar 1761 zijn uitgekomen.* Rotterdam, 1773.

VANDER AA, (editor, publisher). *Naaukeurige Versameling der Gedenk-waardigste Zee en Land Reysen na Oost en West Indien.* Leyden, 1707.

VATH, A., S. J., *Der Hl. Thomas der Apostel Indiens: Ein Untersuchung ueber den historischen Gehalt der Thomas Legende.* Aachen, 1925.

VIGNAUD, H., *Americ Vespuce.* Paris, 1917.

VOGEL, J., *Rom und die Ostkirchen.* Asschaffenburg, 1959.

VOSTE, J., *La Confession chez les Nestoriens note sur le ms. Vat. Syr. 505.* in *Angelicum*, 1930.

VARTHEMA, L. *Les Voyages be Ludivico di Varthema.* Paris, 1888.

VRIES, W. de, *Der Kirchenbegriff der von Rom getrennten Syrer*, Roma, 1955.

VRIES, W. de, *Der Christliche Osten in Geschichte und Gegenwart.* Würzburg, 1951.

VRIES, W. de, *Die Entstehung der Patriarchat des Ostens und Ihre Verhältnis zur päplichen Vollgewalt.* in *Skolastik*, 1962.

VRIES, W. de, *Orient et Occident, les structures ecclesiales vues dans l'histoire des premiers concils oecumenique.* Paris, 1974.

VRIES, W. de, *Rom und die Patriarchat des Osten.* Freiburg 1963.

VRIES, W. de, *Sakramentaltheologie bei den Nestorianern.* Roma, 1947.

WERNER, R., *Etudes sur le "Fasc. Temp." edition de Henri Wircburg, moin au priere de Rougemont, 1481.* Chateau d'Oex, 1937.

WICKI, J., S. J., *Documenta Indica.* 7 Vols. Rome, 1948-62.

YULE, H., and BURNELL, A. C., *Hobson-Jobson - A glossary of Colloquial Anglo-Indian Words and Phrases and of Kindred Terms, Etymological, Historical, Geographical and Discursive.* London, 1902.

ZAIN AL - DIN, A., *Historia dos Portugueses no Malabar. Manusscripto arabe do seculo XVI.* Trad. D. Lopes. Lisbon, 1898.

ZANARINI, G., *Pape et Patriarches.* Paris, 1962.

ZINADIM, *Historia dos Portugueses no Malabar,* trad. & ed. D. Lopes. Lisbon, 1898.

ZURLA, *Dei Viaggi e della Scoperte Africane di Ca da Mosto.* Venice, 1815.

Index

A

Advent 98, 174, 177.
Alexander, Pope 63, 71, 78, 79, 84, 170, 171, 233.
Animals of Cranganore 99, 186, 187. 188, 189, 243.
Anonymous Narrative 64, 65, 72, 73, 74, 75, 76, 77, 79, 264, 265, 266, 267, 268.
Antioch 79, 170, 171, 233.
Arabia 180, 183, 225, 239.
Arabs 155, 197.
Armania 58, 75, 79, 168, 169, 170, 173, 231, 233, 274, 276.
Ascension 176, 177, 178, 237, 283.
Assemanus 66, 80, 81, 262.
Assumption 176, 177, 237, 283.
Astley 84, 85.

B

Babylon 60, 71, 80, 81, 195, 247, 251, 263, 268.
Barros 62, 65, 69, 72, 75, 76, 80, 81, 87, 268.
Baufer 198, 199, 249.
Betrosia (Gedrosia) 206, 207, 253. 292.
Bible 178, 282.
Bishops 71, 78, 130, 131, 168, 169, 274.
Bisnagar 63, 257, 259.
Bread, Unleavened 235.
Brunet 11, 19, 20, 21, 24 44.

C

Cabral 5, 7, 10, 13, 14, 15, 27, 28, 47, 60, 62, 63, 64, 66, 68, 69, 71, 72, 73, 74, 76, 77, 82, 92, 94, 263, 264, 265, 268.
Ca da Mosto 13, 14, 27, 28, 47, 310, 316.
Cairo 60, 154, 194, 195, 203, 211, 251, 253, 255. 257.
Calicut (Calechut, Calichut, Calicuth, Callichut, Colochut)
Calechut 28, 47, 48, 72, 115, 119, 131, 135, 147, 149, 153, 187, 195, 197, 199, 201, 203, 205, 209, 217, 265, 314.
Calichut 14, 15, 26, 28, 115, 119, 130, 134, 146, 148, 152, 186, 194, 196, 198, 208, 216, 299, 309.
Calicut 26, 28, 32, 47, 60, 62, 63, 64, 72, 73, 80, 94, 100, 264, 265, 266, 267. 290, 303, 307, 327.
Calicuth 115, 119, 220, 221, 222, 223, 246, 247, 248, 249, 256, 257.
Callichut 14, 16, 299.
Camus 11, 19, 24, 29, 30, 39, 43, 44.

INDEX 339

Cambay 60, 63, 64, 186, 187, 253. 257, 288.
Cannannor 249.
Cape Mogalistan 204, 205, 253.
Capricon 176, 180, 181.
Caravels 89, 146, 148, 262.
Cardinal 130, 131, 168, 169, 231.
Catholicos 58, 59, 63, 231, 233, 275.
Ceylon 61, 64.
Chastity of priests 176, 177.
China 61, 85, 93, 166, 169, 174, 180, 183, 194, 195, 196, 199, 202, 203, 216, 217, 247, 249. 257, 259, 273, 275.
Christians 65, 130, 199, 200, 201, 223, 227, 229, 233, 235, 251.
Church 257, 259
Cochin 26, 32, 62, 63, 73, 74, (Cuchin) 76, 92, 94, 96, 129, 149, 151, 212, 213, 214, 215, 220, 221, 257, 259, 266, 293.
Coins 184, 185, 241, 243.
Colochut 119, 148.
Confession 235, 279, 280.
Continence of monk 176, 179.
Columbus 14, 18, 27, 28, 31, 57.
Communion 279, 280.
Coonan Cross Oath 275.
Caranganor 50, 66, 113, 114, 119, 130, 132, 148, 152, 156, 164, 166, 168 180, 186, 194, 212, 221, 222, 223, 224, 225, 226, 227, 229, 230, 231, 237, 238, 239, 246, 247, 248, 249, 257, 267.
Caranganora 49, 58, 74, 119, 149, 153, 157, 165, 167, 169, 180, 181, 195, 197, 213.
Cranganore (Caranganor, Caranganora) 60, 61, 62, 63, 64, 65, 66, 71,

Cranganore 73, 74, 75, 81, 82, 91, 92, 93, 94, 95, 96, 97, 98, 99, 101, 108, 119, 120, 121, 267, 275.
Customs 63, 95, 96, 133, 157, 162, 163, 200, 203, 251, 253.

D

Damascus 194, 195.
Deacon 279.
De Barros (see Barros)
Diongul 255, 257.
Division of the year 178, 179.
Divorce 179.
Doria 5, 69, 262.
Ducat 184,
Dutch text 82, 83, 88, 90, 92, 139, 140, 141, 143, 220, 239, 261.

E

Easter 174, 176, 177, 237.
Elephant 188, 189.
Epiphany 176, 177, 283.
Equinox 180, 181.
Erythean sea 183.
Ethiopian sea 255.
Eucharist 176, 179, 235, 279, 280.
Extreme unction 281.

F

Faith 95, 152, 153.
Fariay Sousa 65, 66, 75, 81,
Faillam 180, 183.
Fasiculus temporum 4, 8, 9, 52, 53, 65, 66, 68, 69, 106, 140.
Feast of Resurrection 176, 177.

G

Geography 190, 191.
German 4, 5, 7, 8, 9, 52, 58, 59, 81, 262.

Germann W. 4, 7, 8, 59, 65, 68, 69, 70, 80, 81.
Gentiles 152, 154, 155, 156, 160, 161, 162, 163, 164, 165, 166.
Good Friday 174, 177, 237.
Gouvea 4, 7, 8, 9, 62, 64, 65, 75, 76, 268.
Greenlee W. B. 5, 11, 12, 16, 64, 65, 68, 69, 72, 73, 74, 76, 77, 263, 264, 266, 268, 269, 270, 272, 287, 288, 294.
Guzurath 60, 64, 206, 207, 209, 210, 211, 249, 253, 255, 257.

H

Harissee 11, 12, 19, 20, 21, 22, 24, 29, 44.
Hen 188, 189.
Hindus 92, 95, 96, 197, 201, 203.
Hough 81.
Humboldt 11, 18, 19, 20, 21, 22, 23, 24, 29, 44.

I

Idols 253, 255, 259.
Indian nuts 190, 191.
Inhabitants 243, 245, 247, 253, 255.
Itinerarium 3, 4, 6, 8, 10, 11, 12, 17, 18, 23, 24, 25, 26, 27, 28, 29, 30, 31, 32, 33, 34, 35, 36, 37, 38, 39, 40, 41, 42, 43, 45, 46, 49, 51, 52, 53, 57, 69, 74, 88, 129, 141, 142, 153, 157, 163, 167, 173, 181, 185, 189, 193, 197, 205, 211, 212, 213, 266, 269, 278.
Italian text 14, 78, 82, 83, 84, 86, 87, 89, 90, 91, 92, 93, Italian text 129, 139, 140, 141, 142, 143, 172, 182, 195, 227, 257, 261,

J

Jacobita 168, 169, 231.
Jack fruit (figs) 189.
Jerusalem 62, 73, 74, 75, 77, 78, 79, 80, 94, 148, 149, 150, 221, 263, 267, 268.
Jews 65, 149, 154, 155, 200, 201, 225, 270.
Joseph the Indian 9, 12, 17, 28, 37, 39, 42, 43, 46, 48, 51, 52, 57, 59, 60, 61, 62, 63, 64, 65, 67, 68, 69, 70, 71, 72, 74, 75, 76, 78, 79, 80, 83, 86, 146, 147, 223, 233, 262, 281.
(See also Narratives of Joseph the Indian)
July 3 176, 177, 284.

K

King 96, 146, 247, 249, 251.
King Manuel (Emanuel I) 262.
King John II 262.
King Narsindus 249, 257, 259.
King Hemanuel 146, 147.
King of Portugal 146.

L

Latin Text 82, 83, 84, 85, 86, 91, 93, 140, 172, 227, 239, 257, 261, 277.
Language 84, 85, 86, 87.
Lent 177.
Lisbon 14, 16, 26, 28, 47, 57, 62, 64, 66, 71, 74, 76, 77, 78, 81, 82, 84, 87, 94, 147, 150, 151, 221, 223, 262, 265.

M

Maia 257
Mailapur 257, 259.
Malasines 198, 199, 249.
Malabar Church 9, 69, 273,278, 280, 285.
Malabar 60, 62, 63, 64, 86, 94, 95, 263, 270, 273, 274, 275, 276, 279, 280, 281, 282.
Malabar coast 247, 270.
Mailapet (Mailapetam) 198, 199.
Marriage 176, 179.
Mathias (companion of Joseph) 65, 66, 67, 68, 75, 76.
Marco Polo 21, 45, 93, 168, 231, 233, 275, 276.
Malayalam 86, 274.
Malnar 97.
Madrignanus 23, 25, 26, 29, 30, 32, 33, 39, 40. 52.
Mesopotamia 52, 58.
Merchants 247, 249.
Meilopetam 249.
Milibar 16, 152, 153.
Michael Hass 49
Moors 154, 178, 194, 195, 197, 200, 201, 237, 247, 249, 253, 254, 270.
Money 184, 185.
Monks 176, 177.
Montalboddo 12,13,17,18,19,20, 21,22,23,24,25,26,30, 33,39,40,41.
Mundadan (Mathias) 58,59,65, 68,70,71,73,75,77,81, 262,266,268.274,275, 279.280,281,282,284, 285.
Mylapore 61, 63, 101.

N

Nairs 96, 225.
Nativity of the Lord (of our Lady) 176, 177, 237.
Narratives of Joseph 3, 4, 5, 6, 7, 8, 9, 10, 11, 12, 15, 31,67,69,74,76,78, 80, 81,82,83,84,85,86, 87, 88, 90, 91, 92, 93, 94, 95, 96. 139, 140, 141, 219, 235, 261, 287.
Nagam Aiya 4, 9, 66. 67, 262.
Nestorian 231, 233, 273, 276.
New Testament 176, 179.
Nuns 179.
Novus Orbis 4, 9, 37, 42, 43, 44, 45, 46, 48, 49, 50, 52, 53, 65, 66, 67, 68, 69, 70, 74, 77, 87, 88, 141, 142, 167, 262. 266, 267. 273, 275, 276.
Nuiram 96, 157.
Nuirinam 96, 156.

O

Octave of Easter 176, 177.
Orumus 58, 60, 64, 135, 164, 165, 168, 169, 186, 187, 204, 205, 206, 212, 229, 231, 243, 253, 257 273.
Oriza 257, 259.
Ornus 273.
Ornaments 257.
Osorius 276.

P

Paesi 2, 3, 4, 5, 8, 10, 11, 13, 16, 17. 18, 20, 21, 22, 23, 24, 25, 27, 29, 30, 31, 32, 33, 34, 35, 36, 37, 38, 39, 40. 41, 42, 49, 51, 52, 53, 68, 69, 70, 74, 90, 129,141, 142, 150, 154, 156, 162, 166, 172, 180, 184, 188, 192, 196, 202,

342   INDIA IN 1500 AD

Paesi   204, 210 212, 266, 269, 283.
Patriarch 58, 75, 78, 80, 168, 169, 233, 274, 275.
Param 241.
Palms 190, 191.
Parente, Parant, 184, 185.
Persia (Persian) 154, 180, 183, 194, 195, 292, 203, 225, 239, 276.
Penteado 59, 71, 81.
Pedro Aliares 62, 63.
Pepper 61, 194, 195.
Persia 286.
Persian gulf 205, 210, 211, 251, 253.
Persians 155, 203.
Pizhamulal 280.
Portugal 8, 26, 59, 60, 62 64, 66, 67, 71, 74, 75, 76 77, 81, 94, 130, 146, 151.
Podipara P. J. 65, 69, 68 262, 273, 274, 275.
Portuguese 3, 14, 53, 69, 86, 87, 88, 89, 146, 148, 154, 160, 166, 221, 257, 262, 263, 274, 275, 280, 281.
Portuguese influence 88, 90, 181.
Prester John 62.
Proletariate 157.
Priest Joseph 262.
Ptolemy 60.

R

Redouer 17
Red sea 180, 210.
Religious life 92, 96.
Religion 249.
Resurrection 176, 177, 237, 283.
Rice 188, 189.
Rice bread 188, 189.
River Meli (May) 257.
River Indus 249, 259.

Rome 8, 39, 62, 74, 79, 82, 83, 84, 87, 94, 130, 146, 147, 150, 171, 202, 205, 221, 263, 266.
Ros S. J. 280
Rolevinck 4.
Rothschild 11.

S

Sacrament 235.
Sacrifice 225.
Sacerdotal vestment 159.
Samotra 259.
Sarapho (saraphum) 184, 185, 288.
Sayla 259.
Schurhammer 9, 58, 59, 65, 68, 69, 70, 81, 262.
Scientific honesty 85, 92, 93.
Ship (construction & Launching) 71, 72, 92, 180, 181, 182, 183, 241, 247, 255, 262.
Simon the Magnus 233.
Simon Mar 58.
Social class (custom) 95, 96.
Soldiers 243.
Sonderlinge Reysen 4, 10, 39, 50, 52, 53, 57, 83, 88, 226, 233, 237, 273.
Sources (Different immediate sources) 191.
Sousa (Flora) 81.
Spices 247.
Strabo (Book XV) 93, 190, 191, 200, 203, 243, 251.
Sugar 188, 189, 192, 193.
Sumatra 61, 64, 217.
Syria 202, 151.
Symphony 159.
Syriac 87, 278, 281, 281, 283.
Syrians 155, 197, 270.
Synod of Diamper 279, 282.

T

Tambram 96, 158, 159, 225.
Taprobana 180, 183, 216, 239, 259, 287.
Temples 95, 156, 225, 227.
Thacher 11.
Thomas St. (commemoration) 176, 177, 237, 259.
Thomas Christians St. 12, 59, 60, 61, 63, 68, 69, 71, 73, 75, 78, 86, 92, 94, 95, 140, 276, 282.
Tomb of St. Thomas 294
Three letters of Mar Jacob 9, 59.
Trinity 176, 177.
Traditions (of St. Thomas Christians) 60, 265.
Tiraboshi 11, 24, 29, 30, 39.

V

Vander Aa. 7.
Vasco da Gama 14, 16, 27, 28, 47, 60, 71, 262, 263.
Venice 8, 16, 19, 20, 60, 62, 71, 74, 77, 78, 79, 81, 82, 83, 84, 89, 94, 147, 150, 151, 202, 205, 223, 251, 259, 263, 269.
Vespucci 13, 15, 18, 20, 27, 30, 31, 45, 47, 48, 297, 303, 307, 309, 311, 316, 321, 327.
Vignaud 11, 12, 19, 22, 24, 25, 30, 31, 44.
Vinegar 61, 132, 192, 193.

W

Weapon 186, 187.
Wine 193.

Z

Zamorin 62, 92, 94.
Zaraph 240, 241.
Zorzi Alexander 18, 19, 20, 21, 22, 23.